THE

# CELESTIAL TELEGRAPH;

OR,

# SECRETS OF THE LIFE TO COME,

REVEALED THROUGH

# MAGNETISM;

WHEREIN THE EXISTENCE, THE FORM, AND THE OCCUPATIONS, OF THE SOUL AFTER ITS SEPARATION FROM THE BODY ARE PROVED BY MANY YEARS' EXPERIMENTS, BY THE MEANS OF

## EIGHT ECSTATIC SOMNAMBULISTS,

WHO HAD

## EIGHTY PERCEPTIONS OF THIRTY-SIX DECEASED PERSONS OF VARIOUS CONDITIONS:

A DESCRIPTION OF THEM, THEIR CONVERSATION, ETC.,

WITH

PROOFS OF THEIR EXISTENCE IN THE SPIRITUAL WORLD.

BY L. ALPH. CAHAGNET.

FIRST AMERICAN EDITION.

NEW YORK:
J. S. REDFIELD, CLINTON HALL,
CORNER OF NASSAU AND BEEKMAN STREETS.
ROCHESTER: D. M. DEWEY.

1851.

# INTRODUCTION.

"Death is but one of the hours of our dial, and our dial must turn for ever."—SAINT MARTIN.

THE object of this work is not a desire to create or annihilate such or such a system to favor any particular religion or creed, more or less prominent in our age; its sole object is to commune with men who, like me, seek the truth with all the strength of their soul. Pursue the track wherein I believe it to be, and you will find it. Be prudent; admit, reject naught without mature examination, and what you do not comprehend never proclaim to be impossible!

Somnambulism, *ecstasy*, promoted by magnetism, are the only means of attaining the ends I have proposed to myself; any other state, effected by the ordinary means of narcotics, leaves the individual too much dependent on the resources of his belief, the influence of desires, and naught but very suspicious results are obtained. If, on the contrary, divers subjects, taken from among all the conditions of civilized life, are directed by men who have no other object but that of procuring information, the results will be more complete;—and why? because the isolated ecstatic is like unto a frail skiff on a boundless ocean, having no decided course; the account that he will give of his voyage will portray the *ensemble* of the picture he has seen, without describing its parts; if he is conducted by a will stronger than his own toward a proposed object, we shall arrive at the truth.

Once in this track, it would be wrong in us to be stopped by the desire of knowing, comprehending, and defining the existence of God; to doubt him, would be to erase one's self from the list of reasonable beings; to demonstrate him, would be to suppose him incapable of doing so himself; to speak of his goodness, his justice, that is but right! but of his wrath, that would be assimilating him to ourselves; to give him the form of the sun, of a man, of a tortoise, of vegetables, would be to repeat a multitude of systems, all of which do but end in keeping our language in an eternal movement, and demonstrate how foolish man is to wish to explain what he can not rationally and mathematically comprehend; we will restrict ourselves to the confession that, before explaining God, we should wish to be able to explain ourselves.

The word God, or Jehovah, designates a being to whom we attribute the innumerable mysteries surrounding us!—a thinking being, the author of all, the central focus toward which all beings gravitate, and to which all are indebted for being what they are. This ought to suffice us.

Immersed in these explorations, we will not imitate prophets or their commentators, who have written only for a few, whose intelligence more or less expanded, alone profited by their writings. No symbolical, cabalistical, or mystical figures;—such is not my purpose. I desire, if possible, to say to all beings: "This work will offer you the proof of a better world than ours, wherein you will live after having left your body in this, and wherein a God, infinitely good, will reward you a hundredfold for the evils it was profitable for you to suffer in this world of grief. I am about to prove to you that your relations, your friends, therein await you with impatience; that you can, although on this globe, enter into communication with them, speak to them, and obtain from them the information you deem fit; to effect this, deny not the existence of the soul, or at least strive conscientiously to obtain the proofs you desire; by somnambulism you may have as many as you please."

I can not pass over the word *soul* without addressing these questions to whomsoever believes not in its existence. What man of sense is there who can answer that there is not a being within our body that seems separate from it, although intimately united to it? This *self* that responds to the least desire of reason, this mover, this mother-thought, around which are grouped the thousand-and-one thoughts constituting our whole existence, something that invariably says to us: "I am here, I exist with you, I am a unity for you and a fraction for the mass; in my unity, I am as complicated as the mass. I am termed soul, spirit, mover, essential part of God, without knowing positively the nature of my essence; whether I be matter in its most ethereal life, or a luminous substance apart, I am the slave of this matter but for a moment in eternity, I undergo its laws only because I am identified with it through necessity; whether I be of its nature or another, there nevertheless comes a moment when I separate from it: what represents death, restores to the earth the atoms which the body borrowed from it, and I restore to space the particle of spiritual substance of which I am formed. I, immortal child of eternity, a traveller halting for a moment on this petty heap of dust, return to my vast domain never more to quit it, and there enjoy the properties with which my Creator has endowed me.

"If matter had me not to animate it, to think in it, and cause it to act, this body, which would be but a compound of material fluids and molecules, according to your philosophy, could be set in motion by the harmony of these same fluids. When I quit the body, with the combinations possessed by chemistry, physics, and medicine, why do they not succeed in reharmonizing these molecules, and restoring to them existence! Galvanism has succeeded in setting in play the nervous mechanism after I had abandoned my envelope; but there stops its power; thought, my inseparable property, can only be communicated by myself; myself, *alone.* I am the grand lever that can cause all these organs with whose ramifications I am acquainted, to perform their functions; no motion can replace me—think and act for me! Wherefore? Because I am the life; because I am an individualized thought, and protected by my Creator. I alone can be this *self,* this spirit, this soul! which can no more end than the nature of its substance, which is whatsoever is! Because you can not see me or touch me with your material organs, you say that I am not a being apart, a power apart.."

Were it necessary to admit only what your material organs

can see and touch, you might deny thought, speech, electricity, galvanism, sympathy, antipathy, attraction, repulsion, the properties of the loadstone, in short, the aggregations of the three kingdoms, from the ethereal molecule in which are found the principles of the diamond, to that of the plant and the animal! How many things, however, exist which the eyes see not, or the hands touch; we can not, in the presence of the effects, deny the causes which we know not how to explain.

Man alone possesses the power of becoming acquainted with the various conditions of the matter constituting him, but not through the ordinary means of material science; to arrive at this knowledge man must divest himself of his envelope, and render himself homogeneous to the state of the thing with which he desires to become acquainted. He may, in his material, *exist*, divide matter *ad infinitum*, combine it, but he can not become acquainted with its life. This life is comprehensible only in the spiritual state wherein is the source of whatsoever exists; we can explain laws only in the state in which we are. Let us not, then, deny the existence of the soul, which we are compelled to acknowledge, though not beholding it.

In the spiritual state the soul represents in man his whole form and each of his parts—his passions and pleasures, superiority, inferiority, and intelligence; finds itself individualized as on earth, has the recollection of its terrestial existence, its family affections and friends, all which will be proved by psychological apparitions and discussions hereafter. My experiments had been followed by no reflections since their commencement, which goes back many years, because I wished to acquire an intimate acquaintance with the subject I proposed treating of; to take my time, in order to judge without enthusiasm the facts, of which I have collected a pretty large number, and learn where to abide. I shall endeavor, therefore, to explain as clearly as possible whatsoever appears to me important and consoling for humanity in each revelation; happy if I succeed in confirming in others that belief which I have acquired of the existence of a world of consolation, and penetrating a few souls with all the happiness which I experience from so sweet a hope!

# THE SECRETS OF THE FUTURE

REVEALED THROUGH

# MAGNETISM.

## FIRST ECSTATIC.

1st Sitting.—Binet (Bruno), my first ecstatic, was a young man, twenty-seven years of age, of mild disposition, and very limited intelligence in point of spiritualism, having read and heard but little of magnetism. He submitted to my action with confidence, and presented me with somewhat rare phenomena; he was not isolated, recollected all he said in his crises, was sent to sleep by a single look from me, underwent the laws of magnetic attraction with a great sensibility, was completely dependent on my influence, and recovered his independence instantaneously; he beheld perfectly the interior of bodies, and gave salutary counsels, possessed a retrospective view of events and actions dating from a few years to half a century, and described them remarkably well; he beheld not objects near him, but distinguished them perfectly well at a distance, and gave me great proofs of singular lucidity. I kept a journal devoted to his material views, from which I have extracted whatsoever related to metaphysics and the spiritual world. It was about a week ago that I was magnetizing him, when I beheld him thrown off his seat as if by a thunderbolt, his countenance inflamed, and himself under the influence of a fear, which he sought to disguise from me under the semblance of a courage he no longer possessed. "What is the matter with you?" said I to him. "I have just heard a voice on my right, that told me your complaint was incurable, and that I am no longer to trouble myself about it; I thought no one was near me, and then I was struck with a commotion that I can not account for."—"Ask who it was spoke to you?" "It was my guide," is the reply.—"What is the guide's name?" "Gabriel."—Bruno answered me in a low voice as the voice spoke to him. He was at least a week in habituating himself to this voice, which was hereafter to be the oracle to answer the questions I put to him with respect to the spiritual world.

As Bruno served me more particularly in medical experiments, and as I was by no means disposed at that period to speak of spiritualism, he invariably reverted to his communications. Whereupon, I took note of them, and assumed that mystical language seriously only when I discovered in them arguments sufficiently strong to be in oppugnancy to my reason.

I numbered these sittings in order to avoid relating the thousand-and-odd details which ordinarily precede and follow these sorts of communications, which we can not always provoke at our will, but which should be seized upon whenever they present themselves. As the multitude of questions which I address to these ecstatics are naturally distanced by intervals which can not be avoided, it will be impossible to find in them the regularity of an ordinary dialogue, seeing that the most precious communications often arrived at the moment I least expected them; therefore, I beg the reader to be patient, not to lose sight of the most trivial questions, which he may afterward arrange so as to form an instructive whole, worthy of meditation.

2. "Could your voice tell me what magnetism is—what its properties are?" "Magnetism is a remedy that can cure all curable diseases."—"Is magnetism a property of the body or the soul?" "It is a property of the soul: the body is the machine through which it filters, the soul is the prime mover."—"What are the other properties of the soul?—is it free to do whatsoever it wills?" "No, the soul is influenced by other souls; it

is the latter that guide it in magnetism, as in all its other actions."—"They are, then, guides similar to yours?" "Yes."—"Have we all any?" "Yes, a good and a bad one."—"Where are they placed?" "My good angel is before me, hovering on the road to virtue, which he points out to me, and the bad one is on my left."—"Is there a means of withdrawing one's self from the influence of the bad one?" "They are there to fulfil their mission; it is ordained so; man can scarcely avoid one more than the other."

3. "You spoke to me of souls the last time, could you tell me what form they take after their separation from the body?" "No answer is made to your question."—"Ask if your father lives, and is happy?" "Yes, my father lives, and is very happy.?"—"Could you see him?" "Yes."—"When?" "He will appear to me suddenly, at the moment I am least thinking of him."—"Do you think there is a means of communicating with angels or spirits?" "Yes."—"What is it?" "Prayer."—"What kind of prayer?" "That from the heart; but, in the state I now am, we have greater facility for being with them—we have only to desire them, and they approach."

4. "Why have you had more difficulty in falling asleep today than at other times?" "It is on you that that depends."—"Why have you moments of excellent lucidity and others far inferior?" "That depends on ourselves."—"We fail, then, in something?" "We should pray."—"When?" "At night, before getting into bed; you on your behalf, I on mine."—"What prayer should be said? Can it be dictated to us?" "No; it must proceed from the heart."—"Should it be said aloud or inwardly?" "Inwardly."—"Are all postures good?" "No; we should pray on our knees, with our eyes to heaven."—"Why rather on our knees than otherwise?" "Because we ought to humble ourselves before the Being to whom we are indebted for life; we owe him submission, and it is not standing with pride, or lying at our ease, that we ought to address a Being so superior, so good; we can well make this slight sacrifice to him who bestows with so much generosity. Infinitely insignificant as we are, prostrate ourselves to the dust,

we can but crawl at his feet."—"Should we also pray to our good angel?" "Yes; not for him who could not accept what belongs to God alone; but being nearer his throne, by his nature and virtue, he serves us as an intermediate, by offering our prayer to God, and the more we place ourselves under his protection, the more he can inspire us with good thoughts."—"You have told me that we had a bad spirit, whose influence we were obliged to undergo; this is not unlike destiny." "Destiny is only in influences, and I will tell you how to provide against bad influence. We conceive a wicked thought; from the first stroke that we feel of its influence, we should have recourse to the good angel, that he may not allow it to take root in us, that it may not return to the charge seven or eight times, until it draws us on to commit the bad action with which it inspires us; we may, by placing ourselves under the protection of our good angel, that is divine protection, avoid the snare laid for our ignorance."—"Suppose that bad actions can not be avoided, as we perceive every day, is he who commits the evil punished for it?" "Yes; for at his death he appears before God, who has ever counselled him to do good, who desires naught but good; he then reprimands him by reminding him of all the bad acts of his life, pointing out to him, with mildness, the road he ought to have taken; recommends him to improve his conduct, and places him in a society suitable to his tastes."—"There is no hell, then, or place of punishment?" "I beg your pardon, there are different places where suffering exists, not as it is presented to us; they are places of trial, wherein you are purified, without suffering, except that of being deprived of the sight of God. As I have told you, God is so good, he has so great love for us that he punishes us merely by a reprimand; but this punishment is very sensitive, seeing that it is inflicted before all in heaven, then it would be an impossibility for us to do evil, since the bad thoughts which engender it are of the domain of the earth, which is the real hell, and rest buried there with our mortal remains. Then, again, in heaven, our whole interior is laid bare; we can not have a thought which may not be instantly perceived by all those around us; even if you had an evil thought, but that is an impossibility—it would be impossible for you to put it in execution: the rest, seeing our body laid bare, and our utter inability to conceal a weak part of it, would advise us to think better."—"You speak of bodies; we have one, then?" "Yes; we are exactly as on earth, dress apart."—"Swedenborg spoke of these things, does your angel know him? Was he inspired by God?" "My angel does know Swedenborg; he was inspired by God."—"Is all that he revealed relative to the spiritual world exact?" "No."—"He has committed errors then?" "No answer is made me to your question."—"You have told me that in heaven all live in society, what do they do there? is prayer your sole occupation?" "Oh, no! one is there as on earth, with one's family, wife, children, friends."—"Can we gratify there our passions for love, reading, music?" "Yes; but not such love as on earth; it is a holy, intimate friendship, a pleasure at finding ourselves reunited to those whom we have always loved; but we know not there the love of woman, in such an acceptation of the word as you, no doubt, mean. We read, play music, have usages as on earth; we demonstrate what we desire to know, with this difference, that there are no haughty masters as on earth, but all are friends, who take a pleasure in serving you; we learn there much quicker than here below—in a few lessons we know what we desire."—"Do we return to the earth?" "No."—"Do we remember what we have done on earth?" "Yes and no. No, because it is a state so different from the terrestrial one, we find ourselves so happy that we are not tempted to think of the earth; but we know that we have lived there, left relations and friends there whom we long to see again."—"How can we meet again among such an immense number, and after a time more or less long?" "That is accomplished by the power of God; it is an enchantment incomprehensible."—"You say that we all meet again in families; but those poor families that have neither father nor mother, who receives them?" "There are no fatherless and motherless children; if they are forsaken by their parents, they find them again in heaven, where nothing is lost; in the meanwhile they are received by their grandfather or grandmother, they find a family awaiting them, and are placed, although among millions and millions of beings, as quickly as you would place a book in your library; I tell you it is so miraculous that it can not be comprehended or explained."—"Is it still Gabriel who tells you these things?" "Yes; then again I am sensible of and comprehend them."

Here are two answers on which I beg to fix for a moment the attention. Bruno says that in heaven it is impossible to have an evil thought, because our interior is laid bare. Swedenborg has already said that in his Treatise on Heaven and Hell; this revelation contains nothing incomprehensible before the communication of thoughts in the somnambulic state.

The second answer is that in heaven we meet again our family and friends as if by enchantment. We behold the same miracle—must we say on earth—through the facility that clairvoyants have of seeing at immense distances, designated places, without having any communication with them.

Bruno, as I have said, has no notion of psychology, is by no means inclined to devotion; I can not influence him by my manner of thinking, which, as will be seen, is almost always heterogeneous to his own. It is in order that the reader may judge of my impartiality that I give an account of all my questions and the answers obtained, without, in the least, perverting their meaning.

5. "I should be much more lucid were you not possessed by an evil spirit."—"What do you mean by that?" "I mean that a person with whom you have no longer friendly relations is the cause of your being beset by an evil spirit."—"What power can this spirit have over me. I in no wise dread him; I have never experienced any effect from him?" "Ah! such are men who dread nothing; but know, once for all, that your power is a complete nullity before the spirit; it is the spirit that moves matter; it is that which possesses action and force, and God alone knows what force a spirit can display? You say that you have never felt the influence of the one I speak

of; do you not recollect that about three years ago, you experienced a painful oppression in your slumbers; you had dreadful visions, and, if you would confess it, you were raised up in your bed, and even now you must experience much difficulty in going to sleep."—"True it is that for a long time I have had at night nervous attacks which I attribute to the weakness of my constitution. I have had also painful dreams; but that does not prove to me that it is a spirit sent especially by the person you have mentioned, who can have caused this trouble." "Let it suffice you to know that you ought to have been aware of the power of a spirit, because you desired to see one, touch one; you have been heard. You do not tell me the whole truth; my guide says so, and he adds that if the angel of light who guides you had not been so powerful you would have seen others; you might have been beaten, thrown out of your bed; you are fortunate at having got off with so little; pray, and you will soon be rid of it."—"I do not very well understand what you tell me; things have passed which in truth have caused me much surprise and suffering; but I always attributed these facts to nervous irritation or some other material cause." "It is true that the sufferings you have experienced are owing to your nervous system: but all that has reference to the intelligence, was under the dependence of this evil spirit."—"You say that it was a spirit sent to me; this person is altogether innocent of intriguing, and I am certain that you are in error." "I will explain to you how it has been brought about. The difference that happened between you and this person, who is several leagues off, took place by correspondence; you wrote something that offended this person, who has ever been jealous of you; he answered you under the influence of the contrariety he experienced. This person has very acrid humors, very ardent desires, he could have wished you at the very deuce: he wrote to you things that gave you much pain; the letter was the conductor of this bad choleric fluid; the nervous state in which you then were conduced to your being invaded by this fluid; the disposition of mind in which you were, independent of this circumstance, facilitated the introduction of this spirit within you; under the nature of this fluid, you directly asked to see spirits, in which you did not then believe, and both circumstances contributed toward placing you in a state of obsession. Drive back with all your might this fluid on the person I have named; pray, and you will be released, and I shall be lucid."

As may be naturally supposed, I made minute researches to confront the date he gave me with that of this *soi-disant* letter. The very next day a person to whom I spoke of this revelation set me on the right track of this quarrel, which dated, indeed, from the time when I received a letter producing such an effect of contrariety on my mind that I passed more than three hours in a wood, a prey to such agitation that I knew not what had become of me. It is true that from this period I had extraordinary visions; it is certain that I experienced effects of attraction in bed though wide awake, that I was obliged, once especially, to cling to it, seeing that I was being carried away, and that half my body was quite out of bed. It is true that at that period I wrote down a few conjurations in order to enter into communication with spirits, and satisfy myself respecting them; then kept a journal of those visions and corporeal phenomena, and afterward classed the facts among those of nervous diseases, and I do not understand how Bruno can otherwise class them; I am unable to perceive in this revelation any communication of thought, since I could not think myself, as I was presumed to be under the influence of possession, and he was totally unacquainted with those facts to which I attached no importance.

6. "To-day will you be able to see your father better than the last time?" "I see him."—"Can you speak to him?" "Yes."—"How is he dressed?" "He is in the same dress as he wore on earth — blue waistcoat, pantaloons of striped velvet, felt hat, somewhat worn."—"Ask him where he is now." "In heaven."—"Is he happy?" "He is very happy."—"What are his occupations?" "He reads a great deal and promenades, as he did on earth."—"Can he protect you?"

"He can give me wholesome advice; he will come and see me again when I ask for him."—"Who, pray, thus awakes you at the moment I least expected it?" "Gabriel."—"For what reason?" "Because he foresees that the evil genius could answer me in his place, and, in order to thwart his designs, he will awake me thus whenever he deems it not fit, for the moment, to answer your questions."

7. "Have evil spirits a chief whom we term the Devil?" "No."—"Have all spirits existed on earth?" "Yes."—"Angels and spirits, are they not equal?" "No: angels and spirits are men who have inhabited the earth, but there is a great difference in their attributions, understanding, and wisdom. The angels are nearer to God, better acquainted with his designs, and put them in execution."—"Have angels wings?" "The wings represented on their shoulders are merely symbols, figurative of the speed with which they clear space, seeing that for them there is no space. Positively speaking, they have none; but to those who believe, and desire to see them with wings, they appear thus."—"Do spirits work in heaven? Do they eat and drink?" "They do in heaven precisely what is done on earth, with this difference, that it is no longer a want, but a pleasure. It is not for money that they work, but for pleasure's sake."—"Can spirits carry material objects?" "Some have this property: their strength is incomprehensible, when they are allowed to make use of it."

8. At this sitting I obtained no information worth mentioning. Bruno is aroused, and if, perchance, I put to him a question previously submitted to him (a circumstance fraught with great difficulties to me, unable as I am to recollect exactly whether I have put such or such a question), he is suddenly aroused, saying, "You have already been answered." This has occurred several times, even in medical consultations. I am consequently, obliged to take every possible precaution.

9. "What is the substance of a spirit?" "It is a substance similar to air, for which reason it can traverse all bodies without encountering obstacles."—"What is the special form of a spirit?" "That of man, since all spirits have been men on

earth; but it can assume the form it desires when disengaged from matter."—"You say that there are wicked spirits around the earth: are there any also in heaven?" "There are no wicked spirits in heaven: they wander around the earth."—"Why is it thus?" "To gratify their desire to do evil, which is rather the accomplishment of a mission, which, when terminated, restores them to the state of the good, and then they go to heaven, as the rest. No one is excluded."—"Who orders them to do evil?" "Evil is useful; without it there would be no good. We could not appreciate the one without the other. Evil is the consequence of good; the good of one is the evil of another, and the latter tends to the good of the former. God has deemed fit thus to act, and we must be satisfied."

10. Bruno is in a powerful ecstasy; he goes to heaven for the first time; sees there his father, who is reading while seated at a small table. "What book is that your father has in his hands?" "It is similar to ours, but the impression is not the same."—"Of what form is the impression?" "There are letters in the form of a D; then, again, others similar to a school-boy's pot-hooks, &c. I can scarcely describe it to you. My father closes the book, and says that we should not comprehend this writing. Suffer me a moment to return to heaven." At the lapse of a quarter of an hour he awakes, looks at his bed with an air of contempt, and exclaims, "Oh! I can very well understand why the dead regret not the earth. Who, pray, would desire to vegetate on this heap of dust after seeing what I have just seen?"—"What, then, have you seen?" "Heaven."—"Well, let me hear all about it." "Oh! I was in a place having no horizon, illumed by a superb light; before me was a being whom I believe to be God, seated on a throne. On his head was a brilliant cap; his beard was gray, *I believe;* his arm resting on that of his fauteuil; and he wore a robe of crimson velvet spangled all over with golden flowers-de-luce. His air was majestic. He was speaking to his ministers, six or seven in number; I did not count them. They were all seated on the steps of the throne, and attired in a robe of the

same stuff and color as that of God; but I do not think I saw any gold embroidery on them. Around them, and in the distance, were a multitude of beings, promenading. Oh! how ugly are the men of earth, compared with those beautiful countenances — those complexions so fair! Over one shoulder they had a covering of gauze in the form of a scarf, then a small robe of gauze so fine that their whole form was easily perceived; their feet were in sandals fastened to buskins; but, oh God, how beautiful it was! I was raised into the air; I beheld the earth under my feet, and all those insignificant beings, men, so vain, so proud, that they appeared to me paltry and mean compared with the divine beings before me! How dirty and dark, too, appears to me this room compared with the places I beheld. Oh! I could have wished never to wake again. I can very well understand the colonel who attaches no value to the 200,000 francs he has lost. What are the riches of the earth compared with those of heaven? What would I not have given could you but have beheld this sublime sight!"—"My dear Bruno, you were in a superior ecstasy. I am sorry that I was not aware of it: I should have counselled you to a thorough observation of many things. We ought, however, to deem ourselves fortunate that you have the power of recollection, as it gives you so much pleasure and me precious information, only I think that you have been mistaken with respect to the personage you take for God; it could not be the Supreme Being. We will inquire by-and-by."

11. "Ask your guide whether it was God whom you, in your ecstasy, saw the other day?" "No, it was Gabriel himself."—"Why did he appear to you thus presiding at his council?" "He was not presiding at a council that day, he wished to give me a sitting."—"For what purpose?" "To display to me the glories and riches that God has in store for those who love him."—"What do you mean by glories and riches?" "I mean the faculties with which the soul obtains what constitutes its joy."—"Is he always attired thus?" "No; it was to impart more charms to my vision."—"Ask him if Gabriel is his real name?" "No; the angels in heaven have

no name; they may take one to visit men: that of Gabriel signifies God's angel of light."

12. "You once told me that Gabriel was also my angel; he may then be the guide of several persons at once." "Thousands." —"But how can that be? It is incomprehensible." "Precisely, because it is extraordinary, it is so; did it seem an easy matter to us, they would not be our superiors; from the fact of their accomplishing things which we do not comprehend, they surpass us."

13. "Ask Gabriel why, despite my wish to believe all I see, all you predict, I am still incredulous, and unable to attain that faith which is said to be so necessary to arrive at great mathematical solutions." "You will believe by-and-by, doubt is not forbidden; the more one has doubted the stronger the faith becomes. You will believe; follow your impulsions, it is no crime. Important revelations are prepared for you, you will be instructed by degrees."

14. "You have told me that you beheld heaven as an immensity without bounds, could you give me a fuller description of it?" "It is an immensity boundless, ever illumed by a most brilliant light, consequently there is no night."—"Is time reckoned there as on earth?" "No."—"Do angels like yours behold God?" "Yes."—"In what form?" "That of the sun."— "Is it our terrestrial sun?" "No; there is in heaven but one sun which is the spiritual sun, in the form in which God appears; our terrestrial sun is itself but the reflector of the rays he receives."—"Are there distances in heaven for those who dwell in a particular place than they are there."—"How are spirits in it?" "They know none; for no sooner do they desire to be found there, assembled or dispersed?" "They are in societies, according to their tastes, and walk about as on earth."—"Are there several heavens?" "Yes; there are three."—"Give me some idea of them." "They are placed one above another like clouds; according to their qualities, men after their death go to one or the other."

15. "You told me there were three heavens placed one above another, like clouds." "Yes; they are kinds of spheres, for

all that exists has a sphere. Gabriel can envelop in his, every being under his ægis; in like manner, man has a particular circle surrounding him, and within which is contained all that it is necessary for him to possess."—"Some authors have already spoken of these kinds of spheres, and even gone so far as to say that man contained within his own a universe in miniature." "Do not let that astonish you; man, it is true, possesses a material universe in miniature."—"Those heavens, no doubt, are the beautiful azure field studded with stars, which we admire above our heads." "No, it is above us, above our earth; but in an atmosphere more pure and of immense extent, and these heavens seem to form but one, they present no difficulty to traverse."—"How after death do we ascend to heaven? "As a bubble, a little air ascending on water."—"Have we a form when quitting the body?" "No; but it delineates itself gradually, and on entering heaven has that of man, which it ever preserves, without, as you may suppose, undergoing change as on earth."

16. Bruno furnishes me with still further details as to spirits. "A spirit is air," said he, "but it can assume the form it desires, carries very heavy burdens. In the state I am now, I am a spirit like them; I am out of my body, I perceive it seated on the chair; I walk about in my room without being seen or felt by you whom I touch. I even see myself at my shopboard preparing to go to work. I see myself wherever I wish; this would make me believe that I am several beings. As images impressed in each place, I regard my soul—at this moment it is similar in everything to anybody, only I perceive in it a whiter brow, and I am more comely than my body."

17. "Why at times do you answer me almost before I have finished questioning you—you can not have time to reproduce my words?" "That astonishes you, and you will be still more astonished when I tell you that I myself am at times a quiet spectator of the words pronounced by my mouth; it often happens that I take no part in the discussions carried on between you and Gabriel; it is he who insinuates himself into my body, answers by my voice your questions, and I find myself a mere

auditor of your discussions; you can not believe this since you do not believe in spirits."—"I think I have sufficiently proved to you that I believed in the existence of the soul after its separation from the body, and consequently in the existence of spirits, since the soul is one; but I can not comprehend and place a blind faith in all you tell me, without annihilating the faculties of the soul: I can not very well appreciate them without unexceptionable proofs." "You will not want for proofs; but they will not always respond to those demanded by material reason, because I have already told you that the two states of being are so incompatible (although linked with each other), that they can not be proved by each other; one appears to exist only by the other, and it is the spiritual which is the real life, the material life being only a copy of the former, and encompassed with errors."

18. For some time I had not magnetized Bruno, when one day he came to me quite ill, and making many apologies for his neglect toward me, begged me to cure him as I had already done several times before. Scarcely was he sent to sleep than he said to me: "You would never believe that the complaint I labor under is caused by evil spirits that have taken up their abode in my stomach." Had I not known Bruno for a kind and frank friend, I should have thought that he wanted to mystify me; but I was assured of his good faith in all he said to me, and could only fancy that he was very susceptible of hallucination. However, it came into my head that Swedenborg affirmed in his writings that spirits often assembled in society in some part of the body. The possessions operated at Loudun, and a thousand other analogous facts seem to impart a sort of truthfulness to this assertion. I let Bruno utter before me his system at his ease, contenting myself with always questioning whenever he appeared obscure. I said to him, therefore, "Explain to me how that appears to you possible." "People often say, my complaint lies here, I have a swelling, a pain, complaints that we attribute to a cold, or something else, when properly speaking, it is the work of spirits that insinuate themselves into our bodies to disturb, by all possible means, the harmony of life, to

create distress and unhappiness, in order to gratify their propensity for mischief and trouble. The world would look upon him as as madman who should say that a spirit, in the form of wind or a swelling, produced the colic or inflammation, in order to paralyze our action by keeping us in bed, or confined to our room at a moment when we ought to be out attending to business, which often, by an apparently trifling delay, suffers much, and sometimes the most important effects thus depend on the most insignificant causes. The cause is otherwise seen, or to speak more correctly, not seen at all, and poor humanity finds itself blinded by its foolish pride, which would be unwilling to descend so low as to admit what I say."

19. "You told me yesterday that spirits in some form or other, introduced themselves into our bodies, to torment us at their pleasure under the mask of disease; we are, then, the veriest slaves of the universe; it is by no means to be presumed that we are the sport of such or such a spirit, according to his caprice." "What I told you yesterday, is the fruit of my knowledge in the state I am; it is my conviction. I speak of what I behold with my own eyes, and I defy any somnambulist, having the light I have, to belie me."—"How is it that a spirit that must have some form, can take that of a trifling swelling, of wind, &c.; it is impossible, incomprehensible!" "It is owing to our inability to comprehend it that they do so; were there nothing miraculous in their actions, they would not be superior to us; could they do the mischief to each other that they do to us, they would not make us their victims, but as they can neither deceive nor influence one another, they of necessity torment us; and, as I have already told you, the man who by their counsels devotes himself to the doing of evil, calls them even to his assistance. When he quits the earth, he takes the place of the spirit who led him into evil, and the latter passes into a sphere where his evil thoughts no longer accompany him; thus proceeds the purification from the earth to God."—"You have, however, told me that wicked spirits had a mission for evil; that this evil was beneficial; that God punished not the guilty." "I told you, it is true, that evil was beneficial, but in order to

be put in execution it must assume a form. It is not your good angel who will give a form to evil; his mission is to give or apply a form to good: it is, therefore, the evil one that is obliged to apply evil in order to satisfy his want of enjoying his work. If he had not the taste of acting thus, evil could not exist; then he can draw from it, and raise up for us a host of evils, each of which represents an evil spirit or its action. The good one acts quite the reverse, and thus it happens that this perpetual conflict of good and evil can not terminate so long as the material man exists. This, then, was the reason for my telling you, and I repeat it, that all the angels and the evil spirits that are on the earth in pairs beside us to lead us to good and evil, as we lead a child, have been men on earth; it is only since they quitted it that they are what they are, and it may easily be divined from his very inclinations what part a man living on earth will play after quitting it: the more he has desired to do evil, the more he will cause to be done when, in his turn, he shall be called upon as a guide, instead of being, as he was on earth, guided; it is a chain that runs *ad infinitum*, many links of which are still hidden from us."—"You just now told me that spirits can not influence each other, how is it that a little ptisan or a cataplasm cures the swelling or inflammation which you represent as an evil spirit?" "I told you that they had no influence over each other in the spiritual world; but on earth it is different, seeing that it is on this continual influence that our life depends; and I will answer you that the remedy you apply is the influence of the good spirit in the form of a flower or grain, and thus it is that they drive each other out by remedial applications, or their contraries, in material forms which they can influence at will."—"In that case all that exists is but a compound of spirits." "Certainly, in so far as they can invest all the forms of it, that there is nothing dead in nature, and that all that exists is divided into two camps, the one good, the other bad, or I should rightly say"——"While you are about it, say; keep back nothing; your system does not displease me." "Well, I will tell you that good and evil are what they are only because we find ourselves in positions wherein we are unable to appreciate their effects; for, according to the position, evil is a good for one, and good is an evil for the other. Such we perceive to be the case with fire, which effects the greatest good when we stand in need of it, and annoys when it is not required; not that I pretend by this that a man who breaks his thigh derives good from it; but, although this accident in our eyes is in the category of evil, the doctor, and all those who live on the evil of others, find therein as much good as the patient does evil: so, judge."—"I acknowledge that you are ingenious." "I am right."—"I don't deny it."

I must not terminate this sitting without making mention of a somewhat similar revelation of which I was once a witness at a party to which I had been invited to see a somnambulist who was singularly susceptible of the physical influence of her magnetizer. A gentleman approaches her to consult her as to an indisposition he experienced, and, I believe, to know at the same time what to think of somnambulism. Scarcely was she in communication with him than she said to him: "Your complaint is not in the least dangerous; it is an inflammation caused by an unfortunate passion you have."—"What passion?" asked he. "You will not take offence if I mention it before company."—"Mention it; I have naught to reproach myself with." "You are too often thirsty."—Every one began to laugh, following the example of the consulter. "I have not always had this failing," replied he. "I perceive it, and I also perceive the cause,"—"What is it?" "A long, long time ago, you passionately loved a young person; she did not return your love, because you were not disposed to wed her, for good reasons which you then had. You left that part of the country in which she lives, and since that time she conceived such a hatred toward you that she wished you all possible harm; you became a victim to her evil influence."—"What do you mean by that?" "I mean that from that period you have been under the influence of an evil spirit, that has disordered your conduct, by kindling in you a fire which you always thought you could extinguish or moderate, by giving yourself up to drink; and, what is more, those desires for drink are in you periodical."—

"What you tell me is exact as to the circumstance and my failing; but I can not believe that such is the real cause." "You clearly perceive, however, that I tell you the truth on one point, I do not deceive you on the other; but don't be down-hearted, there is a remedy."—"Drinking no more, doubtless?" "Oh! you could not leave it off of yourself; there is no power but that I shall point out to you that can set you free."—"Tell me what that power is?" "At night, before going to bed, kneel down, pray to God from the bottom of your heart to deliver you from this failing; then, rise, animate your thoughts by the reçollection of what I tell you, strive to pass into a state of exaltation, then raise your arms, fancying to yourself that this person is present before you, and cast at her, with disdain and wrath, the evil fluid with which you are impregnated, saying, 'Evil spirit who besettest me, flee far from me, in the name of God, the sole Creator, thy master and mine; return to the source whence thou camest.' Pray your good angel to aid you in this operation; do this until you are released, and you will not be long before being so, I assure you."—"How would you have the fluid of which you speak rejoin that woman who is more than a hundred and fifty leagues from here?" "Fancying to yourself that she is in your room, she will no longer be a hundred and fifty leagues off."—"I can't comprehend that." "Act without comprehending, and you will see."

The magnetizer, who believes not in spirits, but takes much delight in rendering his somnambulist cataleptic, resumed his experiments without paying any attention to what he had just heard. As this revelation bore so close an affinity to those of Bruno and my other ecstatics, I took note of it, and now mention it, deeming this to be an appropriate place, in order to fix the thoughts of the reader on this kind of possession. True that this is raising new difficulties as to the existence or non-existence of free-will, and apparently in favor of the latter belief. However, this kind of alienation of the faculties of men could not be generalized, and this power of a few beings over their fellows would rather seem merely an assemblage of two organizations, one of which is destined to subdue or dominate the other for a time and similar enough to the power of magnetism, which is null before an organization that enters not into correspondence with it; unfortunate, indeed, would it be were it otherwise; the mere wish of an enemy would suffice to reduce you to a state the most abject and dependent; I repeat, however, that it is possible.

20. After a moment's concentration, Bruno perceives coming toward him an angel, in celestial costume—transparent robe, wavy hair, feminine physiognomy, legs bare, feet in buskined sandals; this angel carries off Bruno, who tells me he is leaving his body and going away; at the lapse of an instant, he says: "I have traversed clouds; my angel conducted me to my father, and left me alone with him."—"What was your father doing?" "He is still reading."—"Is he happy?" "Yes."—"Does he eat, drink, and sleep?" "He eats, drinks, and sleeps, only when disposed to do so for pleasure's sake, and not through necessity; if he has a mind for a pear or any other fruit, he gathers it and eats it; but I repeat, it is not through necessity, for spirits have no wants of this kind in heaven."—"What are their usages and occupations?" "The same as on earth, what best pleases them."—"What are their acquirements?" "Such as they are pleased to have, they study and learn by themselves what they desire to know."—"Can your father be deceived?" "No."—"Can he answer me a few questions?" "Yes."—"Was it a good spirit that came at the last sitting?" "No, I suspected him; but they are all so very malicious, and wrap themselves up in so much precaution that one has some difficulty in recognising them."—"What now tells you that it is really your father who speaks to you? Can an evil spirit assume his form?" "Yes: but my father will make himself known by placing his hand on his breast, a sign that an evil spirit can not take, because God permits only the good to make use of these kinds of signs:—an angel, for instance, will be recognised by a star, a crescent, a diamond, or precious stone. Were it not for this we should never distinguish between a good and an evil spirit."

21. "I see an angel that I can scarcely fix my eye on. Oh!

it is an angel of light!"—"Ask him his name!" "He answers me, Gabriel; but I can not speak to him, because he himself is speaking to a throng of persons assembled around him; he is holding two crowns which he displays to me; they are for us two."—"When will he give us these crowns?" "In heaven."—"We have plenty of time." "You have less than you imagine."—"How should you know?" "I can perceive it."—"How so?" "I am shown a very brilliant six, which signifies six years; then again I perceive your body before me deprived of life, or at least life quitting it."—"Look at it dying, no doubt it is from a disease of the chest." "No, of the side, which will work its way up to the throat and suffocate you—must I say it—suddenly."—"Look and describe to me this scene." "I perceive your soul in the form of smoke from incense, issuing through all your pores, gradually assuming the form of your body, then you ascend as gradually, traverse the two circles, arrive at the third; you receive the remonstrance due to your faults from the part of God; you are not pure enough to remain in this circle which is the most divine, you descend again to complete your purification; there, I perceive you receiving the crown of a green color, which has been just shown me; you are of a dazzling whiteness; your figure is more graceful, your hair glossy, forehead open, in short like all spirits, without losing the form of your features, they are more delicate, and set off by that celestial whiteness which renders all spirits so beautiful to behold! You give yourself up to the study of books; you have pens, ink, and paper; you write, and as you are very fond of little children, you have several around you; you are holding a little boy who is indebted to you for life; you will not be long before you go up to the higher heaven. How singular it is! I see you in heaven without ceasing to perceive you on earth! You appear to me clad in white like many others."—"You see me read and write; since we obtained a knowledge of all we desire without having recourse to those means, they appear to me useless!" "I have already told you that in heaven we were not as mummies, we possess there the same passions as on earth, especially those which render us as happy as possible; so, you who love study devote yourself to it, you write down your reflections; but, as you may imagine, on subjects otherwise grave and curious than on earth: they are true writings, while on earth they are but romances, trifles; you will know as much as you desire, and you will not fail desiring."—"When my soul left my body, did it appear to you to form a body similar to mine in all its organs?" "I have just told you that it was delineated perfectly well, but became more distinct as it rose, and when at length conveyed to its abode in heaven, it was in all similar to the body, apart the delicacy of the features and the whiteness of the skin. In the circle you will be, you will have the power of visiting the earth."

21*b*. "My guide is near me, have you any questions to put to him?" "Can your guide see matter?" "Yes."—"Other spirits answer the contrary." "Because they have not that power; mine can see it. If certain spirits could not see matter, how would you have them convey objects, cause obsessions, upset furniture, and all material things? To strike a blow on this chest of drawers, it is necessary to see it; to ring this bell it must be seen; to upset this vase it must be known where it stands; to bring a letter or anything else it must be held. My guide says that he can see at will material objects."—"Which is it, matter or spirit, that is sensible?" "It is spirit that renders matter sensible and supports it."—"If spirit supports matter, why should a person whose leg has been amputated stand in need of a wooden leg, seeing that he has a spiritual leg, since, according to you, the soul is in all similar to the body?" "Such person has a spiritual leg that no power in the world can separate from his body; but this leg no longer having the material organs in which it performed its functions, it can not, any more than a workman without tools, do anything where they are necessary."—"If it be matter animated by the spirit which suffers or is sensible, why should this same person suffer at times as if he had his material leg; the spirit then can suffer alone?" "I see at this moment one who has undergone an operation. I perceive his spiritual leg, which is much whiter than the other, I assure you, although I equally perceive the wooden leg that supports him; and my guide makes it clearly perceptible to me that the suffering which this man experiences owes its sensibility merely to its alliance with the material body; it is subject to all the sensations of this material leg of which it is the prolongation; but this painful sensibility can not exist when the perishable body is totally separated from the soul."—"Could you tell me how it was that the fanatics of the 18th century who were subject to convulsive fits, being submitted to tests which metals can not resist, were not crushed by these experiments?" "All that was operated by the will and power of God, and as you are aware, nothing is impossible to him, the spirit withdrew from these bodies; this rendered them insensible, and then God supported them in these cruel experiments; it is impossible for us to comprehend this miracle."—"The spirit of God lent itself, therefore, to such farces?" "I have no answer for your question, God is not an actor, whom we may hiss or applaud!!"

22. "Ask your guide whether we are reunited in heaven to the woman we loved on earth?" "Not always; we are reunited to the woman who was created after our own image, having the same affections, wants, and tastes, as ourselves."—"What am I to understand by this? the wife of the earth may not be the wife of heaven." "No, in heaven, as I have told you, we can neither dissemble nor conceal aught from each other; every one can read in your heart and know your real affections; on earth it is very different, the material body conceals the defects of the soul; we fancy the existence of a mutual feeling, we meet; but as soon as our gross passions are satisfied, directly the body has no longer any want, we resume our liberty of acting, thinking; we no longer dissemble, and perceive too late that we should be best far away from each other. As every one bears with him to heaven his earthly affections, as we can not make a sacrifice of them to any one, but, on the contrary, must gratify them, we no longer seek each other to give rise to mutual vexation, but to add to our bliss; then, the woman whom you have lived with on earth not being what you

could wish, God bestows on you another who is the half of yourself."—"Herein you seem to explain as the Bible—that man was created male and female. Can it be that a material body contains two bodies which undouble themselves at death?" "No, it is not thus man was created male and female; but not androgynous, nor two bodies in each other, as you say, but separately, that is, he is born double and lives separately. Every being has his complement awaiting him in heaven."—"I don't understand this explanation." "I tell you that every being that is born is double, whether man or woman; that we meet each other in heaven even though we may not have met on earth."—"Then, according to you, on earth we are disjoined?" "Yes, the better to make you understand, my guide presents to me a picture showing the manner in which this is performed. I see before me several women, the first of whom being *enceinte* brings into the world a boy who undoubles himself instantly, enabling me to see a little girl who issues from him, resembles him in all, and she enters like a germ into the body of the second woman in order to be bred there and to receive life in its entirety. This little girl will be the complement or wife of the little boy from whom she issued, and whom she would rather take for her little twin-brother; they will rejoin each other in heaven, no matter at what time and in what place they are born, because my guide tells me that the little girl who is the half of the little boy, may, according to the order and will of God, not be bred in due succession nor in the same country, yet for all this they meet again at the same time in heaven; but, though born at a different period, she will, nevertheless, rejoin her half to complete it, and live with it in a union as pure as holy; when this second half is born the same process will be renewed, and from the girl will issue a boy, who can not be completed until there issues from him a half in the same manner, which will be a little girl, and so on *ad infinitum*. Now do you understand? I explain to you herein the mystery of our appearance on earth which is revealed to you."—"I thank you; if it be thus, God is infinitely good!" "Can you comprehend the goodness of God in your wretched state of ignorance? What would the learned say of such a mystery, which they should take for a system, they who have formed, and will continue to form, so many, if they perceived, like me, that there is no possible simple unity, that all is in pairs; each thing to infinity possesses two halves, two sides, the union of the two constitutes happiness, their separation unhappiness."—"Thus you believe that everything has a half of himself undoubled, *ad infinitum?*" "Yes."—"You believe that the first half rejoins or awaits the second?" "Yes."—"That when they meet in heaven their happiness is real, and their union eternal?" "Yes; I neither should nor could have believed this in my ordinary state, because it is a truth, and we accept only errors."

Here is a revelation which I am unable to prop up with my reflection; if not true, it is, at least, consolatory.

23. "The other day, through the medium of my somnambulist, Adéle, I asked the spirit Mallet, whether there were any cities in heaven as on earth; he said he did not know; can your guide tell you?" "Yes; there are cities in heaven for him who desires to dwell in cities. If Mallet did not answer you clearly, it arises from the circumstance of his having no taste for studying and frequenting cities."—"Mallet seems cramped in his answers, I don't know why?" "Because you ask him things which he is not permitted to acquaint you with, and others with which he is unacquainted. I have already told you that a spirit in heaven knew only what it desired to know; its happiness consists in the knowledge of one thing, little matter to it the rest."—"Still, all spirits must behold cities, groups of houses and people, since they are in places inhabited as on earth?" "Spirits see only what they wish to see; if they delight in a house, they see only a house; if in a city, they see a city; the same with gardens, the country, public places, and assemblies; if they wish to travel they do so. There is something of everything in heaven, and there is nothing."—"How nothing? I can not understand how something should be nothing." "But I do, I can understand it; they are images, appearances; they are trees, furniture, effects,

and nothing, since the desire once gone, all disappears, nothing remains; they are images appropriated by the goodness of God to the nature of beings."—"Is it really your guide who answers you these things? You answer me so quick that I much doubt it." "I answer you quicker than I should, were it not my guide who does it in my place."—"Your guide, then, is in you?" "I have already told you that a spirit may be in me, speak through my mouth, without my knowing how; my lips move despite myself, and I articulate words briefly; sometimes I hear words beside me. Frequently I await the answers—sometimes I do not obtain them; but from the moment my guide is not positively in me, he is, perhaps, five hundred leagues off. I communicate with him by a sympathetic thread, a sort of ray; to express my meaning better, I regard myself as the speaking-trumpet in which he speaks at a distance."—"It is very surprising that you should hear thus, and operate by the means of this sympathetic wire." "All appears to you astonishing, but it is not the same with me; a spirit might speak to me from the end of the universe, had the universe an end: distance does not exist for us. What will astonish you still more is, that a spirit can speak with several persons at once, though in different places, and appear to them at once, but know that very often it is only his image, a sort of undoubling of his person, which can assume all forms, costumes, &c., and be at different places without quitting the one he occupies in heaven. I am not the only person whom my guide answers, he has many others under his influence."—"By answering us thus he takes delight, then, in the science of which we speak?" "It is his speciality."—"I push my inquiries further, but the reply is, 'One can not answer those questions, what is revealed to you by other somnambulists is effected by the assistance of spirits whom God appoints to instruct you; spirits do not prejudice each other, and can not always answer what is asked them; as for me I communicate to you a certain light, another does the same in another way. You have no reason to complain, as you know many hidden things.'"

I was for a moment astonished at learning that a spirit can be in different places at once, and speak with several persons; but reflection has confirmed in me this fact, taking invariably for point of departure, and as material proofs what we see somnambulists do on earth for whom distance exists not; they could, therefore, were they in that state, at once see at the same instant a designated place or person, speak with him and give similar information. To these seers a spirit resembles an orator on whom all eyes are fixed, though parting from different points, and in like manner all intelligences, receiving at once the word which is only one for him who utters it, and a thousand times one for the thousand and one persons who have received it. Another point may also be cleared up — the image or undoubling of the man and the thing. We have also material proofs of those facts in magnetic experiments, where the image of a thing remains impressed in the place where it has stood. M. Teste, in his journal, cites, with respect to this, a curious experiment: A female somnambulist enters a room, and exclaims, "What a pretty girl is sitting on that chair!" At this exclamation, M. Teste observes to her that she is mistaken, that no pretty girl is there. Far from giving in to this declaration, she sees one on each chair, and there were six of them. Unable to account for this hallucination, M. Teste contented himself with gathering exact details of the dress of these little girls, and confessed that a little girl precisely similar had been playing for a moment before the somnambulist entered the room, and had jumped on the six chairs, one after the other, sitting down on them. This vision of hers alone would prove this sort of undoubling or image, even did we not possess similar ones every day. There is not a magnetizer who has not in the distant views of his seers discovered a multitude of errors, surrounded with a large number of truths; without endeavoring to explain the cause of this, they pass over it in silence, when, on the contrary, there is often wherewith to amply gratify curiosity. A seer says: "I perceive in this room a commode, a scrutoire," objects not there; you exclaim against the error, the sorry lucidity, without taking into consideration the state of the seer, or whether there have not previously been in the room the articles of furniture which he designates, but which are no longer there. I have made this sort of experiment and researches. I have often recognised that the image of material objects set in a certain place remained there for a long time. Any one may verify the fact, and thereby rectify his judgment on the pretended errors of clairvoyants. There is even another influence which equally leads astray — that is foresight. A somnambulist can see at present at such a place, a house, a garden, which are not there, not even likely to be there; and yet the place, the object, exist for the seer, and will one day exist in all the details given and foreseen.

The third revelation in this sitting is, that in heaven there are only sorts of images. I am unable, as yet, to decide respecting this, without fuller information. Already, on earth, the spirit has the assurance to fancy that it creates what it pleases, a creation unappreciated by our senses, but apparently quite real to the spirit in a state of somnambulism. No one exists who may not have assured himself of the pretended reality of this creation. This creating power, which belongs only to God, which man draws from the world, his type, can attain such a degree of force that matter finds itself dependent and paralyzed by it. All the harmony of its laws finds itself annihilated by the facts of attraction and suspension. It should not be denied that an ecstatic can stand materially on a stool created spiritually. These facts, without saying that in heaven the objects which surround us are the offsprings of our imagination, tend, nevertheless, to prove it; when, on the contrary, being then of the nature of the world of causes, we can dispose of them to our advantage, floating in that atmosphere of images, they group around us, according to the divine thought which presides over them, in order to satisfy our wants by which they find themselves denominated or called.

24. "Since a spirit can introduce itself into our body, and make us speak despite ourselves, can it make us act also?" "Yes."—"This question I put to you has reference to posses-

sions; the possessed have always affirmed what you advance." "It is a truth which, in my ordinary state, I should never wish to believe; but I believe it now because I am fully conscious of it."—"In this kind of possession, since they can make use of our body to operate what they desire, have they any influence over the destiny of man?" "Yes; in this way: A man, such as Napoleon, any other warrior, or a savan, no matter, finds himself destined by the Creator to be born into the material world, and accomplish great things; he is then handed over by God to the care of spirits, who are charged to protect his birth, life, and actions. The father and mother are merely the machines destined alike to co-operate materially with that which is ordained spiritually; then, in this case, there is a spirit specially charged to preside over the introduction of this child into the woman, and watch over its welfare."—"In that case an evil spirit could act a contrary part, and influence in an evil way the rising germ?" "Yes; it is even useful; but God never allows such a being to be born without placing near him a good guide to counteract the evil one."

25. "At the last sitting, you told me that your guide could speak to you at five hundred leagues distance; this revelation for a moment astonished me; but, in presence of daily experiments, by the distant communications that take place, I have yielded to this truth, that there is no distance appreciable to spirits. I return to other revelations you have made me; you told me that in heaven are cities, places, according to the desire of the spirit of each; you told me, also, that one beheld only the object desired, and this would induce me to think that this must be an effect of the creation of the spirit, and not places existing eternally." "They are places that exist eternally; but the facility which one has of communicating with them, and the same facility of no longer seeing them, would make us think that they have no real existence like terrestrial objects. I will give you an example: I am beside you, in any part of heaven; I desire to be on a plain, in a garden, or house, I myself find and see what I desire, without stirring from the spot, if such be my wish; you also form a desire, but you wish to be in a

church, a ballroom, or any other place, you are there instantaneously, without however, quitting me for a moment; in like manner, instead of a library, another will desire to see a picture, these two objects exist together, visible to the two desires, and at the same place. Thus you see it is a mystery altogether incomprehensible, which men will deny, although a grand truth."—"The description you give me would make me doubt whether there be anything real in heaven." "All that is there is more real than on earth, where everything perishes or changes its form. As to heaven, all these objects are imperishable, and constitute your eternal joy: only, not being subject to the same laws as matter, there is no need of pulling down a house to build another in its place; it disappears, and another replaces it. Although disappeared, it nevertheless exists, because it can not be destroyed; but as I repeat to you, it presents no obstacle to the admission of another in its stead."—"Then, in heaven, every one, according to his inclination, may, no doubt, build cities, temples, palaces." "No; the desires which spirits have are communicated to them by God, who is the sole and grand architect. Man fancies himself the artificer of all these things, when he merely forms the wish for them: but the cities there are uniform, the palaces a hundred times finer than all that human conception could bring forth or believe; and all this is appropriated to the tastes and wants of the societies inhabiting them. There is so much harmony between your spiritual tastes that you could not desire what another spirit would not wish, especially—mark it well—if this spirit were a member of your society, who would be, as it were, a fibre of your body; for spirits can not influence each other, and where they foresee what reigns not in accordance with their desires, they associate not. They assemble to exercise usages which are but pleasures, and not wants. In like manner, they isolate themselves, if they think fit."—"If I wish to compose a book and have it read, what means can I employ to gratify this desire?" "You compose your book, you desire to possess five hundred copies of it; you desire to give them away, advertise, or sell them; all this is performed as on earth, with this difference, however, that happiness is the result, and not trouble, as on earth. You possess this work for ever, if such be your wish. The spiritual life may be explained in a few words: you desire only what it is agreeable to you to possess, and the goodness of God gratifies you instantaneously."—"But if I desired the wealth of my neighbor?" "We can desire in heaven only what we are able to obtain; we do not enter heaven with thoughts of robbery, disturbance, falsehood: all such thoughts are of the domain of the earth, and can not accompany us on high."—"You have told me also that a spirit could appear in several places at once; how is that?" "They are only images of the spirit that appear; he may have as many as he pleases, and send them to you."—"Good; but do these images speak?" "Yes."—"They are, then, so many individuals." "No; it is ever the same one."—"All these images, you say, appearing in different places at once, and answering different questions, would make us suppose them masses of spirits, instead of one." "It is difficult enough to explain to you this mystery; but I will endeavor to do so for your instruction. The spirit who directs me, and who is in heaven, can draw from himself, by a sort of radiation, a multitude of threads, extending and serving as a means of communication with those who desire to correspond with him. The spirit can impart to each thread the resemblance and sound of his speech, although, among themselves, spirits speak but little, thought being the only bond of communication. Then he can at the same instant convey his thought, which answers the questions of those in communication with him by means of these sympathetic threads; he is but one, multiplying himself according to circumstances, *ad infinitum*, and is seen by all at once, as the entire audience at a theatre sees an actor. We fancy him in a hundred places at once, when, on the contrary, it is a hundred spirits that are enabled to see him, and in the place where he is; but his image can, in like manner, fulfil this office, and this would make one believe in the existence of a hundred individuals. This image proceeding from him is in correspondence with his thoughts, and can, like him, represent them, for thoughts are unalterable. I am fatigued."

This sitting was the last that Bruno gave me. His summing up has a reference to the observations I made at the close of the twenty-third sitting, to the effect that the image may remain impressed on a place where the object has sojourned, and this proves materially that spirits may possess the power of undoubling themselves better than material objects do. These phenomena can not be explained, nor can they be denied. As I wish to keep within the limits I proposed to myself, to borrow nothing from the books I have read, and which would no more be believed than my word, I cite none of those proofs which, however, are very curious and instructive. Suffice it for me to recommend the reader to experimentalize by himself on all those facts and the following ones, which are not less curious. We can see well only by our own eyes, comprehend only by our own judgment. I shall see hereafter whether I can throw any light on these revelations.

I regretted Bruno, but I have been consoled for his loss by the ecstatic Adèle, who will appear in a proper time and place to reveal as much as it is desirable to the eyes of the studious: the proof of the existence of man after his separation from matter. In the meantime I will introduce a few ecstatics who have furnished me with no less evident proofs of what I propose to myself demonstrating to men.

---

## SECOND ECSTATIC.

26. Mademoiselle Fanny Binet, sister of Bruno, a young girl of seventeen years of age, the very model of candor and virtue, said to me one day: "I had a very extraordinary dream last night; you were magnetizing me and I fell asleep like my brother; I saw on the table a sphere, such as professors have to teach astronomy; a prodigious quantity of circles surrounded it; I saw issuing from this globe a sort of smoke, which you projected into the pit of my stomach." I induced her to be

magnetized, as her dream augured well; she consented to it, and in about twenty minutes fell into an ecstatic sleep. At this sitting and the following ones I sought to turn to account this state, and recognise her speciality; it was ecstacy, and here is the result: "I perceive something coming toward me."—"What is this something?" "It is a person, I believe."—"Look well; have you asked for any one?" "No."—"It is a person of your acquaintance." "No."—"Is it a man?" "Yes."—"What sort of a man?" "His deportment is noble and very imposing; he is wrapped in a beautiful mantle of red velvet, edged with gold; he is sitting on a throne, I believe, covered with blue; he has on his head a large and very beautiful crown of gold; he is holding a little child in his arms; he seems to wish to get rid of it; this child is quite naked."—"Do you see this man's face?" "No, not very distinctly."—"Beg him to draw nearer to you, and tell you who he is." "I don't see him better; he does not approach."—"Then repeat from the bottom of your heart these words, 'In the name of God, thy creator and mine, stranger, whom I behold, if thou comest not from him, and art not a spirit of light, withdraw; I have no need of thy services." "He is gone; but a new face now presents itself much nearer."—"Repeat the same invocation, and you will see how this spirit will act." "It stays; it is a woman. Oh! what a beautiful countenance, never did I see such a one."—"In what position, with respect to you, is she?" "Before me, a little to the right."—"Does she appear to you alive?" "She does, indeed; she is borne on clouds, and quite surrounded with such an azure as I never before saw, so lively, fresh, and transparent is it."—"How is she attired?" "In a beautiful robe of red velvet, descending to her feet, bordered with bands of gold; her hair is black, and falls down upon her shoulders, which are of an incomparable whiteness; on her head is a crown of gold, but much narrower than that of the first figure; she has on a robe of light gauze. But, good heavens, how beautiful she is," timidly said the young girl, her head drooping on her bosom.—"Ask her if she is your angel or guide—request her to speak to you and tell you her name." "Oh! she smiles on me; but I am so overcome with respect and admiration for it, that I don't seem worthy of her answering me."—"Venture, however, she is a celestial creature, who, no doubt, desires only your good, and comes in order to be of service to you; she will answer you." Fanny is so absorbed in admiration that I am obliged to wake her, without obtaining any results but this vision. Scarcely is she awake than she sees herself in the glass, and hides her face in her hands, exclaiming, "Oh, how ugly I am compared to the beautiful creature I saw."—"Eh! what? you recollect then what you have seen?" "I recollect but too well, as it furnishes me with a comparison which is all to my disadvantage."—"You are wrong, I never saw you looking more beautiful than at this moment." It is true that this young person has a prepossessing countenance; she had at this moment that angelic expression that all ecstatics have in the height of ecstacy, and it was impressed on all her features. She could not be induced to look upon herself in such a light, and remained the whole day under the influence of this vision, recounting it in all its details to the persons around her.

27. Fanny heartily desires to see again the same beautiful person; I put the question to her: "Do you see anything?" "Yes; but it is not the same figure."—"How is this one?" "It is a young man who is on his knees, and apparently praying to God with great humility."—"On what is he kneeling?" "On an estrade, to which there are two steps."—"He does not seem to you in the air, then, as the other day?" "No."—"How is he dressed? Give me a description of him." "He is a dark man; on his head is a crown of gold, the form of which is very different from that worn by the last apparition; he has on him a beautiful mantle of red velvet, worked all over with stars of gold, and descending to his feet in the form of a robe *à queue;* I perceive a white robe under this mantle; his skin is very white."—"Make an effort to speak to him; tell him to look at you?" "I dare not; he seems so deeply absorbed in prayer that it would be more than indiscreet in me to disturb him; he looks very happy, and I am not less so at gazing at him."—Bruno, Fanny's brother was

present when I magnetized his sister, and desired to be sent to sleep with her. He soon beheld the vision of his sister, and gave a full description of it almost in the same words as Fanny, only he beheld the hands of the apparition joined below, while Fanny saw them raised on high. "Who is this young man?" asked I of Bruno. "It is Gabriel."—"What is he doing?" "Praying for us, and giving us at the same time a lesson of humility."—"Your sister, considering her religious practices, might dispense with this lesson; but to you it is necessary." "It is necessary to all three of us, we *none* of us know how to *pray*."—"How is it that you see his hands in a different position to what your sister does?" "Because he never shows himself to two persons at once precisely in the same position."—"How is that?" "Because we should believe in influence and fascination, and that proves to me that what I told you, some time ago, respecting the power they had of undoubling themselves."—I woke them both.

I tried several times to magnetize Fanny, and reconduct her to her visions, but I could not succeed; she had no longer any wish to be sent to sleep. I have thought fit to make mention of these two ecstasies, as one can not collect too many proofs of spiritual apparitions. Here is a fact contradicting what many magnetizers advance, when they affirm that all these visions are merely the fruit of a fatigued or disordered imagination, and that clairvoyantes possess the faculty of creating for themselves images; on this last point, I agree with them. Thus a clairvoyante who has created for himself such visions will ever have them at his disposition, and see them whenever he pleases, obtain from them answers sympathizing with his thoughts and his tastes; but Fanny is not in such a position; she sees not what she desires, and sees what she does not expect. It is not for want of being in the lucid state, as we may believe, since in these two visions she sees to the same degree, and with the same facility. Moreover, we have other facts to set forth which will easily do away with this objection.

## THIRD ECSTATIC.

28. A YOUNG lady, named Françoise, having consulted my somnambulist Adèle on the state of her health, the latter advised her to get magnetized. She was in a hopeless condition, and begged me to cure her if I could; I undertook her case, and she derived great benefit from my treatment. Without being cured, on account of the disordered state of her organs, she furnished me, after a few magnetizations, with the following phenomena :—

At one sitting, she tells me that she can see her father and mother, who had been dead a long time, that they appear to her really alive. Her mother was surrounded by a beautiful blue sky, on her right, and ventured not to approach her; she was precisely in the same dress as she wore before her death; her father, too, was attired as on earth, and sought to conceal himself behind a bush on her left. She contemplated them a long time without speaking to them. This was the first day she had been clairvoyant, and perceived her hopeless condition, assuring me that if I continued to magnetize her I should have to take the greatest precautions, for my life was at stake, as I had been already told by two clairvoyants. I took no further account of these warnings than by guarding against her baneful emanations. On awaking, she recollected having seen her father and mother, but had not the least recollection of her hopeless condition, or what she had said respecting it.

29. After a moment's sleep, "I hear," said she, "the voice of God telling me that my niece, who is at this moment in her confinement, will die in three weeks; she can not get over it!" Françoise was very fond of this niece; she began to cry bitterly. I wished to make her believe that it was a mere rambling of her imagination, occasioned by the warm affection she felt for her niece; that it was not the voice of God she had heard. She was highly offended at my doubts, and replied—"It was assuredly God who spoke to me; they who live long enough will see."

30. "There's my father," said she; "I know not why he dares not approach me."—"Ask him why?" "He answers me that he desired to see me before his death, and that I did not come to receive his last farewell. He seems angry with me."—After this reproach he moves away; then appears before her a little girl she had had, and lost at the age of eighteen months, while out at nurse; the child seemed to her bigger than when she parted with it, being then only six days old.—"How does this child appear to you?" "Very well; only she has a somewhat suffering air; she is naked, has little wings, and a pink cap on her head."—"What! naked, and a cap on her head?" "Yes, 'tis just so that I see her."—"Ask her where she is?" "In heaven."—"With whom?" "Her grandmother."—"What does she do there?" "She plays with little girls whom she delights to teaze."—"She appears to you suffering, ask her whether she suffers?" "She longs for me; but, that apart, suffers not; she says she is very happy; she has often seen God, and goes to him."—"How does the Deity appear to her?" "Like a man amidst a cloud of dazzling whiteness. She tells me that I shall live a long time yet in pain."—"Why is not your grandmother with this child, since she is under her care; you should see her at least?" "She tells me that at this moment she is praying to God for me; my little girl has blue eyes; I don't know what color they were. Here is a little boy whom I don't know, but he calls himself my nephew; he died when nine years old, of convulsions, brought on by fits of passion, which have not yet left him, although dead. He says that he has at times seen God; he entertains the hope of being with him by-and-by, when he improves in disposition." He announces to Françoise that his mother is suffering from a disease in the chest that will by-and-by become a catarrh. Françoise sees many persons who claim relationship with her, although she does not know them; she does not even remember ever having seen them; she desires to see her daughter when awake, and points out the means of effecting this, which succeeds perfectly well; she no longer recollects anything. This greatly astonishes her, and

especially the cap which she sees when awake on her child's head.

31. Françoise says that she hears again the voice of God, telling her that the little girl her niece is brought to bed with will die soon after her. "Have you any presentiments of these events when awake?" "No, none; my niece is not well, but still I have no reason to be alarmed at her condition."—"And her little girl?" "She is at nurse, and I see her only in my sleep; but nothing makes me forebode that she will die soon."—"Your nephew told you the last time that his mother, your sister, was ill; did you know it?" "I knew it only to-day; I have heard from her, and she is not well; but before I knew nothing about it."—"Could you learn why your little girl appeared to you naked, and with only a pink cap on her head?" "I will ask her."—After a momentary pause she said to me: "I gave her nurse some good baby-linen, which she returned to me after the child's death. I desired her to put in the coffin one of the child's best caps; she afterward told me that she had done so, but I had my doubts about the matter, and presumed that she had not, especially with respect to the cap in which the child appears to me at this moment, by the permission of God, who desires that I should no longer deem this woman guilty of theft. I could never have believed that she would have acted thus, especially with an expensive cap like this, and having such a large family, to whom it would have been more useful than to this child."

I had no more revelations from Françoise; she got better, and I saw her no more. I will make a few observations on what has been just stated. Françoise possessed a singular clairvoyance for distant views, reproduced conversations held in remote places, of which I obtained unanswerable proofs; she was of a frank disposition, and by no means cunning; she did not deceive me when announcing her sister's illness, of which she had no knowledge till two days after. Was it really her little deceased nephew, whom she had never seen, that confided this to her? or was it a *view at distance* that she had taken? One can only decide from her good faith and aversion to falsehood. I believe that this child appeared to her because she said that he was still irascible, a truth that will be proved by-and-by. Man parts not at once with his manners and propensities on entering the next world, a thing that she could not possibly learn or perceive in my thought, seeing that then I neither knew nor suspected such things, and even now can scarcely comprehend. I also believe in this revelation, because I have had similar ones since which have determined me not to reject it. I therefore beg the reader not to lose sight of this observation.

A voice, which she takes to be that of God, announces to her that her niece and daughter will die within a short time of each other. This prediction was literally accomplished.

She perceives her little girl, who had been dead a very long time. The particularity of the cap which Françoise could not invent in order either to appear ridiculous in my eyes, or to make me appear so (by admitting such thoughts we might doubt our own existence, if everywhere we perceived but cunning and falsehood), this particularity alone is an undeniable proof of the existence of the spiritual world; to support it with commentaries would be injuring it; let us, therefore, preserve it in all its purity. A man may doubt and cry out hallucination, on seeing with his eyes, and touching with his hands a person dead, because images may, for a moment, paralyze our senses; such a man will gradually lose the impression of what he has seen, and end by doubting himself of his own good sense. It is not the same when it is reasoning that speaks, and is maintained by facts which he can not destroy, despite his inclination. A man vanquished by reasoning will be for ever vanquished, and a man overcome by the senses will easily recover from his state which he will class among those of fear, hallucination, and absence of mind.

## FOURTH ECSTATIC.

32. BEING one day at Colonel R—'s, I saw a lady who had been magnetized during six months for a malady by this gentleman, and afterward by several somnambulists; she had never slept despite their assurance that she would one day sleep. She begged me, after hearing what had been said respecting me, to try and send her to sleep. In the course of five minutes she slept and was in the state of a somnambulist. "Why have you not slept until to-day?" "You alone were able to send me to sleep, because your fluid is in much better communication with mine than those of the persons who have hitherto magnetized me." This lady, the wife of one of the first artists of the capital, had received a good education, and, though she had been cured by magnetism, she could not altogether believe in the marvellous effects of somnambulism; she wished to judge for herself, and this no one was better enabled to do, considering the reiterated physical experiments I made on her. Her speciality was for maladies, and the communication of thoughts; I magnetized her for some time, and she presented me at one sitting with a scene that I will relate.

33. "Madame," said I to her, "hitherto we have not occupied ourselves with serious things in your sleep; you have received a good education, which has developed in you very skeptical thoughts; you are strong-minded, you would not allow yourself to be imposed upon by mere reveries; will you endeavor to enter into communication with the inhabitants of the other world?" "I do not believe in their existence; but if you can *let me see them,* I shall be most happy."—"In that case, desire with all your heart to see your angel, I will request him to appear to you." "Here he is."—"Already?" "Yes."—"Give me a description of him?" "His countenance seems to me noble and gracious, though rather stern."—"Angels, it is said, are not ordinarily stern; no doubt it is an evil spirit, who, as usual, presents himself first; if he is not an angel of light, pray God that he may disappear." "He is gone."—

"Come, madame, no error on the part of your imagination; you are in a condition to enter into communication with the inhabitants of the other world; be pleased to regard with circumspection that you may be the better convinced of the results we shall obtain." "I saw perfectly well this person, whose sombre and stern physiognomy struck me so forcibly that I have no wish to recommence the trial. I should prefer seeing another, particularly my father, who has been dead a very long time, in order to assure myself whether or not he still lives; let us leave the angels."—"Since you prefer seeing your father, call him." "Oh! here is another, a little angel—oh! oh!" Madame F. then goes off into a state difficult to describe; she weeps, calls on me to rouse her, falls back with her head against the wall, her bosom swollen by sobs; she seems to suffocate under the weight of her grief, and it is only at the expiration of a few minutes that I can obtain an answer to this question."—"What, then, do you see?" "My son! my poor little Ernest; wake me!"—"Wake you because you see your son; what is there so dreadful in seeing one's son? How do you see him, alive or dead?" "Alive; although he has been dead these fourteen years."—"A reason the more to rejoice at seeing your child again; what age was he at his death?" "Six months."—"How old does he seem to you now?" "About three years old."—"Since he would now be fourteen, why does he appear to you only three years of age? one would think that he would rather appear to you not more than six months old." "God wills it thus; children that die before they are three years old, seem not to exceed that age."—"How is he dressed?" "He is quite naked; he has little wings."—"Are you quite sure he is your son? Repeat the same invocation as that you addressed to the wicked angel." "Oh! it is really my son; he stays, assuredly; I can recognise him; how fair he is!" And she continued weeping.—"Would you like to see him when you are wide awake, to satisfy your curiosity and overcome your incredulity?" "Oh! yes." She becomes somewhat calm. I ask her if she can still see her son. "Yes; he is calling to some one who seems to be unwilling to advance."—"Do you wish to see another person?" "Yes; a friend whom I lost a very long time ago; but *I can not see her*."—"You ought not to have asked for this friend before obtaining the result of your first wish, which was to see your father; you ought to have waited for him." "It is he whom my son is calling; he has no wish to come." —"That is, as I repeat to you, because you have a greater desire to see another person in preference to him." She awaits a few minutes longer, but her father does not appear. She requests me to wake her. When I believe her to be thoroughly aroused, I put to her several questions which prove to me, as before, that she has no recollection of what she has seen or said. She fixes her eyes on one point on her right, and cries out, "Wake me, then." I disengage her as quickly as possible, her eyes still remaining fixed in the same direction. I ask her what she perceives there. "I don't know; it is a dark point that draws my attention thither, and I am unable to turn my eyes away."—"Look at me." She does so, and exclaims, "What does all this mean, monsieur?" "I know less than you, madame, but you will explain it to me presently." I place my hand on the region of her heart, and she then cries out that she perceives her son amid the clouds that attracted her attention; and says to me, "It is my first child, whom I thought little of, having at his death bestowed all my affections on his brothers and sister. It is very astonishing that this child, who was then but six months old and would now be fourteen years of age, should appear in your room: I should like to know what this means!" "It means what you sought to know, madame, that the dead exist as well as we do; you desired, in your sleep, to see your father, no doubt he preferred sending you this child, whom you say you no longer thought of, in order that you may not think that in desiring to see your father, and having seen him, that is a mere effect of the imagination or hallucination. You expressed a wish to see this child when you were awaked in order to remove all your doubts in this respect; you ought to be satisfied."—"Did you really see him?" "Yes, monsieur."—"Did you really recognise him?"

"Yes, but you, did you not see him?" "No, madame, I was not in your state."—"How surprising all this is! it is enough to derange the strongest mind. *Assuredly I saw him;* I dare not think of it, 'tis miraculous; a child that I had not thought of for so many years!" "He still thinks of you, madame; those in heaven are not so forgetful as we are." The effect experienced by this lady was not the same as in her sleep, she looked upon her son without emotion, matter had resumed its sway. She quitted me inveighing against magic and natural philosophy; I did not become attached to this somnambulist, as it required much labor to obtain from her satisfactory results. This sitting is not devoid of interest, and proves again that the desire is not always the sole mover of spiritual visions. This lady desires to see her father, and she sees a little creature that she was far from thinking of at the moment; a scene ensues. The father seems unwilling to obey the request of the mother and son, the latter appears with little wings; like the child of Françoise he is about three years old; like the other, he is naked! Hence, conformity of apparition. It is to be attributed to this, that appearing in a more advanced age, they would be less easily recognised, or do they remain in this state of innocence? We shall see hereafter in a revelation of the same kind. This lady, I think, was not gifted with an inventive imagination, since she thought she should see nothing, and what she did see she sought not, without being able to obtain what she desired. This is a very singular apparition, and sets all doubt aside.

## FIFTH ECSTATIC.

34. I HAD been devoting for some time my attention to a young person afflicted with a disease of the chest;—one day, Madame Reviere, her aunt, who was always present at my sittings, requested me to try and send her to sleep: I succeeded in doing so. After being acted upon magnetically for about twenty minutes, she was in a state of somnambulism, and begged of me not to question her, but leave her in the happy state she then was. Scarcely had a few minutes elapsed before I could perceive that she was in an ecstatic state, from which I roused her when I thought necessary, knowing that it is often dangerous to prolong it; she bitterly reproached me on my want of patience, saying, that she had never experienced like happiness. "Where were you and what have you seen?" asked I. "I was in a magnificent open country, illumed by a superb day-light, the vegetation was admirably rich! I felt that I had abandoned my body, and I proceeded toward a spot where I beheld beautiful sheep grazing, and judge of my surprise, when I perceived my good father watching them. When I begged of you to leave me alone for a moment, I had been wishing to see my father, having heard you say that in this state, one can see and speak with the dead. I had reason to be astonished at perceiving him watching a flock. It is no dream; and had you not interrupted me, I should have spoken to him."—"We will recommence the experiment when you please, madame. Did your father ever tend flocks?" "Oh! no; I am certain that I was not dreaming, I saw perfectly well, and experienced a happiness unknown to me. Were I at liberty to open my eyes I should believe that they are not closed, so conscious am I of being in my normal condition; *I beg you will open them for me*, for it is singular enough, that I can't do it myself."

When this lady was roused she had a perfect recollection of her ecstasy, and was not less surprised at it than when in her sleep ; she could not conceive why her father had appeared to her as the keeper of a flock. I told her that the ecstatics I had hitherto known assured me that in the other world every one was occupied agreeably to his tastes. "In that case," replied she, "he would be a trader, for I never knew him to quit Paris, and am not aware that he had any taste for rural pursuits." That very day this lady recounted her vision to her mother, whom she expressly went to in order to inquire whether her father had ever been a shepherd. Her mother replied that to her knowledge he had never been engaged in a like occupation; but that she perfectly remembered having heard him say that when very young, he had an uncle in the country at whose house he often passed some time and took delight in playing the part of a little shepherd ; that he had even told her that he had never been so happy as at that period, amid his little flock. The surprise, as may be supposed, was great on both sides; but for me this revelation was useful, inasmuch as it proved to me that what Swedenborg said (I had studied him after acquiring by myself proofs of a spiritual existence) was correct on this point. Bruno had often said to me: "It is ordained that you shall believe in these mysteries! You will believe in them because in your respect means will be employed that will leave no room for doubt. You shall have proofs!" He was not deceived; for ten years have I been collecting facts of this kind. This lady having removed to a distance I obtained from her but one sitting.

## SIXTH ECSTATIC.

35. We are now come to our best and most powerful ecstatic; the one whose light has opened our eyes; the one who refuses no spiritual experiment. Theology, metaphysics, psychology, she answers all in a sense tinctured with neither pride nor error. Should the materialist not obtain from her the proofs he desires, he can not accuse her of entangling the question, or of bad faith. For several years past, in her magnetic sleep, she lives with the beings of the other world; give her but the Christian and surname of the deceased persons, no matter at what period we desire her to perceive or consult, and she sees and converses with them at will. Hitherto, she has never failed in one experiment, and we shall be astonished at her clairvoyance, and the exact details she gives of persons who have departed this life.

Adèle Magnot, whom I have known for a long time, is a somnambulist by birth. In her childhood she was sorely afflicted with somnambulic fits, compelling her to get up at night to terminate or continue her day's labors. I advised her to be magnetized, in order to cure, or, at least, divert the course of her fits of somnambulism; she consented to it, and since then her sleep is undisturbed. From the first sitting she was a somnambulist, and her first speciality is for maladies. She possesses, in this respect, a clairvoyance equivalent to that she has for spiritual views, and for which, from her charitable disposition, she had more taste. No interested views have ever guided her; she gives and receives not. I kept a journal devoted to all she could tell me or do in her slumbers, and will now collect from it whatsoever bears upon spiritualism. I again claim the indulgence of the reader for a work which is above my knowledge and strength; let none behold in me, as I have said at the commencement, any other pride but that of opening or strengthening, in all who read me, a belief that constitutes all my happiness. It is a debt which I owe to humanity, and would wish to discharge as I best can.

36. Adèle possesses all the qualities desirable in somnambulism; she is wholly isolated, totally independent of the magnetizer, sleeps the desired time, and has no recollection on awaking.

"What is magnetism?" "It is an influence of the nerves conveying the greatest good wherever it is directed, particularly if we are animated with the love of God and what is good."—"And spiritually?" "It is the quintessence of what exists most pure in man; it is a divine influence, the very purity of God."

37. "What creates in you this surprise?" "It is my little niece."—"Who is this niece?" "My sister's little child who died two years ago."—"How old was she then?" "Twelve years old."—"Give me a description of her person." "She is taller than she was on earth; her complexion is of a dazzling whiteness; she is dressed in white."—"Ask her where she lives." "In heaven."—"Is she happy there?" "Yes."—"What does she do there?" "She plays, walks about, and is surrounded by my numerous family, who often speak of me: my mother, father, and brothers, would be glad if I could soon rejoin them."—"The dead remember, then, their earthly existence?" "No one is dead in heaven; all are alive, more alive than we are; they remember the relatives they left on earth, and pray to God for them."—"Do we recollect the details of our past life, or only remember our relatives?" "We do not remember the details that concern evil, or the earthly passions appertaining to it; all is forgotten in this respect."—"Are all happy in heaven?" "Indeed are they; we have no notion of such happiness on earth! we live there in an atmosphere so mild—neither too warm nor too cold. How can we dread leaving this earth! My little niece recommends me to pray if I wish to go to heaven with her: it was for that that she came to me last night at a moment when I was in a similar state to what I am now, and exhorted me to go and fetch a small chaplet which she wore on her neck before her death, and pray to God with it. This I did, though it was hidden in my commode. She pretends that it was the prayer that procured me a speed-

ier admission into this state, and the happiness of seeing each other again. My surprise was great when in the morning I found this chaplet in my bed. I should wish to remember this particularity, in order to remove the inquietude it has caused me."—"You knew, then, perfectly well how to find it, despite the darkness?" "In the state I was, there was no darkness for me."—"It is necessary, then, to enter into this state, in order to see and speak to spirits?" "Yes; without that it is impossible to see them."—"Some persons, however, when wide awake, have seen them?" "They seemed awake, but they were, although in communication with the two worlds, in a state which is not normal."—"Is it really her hand that you seemed to clasp in yours?" "Oh, it is indeed! I feel it better than yours, as she presses it affectionately."—"Ask your niece if it is true that we all have two angels beside us?" "No, we have but one; the other is not an angel; it is an evil spirit."—"Can you see your angel?" "No; *she tells me* that it is near my right shoulder, but I see nothing."

38. "Do you think you will soon see your mother?" "I don't know; but here is my little niece; she tells me I must pray; to hear her, we should do naught but pray; we can not, however, be continually praying."—"Perhaps you don't pray often enough." "I pray as every one does, morning and night."—"When she speaks to you, has she a childish or rational air?" "She looks just as frolicksome as when she was on earth, is always wishing to be off, and laughs heartily at my questions and ignorance! You don't hear her then laugh?"—"You know that I am not in your state." "True; let her go, as she will not answer my questions."—"You seem very blunt with this young girl, who seems so glad to see you; that is not right!"

39. Louise, Adèle's niece, comes in haste to tell her that her brother is about to appear to her. "Oh, here he is! It is my brother Alphonse, who died in Africa."—"When?" "Four years ago."—"On what day?" "I don't know."—"Ask him." "The 11th August."—"How is he attired?" "In the uniform of a dragoon."—"Is that his dress in heaven?" "No; it is

that of the corps in which he served before his death, and it was in this costume that I saw him on earth."—"Why is he dressed thus?" "Spirits must surely appear in the costume and condition by which they were known on earth, otherwise we should be unable to recognise them."—"Since you did not ask for him who told him to come and see you?" "My little niece."—"Is she with him at this moment?" "Yes; but how beautiful she is! her fine black hair falls in ringlets on her shoulders, as on the day of her first communion."—"And Alphonse, does he appear to you handsome?" "Oh! indeed he does. His forehead, which was, however, very dark, appears to me as white as snow; he tells me that it will not be long before I see my mother, father, and brother-in-law. I have no wish, however, to see the last-named one; he was too wicked on earth."—"If in heaven there is no wickedness, you must not think of the past." "I won't see him!"—Adèle stretches out her arm to detain her niece, who has just quitted her, despite her efforts; it is surprising to see the mimickry, the apparent mutual understanding, the contrariety; one can not doubt the reality of the scenes in which the imagination, as we may believe, is not always strongest, for nothing appears to respond to the caprices of the clairvoyant.

40. Louise, true to the promise she had made Adèle at the last sitting, announces to her her second brother. "What brother is this?" "It is Jean Marie, who also died in Africa, three years ago."—Adèle contemplates with delight these three members of her family; the latter is also in the uniform of a dragoon; she talks, as in the preceding sittings, a long time with them, acquaints me not with the subject of their conversation. "What do your brothers do in heaven?" "They amuse themselves, promenade."—"We can neither amuse ourselves nor promenade a whole eternity without an object." "Oh! they play music, study the sciences; they occupy themselves better, and with more pleasure, than we do."

41. "Here they are."—"Do they appear glad to see you?" "They do, indeed."—"Is your niece with them?" "No."—"Are they glad that they are dead?" "Who would not be?

They are so happy. I am going to see my mother, they tell me."—Adèle awaits a moment, then suddenly extends her arms, and seems to embrace her mother; her heart beats violently, her physiognomy is expressive, she is quite joyous and sheds tears. "Does your mother seem to be as glad to see you as you her?" "Oh! yes."—"What does she do in heaven?" "She is with my father, my brothers, in short, with my whole family; she is very uneasy about me, but withal very happy. She reads, and delights in hearing my brothers play music."—"There are books, then, in heaven." "I beg you to believe that there are, and not such romances as on earth."—"Of what do they treat?" "Of the mysteries of God, and of science; but they are not written as on earth, my mother tells me. How I should like to be with them. Let me go, I should soon be in heaven."—"Yours is a very generous idea; what should I do with your body?" "Bury it, or do what you please with it."—"And what should I say to justice?" "That I am gone."—Adèle makes a few efforts to rise to the highest degree of ecstasy. I wake her.

42. "You were not very reasonable in your last sleep, it was a suicide you would have committed, and you know that is very wrong!" "True, but once committed, one must needs enter like the rest."—"What is the punishment that God reserves for suicide?" "That which he inflicts on all those who do evil, a public reprimand; after that, God renders it impossible for them to do evil, by consigning them to a place apart."—"What sort of place is it? Is it the hell of which men speak?" "There is no such hell as is depicted on earth; there are places of purification, which are termed places of punishment, because one is there deprived of the sight of God and his divine light; but those who are there are happy."—"And all great criminals, where are they?" "In similar places, assembled in society; but, as God is so good, he provides for all, prevents evil, and re-establishes good in the hearts of all."—"We are, then, in societies in heaven." "We seek one another, and assemble together according to our tastes."—"Is there any disturbance sometimes in these societies?" "No,

because the thoughts of every one are laid bare; consequently, none can be deceived. The criminal, the passionate man, the virtuous and good man, can not, the one any more than the other, appear what they are not, or disguise their thoughts as on earth; it is a sort of stamp engraved within us, and not to be effaced."—"In that case we ought to recollect all we have done on earth." "No; for the simple reason that we set no value on it, all that is forgotten; we no longer occupy ourselves with such things; we merely study the thoughts, the affections present and necessary to the common happiness; we pity those who are still on earth, pray to God for them, and are delighted when they rejoin us; for them it is a time of trial, which each must undergo in his turn."—"Do we meet again among friends?" "Yes; but, if the affections are different, we separate, each to enjoy apart what is agreeable to him."—"We receive there instruction as on earth, I suppose, as every one is not learned on entering heaven, the child as well as the old man." "Instruction is not the same there as on earth, because, on our arrival, our spirit comprehends forthwith whatever it desires to know; we speak there but one language, which is that of thought; all, from the infant to the old man, can speak and comprehend it from their very entrance; in like manner, all can read. It is only for the superior sciences, the knowledge of the laws of the spiritual world and the mysteries of God, that there are teachers, who are more like friends than masters, and we learn in a short time what we desire to know." —"Who tells you these things?" "My mother, who gives me to understand that I want to learn a great deal in one day."—"Ask your mother whether we see God in heaven." "Yes." —"In what form?" "That of a sun, so dazzling that we can not fix our eye on it; no one can form an idea of its brilliancy."

The answers at this sitting are so much the more astonishing, as Adèle, in her state of vigil, is unacquainted with my way of thinking on spiritual things, and which is not exactly in accordance with what she tells me in her sleep; I can not, therefore, influence her in this respect; she has not the speciality for the communication of thoughts, and this should remove the idea, which might be conceived, of her reading in mine. I have sufficiently studied her to this effect in circumstances wherein she had a powerful interest to do so, but never was I ablé to succeed in making her comprehend a single thought. I have equally maintained the greatest reserve, by never recounting what my somnambulists tell me in their sleep. How does she happen to accord so well with Bruno and others who preceded him, and especially in all the reiterated questions that I shall address, by-and-by, to various deceased personages?—questions far beyond the ordinary intelligence of Adèle.

43. "Here is my mother" (same emotion as usual). She announces to me the arrival of her father. "Here he is!" Adèle opens her arms, as she did at the first visit of her mother; her agitation and joy are no less great; she clasps her hands, and humbly bends her head to receive her father's blessing; then talks of family affairs; her brothers are present. What surprises me most is, that she could see all her relations only at intervals of time—more or less long; had it been merely the fruit of imagination in her, she could have seen them at the same sitting, or the following one, at least; but their arrival was announced by her niece, or her brothers, at fixed periods.

44. Can your mother answer me a few questions?" "Yes; according to the nature of them."—"Can she tell me what sort of sensations we experience when dying?" "We experience a painful sensation, for the internal quits not the external body without suffering; but scarcely is it disengaged, than it thinks no more of it, and finds itself of inconceivable lightness; it ascends forthwith to heaven, where it is reunited to its family. All this takes place in so short a time that it knows not how it could have been accomplished."—"In what form does the soul quit the body?" "In that of the body."—"Is it composed, like the body, of all its exterior and interior organs, such as arms, legs, heart, lungs, and all the other viscera." "The soul is in all similar to the body; one can not be better assured of it, since we see all these interior organs like

the works of a watch under a glass."—"But how does such a body manage to penetrate matter without obstacles, and unperceived?" "As my relations, who are four in number, here present, and unseen by you; there are no obstacles for the spirit."—"Is it really your mother who still answers you?" "Yes; and my father and brothers applaud."—"Since I have just asked you a few particulars as to our exit from the world, I should wish to obtain others on our entrance into it?" Adèle seems embarrassed; modesty apparently commands her to elude my questions. I reassure her as to my intentions, telling her I only seek for instruction. "God creates, man sows, and woman performs the office of a hen; she broods. God does the rest."—"Has the germ any form?" "Yes; the human form."—"Woman then stands for naught in this creation?" "The woman broods; supplies the juices necessary for the material body, that's all. My mother is going away."

45. "Are all your relatives with you?" "There are four of them present."—"Do you expect others?" "I expect my sister, who also is dead, and whom I have not yet seen. Oh! here she is! and how beautiful! Goodness me! how we improve in looks after death!"—"How is she attired?" "In her betrothal dress; she died on the eve of the day fixed for her wedding; she is in white; her hair is turned back: she is also barefooted, like my little niece. How droll."—"Ask them why they have not chaussures?" "My mother answers, that where they are, there are no stones."—"On what, then, are they?" "On a beautiful green turf."—"What have they around them?" "A vast and beautiful blue horizon."—"What kind of light illumes this horizon?" "A very pure light, which I may compare to that at the close of a fine summer day."—"You once told me that, in order to have the perception of spiritual bodies, we had to enter a state necessary for that purpose. Is it the same with them, or do they see our material bodies?" "Spirits see only our spiritual bodies; but no sooner do we desire to see a deceased relative, than he is forthwith with us. If we can enter into this state, we see him; if not, it is not he who is at default, but we who can not see him."—"Your father's coun-

tenance; does it seem to you, as on earth, older than your brother's?" "Yes; and that you ought easily to conceive, it being absolutely necessary that the dead should appear to us just as they were on earth, in order to be recognised; but it is not their real heavenly countenance. There they all appear to be of the same age, excepting those who die when children: in that case, they continue growing, and become like the rest in respect to the uniformity of age stamped on their physiognomy. Although they all appear to be of the same age, each preserves his individual look, apart the beauty which is common to them all, and which surpasses all that the imagination can conceive on earth."—"What appears to be the general age?" "Thirty to forty; but this age would be taken by us for about twenty."—"Negroes, I suppose, are of a beautiful black there?" "The souls of negroes are as white as ours; it is only in the skin they differ from us; but in heaven every one is white."—"Since we meet again in families, no doubt the husband rejoins his wife?" "Yes; but they do not live as on earth, on our impure love; they live like brother and sister."—"What! there is no love in heaven?" "There is a love unknown to the earth, and incomprehensible to those who are on the earth; it may be compared to a chaste and pure friendship."—"Are all beings assembled there in pairs?" "Yes."—"But there are beings that delight in isolation, and have never known love on earth; they have loved no one?" "Not a being exists but has loved some one on earth, or felt the want of loving; this want has ever existed, and, perhaps, there are no beings in existence who may not have said to themselves, 'I should have dearly loved such a woman, or such a man.' This union of two beings is the foundation of all happiness."—"I am aware of that; but it seems to me that there is one difficulty: many beings have not loved because they could not love conjointly the same person, and hence spring the rivalries which cause so much trouble." "It is not thus in heaven. Analyze earthly love, which is a passion of possession, and you will find that it is in order to possess the same woman to one's self that rivalry springs up: in heaven it is the contrary; we love not for the happiness of possessing, but for that of loving."—"You have, however, told me, that in heaven we are in pairs, a proof that we possess there, as on earth, the object of our affections. Then, again, a woman who has had two or three husbands, how is that managed? I think you will be puzzled to give me an answer?" "By no means; every being is created double, and sooner or later united to his half; but in the world of spirits, of which we now speak, we know not earthly love, or the want of being united to the object of our affection. Thus, we dream not there as on earth of the possession of the being that often remains long unknown to us; and then, again, we love those around us like brothers and sisters."—"You told me that your brother was united there to his betrothed?" "Yes; because it is she who is his half; but every one meets not forthwith with his own, and such union is in nowise similar to our earthly love. A woman might be loved by a score of men, since none would desire to possess her to himself alone. You perceive, therefore, that you can not comprehend such mysteries."—"I fully comprehend that the idea of possession, in love, as in everything else, is the foundation of all earthly troubles; but if this affection is at times misplaced, it, nevertheless, procures for the man and the woman a happiness which it seems to me no easy matter to replace by aught else?" "It is not said that it is replaced, since, on the contrary, I have already told you, that in heaven all beings, without distinction, were completed there; but I replied to your question of a woman who has had several husbands. In heaven, she may love them all at once, as a mother loves all her children, and may be loved by them all, as this mother is loved by all her children. Were there a hundred to love her, they would not be too many; if the whole hundred wish always to be in her presence and enjoy the pleasure of her conversation, they may all do so, without jealousy, since we possess all that we can desire to possess. So much for the heaven of spirits. But in the superior heaven, where the reunion, the junction, of bodies is definitely effected, each is penetrated with a holy love for his partner, whom none can either envy or dispute with you, each having his own, from whom he could not divert the least affection."

46. "You told me at the last sitting that spirits could pass without difficulty through all bodies; this would induce the belief that their substance is but a compound of air; can these spirits assume any other form besides the human one?" "Yes, whatever form they desire, especially evil spirits, who take delight in all sorts of disguises."—"This would make me believe in the malicious spirits who cause those apparitions so industriously circulated in the country." "It is a reality; they take delight only in troubles of this kind."—"Do you believe that these spirits have the strength to upset articles of furniture and a thousand other things, as it is said? I can not accord such power to air, a light fluid can not disturb a heavy one." "You don't believe it! it is, however, this light fluid, as you term it, that imparts motion to your body, and can also, by transporting it from one place to another, charge it with a heavy burden, without your knowing that it is the spirit alone that possesses the strength to move this matter, though shackled as it is by its bonds. Why should you refuse it a double or triple force when it is freed from it? Know that the spirit can bear the heaviest burdens, light fluid as you believe it to be, and can effect things of which you have no conception."—"I accorded it this power within us because we furnish it with organs and fluids wherewith to operate, but I do not think that out of matter it has any power over it." "It is as I have just told you; you can not conceive that it has the same organs, that it is it which is the life, the strength, the action, the mover of matter; and what has moved it a minute can also move it an eternity."—"Can these spirits, as it is affirmed, repair to your orders to obey you?" "They desire nothing better; they obey you a few instants in order to draw you into their society, and become, at a later period, their slaves."—"What do you mean by that?—they have a leader, then?" "No, they are all free and independent; but you become their slaves, as the gambler is the slave of the places he frequents, of the passions, the consequences, of which he undergoes; they

aided you to do evil, after your death you aid them to do what you took a delight in seeing them do for you."—"Many persons doubt what you now say, because they have sought to enter into communication with them and have not succeeded." "That may be accounted for thus: in the first place, their good angel diverted them from such a course; secondly, if you ask for a spirit out of the mass, as you would for a soldier out of an army, none will answer only to his name; we should know, therefore, to whom we address ourselves; do so in proper form, and not make the request while dreading its execution. A truce to such conversation; I don't like it."—"Can you tell me the name of my angel?" "Gabriel."—"And the name of yours?" "Raphael."—"There are, then, many angels named Gabriel?" "There is no dearth of them—it is a society."—"Can an angel convey messages and objects, as some religious persons and magnetizers have said?" "Yes, but that happens very seldom; it can be effected only by quite a special protection of God. My mother tells me that I wish to know a great deal." "Tell her that it is in order to instruct yourself, and avoid being laughed at by your brothers for your ignorance."—"Could your mother be deceived?" "No."—"And your niece?" "She might, because she is yery young and thoughtless; no doubt she has been forbidden to speak to me, as she is much more quiet now."

47. For several sittings Adèle's mother did not come, but at this one she appears, and complains to her daughter of my incredulity in her presence, telling her that I had carried my doubts so far the last time as to try and lay hold of her with my hand; that if ever I recommend such an experiment she would come no more to visit her; that I ought to have as much confidence in her as she had in me; and that, moreover, I could never feel or touch a spirit. Adèle is very much astonished at this communication. I wish to assure her of the contrary, but she believes her mother in preference to me. It is quite true that I mechanically put out my arm toward the spot where I supposed Adèle's mother to be, without for a moment considering that I could not feel a spiritual body; but this silly experi-

ment on my part has presented me with a solution which I was far from expecting, as it assures me that no other being but Adèle's mother could have been acquainted with my then present thoughts. Adèle, as I have observed, not having this speciality, and had she possessed it she would have given me to understand forthwith that I was doing a silly act; neither has she the speciality of seeing bodies or objects present, she sees only the interior of sick persons: she could not be aware of this incident, and, had she divined it, she is incapable of dissembling so far with me. We shall see, by-and-by, that she is worthy of all confidence; a single fact of this nature proved may admit a hundred. This sitting was to be pregnant with good results: Adèle's mother predicting that one of her daughters, Adèle's sister, would get married in a short time, that she would not be the first to acquaint her with this change in her position, but that her brother, who was in the country, would bring her the news. She also tells her the name of the person to whom her sister was to be married, though he was then unknown to both the latter and Adèle. Her father informs her, at the same time, that she will shortly hear that another of her sisters had been brought to bed of a girl. The prediction was realized, point for point, two years after, and the communication was perfectly true. Here, then, are three facts emanating from real communications, and not from any other combination.

48. Adèle exclaims: "Oh, here is a pretty little angel! How fair, and how beautiful!"—"Who is it?" "My little godson, who died in my arms when only a fortnight old." "That's three years ago." I had magnetized Bruno the same day with Adèle, he also sees this little angel. He declares that it has wings; Adèle says the contrary. After a moment's contemplation, she appears to be afraid. "What makes you afraid?" "My brother-in-law, who is come to see me, and wants to take me by the hand. I could very well dispense with his visit. I told my parents that I had no wish to see him. Why does he come? I won't have him touch me; let him go. Adèle turns away in a pet from this man, who appears to her

on her left; while, on the contrary, all good spirits ordinarily appear on the right. I observed to her that it is very wrong and unjust on her part; that she ought not, in the state she is, to entertain ill-will toward any one. I desire her to give her hand to her brother-in-law. She obstinately refuses, saying that he is in a position well adapted for his malicious purposes; that he had made her sister miserable; that he still did all he could to inspire her with disagreeable thoughts, but that when he had passed over to the good side she would forgive him. I am obliged to order off this man. One can not take this apparition for an effect of the imagination, as she in nowise desired it, and was horribly surprised and vexed at it. Never before had I seen her so harsh and wilful as toward this man.

49. Second apparition of Adèle's little godson. She seems to take the greatest interest in this little being; and when she beheld him depart it seemed to her that he was going to fall. She followed him, and entered into the complement of ecstasy, from which it was no easy matter for me to withdraw her. She signified her displeasure at my attempts, saying to me as before, " Why force me to return to this world of trouble and misery? I was so happy in accompanying this little being, who has, indeed, pretty little white wings, such as M. Bruno described. It is I who was wrong on this point."—" How far did you go?" " I ascended to a great height, then passed through an immense vault, at the end of which were beautiful gardens, containing all that is remarkable for freshness and elegance. A great many persons were walking in the alleys, some reading, others playing music—all seemed very happy. The harmony among them appeared so perfect, that one could only desire to be with them. I saw my father there, my mother, the whole of my family. I wanted to stay,. but my mother and your will obliged me to descend again."—" How were all those people dressed?" " In a sort of gauze robe, of all colors. Their physiognomy was totally different; but I fully recognised my relations, although if they appeared to us thus attired it would be more difficult to recognise them. God has done right in contriving otherwise."—" How can males be dis-

tinguished from females?" "By their form; for their light dress is no mark of distinction. If the passions were the same in heaven as on earth, we should be ashamed to see ourselves thus. No attention is paid there to such things."—"Bruno has already told me the same thing; this attire, however, is very indecent." "Yes, for us here below, where love exists, with its impure empire; but there, no such thoughts are entertained."

50. "Here is the partner of my brother Alphonse, Rosine, one of my old friends, who was betrothed to him, as I have told you, before he set off for Africa; she died four years after him."—"Ask her if she is disposed to answer a few questions I wish to put to her." "Yes."—"Since you told me that she is united to her betrothed in heaven, would she tell you how this reunion, which is now a real union, was accomplished? Were there any ceremonies for this purpose?" "Good heavens! no. Alphonse awaited Rosine, because he knew her end was approaching. No sooner had she entered than they were reunited without any ceremony—without requiring the approbation or consent of a third party; they were reunited to each other as friends, and not as lovers, as she also says that there is no love in heaven. They are like brother and sister, perfectly in accord, since it can not be otherwise."—"Do they sleep together?" "We do not go to bed in heaven; there is no night as on earth; we merely repose when we desire it, for it is not fatigue that compels us to do so."—"Does Rosine repose beside her friend?" "Certainly."—"On what?" "On a divan, cushions, whatever she pleases."—"Are they always together?" "No, she goes to see him, and he her."—"Have they a room for two?" "No, they live in families and societies."—"There are no rooms, then, in which we can meditate apart?" "Positively speaking, there are no houses as on earth, but separations that stand in their stead, which every one may occupy according to his taste; but nothing on earth can be compared to them in beauty and magnificence."—"We may, then, meditate or perform usages agreeable to us for an infinite time?" "Yes, we may read a book, a page, a phrase,

for a time without end, seeing that there is no time in heaven, and still less of it, for aught that is agreeable to us; we find incessantly the same pleasure, the same enjoyment in the idea we delight in. My brother-in-law is exasperated at my rancor toward him; but he indemnified himself for it last night, by suggesting to me bad dreams. I dreamed that I was cutting the throat of his daughter, my little niece, who is in heaven and comes to see me habitually; I concealed her thus assassinated under my bed. Good heavens, how I suffered!"—"It was a mere rambling of the imagination; a spirit can not thus influence us, were such the case, we should be slaves, a hundred times worse off than the brutes." "It is so, however, not in all dreams, but in some, spirits prefer the moment when the body is left to repose, without any defence, and when the soul is less vigilant over it, by seeking to avail itself of the body's sleep to give itself up to researches, experiments, travels. Then it is that evil spirits torment us, and we can rid ourselves of their presence only by invoking the name of God who drives them out forthwith. What I tell you is a truth at which I should laugh in my watchful state, but now appreciate at its proper value. It was my brother-in-law who represented to me those horrible images."—"But the good angel, beside us, can he not protect us under such circumstances?" "Not always; our soul stands in need of his counsels for a multitude of other actions, of which it has no recollection; for the spirit sleeps not, and our angel can not always prevent by night, any more than by day, the power of evil spirits."

We are now come, without the least desire, to the persuasions of M. Berbiguer, with his hobgoblins. I have thought fit to give this sitting entire, that every one may judge of it as he pleases. As one of the objects of this work is to engage all magnetizers to make similar researches on the spiritual laws, I doubt not but that many will be found to obtain similar results. In all that has been hitherto told me, it is impossible to perceive aught but mere sickly or dreamy organizations; but there is too much affinity between them not to admit at least a mental indisposition, the symptoms of which should be precisely the same in each individual; but how admit such connection in the ideas, without concluding therefrom that it is the magnetizer himself who insinuates them? In that case I will reply: Do as I do and you will know what to think of it. Continue the perusal of this work to the end, and you will see that a magnetizer is not a god, that his properties must be limited to his belief and his knowledge; but that he is unable to influence what he knows not, what he believes not, and if you meet not with the solution you seek, do not say that my ecstatics were wearisome fools.

51. "My niece tells me that my brother is ill, that he has had medical advice in time, but that he will be attacked again with the same malady and will die young. [This proved to be true.] Here is my mother, she does not seem pleased."—"Perhaps she is displeased at your propensity for the ecstatic state in despite of her counsels; ask her if such be the case." "True; she says that this state is a very dangerous one for me."—"How long ought you to remain in it?" "Five minutes."—"Why does your little godson who comes to see you appear to you as an angel?" "Because he is really one?"—"Why should he be one, any more than your niece?" "Because he had not attained the age of three years at his death."—"Why rather this age than any other?" "My mother tells me that all children that die before this age grow no bigger. God, who dearly loves them on account of the state of purity in which they died (seeing that they have not yet committed any evil), delights in being surrounded by them; they are much nearer to him than any of the rest."

52. "When you rise, through ecstasy, toward heaven, the sensation you experience is, I suppose, similar to that experienced by a person dying." "No; I rise in good health, experience no obstacle, whereas at death, the soul is much more cramped in quitting the body disorganized by illness; then there is suffering, but I feel none in the state I am."—"What effect is produced in you when you behold beneath you the earth, which must appear very obscure compared to the brilliant light of heaven?" "We make no reflections; we neither think of

the earth nor of any one; we rise in a sensation of happiness, of joy impossible to describe, we would wish to remain there." —"May it not be an error of your senses this pretended elevation toward heaven, or rather an interior nervous expansion, illumed by bright electric rays surrounding the soul, which, possibly is, in its corporeal interior, and enjoys the happiness of this sight which it fancies it tastes from without." "How admit such an error, when one feels as I feel, sees what I see; traverses clouds, space, and arrives in the midst of relations, friends, who all stretch out to you their arms, overwhelm you with caresses, and seek by all possible means to prove to you the pleasure they feel in seeing you, and desire with a common accord that you should soon rejoin them. If we look upon all this as error, I know not then how we are to recognise truth." —"There are narcotics which produce hallucinations more or less agreeable, and display to us pictures, scenes, somewhat similar to ecstasy, and such, however, are errors." "There you are again at discussion and doubt. It is a practice with men to treat as errors what they do not comprehend; it is an easy way of settling the matter. Narcotics convey trouble into the nervous system, disturb the soul in its vital functions, throw it into the world of causes, when it makes unheard-of efforts to remain in the world of effects. The soul confounds the domain of the memory; the pictures of the ineffaceable actions which all men have within them, with the pictures of the world of causes in which it wanders for a moment. It can perceive in this state the most burlesque scenes tacked on to rational ones; because it knows not how to separate them, knows not where it is, knows not what they are; the reservoir of its imagination overflows, and hurries it into the absurd. But is it the same in ecstasy: is all that I tell you under the empire of folly? What is predicted to me and which is accomplished, is it of the domain of error? The views at distances, the descriptions of places: what is done or said there; are they errors? All the somnambulists who thus see do they not prove that they are no longer in their body, since they reproduce to you facts, scenes, conversations of which you have never heard speak, and which take place for the first time at the very instant they are communicated to you. What can you say to those facts? Be reasonable, then, and believe that all the *savans* in the world can not deny what I have just cited, and which is operated every day at each instant; they will be obliged to extend the properties of the body, if they are unwilling to give it a soul, and these properties will be as obscure in their solution as those of the soul, or they will accept the latter; then they will give it the power of travelling out of the body, reading thoughts, seeing actions past and future, and when they have acknowledged such a soul, they will not refuse its going in search of repose to a place of recompense for all the sufferings which it has endured in this world of grief."—"I thank you for your ingenious and frank explanation. I have nothing to say against it."

53. "Once more, allow me to make an observation on the last sitting. My reason for doubting that your soul was out of your body, is, that scarcely have I spoken, than you answer me; and I do not perceive your body making any movement when you say that you are receiving the caresses of your relatives." "It is, however, this want of movement in my body, in my grand ecstatic movements, which ought to prove to you that I am no longer in it; when my relatives, on the contrary, come on earth to see me, you perceive my spiritual hand pressing theirs, my body gesticulating, because they are really there present and I also; but when I am in heaven, my body can no longer make the same gestures, since there is no longer a soul within it. If I answer you immediately, it is because I still cling to my body by sympathetic threads which you seem to me to hold like cords, forcing me, when you draw them, to descend to the power of your will."—"In views, at distances, although the somnambulists are in other places, their body is not deprived of movement." "The comparison holds not good. They are on earth at slight distances comparatively with those of heaven; they are not in the ecstatic condition necessary to communicate with heaven, and hence the separation of the soul and body is not the same."—I perceive that Adèle purposes entering into the ecstatic state; I make up my mind to try a decisive exper-

iment, and leave her to her will; I forthwith send Bruno to sleep, put him *en rapport* with her, and beg him to follow her as far as possible, recommending him not to be alarmed, and to warn me only if he should see danger. I wished to be assured by myself of the pretended dangers of ecstasy. Frequently had Adèle told me that she had been on the point of not coming back to re-enter her body, and as I thought that she only wanted to alarm me, I wished to know what opinion to come to. At the lapse of a quarter of an hour, Bruno exclaims in great alarm, "I have lost sight of her!" I had relied upon him, and paid little attention to Adèle, whose body in the meanwhile had grown icy cold; there was no longer any pulse or respiration; her face was of a sallow green, her lips blue, her heart gave no sign of life. I placed before her lips a mirror, but it was by no means tarnished by them. I magnetized her powerfully, in order to bring back her soul into her body, but for five minutes my labor was vain. Bruno, alarmed at my want of success, as well as the persons present at this sitting, tended greatly to disturb me. I thought for a moment that the work was consummated, and that I had an indubitable proof that the soul had departed from her body. I was obliged to request the persons present to pass into another room, in order that I might recover by myself a little energy. At the lapse of a few moments, I entertained the hope that I should not have such a misfortune to deplore; but, physically speaking, I was utterly powerless. Falling on my knees, I asked back of God, in my prayer, the soul that I had in my doubts suffered to depart. I seemed, by an effect of intuition to know that my prayer was heard: after a minute's further anguish, I obtained these words: "Why have you called me back? it was all over with me! but God moved at your prayer, sent me back to you. No more shall I be permitted to return to heaven; I am punished."—"Of what punishment do you speak?" "Raphael has forbidden my mother and all my relations, except Alphonse, to come and see me again, until further orders, and it is to you that I am indebted for this privation. I shall no longer be able to ascend to heaven, but had it not been for you I should have been there now and for ever." It may be naturally supposed that I paid but little attention to her complaints and reproaches.

I was only too happy to hear her speak to me, and promised myself, as my readers may imagine, never to recommence such experiments. I advise those who should be disposed to imitate me, never to make such a trial, for no spectacle can be more alarming, and the issue of such experiment might terminate fatally.

It was all over with her ecstasies, just as she had predicted; no one came any more to see her. Her brother often instructed her in what was agreeable to her; but the self-will of Adèle, and her little regard for his complaisance, drove him away. It was more than six months before she recovered this kind of clairvoyance; I was not sorry for it, as I was determined not to magnetize her again. There was a continual combat of subtlety between us two; if I lost sight of her for an instant, she had ever the same intention, suicide in ecstasy! Several times since she sought to re-enter this state, but she invariably felt a hand which pushed her head forward, sometimes she heard boisterous music, which diverted her from her purpose, and once a voice exclaimed in her ear, "That is forbidden you." It was her brother Alphonse who worked all these miracles; he never came to see her without diverting her by an air on a flute, although before his death he knew not how to play that instrument; he often rendered perceptible to her a divine music, which she could hear, though wide awake, by a secret she had taught me to employ to this effect. She equally saw all her relations after she awoke, a circumstance that excited her astonishment, and made her believe in magic; she could not comprehend, be it understood, these kinds of visions, which made me pass in her eyes for a sorcerer. We are bound to conclude from all these experiments, which lasted whole months, and which I compress into one sitting, that it would be more than ridiculous that a woman so firm should not perceive at will the freaks of her imagination, if such they were; but, on the contrary, that all these facts presented such a variety only the better to dispose me to believe in their merit.

We will pass on to more decisive experiments, in the same kind of clairvoyance, in order that it may not be said, it is her relations whose image is imprinted in her imagination, whom she continually sees; that is not astonishing, and proves naught.

54. New Spiritual Clairvoyance.—Adèle was consulted by an abbé on a speculation. When he learned that she had the facility of conversing with spirits, he expressed a wish for her to see his father, who had been dead some months. "Here he is," said she. "Describe to me his appearance and dress, if you please." Adèle did so, to the great satisfaction of this gentleman, and related to him a few particulars of the life of his father, such as he alone could be acquainted with. Naught more was required to convince the abbé of the excellent clairvoyance of Adèle; consequently he returned a few days after to beg me to put some questions to her on alchemy; I promised him that I would do so with pleasure. Adèle was not at my house that day.

55. "Will you request your brother to come; I have a few questions to put to him?" She requests his attendance, and all at once seems overcome as if with surprise. "What is the matter with you?" asked I. "It is a capuchin friar who is come to me; he is on his knees, and praying to God."—"Who is this friar?" "I don't know whether he is a capuchin, but he has a cowl on his head; I can't see his face."—"Ask him what he wants with you?" "I dare not speak to him."—"In that case I'll send him away." I give the usual command, but the man does not budge. Adèle and I both laugh; she experiences no alarm, still she persists in not speaking to him. At last he disappears, and she again asks for her brother, who forthwith comes. "I beg her to ask him who this man is." "It is," replied he, laughing, "Father Lauriot; I sent him to you that you might question him for the abbé." Adèle laughs at this name, and thinks that her brother is making sport of her. (Lauriot signifies a baker's tub.) "Request your brother to tell you positively the name of this man." "His name was Achilles; he was a priest, and one of the abbé's friends. I

know not whether this gentleman is aware that he devoted himself, when on earth, to hermetic researches; but in heaven he is in societies that follow such pursuits, and for that reason I address him to you."—"You were aware, then, that I was to question you on this subject?" "Yes, I perceived it in your thoughts," replies her brother; "and as I do not trouble myself with such matters, I thought I could not do better than place you in communication with one who could instruct you."—"That being the case, you ought to have warned me, and I should not have given this man so cool a reception." "He will return."—"They make, then, the philosopher's stone in heaven?" "No; but every one occupies himself there according to his taste. He whose whole affection it was on earth takes no delight in making it after his death, but in associating with societies that protect and instruct those on earth who work at it, and have recourse to them."—"The stone, then, exists?" "Yes."—I put several questions to him on this subject, which he answered according to their value.

56. I had acquainted the abbé with this apparition, which he took for an hallucination, never having known a priest by that name. I informed him of the answers I had obtained from Adèle's brother, and these were satisfactory to him. After his departure I determined on sending the young girl to sleep again, that I might obtain from her fuller information. Scarcely asleep, Adèle requested his presence. He came, and I put the following questions: "Is Lauriot your real name?" "I was nicknamed thus."—"What is your family name?" No answer.—"When did you die?" "In 1831."—"Where?" "At the hospital Sainte-Thérèse."—"How old were you?" "Fifty-six."—"In what name is your death registered?" "Achilles." "Do you know the abbé?" "Yes; when he was lying ill at the hospital Sainte-Thérèse, I was one of those with whom he most frequently conversed."—"But he says he does not know you." "He will recollect me."—"You employed your time, then, on earth, in search of the stone?" "I don't come here to answer all the questions you think

fit to put to me; I come out of pure complaisance, and shall answer only what I think fit."—"Then what can you say to the abbé respecting his operations?" "They go on very well. He is in the right road, only let him throw a little more heat into his furnace."—"Do you know how long the abbé has been engaged in his operations?" "Four years."—This man again falls on his knees, recommending an augmentation of heat. "Give me a description of him." "He appeared to me standing. He had on his head a cowl, which he took off to speak to me. He is a dark man; his face is pale and long, and his eyes black. He does not appear to be so old as fifty-six. He is taller than the abbé, and has a somewhat taciturn and very meditative air. He had a small leather cap on his head. I scarcely dare speak to him, though he is far from uncivil in his answers; but his tone is severe, especially when he told me that he should answer at the orders of no one, but at his own pleasure."—"Are you really assured of the truth of this apparition?' "I maintain that this man is still there on his knees before me. Be he a good or an evil spirit, I see him full well, and have really spoken to him. He is calm at this moment. He has a chaplet at his side, to which is attached a medal about the size of a five-franc piece, on which are characters of fantastical forms. They are somewhat like Vs and Ys; I can't very well see."—"Can you see your brother to-day?" "This gentleman tells me that he will not come."

57. I forwarded to the abbé an account in writing of all that I had obtained at this sitting; then, this gentleman, unable to call to mind any such name, proceeded forthwith to the library of the archbishopric, where a register was kept of the priests who died in the diocese of Paris. Next day he came to my house with a copy of the registers for the last three years, but we could neither find such a name nor any one of that age. We were convinced that Adèle had been under the influence of hallucination, a circumstance which had never occurred since she had been a clairvoyante. I was all the more vexed at this as her brother, who had never before deceived

her in any of his revelations and predictions, was the author of this trick, which came somewhat late, but in time to tell me not to cease entertaining distrust of spirits.

58. Two days after this presumed mystification, and still without the knowledge of the abbé, I once more sent Adèle to sleep, requesting her to ask for Father Lauriot.—"Here he is."—"You gave me false information. What was your object in doing so?" "To conceal my name; but I came with a good intention—to oblige by my counsels, and I did so sincerely."—"Why do you conceal your name?" "I have no answer to make to your question. Men forgive not, but God does."—"In short, whoever you be, have you a borrowed name, or any other?" "I was called Lauriot, which was not my name; but I bore that of Achilles, which was my Christian name."—"In what name is your death registered?" "I have no wish to say."—"Why did you not tell me your name at once, without deceiving me as you have done?" "I had not the least intention to deceive you, as I told you that my name was Achilles Lauriot. I was obliged to resort to this subterfuge in order to conceal my real name, which would make you curse me, and take in bad part the good I am willing to do." —"In short, did you really die at Sainte-Thérèse?" "Yes." —"In what year?" "In 1831."—"Was it there that you became acquainted with the abbé?" "It was there that I had much conversation with him respecting the stone. I knew and still know the abbé, who, you may rely upon it, will recollect me."—"In what church were you employed?" "I don't mean to furnish such information."—Adèle again addresses to him a few questions, to which he answers: "Your head is poorly," and then recommences praying. It was true that Adèle had a violent headache brought on by this discussion, which advanced us not a jot. I asked for Adèle's brother, who came immediately.—"Tell us candidly who this man is?" "He is a man who wishes to do good, and is incapable of evil."—"But can't you give us fuller information than he did? Who is he? What was he?" "I can not answer what he is unwilling to answer himself. He is a man who is continually

walking, as on earth; he had no fixed locality there; it is the same with him now in heaven."—"Can you not, as a spirit, read his thoughts?" "When a spirit is unwilling that we should do so, we can not."—"He can, then, conceal them from your researches?" "Yes; but he could not, were he a wicked man; it is because I know his goodness that I addressed him to you." Adèle, provoked at not having a more satisfactory answer, begs her brother never to send this man to her again.

59. As before, I forwarded the particulars of this sitting to the abbé, who came to me two days after, more enlightened on the point. "I now know this man," said he, "he really died at Sainte-Thérèse, not, however, in 1831, but only two years ago, and not at the age of fifty-six, but fifty-four. When I was lying ill at Sainte-Thérèse, I knew this man, who was possessed of great information, was an amateur of magnetism, medicine, and alchemy. He sacrificed his time and fortune in the research of the secrets of nature, invariably maintaining that magnetism conceals mysteries worthy of being fathomed, and that plants concerning the juices of which he had made valuable discoveries, possess virtues which men do not sufficiently study. Ever running from one part of the country to the other, gathering herbs, in the research of the occult sciences; delighting to conceal his name in the blessings he spread around him with profusion, as in the relations he established with the world; he was Peter for one, Philippe for another; it was a sort of mania with him. He usually wore under his bourgeois dress a crape cassock; in short, the multiplicity of his studies deranged his intellects, and he fell into a most painful state of imbecility, was obliged to be nursed at the hospital Sainte-Thérèse, where, in his childish condition, he constantly muffled himself up in a capuchin, and never left off wearing his little leather cap. He had at his side a large chaplet with which he continually prayed; he conversed with spirits and fancied himself God; he was the sport of all, one calling him the "capuchin father," another "Father eternal," and so on. This unfortunate man died in the most frightful misery; he who had been surrounded by a numerous and wealthy family, and a

considerable circle of friends, had not two living beings to follow him to the grave! I was the only one to say a prayer over him! This man, the laughing-stock of his fellow-beings, has, perhaps, preserved an aversion for men; this accounts for his saying that his name would create in them horror! This mania of not disclosing his name, has, perhaps, accompanied him to heaven; the dress is precisely the same as that he wore on earth before his death, and the medal fastened to the chaplet alone confirms me in my recognition of his person, as he bought it on one of the quays, and it was covered with cabalistical characters. The mania he has of never resting in one place, as the brother of your clairvoyante says, is just as it was on earth; in short, he says truly enough that when I was at Sainte-Thérèse, we used to talk of the stone; he was the only one who showed me any friendship at that time. So, after all, it is easy to account for the slight mistake into which he led us. The description given him, joined to what passed at Sainte-Thérèse, would alone be sufficient for me to recognise him, and the particulars he gives as to the time when I commenced my operations, are exact. At first I could not trace the date further back than two years and a quarter, but now I recollect having commenced my experiments on the same work by another system twenty-one months before, and this makes up the four years. I have full confidence in this apparition, and will prepare a few questions which you will have the kindness to put to him by-and-by."

60. The abbé expresses a wish to put the following question to him himself: "Can you give me any proofs that I am not deceived respecting you, and that you are really present at this moment?" "I will tell you that I am right glad at your recollection of me; I was, as I announced, quite sure that you would call me to mind again; you are not mistaken as to my name, which I wish to conceal from every one but you, since you are well acquainted with it; but, as a convincing proof, be pleased to recollect that I was the only person at Sainte-Thérèse to whom you spoke of the work; hereby you will plainly perceive that you are not in error."—"Can you tell

me whether my works are going on right?" "Yes, quite so; but increase the heat five degrees more."—"My fire is not to be measured as ordinary fire." "To you, no; but for me I perceive that what you did this morning ought to be continued, and thus you will obtain the additional heat I recommend." This communication excites the abbé's astonishment; he said to me: "In fact, this morning I did something which must accelerate the heat." Then he continued thus: "I have two operations in hand, one of much later date than the other, which is the best one?" "The last, that on the right."—The abbé had already received the same answer from several clairvoyantes. He goes on putting further questions, needless to mention, at which he appears quite satisfied.

61. A few days after this sitting the abbé submits to me a few doubts he has conceived as to the moral condition of Father Lauriot. To clear up his doubts in this respect he proposes putting a few questions to him in Latin, thus enabling them both to converse in secret on hermetic operations, as neither I nor my clairvoyante was acquainted with Latin. He put his question, which Adèle did her best to reproduce to M. Lauriot; she rendered his answers in French, saying: "Just so, just so." The abbé observed to me that these answers were quite irrelevant to his questions, the purport of which, he tells me (and I believe without disguise), was: "Do you know the lady now present?" The question, under such circumstances, was as absurd as the answer, since he was aware that a spirit can not perceive matter. Adèle observes to M. Lauriot that he answers at random the questions she puts to him in Latin. Then he begins talking Latin to her with a volubility precluding the possibility of her transmitting his long discourse to the abbé. Fatigued with this sort of experiment, she finally refuses to continue, and I take it upon myself to question her in order to re-establish the conversation on a surer footing. "In the state you now are, do you still recollect the Latin tongue?" "Yes, as you may know from my having just answered in that tongue."—"The answers are not such as we desired." "The abbé knows that we took a three days' trip together to Ver-

sailles, and that it was then I made him acquainted with the matter."—"Monsieur says that he certainly did take a trip with you, not to Versailles, however, but to Saint Cloud—not of three days, but one only; that you spoke to him on the matter, but did not make him acquainted with it. You, perceive, therefore, that you commit errors which ought not to be. We always see you on your knees; you do nothing but pray, then?" "I pray to God for men in general, and for my relations."—"You have, then, relations on earth?" "Yes."—"Have you any brothers?" "No."—"Sisters?" "Yes."—"Is your mother dead?" "No."—"The abbé says the contrary; your mother died before you. It is quite true that your father is dead, that you have no brother, and only one sister; but, as to your mother, you are mistaken." After this fresh mistake we conclude that the man is not altogether in his right senses; the abbé observing to me that his mother died while he was in a state of insanity, and this accounts for his having no knowledge of her death. We request the presence of Adèle's brother to whom we put the following question: "This man, no doubt, is deranged?" "He is a very honest man, thoroughly good, and remarkably well-informed, but has at times rambling ideas; he is constantly running about, resting nowhere long at a time; he is seen by us everywhere."—"This man had on earth hallucinations, which he has, doubtless preserved?" "He has preserved, as I have told you, his strongest predilections, and his mind seems in consequence disordered."—"Those who die deranged are not, then, restored to a sane condition?" "No, their infirmity constitutes their chief happiness; they meet together, think alike, and are happy."—"But comes there a time when these men recover their reason?" "Yes, God purifies them gradually, and they enter a more enlightened circle."—"We can not trust to this man, who would make us participate in his errors in operations where none should exist." "I will send you another, who has had some experience in the same kind of operations; after putting his clairvoyance to the test, you will attend to his counsels, if you think fit; as for me,

I have already told you, I do not devote myself to such pursuits."

62. Curious to know what sort of personage Alphonse was to send us, I demanded his presence; but to my surprise, Father Lauriot again made his appearance. The obliging air he assumes delights Adèle, and, at my request, she consents not to beg of him to withdraw. I held with him the following discourse: "The information you give us is fraught with errors, and this makes us presume that your clairvoyance is not sufficiently powerful to be of use to us." "The abbé is not reasonable. I came to oblige him; he desired to know a heap of things which had nothing to do with the mission I purposed fulfilling; I have been overwhelmed with questions, with a singular suspicion, as if my passage on earth had been agreeable enough to me to preserve an exact recollection of it; what more could I do than appear in the same garb that I wore on earth in my folly, and say that I had known the abbé at the hospital, and furnish him with the particulars. He has the certainty of my having spoken the truth, that I died there; what more did he want? He ought not to overwhelm me with questions that demand, on my part, researches which would snatch a few instants from the happiness which I enjoy, and which I can not sacrifice to such trifles. You believe that, because I died insane, I am so now? undeceive yourself; I may seem absent in mind, but I could wish that the men of the earth were not more insane than I am, and knew what is known in the state I am."—"The abbé would have wished you to inspect his works." "I can not inspect them, excepting in his thoughts, because it is not in the power of a spirit to perceive matter."—"I thought the contrary, as, in order to predict material events, a spirit must see them." "It is an error; he perceives the causes of them, sums them up, and comments upon them according to his judgment."—"Is insanity an influence of matter or spirit?" "Of both, though matter plays the principal part in it, that only being diseased from the impediments it opposes to the spirit in the ascension of ideas. The latter being obstructed in their course, convey the greatest

trouble to the harmony of the system. Frequently, a single idea, on which the mind is fatigued, suffices to convey all this disorder into the intelligence."—"Are you happy in heaven?" "Yes; this happiness can not be described."—"What are your occupations?" "Reading, prayer, study, promenading—in short, whatever I desire to do or obtain, I both do and obtain."

We have just made acquaintance, I believe, with one of the most curious apparitions in this book. Should any doubts remain as to M. Lauriot's sanity of mind, it is easy to destroy them in part; but there can be none as to his identity. We have had then the apparition of one, a perfect stranger to us, a man whom we did not ask for. Ten days were passed in troublesome researches before his friend could fully recognise him. It remains to be settled how Adèle's brother could have sent to us a man known to the abbé. The latter and Alphonse had never seen or been acquainted with each other on earth; neither had Adèle even seen the abbé or any of his friends. Explain this who can. Let us pass on to a second question. Why was this man so obscure in certain communications, and so true in others? Either he really preserved his earthly mania of concealing his name, or fancied this name incurred public reproach. The first supposition is the most feasible one, since the abbé makes honorable mention of him in the conversation held in Latin. Wherefore do we perceive in it so many errors? Either Adèle was a bad interpreter, or M. Lauriot did not think fit to answer these questions, or possibly the abbé hid from me the truth, struck as he must have been with the idea, that he placed me in communication, without having foreseen it, with a man whose indiscretion might one day make me acquainted with things which he had no wish that I should know. I believe the abbé honest and true, from the eagerness he displayed in this circumstance, to throw the best light he could on this apparition; and therefore conclude that M. Lauriot, not thoroughly comprehending the questions, having, like all spirits, but a very imperfect recollection of their earthly actions, must be likely enough to make mistakes on this subject; his justification even stands in no need of commentaries. Remains his mother, who died before him, a circumstance which could not be forgotten by a man of sound mind; but being at that period under the influence of hallucination, he had no knowledge of her death. He is now in a somewhat similar frame of mind, and has not troubled himself about it. He has been dead two years, which are for him but a second. Under the influence of the moral sufferings which have just quitted him, and under those of the happiness in which he lives, he may well be ignorant of a particular of which he had been unable to think. After what we begin to know respecting the properties of the spiritual life, we ought to be less exigent; it remains indubitably proved to us, by the singular description, the chaplet, the medal, the small leather cap, the appearance, the stature, &c., that he is the man whom the abbé knew. Should not this be sufficient, there remain for us the conversation, the particularities at the hospital Sainte-Thérèse. The jaunt to Saint Cloud is not the less true, though badly described; the precise date of the works, the recommendation to continue what he had done that very morning of which he alone was aware, the exact description of the work which other clairvoyantes supposed to be the best, the explanations not less exact as to the members of his family, alive and dead, with the exception of his mother. I do not think it necessary to insist on these particulars to admit this apparition into the rank of the most conclusive ones. The abbé accepted it frankly as such, as well as myself; but we are about to see that it did not answer his expectations.

63. Before introducing other personages, I ought to give an account of another apparition of M. Lauriot, the results of which are as follows: "I told you at the last sitting that we could not accept your advice. You have not been asked for, why did you come?" Adèle says that she takes a delight in seeing this man, whose goodness she can appreciate to its full extent, and that he may come to her at all times without the risk of her driving him away.—"Then ask him why he told you that his mother was not dead, since she died before him?" "He answers that he did not say so; that I wrongly interpreted

his words, as he knew very well that she was dead, and could not have said the contrary."—"And the Latin which he answered you at random?" "I can not understand material words, and you did not transmit to me those that were addressed to me; you said to me, 'They speak Latin to you.' I thought it was on the subject of the works; hence it was that I replied to you affirmatively."—"Why did you not reproduce the abbé's words to M. Lauriot?" "Because it was a wearisome task; as I was conscious that I had to do with a man who believes in nothing, I preferred committing an error to continuing this kind of communication."—I observed to Adèle that she did wrong; that she ought rather to have said, that such a mode of speaking was not agreeable to her, and that I perceived that M. Lauriot could easily have answered the observations of the abbé (who, after hearing him, thought like me, that M. Lauriot was still insane). Thus terminated the apparitions of this personage.

64. "Here is the gentleman that my brother said he would send to me."—"What is his name?" "He answers, that we do not and should not know him."—"Has he lived on earth?" "Yes; but he is a foreigner."—"Where was he born?" "In Spain."—"Where did he die?" "In Spain."—"In what city?" "He has no information to give on this point; we should not know him."—"Give me a description of him." "He is tall, stout, and may be about seventy-five; his hair is still very black, although there are a few white hairs in his beard; he is very fresh, and has the appearance of having been a rich and very respectable man."—I put several questions to this gentleman, all which he answered very correctly; but it would be superfluous to mention them here. Having no wish to make this work a treatise on alchemy, I reserve the information given me for a separate work. I made the abbé acquainted with this new apparition in all its details, and he appeared satisfied. We devoted a few sittings to conversation with this man, whom we found obliging and sensible; but the abbé, who was very changeable, incredulous, and inconstant, proposed to me a decisive experiment, which I accepted as much for my own instruction as to afford him pleasure; for man can not too highly cherish within

him a belief in the spiritual world, by making experiments called for by the least of his doubts. We were agreed on this point, both the abbé and myself. I had doubted, and at times still doubted, for a pure spiritualist is not to be instantaneously made out of an extra-materialist, and the abbé had one doubt more than I; as he feared on my part charlatanism. He had a right to do so, as he knew me not, and I, for my part, was glad to meet with such a man whose doubts were to turn to my advantage.

65. The abbe said to me, "You will have the goodness to ask, at the next sitting, for M. De Mallet (Christophe Edouard), and send me word whether he appeared, and in what condition." I much doubted this experiment, for which we had so little information to work upon. I asked for him, however, and, to my great satisfaction he appeared. I ask this gentleman if he will be good enough to answer a few questions which the abbé desires to put to him?" "Yes," replied he; I told him that at the first sitting they would discourse together; meanwhile I beg Adèle to give me a description of this gentleman. "He is a priest, or, at least, he wears the costume of one; a black robe, without surplice: he is a little taller than the abbé, stout in proportion; he has a noble countenance, a prominent nose, the nostrils somewhat pinched up; he has a mark on his cheek, under the left eye; his hair is gray, and he may be sixty."—"Are you quite sure that he has a mark on his left cheek, under the eye?"—"Yes; it is evident enough." "What kind of mark, a pockmark?"—"I can not see because he is a pretty good distance off; but I am certain that he has a mark of some kind." This gentleman retires. Adèle is afraid that the abbé should raise any difficulties as to this apparition, and says that she won't ask for any more if she has been deceived.

66. I had sent an account of this sitting to the abbé, but I neither saw him nor heard from him. I thought that Adèle had made some mistake. Three days after he arrived with his servant-girl, who brought me a portrait of M. Mallet, which he had been to borrow of one of his friends. Only judge of my surprise, equal to his, when I beheld feature for feature the

man so well depicted by Adèle, and especially the mark, which was no less than the scar of a sabre wound, which this gentleman had received in the army. The abbé said to me: "I may now acquaint you with the history of the count de Mallet. He was one of the grand dignitaries of the empire, having held a very high rank in the army. At the death of his wife he embraced the church party with not less zeal than he had served the empire. He was superior of the nuns of Sainte Marie de Lorette, and died in the parish of Saint Sulpice, the 26th August, at the age of sixty, regretted by the upright and good; he devoted much time to metaphysics, and wrote a work on this science, which I will lend you; it is the fruit of elevated and not superstitious reasonings."

The abbé is quite delighted at this experiment; he can no longer doubt the truth of these apparitions, convinced as he is, that I did not know this gentleman, seeing that I had no particulars furnished me respecting him, that he had expressly avoided being present at this sitting, in order not to establish any communication of thoughts. What astonished him most was this mark—this gash—and he himself did not know whether it was under the right eye or the left; to make sure of it he had been to borrow the portrait which he showed me, in order that I might judge of the correct likeness of the apparition; he looked upon this fact as conclusive, and declared himself convinced. He wished me to send Adèle to sleep, in order to put a few questions to her. I forthwith complied with his request. Adèle was struck at the likeness of the portrait which she had seen before going to sleep, to that of M. Mallet. The latter answered the questions of the abbé with an exactitude that enraptured the priest, who also put to him the following one: "M——, the person who lent me your portrait, and was one of your friends on earth, has begged of me to ask you whether you had anything to say to him?"—"Yes; let him take good care of his health, he is poorly." "The abbé thought that this answer accorded but little with what he had just seen of this person, who was not in the least indisposed; then he left me. The abbé returned the next day to tell me that he had imparted to his friend the advice of M. Mallet, and, to his great astonishment, found that he had really been unwell for a fortnight, that he had been obliged to neglect his business, and that his maid-servant was saying to him only three days ago—If M. Mallet were still alive, assuredly he would recommend you to take better care of yourself. This particularity conferred more value on the revelation than we had at first thought.

67. After having asked of M. Mallet what the abbé desired to know, I put to him in my turn the following questions: "The D'Orval predictions, as they are termed, in which you had so great faith when on earth, that you even had them reprinted in 1840, what do you think of them now? Do you still believe in them?" "Yes."—"Can you foresee whether the events, of which they make mention, will come to pass?" "Yes; but those predictions are exaggerated."—"Those concerning the destruction of Paris, will they take place?" "Yes; but not to so great an extent as is predicted."—"When will that happen?" "I can not answer your question."—"By what scourge will it happen? Fire or war?" "By a revolution."

* * * * * *

"What government will reign then?" "It is then that it will be said: '*Come, young prince,*' as the prediction says."—"Do you know whether the son of Louis XVI. is dead?" "No, he is not dead."—"Do you know him? Is the Baron of Richemont this son?" "I don't know."—"Do you think that it is the people alone that will cause all the disorders predicted? The people and the foreigner?"—"Of how many is a number composed?" "Of 20." * * * "For my personal safety, I should like to know when this will happen." "The events preceding such catastrophe will be a sufficient warning."—"Will the banishment of the priests take place?" "The priests will escape from France."—"The end of the world, announced in eighty years, will it take place?" "You will not then be on earth, wherefore trouble yourself about it?"—"So you look upon these prophecies as true?" "Yes, in the main, but not in the exaggerations. There will be mischief enough without making more of it." Adèle says that this gentleman has no wish to alarm any one.

68. M. Mallet is preceded, according to Adèle, by a light which she has hitherto perceived only before her mother. I ask this gentleman if he is disposed to answer a few psychological questions? "That depends on the nature of them."— "Have we a soul?" "You perceive it, since I am one."— "What is the form of it?" "That of the body—that which I at this moment bear."—"Whither does it go after its separation from the body?" "Into celestial places."—"What does it do in those places?—does it eat and drink?" "It satisfies its principal affections."—"Are there good and bad places?" "Yes."—"Are the bad ones what Christians denominate hell?" "Yes."—"Are we burned there, as they, say?" "They say what they do not believe."—"But you were a priest, you yourself taught this doctrine?" "I never believed in it."— "Then what do we do in these bad places, do we suffer there?" "We satisfy there our affections; are happy there, although they are places of purification, in which God places us to call us in due time to him, when he forgives us."—"Are they places or states in which the soul is?" "Places."—"Do we remain in them for ever?" "In the good places, yes; and, as I have just told you, not in the bad ones."—"In what does the knowledge of the soul consist in those places?" "In what it desires to possess, and what it acquires at will." Adèle is unwilling to be importunate. I receive these revelations with confidence, because they appear independent of all sectarian calculation, and are of much greater value in the mouth of a priest who has enjoyed an honorable reputation on earth than in that of any other person.

69. "Has the soul any recollection of the earth and of what it was there?" "Yes."—"Can it perceive matter?" "No."— "Does it regret the material life?" "No."—"Can it at will visit its relations, its friends?" "Yes; when it is requested in the state necessary to be seen as your clairvoyante is."— "Can it in aught influence their existence?" "Yes; in the

good which it invariably counsels them to do.'" "Can it inform them of any particularity in their destiny?" "Yes; but it does so with much prudence, especially when it foresees the effect that the revelation will create in the moral being; for this reason it is compelled not to tell all."—"Does it suffer much in quitting its body?" "More or less."—"Is it long before it becomes acquainted with the state into which it enters?" "It becomes acquainted with it immediately."—"You have just told me that a spirit can not perceive matter; how can you come into this house, close to us, without seeing us?" "I am conscious of this young lady's spirit which attracts me, and I find myself with her, agreeably to her desire and mine."—"Still, proofs exist that some spirits see matter, since they upset articles of furniture, vases, &c., convey messages and objects." "Those are evil spirits that are in the circle surrounding the earth, that still hover over it, and do these things."—"It is not only evil spirits, however, that possess this property. I have read several works of saints who have performed or seen some of those phenomena. M. Billot, a very pious man, has received messages of the kind from the hands even of angels?" "It is very seldom that the Deity permits these kind of conveyances; they can not take place unknown to heaven."—"M. Possin not long ago said that he received a crown through the medium of his clairvoyante?" "There has been nothing similar to this in heaven of late."—"In short, we have also a *curé* who, in a small provincial parish where there was a scarcity of corn, had his granary filled agreeably to his wishes; he distributed this godsend among his parishioners, and yet, it is said, the granary was not exhausted. There are multitudes of similar facts in the holy books?" "There are many things written which have never existed; many others which are, as I have told you, the province of spirits occupied in things of this kind; but in order for a man to obtain such favors from heaven, his soul must be very pure, have in view but the happiness of his fellow-beings, and an ardent desire to render himself acceptable to God. Such men and such facts are rare; but they do exist and have existed. We should ever suspect conveyances and messages of this kind, as they are frequently but a stratagem of evil spirits that wish to flatter our pride and incredulity the better to obtain dominion over us."—"In short, since you say that such things may exist through the intercession of angels, as through that of evil spirits, it must needs be that they see the object which they convey?" "Certainly they see it; but they take it from the earth, for in heaven there is nothing material; when such a thing happens, it is, as I have told you, as great a miracle for heaven as for the earth."—"You conclude that the spirits of heaven do not perceive matter?" "I have told you so, saving under the conditions which I have just made known to you."—"You told me that you felt yourself attracted by the will of my clairvoyante; could you not correspond in thought with me, by answering through her the questions I should mentally transmit to you?" "I could do so; but that presents difficulties which would bring in their train errors, and require much more time, inasmuch as you are not in the spiritual state, and such communication is too difficult." I deem it fit to address these questions to M. Mallet, although we have already seen them addressed to other spirits; we can not receive too many confirmations in this respect; we should question all persuasions, in order to come to a correct understanding.

70. M. Mallet is more or less time before appearing. He invariably gives Adèle his blessing at his coming and going; it seems, from what the abbé tells us, that such was a practice with him on earth. I shall pass over the abbé's questions, which have no reference whatever to what I desire to know about the spiritual world.—"What do you think of possessions, particularly the Loudun ones?" "They are merely the malicious tricks of evil spirits, because the good spirits do naught but good."—"What do you think of the *convulsionnaires* of Saint-Médard, &c.?" "Among them are found both good and very wicked actions; things incredible appertaining to good and to evil spirits, deeds ordained by God, others which are condemned by him. We even appreciate all those things only by a judgment enlightened by the Divine light, and disengaged from all haughty and egotistical calculation. I can an-

swer all you ask me only by counselling you to be circumspect, and to pray to God to enlighten your intelligence."—"Do you think that we can render ourselves invisible to several persons at once?" "Yes, by drugs and pacts with evil spirits; but there is naught so displeasing to God as those things by which we may do all possible harm."—"Could you tell me this secret, I believe myself incapable of abusing it?" "You are incapable of it, at this moment, because you do not possess it; but no sooner should you know it than the pride of having such power at your command would take possession of you and lead you to do evil, as the rest. God suffers not the good spirits to divulge those things."—"Fascination plays the principal part in it, does it not?" "Did you send for me merely to read you a course of magic?"—"No; but in order to know what to think of those mysteries; so many things have been written on this subject that I should wish to be enabled to form an opinion respecting them." "Do not trouble yourself about them. There are many good things written; but there are also many falsehoods, and wicked doctrines. Say no more about them."

71. A friend of mine, M. Renard de Rambouillet, to whom I regularly communicate the contents of my journal, requested me to put the following questions to M. Mallet. Desiring to know what a catholic priest could reveal of heaven, I comply with his wishes at this sitting: "I desire the truth with all my heart. Would M. Mallet be so kind as to instruct me in it through you, by answering a few questions which are put to me by a friend?" "M. Mallet answers that he will do so, according to the will of God."—"How do you find yourself in the world you live in?" "Quite comfortable and happy."—"Are you really what we term, and what you termed, a soul, when you were on earth?" "Yes."—"The form of your soul, is it still precisely the same as that of the body it dwelt in?" "Yes."—"Do you sleep? do you eat?" (This question is often repeated, because it is a very natural one, and the first to present itself as the most necessary one, in any style of existence.) "Sleep and eat who please; it is not a necessity as on earth, but a real pleasure to those who do so?"—"Do you live in a

house, as on earth?" "I am in a house; there are houses in this world, as on earth."—"Are there also towns and villages?" "I know not what towns are termed in heaven; suffice it to say that there are houses. I do not busy myself with the rest."—"What are your ordinary occupations?" "I read, write, and pass a part of my time in giving good advice to the wicked?"—"You can then communicate with them?" "Yes, with their spirit."—"Who supplies you with those books and houses? Do you build them, as on earth?" "Those houses, and all that exists in heaven, are unalterable, indestructible, imperishable, have been created by God from all time, and can undergo no alteration."—"Are unions or marriages formed in the place where you are?" "We marry, as on earth, with this difference, that it is for eternity. We can never more separate, inasmuch as we can not be united, unless an exact resemblance exists in the affections, the mode of thinking, and all that constitutes perfect happiness."—"Is the woman we have married on earth the one who becomes our wife in heaven?" "Not always. We are much better acquainted with the affections and defects of each other, and God would not suffer an unequal match, as on earth?"—"When you desire it, are you in the company of friends, relations, dead like yourself?" "Yes; but if our ideas do not accord, we can not remain together—we separate."—"Are many languages spoken in the other world?" "I have never spoken any other language but the one I now speak to you; but, between ourselves, we mutually comprehend without speaking; it is seldom that we make use of speech."—"Do you remain a long time in the state you are in?" "Our happiness is so great that none desire to change it; when we have all we desire, there is nothing more to wish for."—"Can spirits visit the globes, as the moon, the stars?" "By the permission of the Deity, they go wherever they desire."—Adèle tells me that I abuse the complaisance of M. Mallet, whose venerable looks, fraught with goodness, inspire her with respect. I put this last question: "Has God appeared to you? In what form?" "I have never absolutely seen God."—Adèle is unwilling to continue, and this gives rise to a dispute between us two; I making the observation that if I put questions to a spirit it is in order to gain information with respect to the future life through his light; that being aware of my ignorance and the purity of my intentions, he can not take offence. "What he sees, before all, is your incredulity. When one knows what I know there is but little inclination to abuse the complaisance of a venerable man, who, in a few hours, will pass in your eyes for an hallucination, and his answers for errors of my imagination. Spirits no longer cling to the things of the earth; they trouble themselves no more about them than we should of a street we had passed through twenty years ago. Can we think with pleasure, of the scenes of life which have caused us troubles? No; what exists within us is indifference for the past, and this indifference is still greater in spirits that are never to revisit the earth; you, not long ago, sufficiently tormented my brother by your questions, fraught with doubt. Spirits may be deceived, though such would not be the case did they set more value on the things of the earth; they are not criminals put to the question; and bear this ever in mind, if you don't wish to drive away all the spirits who may come to see you, but to obtain from them right resolutions, lay aside in their presence doubt and objection." This long moral lesson of Adèle naturally surprised me; it is true that I had just started several objections, and intended asking for fresh proofs. So difficult is it, I repeat, to convince an unbeliever and draw a parallel between the future life and the present one; our carping reasoning is, above all things, least suited to a good clairvoyante; we can not, in the presence of such traits, for ever say that the clairvoyante is the mirror of the magnetizer's thoughts; in such a case, Adèle would invariably agree with me. True, there are somnambulists of this kind, but she is not one of them. I have put her in communication with other magnetizers, who, no more than I, have been able to influence in aught her will. She is isolated on this head, and wholly independent of all influence; her system is not always mine; she has no knowledge of psychology; and the answers just given by M. Mallet sufficiently prove that she interlards them with naught of her own; she has too much respect for churchmen to misconstrue their words to the profit of my persuasions, which she oppugns, in order to establish in their stead those we have just heard, and which, as we perceive, are by no means in conformity with those of the church, as I have nowhere seen that the church admits houses, occupations, affections, and marriages in heaven. I have seen these things only in Swedenborg, and these revelations seemed to me so foreign to what I then believed (in annihilation, like the materialists), that I can admit them only from the multiplicity of those made to me by persons of all creeds, whom I can not, wish not to, influence; and from the comparisons which reasoning should make between the material magnetic effects which we see every day, and those spiritual ones which seem to be the source of the causes, while ours are but the effects. As there can be no effects without causes, and the latter must be the type of the effects, the spirit, being itself a cause, must return into the sphere where all is, and whence all is manifested. We shall naturally find there houses, gardens, men, and usages.

72. The 8th of July, 1846, I magnetize Adèle in order to put her in communication with the soul of a young woman who died on the 2d of the same month at the age of twenty-four. Her presence was scarcely requested when she appeared with an infant in her arms, which she had lost almost at its birth; the apparition of this child astonished us, inasmuch as we little expected it. Adèle is not much disposed to ask her any questions, saying to me: "Leave me an instant with her, and give her time at least to recollect herself in her new state." Adèle experiences a painful emotion at the apparition of this woman, whose name was Eliza, and weeps bitterly. These tears were sufficient evidence of her good faith; Eliza appears to her clad in white, with a crown on her head; she says that she is very happy, and can not understand why she was afraid to die. She wished she had quitted the earth sooner. She says to Adèle: "When you followed me to the grave, you entertained the thought of placing a *souvenir* on my tomb: it would afford me

much pleasure if you would do so." I ask Adèle whether she had had a like thought? "Yes, I bargained for a small medallion but did not purchase it." I beg Adèle to swear to me by the ashes of her mother, that what she just told me is exact, and that it was really Eliza who divined her thought. Adèle fervently protests to me that she has told the truth, and that in such a circumstance it would be a sacrilegious falsehood to deceive me. "I do not think you have deceived me; but, possibly, you asked her if she would wish for this medallion which you had a mind to buy for her?" "No, it was she who told me of it, I no longer thought of it."—"Does Eliza attach any value to her body, that she desires to see it adorned with a medallion?" "No; but the dead always like to *perceive* kind tokens of remembrance in the hearts of those they have left behind." Eliza's husband was present at this sitting, and could not believe in such apparitions; he said to me: "Adèle watched over the last moments of Eliza; she was struck at such a death; the attachment she bore my wife may possibly react on her imagination; could you furnish me with another proof of the truth of those apparitions?" "Yes, on one condition, which is, that you consider well of the person whose apparition you request; you will so manage that we shall have never seen nor heard of this person; take all your precautions; I will only ask you for the name. After this proof, ask no more, endeavor to make it conformable to your wishes. Ah! I will prepare this for you, and to-morrow we'll see."—"Very well."

73. M. Demarest, Eliza's husband, came the next day, according to appointment. I magnetized Adèle. He then said to me, "I lost a sister, whose name I hand you; be so kind as to request her attendance." "Here she is."—"Give me a description of her?" said he. (He was not *en rapport* with Adèle.) The latter replied, "She is rather taller than this gentleman, her brother; her hair is of a dark flaxen color, her face is long, and she has large blue eyes of a very sweet expression." On the observation of M. Demarest, as to whether Adèle has a good view of her eyes, the latter draws nearer to

her the gentleman's sister, and says that "the right eye seems to her as if somewhat dimmed." "It is a web," said this gentleman, "that grew in her eye, in consequence of an accident." —"Her mouth is small," resumes Adèle, "skin very white, complexion pale, but the cheeks are somewhat flushed like those of consumptive persons, and her deportment is melancholy." Adèle feels conscious that she must have been dearly loved on earth, and she reckons her about eighteen years of age. There is in her voice something sweet, but drawling. She tells her brother that their father, supposed by those around him to be on his death-bed, sixty leagues from Paris, was out of danger; that he should be consoled for the loss of Eliza; that she herself appeared to him expressly to convince him of the reality of another existence after death. She was accompanied by a young girl whom her brother could not recognise from the description given of her by Adèle, and whom his sister said was one of her old school friends. M. Demarest acknowledged all the details of the description as exact apart the age, which Adèle gave her as an approximation to the real one, his sister being twenty-one when she died; apart, the color of the hair, which, said he, was of a chestnut color; Adèle saw it of a dark flaxen; then again the eye, which she had not discovered at once, inasmuch as this person was on one side and at a distance from Adèle; the rest was very exact, even to the revelation of the recovery of their father, which they did not hear of till some days afterward. Would it be believed, these three facts sufficed M. Demarest to doubt the reality of the apparition. A somnambulist who makes a mistake of three years in the appreciation of age, and this gentleman declares that his sister was not *that age;* then again, as to a shade more or less dark of the hair, and a slight delay in the discovery of a web in the eye! this is sufficient for this man to doubt so detailed an apparition; all the other particularities, even to the tone of her voice, are strictly exact; her father, whom he thought dead, and whose recovery was announced to him, sufficed not this uneasy and suspicious man; as much less was required to make me believe, and I had been as far off as he from such persuasions. I will observe that at the sitting he believed, and was greatly astonished; it was only at a later period that these facts disappeared from his memory to make way for these three trifling objections.* We can not say, after such a sitting, that Adèle saw or read his thoughts, had it been so they would have agreed as to the age, the color of the hair; and, above all, the eye, which was the most distinctive sign of the apparition, would have been cited first. Men of right understanding, who consider well of this apparition, will, I think, come to a different conclusion, particularly if I inform them that I had a little somnambulist, ten years of age (he will be seen hereafter), possessing the speciality of views at distances, who one day, placed *en rapport* with this M. Demarest, and visiting his abode, made the remark that he saw on a small table a blue surtout. M. Demarest would not accept this view, because, instead of a surtout it was a paletot. A small sou of ten centimes, no longer circulated but for a liard, being put in a box, the child says, "I see a liard," whereupon this gentleman exclaimed, "This child is not asleep; he knows not what he says."

74. M. Renard, of whom I have already spoken, a man to whom I am indebted for the little knowledge I possess in magnetism, being called to Paris on business, begged me to send Adèle to sleep and give him a sitting similar to what he had read of in my journal. I was most happy to comply with the wishes of so sincere a friend, and so judicious and well-informed a man. Scarcely was Adèle asleep than he asked for a person named Desforges, an old friend of his, who had been dead fifteen years. Desforges appeared. M. Renard had so minute a description given him of his friend, that left no doubt as to the reality of this apparition. A dispute took place between him and Adèle (though he was not *en rapport* with her)

* Eight days had not elapsed before Eliza took upon herself the task of proving to her husband that she existed as really and more so than he, by apparitions he had of her in his watchful state and in his sleep. Many things occurred in this respect that troubled him very much, and dissipated in him all doubts as to a future life.

as to the dress of this person: Adèle maintaining that he appeared to her in a blouse slit in front, while M. Renard declared that he had never seen him in such an article of dress; and that he usually wore a jacket or round vest. After puzzling his brains for some time, M. Renard recollected in fact that some time before he left his friend, people began to wear in his part of the country blouses of this kind, and that he wore such a one as Adèle described. It would be useless to mention the minute details, attitudes, language, &c., with which Adèle persuades persons consulting her on such a point. There remained naught for M. Renard to desire. He was sensibly moved at this apparition; M. Desforges was, on earth, a very studious man, well informed in physics and the occult sciences. M. Renard feels disposed to avail himself of his presence in order to ask him for some information respecting the fabrication of magic glasses. M. Desforges answers: "Why do you trouble yourself about such trifles, that would only tend to injure you in the minds of the fools around you; do you not appear to them superior and incomprehensible enough already? what would you be then? you would pass for a sorcerer, thus incurring their hatred and bringing on yourself disputes that would trouble the short time remaining you to pass among them; believe me, as a true friend, do not trouble yourself about such matters, it will not be long before you rejoin me, and then you will know whatever you desire." Upon a fresh observation of M. Renard, his friend replies to him: "Such kinds of experiments ever bring in their train vexations which, when too late, we would have wished to avoid. For these mirrors to have an absolute and a general property, it is necessary to be in correspondence with spirits that make you pay dear in the end for the slight complaisance they have shown you."

M. Renard expresses a wish to have M. Emmanuel Swedenborg summoned. Adèle sees him, gives a description of him, which M. Renard acknowledges to be conformable to his ideas; it ran thus: "I see a fine portly man; he has brown hair, an austere countenance; though by no means intimidating, and thick eyebrows. What a droll dress! he wears a coat such as no one sees now-a-days, has trimmings to his sleeves which are very large and tucked up, and lined with a different colored stuff to that of his coat. Ha! what large buttons! He has buckles on his shoes too."—"How old does he look?" asks M. Renard. "About sixty-six." M. Renard says that he was more than eighty when he died; but that in his part of the country (the North) men do not show their age. Adèle adds that his hair is curled, and that he appears of a green old age.

M. Renard receives a little advice from Adèle as to the state of his health, proving to him that, independently of her spiritual clairvoyance, she possesses in an equal degree the same faculty in respect to the ailments of the body.

75. Adèle again requested the presence of Eliza, who came immediately with her infant, which she gave to Adèle to kiss; then she sat down in the lap of our clairvoyante (apparently not much to the satisfaction of the latter). She put to her the following questions: "You told me, last time, that you saw in my thought that I had the intention to place a medallion on your tomb; your soul, then, followed your body to the grave?" "Yes, I knew also that my aunt, who was with you, desired to place on it a bouquet of flowers." This second communication is quite true. "How do you find yourself now?" "Very happy."—"What are your occupations?" "I promenade; all that I behold appears to me so pretty that I am never tired of admiring what is around me." Adèle suddenly exclaims: "Ah, the glutton! she is eating a beautiful peach; I will recognise her in that, promenading and gluttonizing; such are her pleasures, she'll never forsake them."—"Would Eliza be so kind as to tell me what sort of feeling she experienced at the moment of her death, and how her resurrection was effected?" "I found myself in heaven, as if waking out of sleep; I still thought all of you at my bedside; I called to you, when other persons who were around me told me that I was no longer on earth, that I had just died; I could not believe what was told me; but at length I perceived that I was no longer among you, on beholding my father and my child, who have not quitted me since that day. I saw, also, the little companion beside me,

who has been dead these five years. I knew her in the hôuse where I was brought up, and where she died; her name was Héloise."—"Adèle tells me that she perceives beside Eliza this young girl, who is very pretty, and looks very amiable; she is fair. Were it necessary for me to add a proof to those I possess in abundance, I should make inquiries respecting this young person. I ask Eliza if her husband will not fall ill from the grief caused by her death?"—"'Twill be nothing," said she; "when he returns from the country he'll think no more of it."—Eliza knew of this journey, as she had known of Adèle's and her aunt's thoughts. I wish to put more questions to her; but Adèle says to me: "Let her promenade a little; she has but just entered heaven; she can not answer all." I ask her whether, on her entering heaven, she saw God? "No," said she, "I have not seen him yet."—"Have you seen any angels?" "No; but persons who speak to you in the name of God, as coming from him; and I do not think those persons are angels."

76. I ask again for M. Swedenborg. He appears.—"You will have the goodness to answer a few questions as to the spiritual world, now that you inhabit it; your answers would carry greater weight with them in your present state."—M. Renard attended at this sitting. We ask M. Swedenborg if he has nothing to rectify in the writings he left on earth, treating of the spiritual world? He answers, that they contain a few errors of little importance. He says that he is not satisfied with some of his disciples, who do not conduct themselves as they ought. M. Swedenborg promises to return to us when we stand in need of him. Adèle says: "He lays his hands on us as if to give us his blessing, and goes away."—We consulted together, M. Renard and I, as to what we ought to think of the apparition of this great ecstatico-prophet. Was it really he? We had not the least doubt of it; but we might be imposed upon by an evil spirit; in that case, said we, God, whom we will call to our aid, and M. Swedenborg, will not suffer us to be deceived thus. Moreover, we shall discover him sooner or later, and know what value to set on his revelations; but I

ought to observe, that if an evil spirit has the power of presenting himself in the place of a good one, he may be driven away by a command, in the name of God. Such a course has invariably succeeded with me and it is what I do at each apparition. Once the person summoned is seen, we should demand of him a token of recognition, which he displays to you, whether by a particular sign, a jewel, or aught else, God never suffering evil spirits to counterfeit in this respect. Neither should we suppose, because an evil spirit may happen to commit a few mistakes in his revelations, especially in his earthly reminiscences, mistakes to which they are very liable, that it is an evil spirit that deceives us. No: we must expect miscalculations. Spirits *can not answer all that is asked them*, because their knowledge is confined to their peculiar affection. Thus, we should seek spirits that participate in ours, if we desire to obtain correct solutions; but it seldom happens, however, that relations or friends are replaced by malicious spirits.

77. I summon M. Swedenborg, who forthwith presents himself. I order him, in the name of God, to withdraw if he is a false spirit; on the contrary, he advances, takes Adèle by the hand, and says to her: "Fear naught, I am indeed Swedenborg."—"Could you be replaced by an evil spirit?" "No; so long as you desire my presence, with the pure intention of instructing yourself, I will come; but if on the contrary, you act with contempt and authority, I should not present myself, and another would come, in order to deceive you."—"Can you communicate with me by thought, through the medium of my clairvoyante?" "No; your thought is too deeply buried in matter. I could do so; but it is best to avail ourselves of this young lady in order to avoid mistakes."—"Could you inform me of a means whereby I could enter into the state necessary to communicate directly with you, by the aid of certain narcotic combinations?" "The only practicable means is magnetism; any other state, provoked by narcotics, irritates the nerves, influences the ideas by disorganizing them, and can not, consequently, be so good as the magnetic state."—"I ask you this, because I should wish to be enabled to express to you questions myself to pre-

vent the possibility of their being altered?" "In that case, I advise you to get powerfully magnetized behind your ears; it is your sensitive part, and probably you will succeed."—"Can you answer this question, Did God create man male and female, as the Bible says?" "The Bible is an excellent book, containing very good things for study. God did create a man and a woman."—"Do you mean thereby that every man whom God has created, has a woman equally created for him?" "Yes, every being has his complement; woman and man are created in pairs."—"These two beings, are they born and do they die at the same time?" "Time stands for naught in the matter; they meet again in heaven when God wills it."—"These two beings, are they in every respect similar in thought and form?" "Yes."—"In their intimate union are they acquainted with love in its carnal acts as on earth?" "Heavenly love can not be described by material language, it is an inexplicable sensation."—"Are single persons seen in heaven?" "Yes, but no being can be perfectly happy without being reunited to its half, which is its complement of life."—"Can they be separated by a caprice depending, or not depending, on them?" "No, we can not be separated from what constitutes our happiness."—"Can the happiness of souls at rest be influenced in heaven by evil spirits?" "No; they are separate, and an inferior spirit can in nowise trouble the superior spirit."—"Have you the conviction that we return not to a second material existence?" "We are in heaven for eternity."—"Can we count the time we pass in this state of happiness and the spaces we travel over?" "Time is not reckoned there; a thousand years are as one day in eternity; space presenting no difficulty to its being cleared is not measured there. The body is so light that it finds itself conveyed wherever it desires without perceiving the distance over which it has travelled."—"Independent of the affections, are there any states through which we must pass to arrive at this superior degree of felicity?" "The affection constitutes the states. The latter succeed each other according to the strength of the affection which engenders them, and leads them to the height of happiness."

78. "Does a lunatic forthwith recover the use of his reason?" "He recovers his reason, but he requires more or less time to arrange his ideas which continue yet awhile more or less disorganized."—"Does insanity proceed from matter or spirit?" "It proceeds from the spirit."—"I was told that it proceeded from both." "Certainly, matter clogs the spirit; but we have sufficient proof that the spirit only remains affected, from the fact of its being still affected after its separation from matter."—"How do you think this is brought about?" "A man ardently devoted to study fatigues his ideas, and the too great contention of spirit on a single one disorganizes the rest."—"We have, also, other cases of insanity in being not devoted to study, which are often produced by very material accidents, falls, fears, afflicting news, &c." "Such accidents are only secondary causes, which would have produced no effect on well-organized brains; there are many men whose external appearance conceal from our judgment very vigorous thoughts, no matter their tendency; they are pent-up thoughts, which, on a sudden commotion, overflow the other ideas and disorganize the whole individual."—"Can evil spirits derange our intellects on earth?" "No."—"Can they hallucinate us by apparitions, removal of furniture, noises, and a thousand other things of this kind?" "They can do so only in the conditions wherein you find yourself impressionable, but most frequently these hallucinations are to be attributed to *material persons* of a very evil influence, who, by their property, or those which they obtain through pacts formed with spirits that possess this affection, take delight in deranging our ideas and tormenting us; the influence of poisons has much to do with it."—"I did not believe in such pacts." "They exist, but naught is more displeasing to God."—"What is the means of ridding one's self of such a possession?" "Doing as you do when an evil spirit appears before your clairvoyante, command it, in the name of God, to withdraw."—"In the possession of Loudun and others, such means did not always suffice."—"In many possessions there have often been too many interests at stake; the prayers were not always as pure as they seemed to be, for the power of God inundates all the powers

of the universe, and no possession could resist were he invoked from the bottom of the heart. It is the sole and noblest power given to man to make use of."—"What do you think of talismans?" "There are very good ones, but we must deserve them: it is a gift of God."—"Could you give me the design of a good one?" "I can not; but there is one worth them all, placing ourselves under the Divine protection, with purity of heart; no other is equal to this."—"What do you think of perception obtained by the means of what are called magic glasses, which are made use of to discover thieves or hidden things, and useful to our safety?" "They exist."—"What spirits can facilitate operations of this sort?" "The good and the bad."—"Could you tell me this secret?" "Yes; but I must first study you, then we will see."—"What do you think of astrology?" Adèle says that M. Swedenborg answers only by a gesture, apparently signifying his doubt in respect to this, and that he does not occupy himself with it. Adèle finds me also wearisome; I put, however, this question: "What do you think of alchemy?" "The stone exists; this also is a gift of God. We must be very pure to possess it." We have a long discourse on this subject, which I can not report.

79. "You told me, at the last sitting, that you would consider whether I was worthy of possessing the secret of the magic mirror, may I hope to receive from your generosity this revelation?" "Yes. 'T is very difficult of execution; you will go to work in this way:—

* * * * * * * * * * *

I had a very good one."—"Since your death, have you increased your stock of knowledge, which, on earth, was already very considerable?" "No, on the contrary, I have lost more than I have gained of that description which is no longer my affection; when on earth, I wished to instruct men in what it was useful for them to know; but now this desire no longer pursues me, and all the knowledge necessary to material life ceased being explained to me when I went to heaven."—"What is your predominant affection now?" "I am in the society of a few friends; we occupy ourselves with celestial philosophy; in the state I am, we know whatever we desire to know, and this is a continual source of felicity."—"Have you any knowledge of the primitive creation of man?" "Yes; but I do not think fit to explain it to you."—"Could you explain to me his properties and relations with the universe; men believe now in a system, and you seem to approve of such a one in your works, which demonstrates man as representing in miniature the entire universe?" "Man is really a representative of what may be confined to his globe, seeing that he possesses within him all the essences composing it; but there ends his resemblance with the universe."—"Some have gone so far to say that he had in him, independently of all that exists materially, places, actions, universal thoughts, inasmuch as he finds himself in the places he desires to see; knows the actions and thoughts which exist and no longer exist. How explain such a power?" "The material man is a compound *of all that exists materially;* that is to say, he has in him the essences of each of the kingdoms, but not places and distances. The spiritual man has alone the faculty of knowing places, actions, and thoughts, which are rightly without the material body and not in it; as the terrestrial essences, he may clear these distances, which for him exist not; he may know past actions, since for him there is nothing annihilated, but the present, the past, and the future are only a condition of being presented to him by matter. He may communicate with all these things, which are so many unities without, and form but one with him, according to the power of his desire."—"Were you acquainted with magnetism before your death; you seem to indicate as much in your works?" "I was not acquainted with its properties in all their development, I had but a confused knowledge of them."—"You equally appear to indicate in them phrenology, by saying that thoughts are agglomerated in the head in kinds of societies, separately incased?" "Our head is but a compound of confused thoughts, which, when not directed and incased by the spiritual man with discernment, lead to the love of evil."—"Could you give me a clear description as to the nature of thoughts?" "God, in creating man, *provided us all with an equal number of thoughts; there exists not a single being who possesses one more than another.* It is for man to separate the good from the bad, if he wishes to be honest and eschew evil."—"How should he manage, since he appears not free to act according to his wishes?" "He could do so by dismissing the first thought that leads him toward evil. If, on the contrary, he does not repel it, by asking of God the strength necessary to do so, this thought engenders others, which, in a short time, form a mass of thoughts leading man toward evil or good."—"The thoughts, then, according to you, engender like living beings?" "They assemble and engender of each other. I will endeavor to give you a material example: Get a couple of ants (seeing that everything is by pairs in the creation), separate them, instead of bringing them together, by putting them each in a small hole; they will be quite at their ease, and will not propagate; if, on the contrary, you bring them together both in the same hole, in a short time the society they have engendered, unable any longer to contain itself in this hole, will burst forth, seeking elsewhere a more suitable space. In like manner with the thoughts; master the first one by preventing it from uniting with another, and you will have no trouble to fear."—"I approve of your comparison; but since God is the author, the creator of all things, he has deemed fit, then, to create good and evil thoughts? Were it not for this assemblage of good and evil, half the human species distributed as kings, judges, priests, soldiers, intrusted with the keeping of the other half, would be useless?" "I have told you that every man possessed the same quantity of thoughts, which he was at liberty to class and govern according to his idea. If the Deity has deemed fit to create such or such thoughts, he owes us no account of it, since he does not render us responsible for the direction we have given them by not punishing us for them."—"These thoughts, which, from your comparisons are naught less than living beings, coupling and engendering, under what form are they seen in heaven and on earth?" "On earth they represent, *en tableau,* the action they concur in causing to be executed, and in heaven they are represented as characters written in gold."—Adèle is surprised at not having seen, when she went to heaven to see her relations, such a representation of thoughts. M. Swedenborg tells her that she was unable to see them, inasmuch as she was still in a state wherein a diaphanous body is imperceptible. "I saw," replies she, "in the body of my relations as in crystal!" He answers: "You saw what might be compared to crystal; but, were you to see a diaphanous body in all its brightness, you would find it infinitely superior."—"Where does that writing in gold appear to be placed?" "In the heart and the head."—"Are the bad thoughts also represented in the same way?" "Yes, but the bad ones can not enter heaven."

80. "Do you still think, as you seem to affirm in your books, that heaven has the form of a man?" "Heaven has not the form of a man. I made use of this figurative comparison only the better to make my readers comprehend the affinities of the affections of the soul with the organs of the body of which I represented heaven as a type."—"You told me at the last sitting that it was seen *en tableaux* how earthly thoughts are accomplished; but our clairvoyantes go so far as to tell us or predict to us words which will not be pronounced till a period very remote. How can speech be represented?" "Clairvoyantes have two ways of becoming acquainted with thoughts: 1st, by sensation; 2d, by view in pictures. Future speech as present is not more difficult to be represented in pictures than actions; speech is the picture or description of an action and every action may be represented in a picture. I will take for example, slander: you say of a person that he is a thief, an idle fellow, or so forth; the person who shall pronounce these words is seen pointing out him whom he slanders, and the latter doing the action of which the former speaks; and the clairvoyante, judging from the apparent degree of candor the person slandered may tell whether it is a truth or a falsehood. Sensation is more difficult to be defined; there must be an intimate relation with the person and the events."—"Are the thoughts liable to external influences?" "Yes, by the good and the evil spirits."—"We see every day actions committed which

appear to be the result of an instantaneous thought: are they to be attributed to the influence of spirits?" "No, not always; the influence of spirits consists in the enhancing or abasing of a thought, or they contrive to prevent the effect of it, for some purpose or other; but there is limited their power. The spiritual man is ever free to appreciate it at its exact value, there is naught instantaneous in his actions; all that appears externally is the fruit of interior combinations, sometimes unknown to the material body, hence they are fancied to be instantaneous." —"What makes me disbelieve in free-will are the predictions of clairvoyantes who, very often announce to us things that we have no reason to suppose will happen. How can that be? Make me understand it." "As I have already told you, the thoughts agglomerate around a mother-thought, a type which it is easy to recognise. The clairvoyante sees this progression of ideas and can judge with assurance in what time they will overflow, in order then to hurry on, by the trouble they convey into the harmony of the material body, the latter to execute the action they are preparing. The prettiest equally as the strongest thoughts have all one and the same source and object." —"Your solution is a very good one for animated matter; but we have also predictions as to whole nations and individual beings still unborn, how can that which does not yet exist be seen?" "There exists not an action but what has ever existed, either in germ or vibration; for the clairvoyante time exists not. I repeat to you, if his attention is directed to dates, epochs, he sees in the world of causes that which will happen at such a period; he is also and most frequently apprized of these predictions by the divine power which desires that they should be known beforehand, that men may prepare themselves to receive or execute them."—"I am too much obliged to you for your revelations to have the least wish to raise objections to what you say to me; but if God permits these things to be known of men, it is in some sort saying to them, you can not hinder them, and all this proves not free-will. I will make but one objection more: if we have not the intelligence of directing aright our thoughts, and have beside us a guide who can influence us to this effect, why does he not employ his power at this moment in order to be of service to us?" "He ever employs it; but his power is submitted to yours, which repels it, because it sympathizes not with it, with that affection especially which predominates in you for the execution of your project." —"You conclude that man is free?" "All men, on coming into the world, having respectively the same number of thoughts, may dispose of them at will; far from free would he indeed be who had not all that is necessary for liberty; but if you are in a library containing all sorts of works, you consult the one which is to your taste; you can not in aught reproach the library which contains all that it is possible for you to desire. What makes you believe that man is not free is, that the exterior has no knowledge of the affections of the soul, which prepares the execution of them."

81. "Does matter really exist, in the full acceptation of the word, for the spirit, which is no longer subjected to its laws, as it exists, for the spirit which groans in its bosom?" "Matter is quite as existent for us as for you."—"Do you behold, in your state, this firmament studded with stars that you admired so much on earth." "I behold it better than when I was on earth."—"Since that you have a constant daylight, how do you distinguish these stars?" "A spirit perceives whatever it desires, without the least fatigue."—"Are these stars inhabited?" "Yes."—"By whom?" "By spirits."—"What! spirits; not men, then, like us?" "No, spirits, like me."—"These stars, then, are not material, as it is said?" "They are adapted to our substance."—"I thought that the spirit, after its separation from the body, hovered in the atmosphere surrounding the globe it inhabited, itself being a compound of air floating in its substance, and that it was as well there as on a more solid globe?" "You are wrong; the spirit for you is a substance comparable to air; but for us, it is a substance demanding space, in spite of the belief of men who think that a spirit, because it penetrates matter without the least difficulty, takes up no space; our bodies take up as much room as on earth, and as such countless myriads of human

beings have died, if there were not other worlds created by the goodness of God, the space of your atmosphere, or earth, would no longer suffice, as well for the spirits as the places surrounding them."—"I thought the stars material globes, as you yourself advanced?" "I committed many errors.—I was a man—that accounts for it."—"You have also said that the sun was pure fire, what do you think of it now?" "The sun that you behold is the God of heaven and earth."—"What do you mean by that?" "Spirits know no other, and God has never been seen in any other form."

82. On reflecting upon what had been told me in the preceding sitting, I needed more ample explanations, as I could not but suspect that we had made some mistake as to the stars, which, according to revelation, are not, as astronomy supposes, material globes. I longed to obtain more precise information.—"You told me, the other day, that the stars were inhabited by spirits; is there no other material globe in the universe but our own?" "There are many others besides yours."—"What are those stars of which you spoke to me?" "What we name stars are spiritual globes."—"Has each material globe a spiritual one?" "Yes."—"Does this spiritual globe form a continuation of the material one?" "No, it is very remote from it; the distance would appear immense to you, material men, but it is nothing for us."—"Do we go, out of preference, into one globe more than another?" "We go to the one we desire to go to; God has set no bounds to our desires?"—"Where are these globes situated?" "In heaven."—"Those, then, are the globes which we see over our heads, and name stars?" "You can not see these globes, inasmuch as they are spiritual; those are material globes which you see and name stars; but in reality there are no stars except in the world of spirits."—"In that case I perceive that I explained myself badly, or was mistaken. According to what you tell me, the material world has its firmament filled with material globes named stars, and the spiritual one has also its firmament and stars?" "Yes; but know that we name not firmament that material immensity which is over our heads; ours is an infinite space, strewed with worlds, like

yours; we know but one firmament, which is the spiritual firmament."—"Where, then, is this firmament?" "Far beyond the immense space which your eyes can perceive."—"Are there many material luminous globes, similar to that we name the sun?" "No, there is but one sun, which is spiritual; which is the God of heaven and earth, which enlightens all that exists."—"You were acquainted on earth with astronomy, and you know that it admits many luminous globes, as the centre of worlds grouped around them, and to which they give light?" "Astronomy is mistaken; there is but one orb which lights up the universe!"—"How is it that being lighted up only by one sun, the spiritual world can enjoy continual light?" "We are much nearer to this sun than you are; our globe turns not like yours—it is not opaque like yours—hence it is that it presents no obstacle to the light which traverses it in every direction as through a glass. Its essence is in affinity with this light and can not alter its rays."—"The spiritual earths, are they in every respect comparable to ours?" "The globes which we inhabit can not be compared with yours, which is not worthy of the comparison."

83. "I was once told by the ecstatico Bruno, that spirits possessed forthwith whatever they desired; for instance, two spirits assembled in one place, desiring to be, one on a plain, the other at sea, could, without quitting each other, find themselves in the places, though so incompatible, which they desired. Would not such places be mere imaginary creation of the spirit, and having no real existence in heaven?" "Your question embraces one of the greatest mysteries of heaven. All is not quite exact in what was told you; it is true, however, that four persons around a tree, from which each shall desire to gather different fruit, one will be able to gather from it a peach; the second, cherries; the third plums, and the fourth apples, which all shall eat with equal pleasure; but what you say, that two spirits can perceive at the same point two different places, is not correct, as this would annihilate places and the spaces separating them. It is otherwise, for places really exist; but by a mystery not less great, these two

friends shall transport themselves into the places they desire, without, however, quitting each other, inasmuch as they have not the desire to do so. This it is that would make those unacquainted with the mystery believe that places exist not, as you say. They have the faculty, which you possess on earth, of being in different places, answering a person, and putting questions to another who is really very far from you."—"I was also told that if a spirit, in heaven, desires a library in his apartment, and that, this desire gratified, he wishes to replace this library by something else, that he had no need of disturbing the former, which would disappear as if it had not existed?" "It disappears as it came, certainly; they are of a nature so light, so incomprehensible, that they exist, or can exist, only for us, only by our desire; hence springs celestial felicity, that is, possessing whatever we desire. Being deprived of nothing, we can experience no pain; being embarrassed with nothing, we experience no inconvenience. Places really exist, but objects exist only according to the desires, or at least, we obtain possession of them only according to the desires, by the infinite goodness of God."—"Since your death, have you experienced any inconvenience, fatigue, or contrarieties?" "I have been so happy since then that I should not be able to tell you whether it was only the other day that I quitted the earth; time is no longer aught for us: the spirit suffers only when imprisoned in matter; but in heaven, there is no longer a thought that can grieve you."—"You are convinced that we never more appear on earth, to be again materialized?" "We are born, and die but once; when we are in heaven, it is for eternity."—"Do we well recollect our earthly existence?" "Yes, and our anterior one also."—"What anterior existence? Have we then already existed on any globe before appearing on earth?" "Before appearing on earth man lived in a spiritual world similar to the one in which he lives on quitting the earth. Each awaits his turn in this world to appear on earth, an appearance necessary; a life of trials, none can escape it."

Adèle observes to me that her brother had already told her

as much; that she gave no credit to it, but was glad to hear M. Swedenborg say the same thing. "I was shown," said she, "a little girl who was one day to be born, and who is still in this spiritual world: this is extraordinary. As it seemed to me a very fine child, I would have taken it in my arms and kissed it; I was unable to do so, however, and asking my brother the cause, he told me that, not having yet appeared on earth, no earthly spirit could feel or touch her. I have taken down a description of this child, and should be much pleased to see it when born."

84. Adèle expresses a wish to see Eliza, whom we have already seen. She appears, and I say to her: "It is now about six months since you left us; tell us all about what you have been doing since then, and what your present occupations are." "I should be very much puzzled to tell you; I am so happy, that it seems to me that it was only the other day I left you." Adèle says that, as before, she perceives she is eating a peach. I make the observation to Adèle that it seemed to me that, in heaven, there must surely be some change in pleasure. She replies: "On earth, where we vegetate a few seconds, we hasten to enjoy pleasures; but they, know you not, that they have before them eternity!"

I asked Adèle what impression she experienced at the approach of a spirit. She replied: "I am fearful, timid, and bashful, while it is speaking to me; I find myself but little worthy of approaching so near to beings so pure, so beautiful, so sylph-like, and with such benignant looks; I compare myself, in their presence, to a lifeless block, and am at times glad when they depart, that I may no longer behold so coarse a contrast; their visit leaves the mind in a sweet calm, the air seems more pure; in short, one is quite happy!"

85. "M. Swedenborg, you told me that we had already lived on another globe before appearing on earth: could you furnish me with any information respecting this existence?" "What kind of information do you desire?"—"Could you tell me the names of these globes?" "They are names unknown upon earth."—"Did we exist there in the human form?" "Yes."—"What did we do on these globes? did we marry there?

had we a family? a form of worship? usages?" "The life anterior, which we have all passed through, was, so to speak, a life of nothingness, of child-birth, of happiness, like that which we enjoy on our exit from the earth; but this happiness can not be comprehended, because it is not accompanied with actions and sensations to prove its sweet and true reality, wherefore God has deemed fit that we should pass through three successive lives: the first life on the globes of which I speak to you, not unlike the one depicted to you through Adam—a life unknown, a life of beatitude, devoid of sensation; the second is the one you enjoy, a life of action, sensation, affection—a painful life placed between the two, to demonstrate, through its contrast, the sweetness of the third, and to delineate the wants, joys, and troubles, which establish, as you perceive, this necessary contrast, in order that we may become acquainted with good and evil, for without evil in this troublesome life we should not be able to appreciate the happy state reserved for us."—"You have just told me that the future life is similar to the anterior one." "Yes, by the spiritual state in which we find ourselves, for it is only on earth that we are material. The first life offers the same joys as the future one; but I observed to you that we could appreciate them only through the comparison of the material life, which it was necessary to have lived in order to be conscious of this happy state, and to delineate its actions and affections."—"On these globes are we in families?" "No, we are pell-mell, all friends: it is only on earth where families, societies, pleasures, and pains, are delineated."—"This first world, may it be in the material sun which we behold?" "No, there is no material sun; I reiterate to you that there is but one sun, which is the spiritual sun."—"Be so indulgent as to listen to me, that I may make you understand me: this luminous globe, which you perceived when on earth, and named, like us, the sun, is it an earth like ours?" "No; this orb, which you term the sun, is not an earth—not a globe; it is but a very feeble ray of the spiritual sun, which penetrates on earth through space, as a candle behind a door in which is a small crevice; this crevice would appear to you as fire, letting pass this luminous ray, which would give light to the places on which it fell. This fiction should represent to you what you believe a sun, an earth, or a globe, to be."—" So I am to understand that this luminous orb, which we term the sun, is but a ray of the grand spiritual sun?" "Exactly so; but a ray so faint, that it is scarcely comparable to a small live coal in a large fire."—" And those other globes, all which appear to us more or less luminous, whence do they borrow their light?" "From the same ray; there are not two of them for your terrestrial system; this one suffices, and, according to their position, they reflect to you, more or less, the spiritual light which lightens them as well as you."—" Are these globes inhabited?" "Yes." —" Could you give me any notion of them?" "No, because I do not occupy myself with them; I have enough to do to occupy myself with the spiritual worlds, without thinking of those I shall never see again."—" Are the worlds that you inhabit very far from the spiritual sun?" "They are as far from it as they are from terrestrial bodies, and were they to approach nearer to it they would be consumed."

86. "All the beings that inhabit the universe, were they created by God at a single throw?" "Yes, they were created at his word."—" All the beings that people the different material worlds, do they bear the human form?" "Yes, as to those that are of the same species; apart the types."—" Are they all subject to the same laws of creation and death as we?" "Yes." —" Have they, like us, places whither they go after their death?" "Yes, and they are quite as happy; for God has in view only the happiness of us all." To be still further assured that I have made no mistake in the details given me by M. Swedenborg on the sun, I ask him for fresh ones, which have the same result. He says to me: "Why, you understand nothing, then; you ask the same question twice over! No, your sun is not an earth, is not a globe, but simply a ray of the spiritual sun. No, there is no globe of fire among your stars; they borrow all their light from these same rays." Not being so well prepared as to be enabled to judge of the value of this revelation, I leave it to those who have the capacity of so doing.

87. "You have told me that our earthly existence was necessary to delineate our actions and enable us to comprehend the anterior and future happiness of spiritual existences; but children that die before they are able to appreciate the material existence, how can they judge of it?" "All children that die before the age of three years are protected by God, who dearly loves them; they are little angels that remain in this state of innocence, and stand in no need, in order to be happy, of having lived longer a material life."—"What is their knowledge?" "They are not so elevated as the angels, nor as those who die at a more advanced age, because the latter acquire knowledge according to that they had acquired on earth; this, however, is no bar to their being very happy. In their angelic infantile state, they are aware that they have lived on earth and in the life anterior; to this are confined all their desires of knowledge. They prefer the innocence surrounding them to any other state." —"And still-born children, what becomes of them?" "It is with them as with the foregoing ones."—"Wherefore this difference of existence between the old man and the child?" "It is by a protection of God that the child lived not a longer time upon earth, whereon it desired not to appear; but as it is a law generally applicable to all spirits that they should come upon earth, God condemns men to pass thereon a time proportionate to the desire they had to quit their first existence, in which they found themselves unhappy, and the more they were so, the more fit God deems it to let them sojourn in this material life, in order that they may drink plentifully of all its sorrows, and find the future life sweet and agreeable."—"In that case it is a kind of punishment?" "It is an imposition, and not a punishment; it is a necessity."—"Then, according to what you say, the more we have desired to come upon earth, the longer we remain upon it?" "Yes, but we are no more acquainted with its painful existence than are you in your material state with the joys of the future life."—"What say those whom we thus quit to appear on earth? Do we seem to them dead, as we are thought when we quit the earth?" "No; every one knows that he must come upon earth, and awaits his turn."—

"You have said in your Celestial Arcana that man had two memories, which he took with him into the future life, one corporeal and the other spiritual, do you still think the same?" "Yes; but these two memories form but one."—"I can understand what the material memory may include; but I do not perceive what peculiarity the spiritual memory can contain; can you explain it to me?" "Yes; the spiritual memory, or that of the soul, is the recollection of its life anterior to the material life; the soul, though in the material body, is well aware that it has lived in another world, and that it must quit this world to enter into a future one; but it can no more communicate to its body its inmost thoughts than the tortoise can inform its shell of what it thinks. As the tortoise, it drags along, with difficulty, this necessary and cramping prison, which prevents it from rising to the object of its desires, as it was enabled to do primitively, for, as to it, to desire and to possess was the same thing. In its prison, it is very different; it is wholly clogged, makes unheard-of efforts to procure for itself, through the view of its material body, the faculty of seeing or possessing imperfect objects, and, again, its desires are at each instant but ill understood by the body, whose tortuous ligaments suffer only perverted thoughts to reach exteriorly. It is so contraried at such restraint that this reacts on the harmony of its desires, which are ever troubled and deceived, thus rendering it as it were insane. Could it quit this body it would soon do so; but the Divine power keeps it imprisoned the time necessary for its purification; it can but form wishes and undergo its sad position."—"Are spirits in your state permitted to make use of these two memories?" "Yes, since they exist eternally; but that of the material life is so opposed to being exercised that we never force it; all the oddities we have been guilty of in this existence are so repugnant to behold that the spirit is ashamed of them, and unwilling to call them again to mind."—"I have been already told that a spirit could appear in several places, and answer several persons at once; could you explain to me how this can be?" "A spirit can be but in one place and answer but one person at the same time; its material body can, it is true, be in another place, but the spirit sees, and is only in one place at a time. What would incline to a contrary belief is the facility with which it finds itself there. This swiftness is inestimable by the laws of time; hence we fancy, because in less than a second it can be swifter than our thought, in several cities successively, that it really is in several at once: but it is otherwise; only being as I am, disengaged from matter, I have a faculty the more, that of responding, by thought, to those who question me, much more quickly than you can by speech, and this would give me the time to answer another person, while you are reproducing my words; thus this would be taken for several answers at once, whereas it is otherwise."—"On the earth we have examples, however, of such undoublings?" "It is the spirit that makes you believe this, because it can represent its body in a place where it really is not; but neither is in more than one place at a time."—"In magnetism, we often perceive impressions of images or objects that have stood in places where they no longer are, when the clairvoyante perceives them still there." "The soul always leaves behind it something of itself, wherever it rests—a sort of image; but the spirit of the person may still very well be present, when its body is no longer there. The clairvoyante may also communicate, by the aid of this impression, with the spirit that has left it, and fancy that it is really present in this place, inasmuch as there is no time nor space for it. It is impossible to explain this to you otherwise, because a spirit can not positively be in more than one place at a time."—"I have still a question to put to you respecting the ray, of which we have before spoken, and which lightens us as a sun; can you tell me why our astronomers perceive spots on its image, reflected by their instruments?" "There are and can be no spots in this ray; no doubt it is the interposition of certain material globes, which check its passage, and appear to them like spots or dark points."—"If, as you have told me, we are all created male and female, or in pairs, and reunited in heaven to our half, how is it with respect to children dead in embryo, or at an age wherein this necessity of completing themselves is not yet formed?" "It is with children as with grown up persons, those dead, after the age of three years, grow up and complete themselves, and those under that age are coupled in like manner to beings of their own age; their felicity is not less great than ours. The Deity, in his works, has displayed the greatest impartiality; we are all equal in happiness, children and men, rich and poor; in heaven is perfect equality!"

### REFLECTIONS ON WHAT HAS BEEN COMMUNICATED TO ME BY M. SWEDENBORG AT THE FOREGOING SITTINGS.

I HAD never read any of the productions of this celebrated ecstatico-prophet, excepting his "Treatise on Heaven and Hell," a work which assuredly, for a materialist, offers not very mathematical solutions. It has been seen that I made a few observations to Bruno on this subject, when his guide told him something relative to what I had superficially read in this work; accordingly, when my friend, M. Renard, who had come from Rambouillet expressly to see my ecstatic Adèle, solicited the apparition of M. Swedenborg, I purposed, if I had the honor to converse with him, submitting to him whatever I could not admit in the little I knew of his writings; reflection proved to me, however, from all I had seen and heard for ten years, that it would not be right to reject with silly pride facts which, quite inexplicable as they are to matter, are not the less true; I was hunted, harassed, by my clairvoyantes to surrender to these truths, the genuineness of which I had combated from the very first; consequently, I lent an ear. My hand on my heart, either I was a madman or what I heard was possible; the unity that reigned in all that my somnambulists told me made me no longer hesitate a moment, this kind of madness appearing to me as rational as our reason; I perceived that it was far best that the latter should be subdued by such truths than by aught that could impose on the senses. For had I seen with my own eyes, and touched with my own hands, an apparition, or a thousand other similar facts, I should have thought it mere hallucination, and in a few days, have said: All madmen see like things, I have been mad for a moment; but it is otherwise with reason, when satisfied on all points; when I read over again every day these revelations, which, to me, are much more palpable proofs than even apparitions, I remain convinced that this kind of madness is very reasonable and consoling, and M. Swedenborg is for me the god of ecstatics; I now read his works with pleasure, because I have already obtained similar secrets without being acquainted with his; If I am puzzled to comprehend others, I have the assistance of magnetism, which I advise all to make use of, as now-a-days we must have persuasions based on proofs: — let us not believe all that is told us; let us simply believe our own judgment!

Should any one succeed in explaining the spiritual phenomena of somnambulism otherwise than by the existence of spirits and their influence; if it can be proved to me how thousands of clairvoyantes, in every corner of the globe which we inhabit, and in every religious condition of life, can so perfectly agree on the main point of the question, namely, that we have a soul bearing the human form, for which is reserved a happy and immortal life! and the recollection of its *self*, the philosophical trinity of all clairvoyantes! — if, I say, their error is proved to me, I will forthwith burn this work, and put myself under medical treatment, as I must be disordered, and have been, though involuntarily, under the influence of hallucination; but, as I know that it is not given to man to annihilate this truth, I have consequently a right to admit that this soul, in the human form, living in a future life, having recollection of its *self*, can not exist without usages — can not be unhappy because it must have compensation for what it has suffered on earth; a just God can not act otherwise!

I have, therefore, collected with pleasure all we have just read of the grand ecstatico-prophet. We can not doubt the purity of his intentions; nothing in his teachings can give rise to the suspicion that he aims at deceiving us; either he preaches error in the interest of an infernal spirit, or he preaches the truth for the love of God! If he preaches for evil, he goes to work in a very sorry way, by vaunting only the bounty of the Creator and the respect due to his omnipotence. If he preaches for the love of God, he owes it to truth to retract a few errors he may have committed in his books; as he says himself, *I was a man!* We see what he says of the creation of man, male and female; it can not be otherwise. If two sexes exist, it must be with a view of union, and to unite there must be homogeneousness; one must have been created for the other, as its complement, as the part most in harmony with its *self* and its affections. As there is diversity in the creation, by the types, thoughts, affections, we can not suppose that an affection has been created in order not to exist, it can exist only by what constitutes its life, which is the possession of what it desires, and it can not desire anything which wounds its harmony, since on this harmony depends its happiness. It is necessary, therefore, that the object of its affection be similar to itself, or sincere, durable, eternal union is not possible; 'twould be just as on earth, trouble and disorganization! We have already seen that Bruno's guide perfectly agrees with M. Swedenborg, and every one will perceive that it must be thus — it is only with our own image, male or female, that we can find concord and happiness!

We will next pass on to the revelation on insanity; he tells us that it leaves a trouble in the spirit after its separation from the body. We have had a proof of this in the apparition of M. Lauriot, who came very *apropos* to remove all doubts in this respect. We have others in the rambling of the thoughts and judgment daily presented to us by clairvoyantes in their confidences and their appreciations. Whoever should think of invariably obtaining from spirits precise information would be greatly mistaken. Should we from this suppose that we have had to do with evil spirits the mistake would be the same; it must be ever borne in mind that they can answer only according to their affection — only on such matters as God permits them to speak — only according to the justness of their judgment, which attains not at once to the plenitude of universal knowledge — only according to the goodness of their memory, their taste in cultivating it, and a thousand others fetters which we believe we should refuse them as spirits. If these impediments did not exist, the secrets of heaven would be those of the earth, and the *rôles* of the two existencess would be changed.

M. Swedenborg equally says that pacts and talismans exist; in this he agrees with M. Mallet and Bruno's guide. I should be tempted to leave this assertion to be judged to whom of right it belongs. It is the sanctuary of cabal: enters not he who wishes; but I can not let slip this opportunity of expressing my thoughts in this respect. We can not admit that there are intermediate beings between the Divinity and the human species, who compound with God by pacts in some interested view; because the Deity, appreciated as he ought to be, can not figure in any affair of this kind. The fatalists, by this judgment, would not assimilate God to a being trafficking in or executing what the foolish or enlightened judgment of a spirit would claim from his goodness or justice, by striking or pardoning a being who may have been more or less the friend or the *protégé* of a spirit. I do not believe in this falling off of the Divine goodness, and the fatalists who are convinced of the human destiny by predictions, have a right to say that man came from the hands of his Creator as a watch from those of the watchmaker, all the works of which concur in attaining a proposed end—namely, to mark the quantities of time; let but a wheel be put out of order by an accident, similar to the pacts in the life of man, the proposed end is annihilated: no more harmony, no more *ensemble*, no more possible movement. Then he says: Pacts and talismans would annihilate the order established by the Creator; they can not exist. Free will exists not, since the most trifling actions of our existence are predicted to us long before their execution; spirits can not intervene in the order of things established by God. They have a right to speak thus; but there exists another manner of viewing the question. God is, indeed, the Creator who can create nothing imperfect; consequently, he has created man as perfect as possible. In this state of perfection which represents the purest happiness, man, from what we have seen, knew not how to taste this sweet position. God beheld himself under the necessity, in order to prove to him how harmonized was his work, and how free he had created him, of creating for him a second state, a less perfect one—the material state, a state of restraint! of grief! pain and trial! and condemning him to pass in this state a time more or less long, in order that man might be confined and dependent in this new state, from which, were it permitted him, he would soon free himself. God has confided this painful infancy to the care of spirits provided with the rights and power necessary to make man sensible of the comparison of this state with the preceding one, and that his only object was thereby to raise him from this sort of fall and prove to him what the liberty he possessed was, compared with the dependence in which he finds himself under the government of spirits whom he has appointed to this guardianship, to transform, restrain our desires and affections, knowing above all that they can not annihilate the creature of his choice, and intrusting them with it only for a limited time, which is but a few seconds in eternity. God, by this proposition, would be by no means accusable. Quite the contrary, he has created us all, without the least distinction, with the same portion of happiness and intelligence, and does what he thinks necessary to penetrate us with it. God, by this proposition, suggested to me by an anterior life, is not the author of our troubles, since he leaves the government of him to man, even man become a spirit, who, by the appreciation it has been in his power to form on earth, directs, unsuspectedly to us, all our actions and thoughts toward one object—happiness. By this same proposition, the cabal would be authorized in its persuasions, its mysteries, pacts, and talismans, as it would ever be possible for the superior spirits that govern us to mitigate at their pleasure our earthly position, elevate more or less our intelligence, according to the dispositions they perceived in us, and the right and good use we made of them.

In such a way do I find explicable the non-existence of free will; for the material man is not free, there can be no doubt of it. And we should see likewise hereby that the Christians who tell us that evil proceeds from, and is produced only by, man, do not deceive us; but it should be the spiritual man who has the government of us, and not the material man. This evil becomes a good, since it is necessary to replace man in the state of happiness from which he has fallen. We ought to complain only of ourselves, accuse only ourselves, and absolve ourselves, if we can. Our material state, buried in the grossest ignorance, permits us not to define evil: what is evil for one is good for another. Even the sun, which is the purest source of terrestrial life, bears the germ of what we call evil, since it burns what it nourishes, destroys what it protects! Evil is only the false position in which we place good; the want of knowing how to appropriate it to ourselves. It is the disorganization of its harmony, the disaggregation of its parts.

We must, therefore, think that cabal and sorcery are the work of spirits, and that if there is nothing very precise and general in their results, it is that the power of such society invoked finds itself dependent, inferior, or friendly, to the society under whose care is placed the individual against whom enchantments or spells remain without effect. Without this proposition we should every day see disappearing, under the baneful influence of a few individuals, thousands of victims! But we are not to deduce from this conclusion that the power of doing evil, whether through magnetism or sorcery, exists not; that cabal has not its powers, its secrets, its laws, and its rites. I repeat it, the essential condition, and one very frequently unknown to the malicious individual, is in the power of the society to which he belongs over that of his victim. We must conclude from all this chaos of evil that God is not the author of it; but that, on the contrary, he is ever our savior when we invoke him with all our heart.

There is nothing incredible in what I have just said, since all religions, in general — sects, societies, governments even — place themselves under the ægis of those spiritual societies and the chiefs who have founded their material societies; so strictly true and rational is the view which appears irrational to man — termed superstitious. In order to develop the proofs of what I advance it would be necessary to write a treatise on purpose; such is not the object of this work, which permits us not to enlarge on every secret, as so doing would only disturb the *ensemble*, already too often interrupted, of our revelations. We will pass on to sittings 79 and 80. The notions supplied by our good Swedenborg on the assemblage of thoughts, their aggregation, must agree with the phrenological system, with the adepts of that of corpuscules, and confirm, above all, that exclamation of the learned English chemist, Davis, after an ecstasy occasioned by the laughing gas: "The whole human organism is but an assemblage of thought!" We see by the notions given us how they are perceived in heaven and on earth; we remain convinced, no matter how they are so, that they are indestructible and survive the actions they have brought forth; we obtain this proof through the revelations made to us by clairvoyantes on the past. This single fact alone suffices to establish the existence of the soul after its separation from the body, and, above all, the unity of its *self;* for, to speak logically, of what use would be the survivorship of these thoughts, these actions, after the annihilation of the being who had been their author? Why should it be impossible for the soul to continue its existence, since all that concurs in surrounding it in its material life exists for eternity? We see every day our clairvoyantes depicting to us as present events, individual actions that took place years ago, and the knowledge of which could not have reached them in any other state. Were this still the effect of the communication of thoughts, it would not the less prove that the memory is perpetually enriched by whatever man has seen, done, known, or thought, that nothing is lost or effaced on these tablets of the book of life! What I have just said is the plainest side of the medal; but the other is much more positive. For it is possible for a clairvoyante (since it is seen every day) to enter into communication with beings that have disappeared centuries ago from our globe, and find again in their memory the most trivial of their earthly actions, which are as unknown to the clairvoyante as to the magnetizer; here, there is no longer any communication of thoughts! They can equally foresee the action which will be executed in a century or two, and the individual who will perform it, &c. In actions which seem most deeply buried in oblivion, we perceive that to the clairvoyante they are as full of life as if they had but just been executed; and we would have the soul alone not to profit by this immortal life, its individuality, its *self*, after its separation from the body, though all that we have just cited is immortal, individualized! For shame! apparitions become useless before such phenomena; wishing to think otherwise is no longer to think.

The 82d sitting offers us the solution of a question which all men have put to themselves without being able to solve it; it is this: If we live after our departure from this globe, whither do we go? We are aware of all the systems to which this question has given birth. India, the cradle of almost all our European religions and beliefs, places our soul in that which most flatters the sectarian spirit—from the sun whence all has emanated and whither all returns, to the tender flower, the caressing animal, these two grand systems of absorption and metempsychosis! China, not less enlightened than India, prefers placing us under the care of its mountains and smiling valleys. The Christians, true mosaic of all these beliefs, place us in hell! under the earth, or in heaven, that azure space over our heads. No one better than the clairvoyante can serve us as a guide in so dark a route; so have we seen M. Swedenborg, ever in accord with the laws of the creation, give spiritual globes to material globes, as a complement of that famous binary, number two, which reigns in the simplest as in the most complicated particle of creation. Every man of good faith who shall recognise in us two distinct beings, one material and the other of an indefinable substance, must admit, in order that this second being exists independent of matter, globes in affinity with its substance, and these globes, every one will perceive, can not be compressed between the atmospheres of ours, but float in atmospheres appropriated to their nature, and this can exist, as he very justly observes, only far beyond the material worlds.

Sitting 83 offers us a solution less comprehensible, as to the manner in which objects are perceived in heaven; how explain what surpasses our intuition? Only, we see that his description corresponds with what our clairvoyantes do daily, when they find a very good piece of sugar in a bit of candle, complete intoxication in a glass of water, an impassable barrier in a train of fluid, &c. We can catch a glimpse of this incredible power or hallucination only in two ways. Man may, after the image of the Eternal, create, by the sole act of his will, by investing his desire with the form necessary to it; or man, in the state wherein is his clairvoyante, may, without suspecting himself, place it in the world of causes. It may be objected, that a magnetizer like the Honorable M. Dupotet, who lately traced a white line on the floor of his apartment, desiring that it should be a road, more or less agreeable, abutting on a precipice, &c., had no other intention than that of delineating or creating this perilous route. I will answer that it is sufficient that M. Dupotet desired to place his clairvoyante in a road which, though existing not materially in our eyes, existed with far superior details in his brain! with an *ensemble* wherein nothing was wanting. Then, will it be thought that M. Dupotet created this image? No, he could but think a thing possible — a thing existing in one of the two worlds; he is too well-informed to think the contrary, for the first act of the thought is of existing from all eternity: the second, investing the form of which it is the soul, by presenting itself thus to the eyes of our spirit; and the third act awaits being materialized by the action, in order to be perceived by the eyes of the body, and what more has M. Dupotet done? He has presented to his clairvoyante a thought invested with his spiritual form! What has the clairvoyante done? He has seen perfectly a road, a precipice, which existed quite as well for him as the Boulevards for us. The precipice would have caused the death of the body, as if it had been material; only, it is necessary, in order to comprehend these truths, never to separate ourselves from the idea that our material body lives only for matter, and that our soul lives only for the spiritual. They are two worlds quite distinct, in which, without in the least suspecting it, we live daily; for how think, without thoughts? and where do we get these thoughts? In their world. What is it? Of their nature. Where is it? Within and without us. How does this world exist? By God, he is the type-world. What is a type-world? A world of form. Then, therefore, a thought, not materialized, nevertheless exists for the clairvoyante, who is ever in this world of thoughts, the causes of all that exists, sees in them their forms, and the simple word forest must represent, in the world of causes, a forest, with all its accidents. Incomprehensible as this proposition may be, we have the proof that it is true. The word forest is the material envelope of the thought itself, which is a forest. Let it not, therefore, be supposed that a clairvoyante who struggles at your feet is hallucinated; he is in the centre of reason, while we stand around the circle. The mere desire of M. Dupotet to fictitiously create a road was sufficient for his thought to place his clairvoyante in a state fit to explore the world of causes where this road exists, since it is a thought, and a thought is a form typical of the thing itself. The clairvoyante finds himself on this road, which causes him, spiritually and materially, the greatest fatigues, which might lead to the death of the body! As, without quitting your abode at Paris, fixing his eyes on your knees, he sees Bordeaux, where you have the assurance that he is, from all that he describes to you. These two terrible problems, which our reason can not admit, will ever be detrimental to its comprehension of these things; for, whoever says that neither time nor space exists for the spirit, says that which is contrary to our reason, though, at the same time, he gives utterance to the greatest spiritual truth.

This is the way in which I am able to explain these phenomena; for God alone creates, and man admires!

We will pass on to the revelation of a life anterior to the material life. No one, I believe, now-a-days, admits that God is continually creating the human species, although a poet has said that the Deity could not think without creating his image.

We generally believe that all created things existed from all eternity, and we ought not to confound, as I have said in the foregoing article, the enjoyment of the sight of the world of causes with the creation of the causes themselves. God can indeed, in a far superior manner to man, enjoy the harmony of his thoughts, which, with him, form but a perfect unity, and which with man form two, because man proceeds from the Divine thought, and is not God; he enjoys like God, when he is spiritualized, the view of the thoughts under their typical forms, but he does not create these thoughts; thus it remains proved to us, that the thoughts of the Eternal Being from all eternity, since they are of him, can not be annihilated without parcelling out the Divine Person; man, who is one of these innumerable thoughts, exists like them from all eternity, he changes his condition like them all when they become materialized, and this gives rise to the belief in a spontaneous birth, because we take the effect for the cause, come to a stop at appearances, and not at the reality. Thus the soul having existed before dwelling in our body, has existed somewhere, in some form or other, and lived a life of activity, for there is no possible repose in nature; all conduces to movement, without the latter it is nothingness, it is the parcelling out of the Great Being; as I have said it is impossible. It must, therefore, be admitted that if the soul has existed from all time, it may have lived under the form of a germ; and again, this form of a germ might be man himself, for every germ has its form within it and all its attributes, so then a form and all its attributes, without movement, without vibration, can not exist. Even though we should assimilate the germ man to the germ flower, it would not the less be proved that these two germs contain within them all that they must one day develop without them, are not the less as complicated as full of life, bound up in their envelope as in their bloom; then we are constrained to admit a prior existence to the material one, and are equally constrained to place ourselves somewhere. This somewhere for us should be a place; this place should be appropriated to our mode of being. Thus, we must have lived in this place, and in order to live it is necessary to act, we have acted; in order to live it is necessary to feel, we have felt, but imperfectly, as has been just proved to us. We stood in need of a new position, in order to render an account to ourselves of the first one; all beings are conscious of this pre-existence, and I can not do better than quote on this head what I am at this very moment reading (six months after the revelation was made to me), in a work of M. Loisson de Guinaumont, entitled "*Somnologie Magnétique*," page 74. Never was description more explicit and of better effect, especially from the affinity it has with this article. It is M—— P——, who speaks in his magnetic sleep, the 21st of May:—

"When God, the essence of love, intelligence, and goodness, created our soul, he created it with a view to final happiness, but he thought proper to leave to our soul the free-will of its destiny; beside the virtues he thought proper to place vices, and leave it the liberty of choice. If we follow the first road we return toward God; but of what nature, then, are the rewards that await us? Here it is that the feebleness of man's imagination and the poverty of his language find an unsurmountable obstacle. How form to himself an idea of celestial joys? of what nature are they? how are we affected by them?

"No images, no words, can give the least idea of them.

"Let us suppose, however, that under the sunny sky of Italy, amid the marble city of Venice, a child belonging to the highest class of the patricians, is just born; this child will grow up surrounded with the love of his parents, in one word, experiencing all the enjoyments that fortune can bestow; arrived at the age of adolescence, this child shall be suddenly, and without transition, snatched from the arms of his parents, and transported by the power of a will, which nothing can oppose, to the depths of Lapland. There, instead of his brilliant sky, instead of all the enjoyments of luxury with which he was before surrounded, he will no longer have but a snowy sky, a hut and garments made of skins; at the same time that he has experienced a change in his condition, he shall have lost even the very recollection of what he previously was. Let us suppose, also, that a confused tradition informs him that there exists a country wherein, instead of this misty sky, a bright and vivifying sun is constantly felt; that instead of those miserable huts there exist marble palaces, adorned with all the magnificence that imagination can conceive; that instead of those miserable hides that cover him, silk, velvet, gold, shine in all parts on the garments of the inhabitants of this country, his confined imagination will not be able to conceive it; but if, by a new transition as rapid as the first, he were restored to his first condition, with the difference only that this time he should preserve the recollection of the miserable life he had led during what he will term his exile, his soul then would be inundated with delight; the joy which he would experience on once more finding all that he had lost, above all, on once more finding his parents full of affection, would annihilate him, if I may so speak, in an ocean of happiness. Well! whatever be the happiness he would experience, it is no more to be compared with the joy we shall one day feel on finding ourselves again in the presence of God, than could the light shed by a candle be compared with that of the sun. Our joy, our happiness, will be augmented by the happiness that God experiences, if I may so speak, on beholding return to him a soul which might have been lost; for the goodness of God, his love for us, is incommensurable."

I repeat it, what can we find more explicit? What a coincidence between this revelation and those we have read, which certainly were not the result of a combination between two magnetizers, who never saw each other, between clairvoyantes who never knew each other, and who accord so well, without communication, since I did not read this work till more than six months after what had been told me on this subject.

By the 85th sitting, we perceive that God, infinitely good, wholly devoid of partiality, invites to the enjoyment of his munificence every being of every globe without distinction of sects; all that tends to good ascends toward him to enjoy the harmony after which it aspires; all that tends to evil performs the opposite evolution by removing farther from the Divine Unity.

M. Swedenborg makes us an unexpected revelation on the nature of the globe, which we take for such, and name the sun; it will be far from satisfying all exigencies and all beliefs, still I know not whether it be possible for man and science to pronounce on this matter which of the two, science or spirit disengaged from material fetters, is most liable to err? I believe that it is science, because the things proved mathematically by it are annulled before the spiritual laws, and what appears rational is not always true. There was a difficulty which prevented me from admitting this revelation, viz., those spots which the solar image leaves on reflectors; we have seen at the 86th sitting what answer he made to this objection, and the fresh assurance he gave that he spoke the truth. Thus all religions that worshipped and still worship the sun, of which Christians are the most devoted disciples, had the intuition of a rational and wise worship, and what appeared to us very ridiculous yesterday may be very sensible to-day. In such way marches human intelligence, which, if it were acquainted with the pure truth as to the mysteries of creation, would flee from it, shun it as a thing heterogeneous to its reason, such being its thirst after ignorance and absurdity! We are about to pass on to a new ecstatic, who, I believe, will not be supposed to have any system of his own on psychology, being but ten years of age. In the little I am about to present, enough will be found to satisfy the studious spiritualists who have read me so far.

---

## SEVENTH ECSTATIC.

88. Emile Rey, ten years of age, of a waggish and very curious disposition, was a little neighbor of mine, and frequently came to spend an evening at my house, when I used to make him recite a few pieces in verse. When I had made the magic glass I have already spoken of, the composition of which was given me by M. Swedenborg, I had a mind to try the first experiment on Emile, though I did not think his turbulent nature well adapted to these kinds of visions, for which a little submission is required. He perceived nothing in it,

but, as I have just said, he was very inattentive. One of his little comrades of a more quiet disposition, perceived in it different things which he desired to see, and this gave me the assurance that my mirror was a good one. I had a mind to try again on Emile, by the experiment of the water-bottle, which Cagliostro often employed to convince his auditors of his magic power: he beheld very distinctly divers remote places; perceiving, from this, that he had propensities for the magnetic sleep, I magnetized him, and in a few minutes he slept; his curious disposition led him to travelling; he acquired, in a very short time, this speciality, and left me no doubt as to the worth of his clairvoyance. It was this child of whom I spoke farther back, whose sleep was called in question by M. Demarest, because, in a distant view at that gentleman's house, he took a surtout for a paletot, and, in a closed box, a small two-sous piece for a liard. I tried to put this child in communication with spirits disengaged from matter; I told him to ask to see his angel. "Here he is."—"How is he dressed?" "He is quite naked."—I repeated a prayer for the dismissal of this spirit if he were not sent by God; Emile said, "I no longer see anything, he is gone." I summon the good one. "Here he is; 'tis no longer the same."—"Why so?" "This one is dressed; he has a blue robe, a pink girdle, beautiful white wings, fine flaxen hair; he is much handsomer than the other!" I desire the latter to be gone, as the former; he remains, and tells Emile that he is sent by God. "By what sign may you be recognised, in case the evil one should think proper to take your place?" He points out to Emile a small white spot on his forehead. "Have you lived on earth?" "Yes."—"When did you die?" "I don't know."—"What do you do in heaven?" "I play there; we have plenty of amusement."—"With whom do you play?" "With children of my own age; I ride on horseback."—I ask Emile how old this angel appears to be. He replies: "About my age."—"Are you fond, too, of riding?" "Very; my angel is on a fine dapple-gray horse."—"What! at this moment?" "Yes."—"What is there in heaven?" "A fine garden, fine fruits, fine flowers."—"Can we eat these fruits and pluck these flowers?" —"No, God forbids it." "Does your angel see the earth?" "No, he can see only heaven."—"Does he see the men of the earth?" "No, he can see but me."—"Can he see me also?" "He could do so, since you are *en rapport* with me."—"Would your angel be so good as to show himself to you when you have been waked up?" "Yes."—I terminate this sitting. Emile, on awaking, perceives his angel when I lay my hand on his heart, as he had recommended me to do; he gives me the same details as to his dress as when sleeping.

89. "Here is my angel."—"What is his name?" "He calls himself Angel."—"He has no name then?" "He has no need of one."—"I should wish him to take one when he comes to see you." "He tells me to call him Aïs."—"Do you still see him on horseback?" "Yes."—"On what does his horse stand?" "On nothing; he has wings also, and he flies." "What do you perceive around him?" "Nothing."—"Could Aïs conduct you to heaven to see that fine garden?" "He tells me that I shall go after my death."—"Why not immediately?—in the state you are, you might go." "He won't let me; he says that my body could not go, only my soul."—"Well! let him conduct it." "He can not, because he fears the wicked angel."—"You have then a good and a bad angel?" "The latter is not an angel, for we have but one we call angel, the other is a wicked spirit."—"Aïs told you that he had dwelt on earth; where did he live?" "In France."—"What city?" "Paris."—"What street?" "Rue Neuves des Petits Champs, No. 9."—"The name of his father?" "Gustave Jules."—"What is he?" "A tailor."—"At what age did he die?" "At the age of eleven years."—"How long ago?" "He does not know."—"When he died, what effect did that create in him?" "None; he found himself forthwith high, very high, then he entered paradise."—"What is paradise?" "'T is the same thing as heaven."—"Is there a hell?" "Yes, but far, very far from heaven."—"What do we do in this hell?" "We burn there."—"Has Aïs seen hell?" "No; never."—"He told you that he played in heaven; with whom?" "With

playfellows and toys."—"Where does he get those toys?" "He desires them, and God gives them to him; but he has not always what he desires."—"When he has no longer a mind for those toys, what does he do with them?"—"He keeps them, because he can neither break them nor destroy them in any way, as on earth."—"Do children grow in heaven?" "Yes."—"Who instructs them?" "Comrades more advanced than they."—"How does Aïs know that it is God who gives him those toys? does he see him give them to him?" "No; he has never seen God, who can not be seen by any one: God is a soul that fills the whole universe, who is everywhere, and whom none can see; but in heaven he is represented by a picture whereon is seen a man bound to a cross."—"Is there any night in heaven?" "Both night and day."—"I have heard say the contrary." "Those who wish to sleep see night, and those who do not wish to sleep always behold day."—"How are we dressed in heaven?" "Every one wears robes."—"What are those robes?" "They are of all colors, blue, pink, red, green."—"How are the men recognised there?" "They are easily recognised by their fringed girdles." "Do we grow old in heaven?" "We do; but we never die again, never, never."—"Are old men to be seen there as on earth?" "Yes."—"I have heard say the contrary." "Aïs will tell us that the next time; he'll ask his companions, who know more about it than he; his father told him not to be long."—"His father, then, is dead, too?" "Yes."—I awake Emile, who, as before, perceives his angel near him an instant.

90. "Did you not know your guide or angel on earth?" "Yes; I went to school with him."—"Did you ask to see him?" "No; I asked to see my angel, and he came."—"You see him with wings; have all the angels wings?" "No; kind Providence gives them to those only who have been religious, and as Aïs was particularly so on earth, he has wings."—"He told you, last time, that he would inquire whether we grow old in heaven, can he answer you to-day?" "Yes; he tells me that in heaven we preserve the countenance we had on earth, and do not change."—"Let us rightly under-

stand each other; you know that on earth old men no longer have any teeth and their skin is wrinkled all over, are they the same in heaven?" "No; every one there has teeth and no wrinkles; we are much handsomer there than on earth."—"In that case we don't grow old?"—"No; but children alter as they grow up; they remain not as they were when they died."—"Could your guide show you your little brothers who are dead?" "Yes."—"To assure myself of this I will summon a person of my acquaintance who is dead, and whose name was Isidore Verdure." "Here he is."—"Already?" "Yes."—"What kind of a man is he?" "He is taller than you, has a black beard, and is dressed in a surtout and a hat."—"Ask him if he knows me?" "He answers that he is your cousin." I cause other questions to be put to him, to which he makes no answer. He is, indeed, the person I asked for, from the answer and details given; for this child knows not how to frame a description, scarcely can he appreciate colors. According to him this man was about thirty-six years of age, his real age was forty. I ask for my cousin's mother. "Here she is," said he.—"What kind of a woman is she?" "She is very small, has gray hair and black eyes." Such, indeed, she was. I can get no other answer from her but to this question: "How many children had you on earth?" "Three," said she. I was aware that she had lost children at a very tender age, but I did not know how many; I inquired of my father who is her brother, he, like the child, told me she had had three.

91. Emile's guide reproaches him for not having conducted him to a remote place whither I had sent him, and of which Emile gave him a fine description; on my observation that he could not have seen those places which are material, he replied that he should have been delighted to accompany him. I comprehended that Emile's guide thought, because he saw Emile disengaged from his body, he could see at will material places, that he would have had the same power. This would tend to prove that the progression of intelligence in heaven is not so extended as one would imagine, and that this child, given

as guide to another child, was himself only a little superior to him in point of wisdom.

Emile's mother having heard say that her son could communicate with spirits, expressed a wish that he should ask to see one of his little brothers; I summoned him without putting Emile *en rapport* with his mother. "Here he is."—"Describe him." "He is taller than I, fair, and blue-eyed; he has a rosy color; he is much handsomer than I, and wears a blue blouse and a sash round his body.''—"When did he die?" "He does not know."—"What did he die of?" "He does not know."—"How old was he when he died?" "Nine years old." Madame Rey says that this description is quite exact, with the exception of the age; she also says, and it is what astonishes her very much, that Emile never knew this child; to be more assured of what she had just heard and what she ought to think of it, she desires that her grandmother, who had been dead upward of twenty years, should appear, if possible. "Here she is."—"Give us a description of her?" "She is very old; her hair is quite white, her eyes black, she has a pimple on her cheek and a scar near her left eye, a cap that ties under the chin, a handkerchief *en fichu* round her neck, and a black gown; she is not very good looking." All this is very exact, even to the scar which was occasioned by a fall on the chimney-corner; as far as regards the left side, Madame Rey is obliged to make inquiries of her mother, and finds it perfectly correct; as to the pimple, they think they can recollect it, but not precisely. She had a very sallow complexion, and this accounts for Emile's description of her looks; she was in mourning for her husband when she died. In short, Madame Rey is confounded with astonishment, she exclaims: "Emile never knew my grandmother, as she died ten years before he was born, he never heard me speak of her but in a vague manner; but how could he know what I did not know myself, I who was obliged to make inquiries to be assured of what he says? It is very astonishing. Ask her what she does?" "She is very happy."—"Where is she?" "In heaven."—"With whom?" "All her grandchildren." "How many of them are there?" "She replies, seven. I say, mother, what, have I seen seven little brothers dead?" "Yes, my child, reckoning with them your little sisters." Emile had never been more explicit or more clairvoyante. Madame Rey smiled with delight, at thinking of all she had just heard, and the sweet hope of a life of felicity, where she might again press all her children to her bosom.

I removed from this house and had no further opportunity of magnetizing Emile, who would, in the course of time, have been an excellent clairvoyante; I much regret him. These slight tokens obtained from a child of ten years of age are by no means out of place in this work; I could leave them to be commented on by the reader, who, if he were initiated into the laws of spiritualism, could do so quite as well as myself; but how avoid adding reflections to reflections on subjects which stand in so much need of them? I was surprised at the apparition of the child that Emile had known on earth, and whom God gave to the latter as a guide; I could not comprehend how a child, who seemed not to know much more than the other, could be his guide, when my worthy friend Renard sent me the celestial secrets of the good Swedenborg, wherein I read what follows as to the state of children in the other life: "When children are not in this state, but in an interior sphere; to wit, in the angelic sphere, they can in no wise be infected by spirits, even though in the midst of them; sometimes, also, the children that are in the other life are sent by the Lord to the children of the earth, although the child on earth is absolutely ignorant of it. The former experience the greatest pleasure at this.

"2296. It has been also shown to me how all is insinuated into them by pleasures and charms suited to their inclinations; in fact, it has been given me to see children clad with the greatest elegance: they had around their breast garlands of flowers that sparkled with ravishing and celestial colors, and, moreover, they had them around their tender arms; it has been given me, also, once to see children, with virgins charged with their education, in a paradisiacal garden, ornamented not with trees but bowers like laurels, forming porticoes, with alleys to lead to the interior," &c., &c.

I solemnly protest that I had never read this work of the great ecstatico-prophet, and I should think, indeed, that my little clairvoyante had not read it at his tender age any more than I. Let us compare what the venerable Swede said a century ago with what we have just read of this child entering into life. Had I not since had a knowledge of these celestial secrets I am conscious that I should not know how to reconcile to myself what was presented to me as strange by this young guide of eleven years of age; I have, therefore, done right to preserve this little journal, which, from what we have just read, proves that Swedenborg saw right, and the latter proves that my clairvoyante was in a good state. We shall no longer be astonished at seeing this guide on a winged courser, especially if we continue the perusal of all that Swedenborg says on the subject. Children, like grown-up persons, enjoy the possession of the objects of their affection, and their spiritual knowledge is very confined, as we have seen by the answers of Emile's guide. How, in presence of such revelations, can we remain shut up in an egotistical materialism; especially when we have it in our power to procure similar ones to those I obtained, surrounded with so much prudence and mistrust? Every one can obtain them by his practice, which will leave him nothing to wish for, and largely indemnify him for his pains. Set to work, you that shall have read me; say not that I was a visionary; neither say that I was a mirror in which my clairvoyantes looked. You will perceive, by yourself, that such logic is totally false, at least you can not accuse me of a want of sincerity and impartiality: my questions are just as I put them; the answers such as were transmitted to me; all that I have been able to collect I give to the reader, keeping nothing back; I wish not to establish a system but a truth, which consists in the existence of the soul and its identity after its separation from the body. Emile's little guide recognises a hell; we can comprehend this belief; he has never seen it, and I should have deemed myself false to truth had I passed over in silence this revelation, which ought to take its place in this work as contrary revelations have taken theirs. The same guide also says that we can not see God, who is a soul, &c., but that he is represented in heaven by a picture whereon is seen a man bound to a cross. Consult the secret 2299 of the aforesaid work of Swedenborg, as to children that have died in Christianity, and the coincidence of these two revelations will be clearly seen. I should never conclude did I wish to fix the reflections of the reader on all that has been unveiled to me; the right-minded will know full well how to draw from it consoling consequences.

Let us pass on to the relations of an eighth ecstatic, belonging to catholicism from conviction.

---

## EIGHTH ECSTATIC.

Madame Gouget, forty-eight years of age, having heard speak of magnetism, had herself magnetized by several persons, the last of whom, according to what she told me in her sleep, had completely upset her. I knew this woman to be a very good kind of person, and was grieved one day, when she came to pay me a visit, to hear her give utterance to a mass of incoherences, as proved to me that she was under a very baneful influence, and that her mind, which already suffered from it, would sooner or later sink under it. She had left off being magnetized; but she felt the want, in order to recover her normal condition, of finding a magnetizer who could rid her of the evil influence of the last one; she begged me to render her this service. Not feeling myself equal to such a task, I gave her the address of the baron Dupotet, to whom she went. He magnetized her, examined her by the power of his art internally, and perceived that she was deranged. He did not refuse her his services (he is known to be too good for that), but this poor woman durst not return to him. She was advised to go to her first magnetizer, but this was needless, inasmuch as the man was unacquainted with magnetism. Grieved at seeing this woman combating the influence of her baneful magnetizer, who employed all the energy of his will to bring her back to him, in order to profit by her at his pleasure, I undertook to snatch her from this secret obsession. I succeeded in doing so at the close of five sittings, and restored the unfortunate creature to a state of thinking and acting as before her disorganization. I have just given a few details which are necessary to persons engaged in magnetism, and which show how scrupulous we ought to be in the choice of a good magnetizer.

The principal speciality of this woman was for views at distance; she beheld the exterior of bodies with remarkable facility, and described maladies perfectly well. I could cite many psychological facts which would not be out of place in this work, but I will content myself with the following ones:—

92. Madame Gouget says that she receives salutary advice from her angel. "Who is your angel?" "Saint Paul."—"There are two Saints Paul, is it the apostle or the hermit?" "The hermit."—"How does he appear to you?" "He is a venerable old man, with a gray beard and a majestic air."—"Ask to see your real angel?" "Here he is."—"Is it still the same?" "Yes."—"Ask for another?" "I see a group of them on my right."—"Beg one of them to approach and tell you his name?" "Here is one."—"Describe him to me." "He is old, very old."—"What do you call old? is his face wrinkled?" "No, but he quitted the earth ages ago."—"Angels have lived, then, on earth?" "Yes."—"Proceed with your description of him." "His hair is red and he has a very fine countenance."—"What is his dress?" "He wears a sort of dress like a priest's chasuble, but it is not one however. I can not describe to you its form—it is not unlike a mantle. He has on a colored gauze scarf which passes over one shoulder and is tied on the opposite side under the arm; his legs are bare and he has a kind of slippers fastened to colored buskins." —"Desire him to go away if he is not an envoy of God."

"Oh! he stays; he is an angel of light, and no power can drive him away from me."—"What is his name?" "He has no name."—"Let him take one." "He tells me to call him the angel of Paradise."—"Since he has been dead so long he ought to be well acquainted with heaven; can he give you a description of it?" "Yes, he is going to show it me."—After her ecstasy, I ask her: "What does he do in heaven?" "He is happy."—"Are there gardens, houses, temples in heaven?" "There are no gardens or houses, but there is a temple where all the angels are assembled."—"A temple is a house." "Yes; there is also one higher, much, very much higher, but into which all enter not that would."—"Where is this temple placed?" "In the third heaven."—"There are several heavens, then?" "Yes; there are three."—"Where are these heavens?" "Very high, very high."—"Is there a hell wherein we are burned?" "No; there is only a purgatory wherein we suffer much at being deprived of the sight of God, momentarily, and this is very painful."—"Are we burned there?" "No; there is no other suffering but what I have just told you."—"Do we remain there eternally?" "No; God is so good that he withdraws us from it."—"In what form is God seen in heaven?" "In the form of a brilliant sun, impossible to describe; its rays are like the purest gold, and so dazzling that we can not look on them; they give out such beautiful colors as we have no conception of upon earth. God is a spirit whom we can see only under this brilliant form."—"Are these things told you or have you seen them?" "My angel tells me, and I have seen them in heaven whither he just now led me. Good God, how beautiful it was! My angel says that here is enough for to-day."

Madame Gouget, once out of this ecstasy, experienced much difficulty, for want of expressions, in telling me what she had seen; she is very religious, and believes in her watchful state the dogmas of her religion, which are by no means in accordance with what she has just said in respect to hell, purgatory, the three heavens, &c. It suffices that this woman renders homage to the Creator, by representing him not as a mischievous and vindictive being, for my receiving her testimony with pleasure. Her angel says that there are no gardens, &c., in heaven, because his principal affection being prayer, he beholds but a temple, where he joins in chorus with the beings who, like him, sing the praises of God. From all that we have read, we perceive that our happiness exists in our principal affection. He who loves solitude would not wish to be in a noisy city; he, on the contrary, who is fond of bustle, diversion, would desire a city. Thus it is that each thing exists for the affection, and what is contrary to it exists not for it; in this sense was it that Madame Gouget answered me hereafter. I stuck to proving that in the three preliminary secrets of the spiritual world she agreed with my other ecstatics, that the soul exists after the death of its body in the form of the latter; that it has a recollection of its *self*.

93. Up to this day I had never desired that my clairvoyantes should see any of the deceased members of my own family, for a reason that will be appreciated, viz., that they might have depicted to me an image engraven in my memory; I had a mind to try Madame Gouget. I asked for my mother by her Christian name and also by her maiden name, and was very much surprised when Madame Gouget told me she saw a very old woman. After a very minute description, and particularly as to a mark that she told me she perceived on the left cheek of this woman, I recognised in her my grandmother, who was precisely as Madame Gouget described her to me. This apparition, uncalled for, and which I was far from expecting, was owing to the resemblance of the names of my mother and grandmother; I ought not to have asked for my mother by her maiden name. I had already fallen into a like error with Adèle, when several members of the same family presented themselves on account of the resemblance in the names. To make sure whether Madame Gouget really beheld my grandmother, I put to her questions the answers to which removed all my doubts in this respect. My mother appeared at the same time, and the portrait she painted of her was quite true.

Madame Gouget offered me also a speciality which all somnambulists possess not to the same degree. I put her *en rapport* with Adèle, and desired she would see the latter at the period she was suffering a cruel malady, twenty years ago; she entered into details on this subject that lasted half an hour, minutely described the places, furniture, personages, words uttered at the time, even to the flowers and legumes in the garden, which certainly no longer exist, as well as a multitude of objects she saw. She even recounted to Adèle particulars as to the very habits of the young girl, trifling things, that no human being would give himself the trouble to commit to writing for the purpose of recollecting them. We were utterly astonished at the perspicuity of these details. "I see you," said she, "in a bed with blue curtains, in a room having two doors. A large clothespress is at the foot of your bed. There is a large fireplace, in which are stout andirons. There is a kind of little white pot before the fire, in which your ptisan is being warmed; it is your mother whom I see, and she has no wish that any one but herself should attend upon you and nurse you. I hear her giving you consolation; she also forbids you to scratch your face, which is the principal seat to which your malady has flown; your eyes are covered with it, you are blind for some time. What kind attentions your good mother pays you! she passes whole nights with you, and will suffer no one to take her place. I see under the bed a pair of light wooden shoes. Over the mantelpiece is an old-fashioned glass, the gilding is all off the frame. There is also a sort of little bureau near the door; we go out by this door to enter another room, and by this we go down into a garden. Ah! I see you there plucking roses, and concealing them under your dress; then gathering fruit, while you look behind you to see that no one is coming. It is especially when you are going to gather some fine chervil that I see you by the wall, under an apricot-tree. Ah! there is a rabbit-hut at the end of the wall, pretty well stocked; there are both large and small rabbits; it has an iron-grated door, a large stone keeps it shut. I see your mother rooting out some fine carrots with a wooden picket; she seems pleased; she is very fond of fine carrots. There are flowers and salad in this alley; there are yellow flowers. Ah! where does this lead to? It is a stable. There is a beautiful vine alongside the wall," &c. Adèle acknowledges the exactitude of all these details. While Madame Gouget is in the garden, Adèle fancies every moment that she is about to tell her that there is a well there; but though passing close by it, she does not perceive it, and this gives rise to Adèle's observation: "If she sees all this in my thought, since I think and wish to draw her attention to this well, why does she not see it?"

This communication is no longer a vision of things and objects existing, since all this disappeared many years ago. Madame Gouget hears the words, sees the gestures as if this scene were full of life. Even though we admit that these things were imprinted in the memory of Adèle, which is true enough, it nevertheless remains to be explained how such an impression should be full of activity at all times. Who causes her to act? and on what site does she stand? We fancy we have said all when we say, she sees in the thought! I think, on the contrary, that we increase the difficulty of answering. If it be possible for the clairvoyante to perceive in the memory facts such as I have just described, and the history of magnetism supplies us with not less incredible ones, it is, therefore, possible for him to find again there all that man has been able to see, hear, say, or do, during his whole life. Partial facts may be imprinted on this memory not only once but thousands of times; and this impression of the shortest scene of our life offers the clairvoyante space enough to discover in it a heaven, an earth, places in which he promenades at his ease. What then is the space that a soul can fill in comparison of that which these images must hold in our memory? Answer, princes of science! it is a spiritualist who asks you this question, and condemns you to the ridicule with which you cover him if you are unable to resolve it. I repeat to you, know that the clairvoyante sees in your thought *what you no longer think, but what you have thought; what you no longer see, but what you have seen; what you no longer hear, but what you have heard.* Thus the secret oaths that you have made to the young girl whom you have deceived! dishonored! abandoned! he sees them and will tell you of them; he sees also the tears that you have caused to be shed; he hears you singing the romance that captivated her heart and you forgot, together with the victim whose image has not left you; you will possess her again in eternity! She forms part of you, you can not shake her off; all is present and full of life to the eyes of the clairvoyante. When the bodies that have committed these actions are gnawed by the worms, he sees them acting, hears them speaking, speaks with them, promenades in places that are no more; he finds of these pictures, of these scenes in the domain of your memory, as many as can pass in the universe! Hear you, the universe! you are, then, a universe, answer? No; since the universe is a compound of a multitude of unities, and that, on the contrary, these unities, these places, these scenes, may exist in you thousands of times! You are, then, a thousand universes! You are still more! Well! if you can not answer this question, study this soul, the masterpiece of creation! you will surely accord it a little of immortality, since the most infamous actions have as much! Say that, in default of better, you will study the revelations that M. Swedenborg has made to me on the subject of the nature of thoughts, which are living beings, engendering, immortalizing themselves, like us. Systems of corpuscules, emanations, images foreknown, demonstrated under a multitude of phases, from Pythagoras to Saint Martin, from M. Delachambre, in his treatise on the System of the Soul, to the learned propositions of Dr. Gall, by his protuberances, progressing, overflowing, and troubling the other localities. This assemblage of atoms can not act without life! The word atom bears with it some kind of form; the word life bears also a *self*. Thus what forms will you give to the thoughts of Dr. Gall? What life will you give to this atom, if not the form of the thing itself? If not a *self* that unites with another *self?* This atom, small as it is, moves toward a certain end, that issues from a will. See at what we arrive, for there is nothing dead in nature; all, therefore, is alive, with a life divided *ad infinitum*. Proceeding from forms to infinity, we perceive that human thoughts and actions are not lost to the clairvoyante—that they are, indeed, acting: in one word, living images; sounds, song, vibrate in his ear! Only think, a sound! which appears to us to have materially entered into vibration twenty years ago, and more, falls with the same force and harmony on the ear of the clairvoyante; it will resound thus to all eternity, and this impression of actions of images will never be effaced! it will ever act; for there is not a particle of the material and spiritual creation at rest; we can not, therefore, deprive these actions, these sounds, these thoughts, these images, in short, with a life not generalized, confounded in the torrent of universal existence, but individualized, having a form proper to them, since the clairvoyante finds them again at all times; they are, therefore, spiritually speaking, as we have been told by Binet's guide, by Messrs. Mallet and Swedenborg, indestructible, unalterable, eternal! However strange this revelation may appear, we have only to reflect in order to admit it; it is not the same, if we wish to explain it. I shall endeavor to do so in a work forming a sequel to this.

To resume: Adèle, who has this speciality only through revelation, in a consultation asked for, in her turn, by Madame Gouget, took her revenge, telling the latter many hidden particularities of her life, which the good woman had some difficulty in calling to mind. Never had I obtained a more curious sitting; self-love was mixed up with it, without turning to jealousy, and I acquired the certainty, and, as I have said, intentionally, that if the last thoughts and actions are reserved with such care in the domain of the memory, and survive the annihilation of the body, wherefore should the soul which has elaborated these thoughts be alone destroyed, or not have the recollection of its *self*, its individuality, since all that constituted this individuality is by no means dispersed in the domain of the universe! but, on the contrary, seems to form in it a bundle more compact, and much better to be appreciated, than in the material life.

I must make a last observation on the manner in which, as

we have seen at the commencement of Madame Gouget's sitting, I wished to dismiss the Saint Paul, in whom I had but little confidence. I desired to appreciate, for the last time, the power of the will of the magnetizer over the magnetized, and perceive how far the influence of the former extended. I acquired the certitude, as every one might, in this kind of researches, that this pretended power of the will lost all its empire in spiritual experiments, for I have maintained many a time, to my clairvoyante's persuasions, which they could not annihilate in me; I have horribly contraried, fatigued them by captious reasonings, and never could obtain their assent to ideas not their own. None would admit the non-existence of free will; not one has represented God otherwise than as a brilliant sun; not one would admit the hell of the catholics; not one would have it that Christ* was the only true God of heaven — Christian spirits and others have all agreed on this head; not one would have the heaven of Christians, or the complete beatitude of a soul devoid of form, that breath, incomprehensible, without some form or other; all, on the contrary, have recognised in the soul the human form; and in heaven, a place wherein there are usages, as on earth, whither all men are called to enjoy a happiness that they deserve, from the evils they have suffered on this globe. They have all been agreed to maintain their thesis of free will, by recognising

* It was said to me: "Confound not the Father with the Son, as Christians do; The sole Creator of the universe never came down on earth to be crucified by men. Christ was the Son of God, as we all are. He accomplished a special mission and returned to the bosom of the Eternal, as we all shall one day return to it!" When I have made the observation that Christians affirm that there is no salvation saving in the divinity of Christ, I have been answered: "Heaven is open, without distinction of sects, to all who believe in the existence of God, serve him with love and respect; heaven is but an assemblage of an infinity of societies, each of which represents creeds and usages peculiar to itself, each society being able to admit into its bosom only beings of similar persuasions, and thus it is that heaven, or the bosom of these societies, is shut against contrary creeds, and all have a right to say, saving Moses, Christ, Mahomet, Luther, Calvin, &c., there is no salvation; that is to say, you will not be admitted into our heaven, our society, the society founded by such or such man, because your persuasions would not accord with it: you would be miserable there yourself, and would trouble others."

places of purification, wherein we suffer from privation of the sight of God, for a period more or less long; but none has recognised an avenging God, wrathful and vindictive; all have made God worthy of being loved, adored, respected, admired. And it is because I ought not, in order to cry up the goodness of God, who can not be extolled by the mouth of a weak mortal, and needs no other advocate but his beneficent acts, it is, I say, in order to combat the errors that have been propagated by all sects down to this very day, with a view to the moralizing of men, and whose maxims are offensive to God, that I have freely committed to writing all that has been told me by my clairvoyantes; and, in order, at the same time, to render homage to the Divine justice, which we can no longer doubt, now that we are acquainted with the object of our material existence. By the revelations that have been made to us on this head, God has no hand in our afflictions, but is all in all in our happiness.

---

## APPENDIX.

M. Renard, the gentleman already mentioned, being aware that I intended publishing by subscription the present work, desired, on a journey he took to Paris, to put further questions to Adèle, in order to judge once more of the value of her perceptions, and at the same time thank this excellent clairvoyante for a prevision she had had in his respect, a prevision which had been realized, and the details of which are as follow:—

At one of the last sittings we had obtained from the venerable Swedenborg, M. Renard had requested me to submit to him a few questions, which were answered agreeably to his wishes; but to one that was addressed to him, as to whether M. Swedenborg had a spouse in heaven, and could address her to us, we were answered, "She is about to present herself from me." What was my surprise when, on asking Adèle to give me some description of her, to hear her say, "Why it is the future partner of M. Renard who is now speaking to me."—"How is that?" resumed I; "it was M. Swedenborg's partner that was asked for." "In faith, I have made a mistake unwittingly," replied she. "I addressed to M. Swedenborg questions on the part of M. Renard; I told him that he would be glad to know his partner. M. Swedenborg, like me, understood it to be M. Renard's spouse that was asked for, and hence the mistake."—"In short," said I, "give me a description of this person." "She is a pretty brunette, with a sweet air, features perfectly regular, fine black eyes, fresh-colored cheeks, a small mouth, rosy lips, and a round dimpled chin; she is not very tall, wears a white robe, and has a crown of white roses on her head. Mind you, she appears to me not as she was on earth, but as she is in the spiritual world."—"Ask her what her name was?" "Juliette Pichot."—"Where was she born?" "At Aurillac, in Auvergne."—"Where did she die?" "At the abode of an old aunt she had at Frénay."—"How old was she?" "Forty-seven."—"How long has she been dead?" "She does not know."—"Did M. Renard know her on earth?" "He knew her at an inn where he came sometimes to take his meals, in a small town near Mans, and where she was a servant."—"What was the sign of the inn?" "The Golden Sun."—"How old was she at that period?" "About sixteen."—"Did M. Renard pay his addresses to her?" "No, he never breathed a word of love to her."—"How will he be able to remember her; he left that part of the country a very long time ago." "She will appear to him, and he will remember her."—"She is, then, the companion destined him by God?" "Yes, she tells me that he will soon* join her."—"Has she anything particular to make known to him?" "No, *she will appear to him in a dream, and awaken him to a remembrance of her.*"

* Whenever a date is demanded of spirits, they all reply, "It will be soon." This word admits not of the same acceptation spiritually as we give it materially. There, where hours and time are not reckoned, the moments appear short; an hour is an age for a happy expectation; a second for a contrary one.

I forwarded to my friend all these details, which, as may be supposed, caused him much surprise; he had not the least recollection of this young girl; he had, indeed, lived at Mans, and travelled in all the small towns dependent on it—had necessarily taken his meals at several inns; but time (a period of thirty years) had effaced, in respect to this, all recollections from his memory. I endeavored, at several succeeding sittings, to obtain more precise dates and places: it was ever the same answer: "Why would you have me trouble myself about this earth where I was so unhappy?—with this condition in which I suffered so much, and with the numerous places at which I was in service? It will not be long before we meet again, and then we shall give up all thoughts of the earth!" I abandoned all research in this respect, and thought no more of the matter, when one day I received from my friend a letter couched in these terms: "I can not, my friend, resist the desire of giving you the analysis of an ecstatic dream, in which I beheld Juliette: I found myself at a large inn, where I called for some refreshment, and was served. Opposite to me, at the same table, was a man with whom I made acquaintance. When he was about to depart, I accompanied him to the street door; he was no sooner gone than a servant-girl whom I had observed going to and fro came up to me, saying: 'I, too, am going away.' I spoke to this girl and advised her to stay; I took her civilly round the waist in order to detain her, and she turned round and fixed her eyes on me. Her countenance was that of a pale brunette, somewhat sickly and expressive of suffering, but having a very tender look. I was greatly moved and my heart bade me give her a parting kiss, but so many persons were passing by that I durst not; at the same time she disengaged herself from my grasp, leaned toward me and said: '*M. Cahagnet, your friend, has told you that an angel awaited you in the spiritual world!!*' Then, taking wing, I lost sight of her. These last words struck me, and I forthwith awoke. Dreams are real excursions in the spiritual world; thus, what your clairvoyante predicted has come to pass. Do not for a moment suppose that it was the thought of this revelation that influenced me; I had long forgotten all about it, since this girl, whom I take to be Juliette, was obliged to remind me, and that in a very, laconic way, of what your clairvoyant had said. The effect of the dream over, I immediately awoke. Modern *savans* have never been able to explain the cause of dreams," &c., &c. Here we have some of those proofs that square not with our material exigencies, but overshoot them. What was Juliette's object in this circumstance? No doubt to represent to M. Renard the inn where she had known him. What did M. Renard do! He could not recognise a place, and a servant-girl who had served him occasionally with refreshments; the personal appearance of M. Renard might have made an impression on her, when probably he had paid no attention to her. Juliette, in this dream, replaces him in the same conditions in which he was thirty years ago; perceiving that he did not seize upon these images, and that his reminiscences remained dumb, she says to him: "*M. Cahagnet, your friend, has told you that an angel awaited you in the spiritual world,*" and she disappears after rousing him! This apparition, which had been predicted by Adèle, but which might be resolved into a simple vision and naught else, made such an impression on my friend, that on his journey to Paris he testified to us all his joy, and declared that he was more convinced by this dream than by anything he could have seen in any other circumstance.

94. M. Renard asks for Juliette: she says that she suggested to him this dream for the purpose of being recognised; that she is often near him, speaking to his spirit, but that he can not materially perceive her presence; she assures him that she will do her best to let him see her again.

We ask for M. Swedenborg. "Here he is."—"M. Renard desires to put a few questions to him." "Let him speak."—"Are spirits sensible of sleep?" "Sleep who will; sleep is not a necessity for the spirit; if the spirit gives itself up to it, it is merely for pleasure's sake. With the material body it is quite the contrary: the latter stands in need of repose while given up to it; the soul, which never sleeps, takes advantage of this repose to distribute and learn its actions, arranges them, prepares them for the day following this rest; the soul can sleep, but it never does; the vital spirits alone that surround it give themselves up to repose."

"You told M. Cahagnet that the star which gave light to our material globe lighted up the whole universe; how can that be?" "I told you, on the contrary, that it was but a ray of the Divine sun that lighted up your planetary system; there are, in like manner, thousands of other rays, departing from the same Divine sun, that light up all the other systems."—"The rays of this star that lights up our earth, are they, like all other spiritual objects, invested with a material substance?" "Yes, the nearer they are to the centre whence they emanate, the purer they are."—"The nations that adore this star ought, in that case, to be nearer the truth?" "All religions that adore God, no matter under what form, are equally acceptable to him."—"The objects found around, and for the use of spirits, according to the thoughts of their affection, were they created before the thoughts of this affection, or are they created only at the very moment of the thought?" "Whatsoever man sees and possesses is within him and without him; it is the fruit of his thoughts which were created by God: man creates nothing; he desires, sees, and possesses the object of his desire."—"But can he perfect the object he perceives, as he does on earth, by cutting stone, polishing wood and metals?" "He can do what he desires, since there are usages; he lives in the spiritual world as on earth; he constructs with materials, if such be his pleasure: if, on the contrary, he desires objects already constructed, he possesses them instantaneously."

95. M. Renard expresses a wish that Adèle should ask for his father. "Here he is."—"Give me a description of him, if you please." (Mr. Renard was not *en rapport* with Adèle.) "He appears to me taller than you," said she, "and stouter; he is dark, has small eyes, a large nose, and an agreeable look; he has a gray vest on him, with pockets behind, and one at the side in which he puts waste paper; he has a waistcoat that comes down very low, and having two pockets; he has blue gaiters on, and I perceive a stick in his hand." M. Renard

says that this description is exact, and begs Adèle to put the following questions to his father: "Are you reunited to my mother, your first wife?" "Yes, there she is," replied he, pointing her out in the distance to Adèle. "Did you love her more than your second wife?" "Yes, for my second did not render me happy."—"Are you happy where you are?" "Yes, I have nothing to wish for." Adèle says that this gentleman is easy of speech, and has a cheerful look; that is exact. What we deem most remarkable in this apparition is the stick, which had become quite a necessary for him in consequence of falls, in which he had had both his legs broken.

M. Renard had no need of this new apparition to believe in the existence of his father; he wished to judge by himself, a second time, of Adèle's excellent clairvoyance, which, far from falling off, continued increasing.

We ask again for M. Swedenborg, to whom we address the following questions: "If we existed on another globe before appearing on earth, we must all be of an equal age?" "Certainly."—"If we are of the same age, one can not be the child of the other?" "No, not spiritually; it is only materially that it is so from necessity."—"If we are equal in age, we should be equal in corpulence?" "Yes, in the spiritual world every one there appears pretty nearly of the same corpulence and age; if there are differences, they exist only in human affections."—"If we are all equally old, and of the same size, there can be no children?" "There are children only for those who desire to see them; but children among each other see themselves as tall as men."—"If it be thus for the equality of ages and forms, it should be the same in regard to intelligence? When a child dies as such on our globe, he ought to recover forthwith all his knowledge, which should be equal to that of the rest?" "No; were it so, it would no longer be a life of progression. To learn constitutes the happiness of spirits; they appeared on earth to delineate there their affections, which multiply to infinity. He who died when a child, knows not what he knows who has seen much and desired much. What all spirits equally know is, that they have all lived on earth and on an anterior globe; they are all acquainted with the language of heaven; but each helps the other to develop his intelligence, which is much quicker than upon earth, but nevertheless leaves a very great difference between the knowledge of each; it is only children under three years of age that, by the effect of the divine thoughts, remain, or appear to remain, in this state of innocence, which they would be unwilling to change."—"I don't understand how an embryo of fifteen days should be able to become acquainted with the earthly sufferings for which it was beneficial, you say, it should be born?" "I have already explained to you that men remained on earth a time proportioned to the desire they had of changing their position; that children, dying as such, had less desire to appear on this earth than others; hence it is that God, who can commit no injustice, leaves them there the time calculated by him as necessary to instruct them in the false position felt there. Do not fancy that the embryo that has not seen the light of your earth has not suffered a sufficient long time to prove to it that it was and is about to be happy. Although in the bosom of its mother, it suffers more than you imagine; for it, it is a prison that may be compared to your prisons on earth, in which, if you passed fifteen days, you would suffer as much and more, perhaps, than a man who thinks it mere sport to spend a few years in one: the last pang is ever the one that makes the deepest impression on us, and renders us forgetful of the rest. Thus the necessary imprisonment of this child in the body of its mother for some time, is as painful to it as long years of earthly existence to others—believe it, all is for the best, and for the justest purpose."—"Still, if this false terrestrial apparition suffices to become acquainted with the painful sensations necessary to our future existence, I don't see why I should vegetate so many years on earth, when I might have undergone the same transformation as this child." "Were such the case, the earth would not be inhabited: you can not comprehend the wise laws of the Infinite, hence you talk in this way. A uniformity, such as you understand it, would be absolute repose—'t would be nothingness; and there is no repose, no nothingness; the variety of forms, of existences, assures you of an eternity of happiness." Adèle is fatigued and unwilling to proceed. I put to her this last question, "If all spirits are equal in age, the name of brothers suits them better than those of fathers, mothers, and children?" "Yes; but such names nevertheless exist for those that take a delight in them."

96. "For some time past I have had a great wish to ask you whether the language spoken among spirits has sounds similar to our languages of the earth?" "On earth, I address to spirits the questions you submit to them in French, and they answer me in that language, but in heaven I do not speak that language; we know, we feel, this penetrates from one heart to another without the assistance of speech."—"Suppose, for instance, I put you in communication with a deceased foreigner, whose language was unknown to you, and he in like manner was ignorant of yours, how would you manage to transmit to him my questions, and he to answer them?" "If your questions were in French they would be understood by the foreign spirit, for deceased spirits understand all languages; but if, on the contrary, the questions were addressed to me in a foreign tongue, I should not rightly comprehend them, consequently I should transmit them incorrectly, as I did to M. Lauriot; hence mistakes would occur. I don't like communications of this kind."—"It is said that there are clairvoyantes who speak languages which they have never learned?" "We can not speak a language which is unknown to us. Those clairvoyantes have a taste for experiments of this kind; to succeed in them, they dispose of the faculty they possess, as spirits disengaged from matter, of comprehending the thoughts. I would not take upon myself to speak any other language than my own, because I am persuaded that if I rightly comprehend the questions put to me, the spirit to whom I submit them will have more facility also in comprehending and answering them." —"Then, to speak to a foreign spirit, you would wish the questions to be put to you in French?" "Yes."—"But how manage to transmit them to him?" "Since I have just told you that spirits comprehend and speak all languages, they have

also the faculty of reading in my thought, and answering the questions put, provided I comprehend it myself. Hence, as I have already told you, the liability to mistakes to which I am exposed like all clairvoyantes; a thought or question not rightly understood, not rightly rendered on both sides, may spoil all." —"Ask for M. Swedenborg." "Here he is."—"All material objects, you have told me, have a spiritual representation?" "Yes."—"So, if spirits desired it, they could see and be present at all our actions?" "Yes, they could, but such is not their practice." "They could equally, if they have taken a fancy to any part of the earth, this room for instance, occupy it, if such was their desire, and be, consequently, with us without our being aware of it?" "They can do whatever they please."—"I would thank M. Swedenborg to answer me a few questions of another kind." "Speak."—"Can he explain to me how a clairvoyante is able to see in his eye whether the latter is disordered?" "It is the spiritual eye that issues from the material one and visits it."—"There are cataleptics who see through the pit of the stomach, or any other part of the body, how is that?" "It happens in this way: the soul no longer being the slave of the organs, as in the material body, it can convey its spiritual view where it thinks fit, especially in the conditions you have just set forth."—"In that case the soul would not, therefore, have a body, alike in all to the material body, for the reproduction of all its organs, if it can transpose them from one point to another, the eye under the foot, for instance?" "The soul does not transpose them for this; it can see where it thinks fit, since there is no obstacle for it; if it can see to the depth of a hundred feet under ground, a sheet of water, or a mine which may happen to be there, it may surely see under its material foot. The soul can see wherever it wishes, be where it seems to it fit, be in all and everywhere, be all and nothing; the soul takes up no material room, is liable to no deterioration, is unalterable, and incomprehensible. If you wish to dwell upon comparisons of volume, size, space, and time, you will never comprehend the spiritual laws; know that the soul can be, without filling it, in the smallest point of the material creation, and can fill the universe by its relations with it."

M. Renard, of an integrity proof against anything, delighted with the results I had obtained, desiring to proclaim them whenever an opportunity occurred, and wishing to support them with all the weight of truth of which he is one of the most fervent disciples, had been long anxious to procure the portrait of the venerable Swedenborg, in order to compare the description given of him by Adèle with the likeness of this great man; for this purpose he applied to the society of the disciples of the New Jerusalem, expressing a wish to purchase the engraving, which, as it is said, so faithfully portrays him. Scarcely had he it in his possession than he forwarded it to me; I exhibited it to Adèle, in her watchful condition, in order that she might compare it with the original in her somnambulic state. I put to her the following questions: "What do you think of the engraving I showed you in your watchful state?" "It is the very image of M. Swedenborg, but he seems to me a little older, although, in the spiritual state in which he appears to me, he is infinitely more handsome than in this engraving; according to the light we are in, the countenance is more or less youthful and fresh."—"You told me at the time that he wore a coat, the facings of which were of a different color; it is not possible to distinguish them in this engraving, would you be so good as to describe to me the colors?" "He appears to me wearing a coat of the cut that I before described to you, similar to that in the engraving, with large buttons; it is of a chestnut color, the facings are green, as well as the trimmings of the sleeves; he has coarse blue breeches on, with knee-buckles, and also buckles to his shoes; he is a strong man; his physiognomy is still imposing to me, although there is nothing harsh or malicious in it, but grave and venerable."—"Do you see him with his hair powdered?" "No, it is curled, as I before told you, and as the engraving represents it; it is brown, and very thick; his eyebrows also are very thick; in short, I had told you all this."—"Do you think that this was the official dress he wore at the Swedish academy?" "No; I asked him before, and he told me that I saw him in his usual dress, which he preferred to any mark of distinction."

These fresh particulars were in nowise necessary to me; the revelations he had made me through the medium of Adèle, which tally so well with his works, which I had not then read, as I have before said, were sufficient to confirm me in the belief that I was not in the presence of a deceiving spirit; the religious sentiments with which all his teachings are stamped are not of a spirit of darkness, and such a spirit, could it have searched into the memory of this great man so far as to reproduce to me what we have read, with so much truth, it would have done the same with respect to his dress, the one not being more impossible than the other; but this supposition would destroy the belief we have in theology, that the inferior spirits can neither influence nor purloin the thoughts of a superior spirit. I merely add this reflection for the sake of a few timorous consciences that see the Evil One everywhere and in all; I am far from addressing it to persons whose minds are free from such childish fears. I have done my best to depict and recognise a man whom I have never seen; assuredly, I can not do more; let those who have it in their power to confront the color of the hair and garments do so, inasmuch as this, I believe, will ever be out of my power.

I advise no one to seek to obtain any other definition of the soul than the one we have just read; it would be fatiguing a clairvoyante to no purpose. We shall never be able to explain the primitive nature or properties of the soul and thoughts by our material solutions; it is the same with respect to the laws that regulate the spiritual world; it is useless perplexing spirits with our *buts*, our *ifs*, our *whys;* let us listen to them, sum up what we see and hear, let us compare, judge, and never finally pronounce, as our judgment may ever be appealed against.

Above all, let us ever bear in mind that in questioning a spirit we are not *the master*, but indeed *the scholar;* should an inferior spirit plunge you into too palpable errors, no longer address him; but *do not contrary him, do not use him roughly!* You know not whom you have to do with; you might be a victim to your silly pride, as well as your clairvoyante.

These precautions are needless in simple apparitions; they

are useful only in the metaphysical discussions you may have with them.

In the captious question I addressed to Adèle on the power with which the spirit disposes to see where he thinks fit, I try (from what she affirms that the soul bears the form of the body) to make her understand that it can not have the visual organ under its feet, but in its head, or in that case this organ would be the soul itself transporting itself wherever it pleases. The answer she gives me is the one she already gave me two years ago, and which has been read in this work. The body of the soul is of a substance similar to crystal, like all around it, and every part of which it can perceive without the least difficulty; this is admissible, since it has this power over matter itself, this proves that there is but one single substance in the creation the degrees of which are more or less luminous for our material state, a substance that the soul can penetrate, whether by lighting them up with its own light, or seeing them by the mere assistance of theirs.

She tells me in the preceding answer that the spiritual eye quits the material one to visit the latter; she means by this, that a somnambulist, to this degree, is himself out of his material body; and hence it is, says she, they can perceive whether a person is asleep or merely pretends to be so, by the mere inspection of the individual's head which appears to them empty if he sleeps magnetically. In this way the body would no longer be an obstacle to the vision. Many other clairvoyantes will, perhaps, say the contrary; judging only from them, although out of their body they perform their functions within; they will ever believe themselves in this body, although they are only intimately united to it, and being instantaneously where they wish to be, they will never be able to explain how they should find themselves entire, present in a remote space, *material, infinitely small*, and find themselves at the same time filling all their material body. Possibly Adèle would have been unable to define this incredible proposition, had not the spirits defined it for her themselves. Oh! abyss of our reason!

## CONCLUSION.

WHAT conclude from such a collection of facts? To pronounce, must we possess a distinguished education? No. Is it more necessary to have a subtle and superior mind? No; it is necessary to stand aloof from all religious parties, implore the divine light of our Divine Master, that he may enlighten our intelligence, bestow on us a sound judgment, strip it of all the passions left in it by false maxims; annihilate ourselves, as it were, before the infinite greatness of the Creator and his creation, instead of proclaiming ourselves, with silly pride, his masterpiece. We must make every effort to shake off, whatever matter teaches and exacts from us by its laws, for the laws of matter are not always in accord with the laws of the spiritual world; they can not, as I have said, fraternize together, though not being disunited, and forming but one inexplicable, yet sensible whole. To form a conclusion on this collection of revelations, we should be wise in the full acceptation of the word, and the wise are rare in our times.

I will not permit myself to pretend to so great an honor, or to add one revelation to another in order to establish a system or beliefs which might possibly be revoked, as not being sufficiently luminous. I leave to each the right of judging, of pronouncing; I will merely beg permission to gather together the principal questions I have put, the whole as laconically as possible, and set down their answers in due order; all this, in a few pages which will close this book, and leave in the intelligence of the reader, without perplexing his memory, a summary of what I have said and heard. Let him take these questions, disorderly as they are, as a model or starting-point for those I advise him to address to clairvoyantes* himself, then he

* After having driven away by prayer the spirit of darkness, invoked the assistance of the divine light, made the clairvoyante swear that he will not alter the truth in the interest of any religion, to render him responsible for his conduct, and, as a greater security, employ the organ of a child to put the questions to the said clairvoyante, who by this means would be isolated from the person consulting him.

will see whether I was wrong in submitting to him this summary of my experiments, or falsified the truth. May he gather from it the sum of happiness which I possess! It is the most ardent wish of a heart that would be glad to see all men a little less wretched and a little more enlightened.

---

## PSYCHOLOGICAL QUESTIONS.

I AM about to submit only questions relative to the existence of the soul after its separation from matter.

1. "Whence comes magnetism?" "From God."

2. "May its action be both good and bad?" "Yes."

3. "What are the conditions to be observed for the good?" "The desire to do good, which proceeds from God."

4. "What are those to be observed for the bad?" "The desire to do evil, which proceeds from man."

5. "Does the body alone possess the power of magnetizing?" "It is in this action but a machine."

6. "What moves this machine?" "Our soul."

7. "The soul, then, stands for something in the action of magnetism?" "It is the principal agent in it."

8. "Is it aided in this operation?" "Yes."

9. "By whom?" "By beings disengaged from matter."

10. "What is its mode of magnetizing?" "Prayer to God, and an ardent desire to relieve."

11. "Has the soul beside it a good and a bad spirit?" "Yes."

12. "Can it avoid the influence of both?" "Yes, in certain cases."

13. "Is it free to act according to its will?" "Yes."

14. "But if it is influenced by spirits?" "It is counselled, and remains at liberty to act."

15. "Has the soul already lived on another globe?" "Yes."

16. "Why did it quit it?" "In consequence of a necessary law imposed by God on all beings, without exception."

17. "What did it do in those places?" "It was very happy there."

18. "In what form did it inhabit them?" "The human form."

19. "Had it a family there as on earth?" "No; it had but friends."

20. "Had it affections there as on earth?" "No; for it nothing was designed but perfect happiness, which it could not appreciate, for want of never having experienced the least obstacle to its desires."

21. "Does it live after the death of its material body?" "Yes."

22. "Whither does it go?" "To heaven."

23. "What sensation does it experience when it quits the earth?" "None, it ascends with all the affections necessary to its new existence, and finds itself placed in heaven."

24. "Is it long before becoming acquainted with this new state?" "It becomes acquainted with it immediately."

25. "Of what form is this heaven? is it not rather a state of the soul?" "It is an immense boundless extent, representing accidents of places as on earth. It is a place which can be appreciated only in a desired state."

26. "Are there several of them?" "There are three."

27. "Are there bad oues?" "There are no bad heavens; there are only places of purification."

28. "For whom are these places of purification?" "For great criminals."

29. "What do they do in these places?" "They suffer at being deprived of the sight of God."

30. "Is there a hell wherein we are burned?" "No."

31. "On entering the heavens does the soul see God?" "Yes."

32. "In what form?" "That of a dazzling sun."

33. "What does he say to it?"* "He reproaches it for its bad conduct on earth before all the assembled spirits, which is very painful to the self-love of the soul receiving these remonstrances; but God is so good, and so dearly loves man, that he pardons it, and consigns it to a place where it is purified and prepared for its admission into heaven."

34. "In what form does the soul live in these places?" "The human form."

35. "Are its organs, in every respect, similar to those of its material body?" "Yes."

* We should be astonished at hearing that a sun spoke, if we had not, to prove it to us, even the declaration of Moses, and that of the prophets and ecstatico-prophets, who all, without exception, hear words issuing from a brilliant light, which they call the voice of Jehovah.

36. "Is it perfectly happy there?" "Yes."

37. "Has it any recollection of having inhabited the earth?" "Yes."

38. "Does it recollect its relations?" "Yes."

39. "Does it regret the earth?" "No."

40. "Can it see the earth at will?" "No."

41. "Can it see its relations and friends there?" "It can only see their spirit."

42. "Can it be of any assistance to them?" "Yes."

43. "In what way?" "By wise counsellings."

44. "In the state of somnambulism, how do they appear to it?" "A beautiful blue sky is seen, and in the distance a small luminous point, which draws near, preceding the person, and admits of your seeing this person before you, or at your side."

45. "In what form do they appear?" "In the corporeal form they had before death."

46. "What is their dress?" "Such as they wore on earth."

47. "Why rather this than any other?" "Because in any other they would be less easily known."

48. "In heaven, do they wear this dress?" "No."

49. "How are they attired there?" "Ordinarily, they have only light gauze robes of different colors, according to the inclination they have for them; their dress is, as on earth, a matter of taste."

50. "What do they do in heaven?" "Whatever is best suited to them; children play, grown-up persons study, play music, and promenade; they do there what they take most pleasure in."

51. "Are they reunited there to their family?" "Yes, those who desire it."

52. "Are they all married there?" "Yes; when God deems fit."

53. "How long a time do we remain in heaven?" "An eternity."

54. "Is there day and night, heat and cold?" "In heaven there is invariably a mild temperature, and a continual day."

55. "Is time reckoned there?" "No."

56. "And space?" "Space is not known, inasmuch as we are instantaneously wherever we wish to be."

57. "Are there houses, cities, gardens, temples?" "There is all that can be desired."

58. "What language is spoken there?" "That of the thought."

59. "Are angels seen there?" "Yes."

60. "Angels or spirits, are they the same thing?" "Angels are more advanced in wisdom than spirits."

61. "Have both inhabited the earth?" "Yes, all heaven contains has lived upon earth."

62. "Do we, after a certain time, inhabit again the earth?" "No."

63. "Are we all equal in heaven?" "Yes, in regard to happiness, and each possesses it in the same degree, but intelligence alone separates us; every one there has not the same amount of instruction."

64. "Are there any baneful spirits?" "Yes."

65. "Do pacts and talismans exist?" "Yes."

66. "Of what use are they?" "To protect you against such or such a thing."

67. "What are their results?" "That you find yourself bound with the spiritual societies that have protected you, and must undergo the consequences of this dependence in which you have placed yourself by doing for others, hereafter, what you were glad they should do for you."

68. "What do you mean by that?" "That when you are in the spiritual world, you must render to man the same service as spirits have rendered you; this makes you dependent."

69. "Is it true that there are obsessions?" "Yes."

70. "By whom are they occasioned?" "By evil spirits."

71. "Those evil spirits, have they a chief named Satan?" "No; every one is at liberty to act as he pleases in the interest of his society's affections."

72. "Can they perform all the incredible things related of them?" "Yes."

73. "What are the means of freeing one's self from them?" "Sincere prayer to God."

74. "Are there any elementary spirits?" "Yes."

75. "What is their form?" "The human form," &c.

Every one may, according to the kind of information he desires, put questions relative to it; but, above all, let him learn to consult the taste of his clairvoyante, and the present affection of the spirit invoked, for were we not to take these precautions we should be cast into a labyrinth of errors, whence we could issue only less enlightened than before; a few truths scattered among these errors would cause the latter to be accepted as true, and this would be a grand miscalculation for the too credulous individual. Spirits taking with them their principal affections, are not totally divested of pride, the greatest sore that gnaws the human species, and they often wish to appear to know more than they really do. We should be firm in our questions, ever mistrustful, yield only to what is beyond our judgment, not carry this mistrust so far as to be unwilling to admit anything, because we can not comprehend what we hear; neither should we reject any revelation, but keep a correct journal of it, change as often as possible our clairvoyantes, question them all in like manner, and judge according to the agreement in their answers. If we have any belief in God, invariably to beseech him from the bottom of our heart to keep away the spirit of darkness from the clairvoyantes; to implore, on the contrary, the spirit of light, and not accept the first spirit that presents himself, no matter his firm and imposing demeanor; you must beg of your clairvoyante to join with you in driving him away with a firm will, if he is not an envoy of God. These are the few words by which, under such circumstances, I operate:—

"In the name of God, thy Creator and mine, I command thee to withdraw, if thou art not sent to us from him!" He who resists this command, if you have a *pure clairvoyante*, is a beneficent spirit; question him. If he commits a few errors do not accuse him of them, he has no intention to deceive you, but he has little relish for such questions, especially if they relate to the earth. Their memory is rich in all that they have seen there, but they like not to search into, or speak of it. His likeness, his dress, the few revelations he may make to you will give you the assurance that he exists. Be not too exigent in his respect, put to him no mistrustful questions, such as, "What is your name?" since he came to his name. "What is your family?" since you know it as well as he; or, should the contrary be the case, you may question him. Ask him not how long he has been dead, he knows nothing about it; leave him at liberty to answer you without interruption, for he reads in your thought: he is of good faith; he thinks that his presence ought to suffice you in all the details that surround him to make you believe in his existence. Have the same good faith, and you will learn more than you could have possibly desired.

To initiate your clairvoyante in this kind of apparition, first look out for a subject as independent as possible of your will; make no physical experiment wherein the communication of thoughts is often necessary. Seek for a natural, voluntary clairvoyante, and not a sickly one, if possible. Conduct his speciality toward these communications, without ever demanding of him any but those appertaining to maladies. Begin by interesting him in an apparition, asking him if he would not be glad to see some departed friend who had been dear to him; he will be curious, his desire will be strong, and the person mentally demanded by you and by him will shortly present himself. Continue this kind of experiment, changing the personage as often as you can. As soon as you perceive that the view of a deceased being greatly affects your clairvoyante, that he appears delighted at seeing him again, tell him to ask this spirit to have the goodness to conduct him into the places he inhabits; he will readily do so, on one condition, which is that the clairvoyante shall descend again to earth, after a short interval of time, not exceeding ten minutes, according to the susceptible nature of the subject. To aid him in his departure, place him under the care of God and his guide; place your hand at some distance from the crown of his head, your fingers downward and brought together to a point, desire them to attract and open the fictitious space necessary to the passage of the soul. When you see him leaning back, his arms languidly dropping down, his face flushed and assuming an expression of beatitude, leave him for the time agreed upon in this ecstatic contemplation. For prudence sake, ever keep your eyes fixed on the plexus, principally the solar or pit of the stomach, retaining by your will sufficient life in the body to prevent all risk. If your clairvoyant should not return at the appointed time, and you perceive that his countenance is getting discolored, assuming a dark sallow hue, proceed no further, death is at hand. Close the door upon him, making with a determined force of will, a few transversal passes over his head and before his face; if it be long before he answers you, do n't be disturbed, do as if you were pulling him from on high with a cord, blow warmly on his heart, and you will see him pass again into the ordinary state of magnetic sleep. Ask him what he has seen, do not laugh, or you will learn nothing. Be of good faith, see in his revelations an act of madness or truth without telling him of it, and think what you please. All the counsels I have just given are dictated only by a wise prudence; there are many ecstatics of different shades, with whom we have no need of this prudence; but there are some with whom we can not be too circumspect, as I well know by experience. We ought to consider ourselves as warned on this head; death or insanity might be the consequence of such attempts. The ecstasy by which we communicate with spirits on earth presents no danger; it is one of the tasks which somnambulists perform with the greatest facility. I also recommend that if the clairvoyante, in speaking with spirits, should solicit from you certain marks of respect or assent to certain gestures, still preserving your dignity as a man, who ought to bend the knee to his Creator only, refuse not doing what could not in the least affect you. Be *confiding, reserved, voluntary, reasonable, devoid of passion,* and you will be indemnified for your pains, rendering yourself more happy than you ever were before; you will be less inclined to curse the earth and its sorrows, inasmuch as you will perceive that those sorrows are beneficial; you will no longer, in your sufferings, accuse God, because you will know that he is infinitely good; you will no longer be puffed up with your knowledge, because the further you go, the more you will perceive that you know nothing; you will patient admire this terrestrial mechanism, so beautiful, so grand, in one point of view, so insignificant in another; you will be in haste to again inhabit your former dwelling and be less attached to your material baubles. You will no longer tremble before your coffin, which is the gate to the temple of happiness wherein you are to live for ever!!

## MAGIC MIRROR.

I PROMISED not to reserve to myself anything I had learned from spirits; I will keep my word by giving to the reader the secret of the magic mirror, revealed to me by M. Swedenborg, who, himself, possessed one, and of which I have already spoken. This mirror is very much like one possessed, in the eighteenth century, at Paris, by a Jew named Léon, which I have seen mentioned somewhere, and which made a great noise at the time. I made two in the way recommended to me, one of which I presented to my friend M. Renard, who, after several experiments, gave a favorable report of it; mine was equally good. This is how we should go to work: Procure a piece of glass as fine as possible, cut it the required size, place it over a very slow fire, at the same time dissolving some very fine black lead in a small quantity of fine oil to give it the consistence of a liquid pomade, which may easily be spread over the glass when well diluted, as it soon is. The glass being hot, incline it on both sides, in order that the mixture may spread of itself all over alike; then, the glass being placed on something quite straight and flat, let the mixture dry without disturbing it; in a few days it will become as hard as pewter, presenting a very fine dark polish; put your glass in a frame, and after well wiping its surface, on which some dross will be found, hang it up on a wall, as you would a looking-glass, but always in a false light. Place the person who desires to see a thief, a spirit, or a place, before this mirror, station yourself behind him, fixing your eyes steadily on the hinder part of the brain, and summon the spirit in a loud voice in the name of God, in a manner imposing to the individual looking in the mirror.

It may be naturally supposed that this kind of experiment requires certain conditions, the first of which is to find an individual endowed with this kind of vision. Nothing is general in psychological facts. There was much talk at one time of the magic mirror of Doctor Dee, which was sold, in 1842 among the curiosities in the possession of Horace Walpole, at Strawberry Hill, for the enormous sum of three hundred and twenty-six francs. It was simply a bit of sea-coal, perfectly polished, cut in a circular form, with a handle; this curiosity formerly figured in the cabinet of the earl of Peterborough. In the catalogue it was thus described: "A black stone, by means of which Doctor Dee evoked spirits." It passed from the hands of the earl into those of Lady Elizabeth Germaine, then became the property of John, last duke of Argyll, whose grandson, Lord Campbell, presented it to Walpole. The author of the "Theatrum Chemicum," Elias Ashmole, speaks of the same mirror in the following terms: "By the aid of this magic stone, we can see whatever persons we desire, no matter in what part of the world they be, and were they hidden in the most retired apartments, or even in the caverns in the bowels of the earth." John Dee, born in London, in 1527, was the son of a wine-merchant; he studied the sciences with success, and devoted himself, at an early period, to judicial astrology; Queen Elizabeth took him under her protection; he composed several useful works, employed much of his time in the science of magic, conjured spirits, made predictions, and beheld the invisible; when he had discovered his mirror he returned thanksgivings to God. He was occupied during his whole life in the search of the philosopher's stone, and died in London at the age of eighty-four, in a state of abject poverty.

The count de Laborde brought us a somewhat similar secret from Egypt. The baron Dupotet communicated a like one to his subscribers, in his *Journal de Magnétisme;* one is much more simplified than the other, and succeeds equally as well. M. de Laborde positively evokes; he makes use of perfumes, stands in need of the co-operation of spirits, and M. Dupotet seems only to employ the magnetism of thought. Cagliostro also employed a magnetism but little suspected, by placing one hand on the head of his pupils. The sorcerers of our country places proceed in like manner with the first mirror met with,

15

imploring the assistance of the spirits that facilitate such experiments. M. de Laborde makes use of a brilliant ink which he puts in the hollow of the looker's hand, and stimulates his nervous system by perfumes. M. Dupotet makes use of a piece of coal with which he describes a circle on the floor, with the intention of making perceptible to the person operated upon such picture as the latter desires; he keeps the subject inclined for this experiment by thought. Sorcerers have their reputation which is of great assistance to them. Certain prepossessions against such or such a person suspected of theft or aught else, their imposing air, their supplication to such spirit familiar to them, without knowing positively the meaning of what they say—this suffices, and they operate! Léon, of whom I have spoken, followed in their steps; prayer, faith, and a disposition of the visual organ, facilitated his experiments. Cagliostro, preceded by his reputation as an incomprehensible man, was often successful in consequence of the tact he displayed in selecting his pupils, the occult magnetism he employed, &c.; but if I ask Messrs. de Laborde, Dupotet, Cagliostro, the sorcerers, Léon and others, whether they saw themselves in their mirrors or reflecting body, they will reply no; therefore, there must be a disposition for this kind of experiment, we must be influenced by an imposing display, an occult magnetism, or the aid of invocations and perfumes. Wherefore, in order to profit by my mirror, I would advise the ceremony to be performed with a certain dignity, and to have recourse only to what may act on the imagination or nerves; as much by a moral or spiritual magnetism as by the assistance of perfumes. All those that bear or shed a sweet, pleasant smell, are suitable for the good spirits, such as incense, musk, gum-lac, &c.; and for evil spirits, the seeds of henbane, hemp, belladonna, anise, or coriander, &c. Each seeks his own atmosphere, or one akin to it; but, above all, shun the assistance of evil spirits. Let the spirit of justice, discretion, humanity, predominate in you: or, otherwise, wo betide you!

It will not, perhaps, be comprehended why I should recommend shunning the invocation of evil spirits, and yet make known the perfumes they delight in. I presume that I shall be thought sufficiently consistent with myself to speak here only of the apparitions we desired to obtain, on the score of thefts, or other crimes, committed to your prejudice. It is the spirits of those culprits who will obey your command to present themselves, and seek the nauseous smell of these perfumes. You have nothing to fear from them, since, on the contrary, they have everything to fear from you. What I recommend you to avoid, when demanding apparitions of those you desire to see, is pronouncing words, the meaning of which is unknown to you, that invite baneful spirits to your assistance. This is true magic.* For the sake of a little earthly glory, lose not celestial happiness. In all our experiments of views at distance on earth, we can dispense with their assistance; we have the power of doing it by ourselves, aided, as I have said, by auxiliaries placing us in the conditions necessary to obtain these results. If I seemed to fear the assistance of strange spirits, it was because the simplest judgment we can pass on the spiritual phenomena of magnetism will prove that spirits exist after being freed from their material envelope; but they can not be immediately delivered from their affection for evil. We should have the conviction that they can not gratify it on the spirits that surround them, and have the same inclinations as they have; we are, therefore, the only beings placed at their disposal, and, under a show of eagerness to be of service, they do not act for the sake of obliging us, inasmuch as their sole happiness consists in doing evil. It is needless entering into further explanation of all that might result from allying ourselves to them.

Magnetism, and all its properties, sufficiently prove the dependence of certain intelligences under the power of the magnetizer, to render us as cautious as possible. The philosophy of this science has so upset every idea hitherto received that we no longer know what to think, what believe, and what do. If

* Confound not angelic magic, the miraculous blessings of God, with the spiritual and the human magic; each has its views and its aim. They are separated into two camps—harmony and trouble.

we dread the services of a friend whom we believe we well know, still more must we dread those of beings unknown! Consult on this head the *Journal of Magnetism*, by M. Dupotet, wherein I read at this very moment: "The souls of the cursed are the first to answer, as they are still disposed to serve sinister projects. Expect from them nothing more; they have only this power." What an authority forthwith comes in support of the counsels I give! Go on, estimable and sincere man, you also have great things to reveal to us! Speak; fear not the name of visionary; it is never too soon to enlighten our brethren; but ever too late when we know them to be in error.

---

## CAN CURES BE PERFORMED THROUGH PRAYER?

HAPPENING to go to work one day at the abode of Madame Ferrière Penona, a lady to whom I am indebted for many marks of kindness, I found her bathed in tears and absorbed in the most profound grief. Venturing to ask her the cause of her sorrow, and whether any misfortune threatened her, she replied: "I have a little niece whom I dearly love, who is, perhaps, at this very moment breathing her last." "How old is the child?" "Fourteen."—"It is hard at such an age to leave the world, and kind parents, whose sole happiness we are! What is her complaint?" "The doctors don't know. My poor brother has just arrived to receive her last embrace; he will assuredly die of grief, as he has but this child, and is dotingly fond of her."—"Do you think there is no remedy?" "The doctors say no, and look upon her as doomed!"—"Has magnetism been tried on her?" "Oh! my brother has no faith in it; he is an old officer, who would think he had run mad were he to take up with such an idea; and then, again, we know no one to whom to apply!"—"I devote much time to this science, and am pretty fortunate; I know not what I feel, but it seems to me that all hope is not lost." "If I could but think so, and you were so good!"—"I should be the happiest of men, madame, could I but dry up your tears!" "What can I do?" "Mention it to your brother." Two mortal hours passed away before coming to an arrangement; the susceptibility of the doctor, the painful position of the relatives were extreme; disorder was in all hearts: at length the doctor said he saw no objection. This news was announced to me by a servant; I hastened off to the hotel, and was ushered to the bedside of the dying child; not a word was uttered by those present; I inspired but little confidence—I wore the livery of a proletarian!

Never did I see a countenance more angelic or interesting—a languishing look which seemed to shun the sight of death to fix itself on a few toys, a few flowers which, like it, were languishingly drooping on the edge of a vase where they were no longer nurtured by the water of heaven. At fourteen, life is so rich in hope and full of emotions! I drew near, asked her how she was, and if she would permit me to take her hand. To what, good heavens! did I speak? Speech was no longer at her service. She let me perceive, by putting out her hand, that I had been understood. The father and the nurse of this interesting child stood by the window, shedding tears. I conveyed my looks on the beautiful eyes of this frail creature. I no longer know what passed within me. I recollect that I spoke to her mentally for some time, lavished on her the most tender consolations, the firmest hope. I implored the mercy of the Lord, and the beneficent influx of the sacred legions of the angels. I attracted her soul to my soul, opened to her my heart to revivify her by the sweet emotions that agitated it; the eyes of her body were closed; mine shed a phosphorescent light wherever they were conveyed; I breathed a sweet odor; a mild atmosphere surrounded me; I was no longer on earth, we were in heaven. Ah! you who laugh at all, respect this recital: it is that of a frank and loving heart, which, for the first time, played the sweet part of a father, and was happy that day, that hour only. It no longer thought of its own painful existence; it was all in that child, and that child was all in it. I will not tell you how long this scene lasted, what thought the persons present, and what I think of it now. *She was saved;* in the evening she took her first meal since a fortnight, slept all night for the first time since a week: and three days after trod with a firm step on the dead leaves in the garden of the Tuileries. I met her but this once: we shall meet again in heaven.

Pray! Essay!

* * * * * * *

I ought to return thanks to the sole and only Creator of the universe for the divine inspiration of this work, as well for myself as for men in general, to whom it will convey the greatest calm by regenerating from the experiments it proposes — faith in the next world, so wavering here below — by imparting to the tender mother, the faithful spouse, the inconsolable lover. the means of beholding in their magnetic sleep the objects of their affection; speaking with them, receiving and giving each other proofs of their mutual attachment and their grateful recollection.

Oh, you cataleptizers of limbs! who would believe you compromised the little you pretend to know, if you bestowed a few minutes on your subjects to pour their hearts into the bosom of those immortal spirits who laugh at your ignorance and foolish pride; you who fling back the cloak of ridicule, which should cover you, on spiritual magnetizers! If there remains but a spark of good faith in you, say with me that *you know nothing, can do nothing, will never know anything;* if you consult not your clairvoyantes on what you are ignorant of, and if you acquire not the proof that you are not empty pitchers, but, on the contrary, that there is in them a being far superior to them; that this being is not a molecule of ambient air which returns into space, after quitting the body it animated, as a drop of water returns to the sea; but is really a being *individualized for eternity*, having a recollection *of its material existence and acquainted with your foolish reasonings;* that this being is beside you, according to your desires, and asks but to answer your questions — if you can not see it or touch it, it is because your prison is too material, your eyes too veiled, and your judgment too vain. I counsel you, therefore, to look well to your decisions, to avoid the two extremes—denying all, as you did, or believing all, as some magnetizers have done. I have said enough in this work not to lead you toward Brahma or Mahomet. Be men! children of God, prostrated at his feet, but not at the feet of your fellow-beings.

I ought also to return thanks to my subscribers, whose intuitive confidence will not, I trust, be abused. Not yet living in a cloudless atmosphere of liberty of conscience, I must be silent as to the names of a few benevolent men who have, more or less, contributed to the publication of this work, by facilitating my acquisition of the number of subscribers I desired, unwilling as I am to render any one responsible for a work which was, possibly, accepted too favorably before being known. Would that I could cite the name of a confiding disciple of Swedenborg, who advanced me the funds necessary for the printing, and that of a generous friend to enlightenment who subscribed a hundred francs!

But shame to the *savans* to whom I addressed myself, and who did not even do me the honor of answering my application! What can be the reason? I wished to prove to them, mathematically, the existence of a soul, of which they speak, but in which they do not believe! I wished to point out to them a school to which men in general should be compelled to resort for new studies. I came humbly to solicit a trifle from philanthropy to aid me in this publication. To whom, alas, did I address myself? I wanted to enlighten those who teach! I asked of those who beg! I offered to bargain with the princes of trade! I ought to exclaim with Saint Martin: "Nothing is easier than to arrive at the door of truths; nothing more rare and difficult than entering it:" and such, indeed, is the case with most of the philosophers of this world!

# CONTENTS OF VOLUME I.

END OF VOLUME I.

# THE SECRETS OF THE FUTURE

REVEALED THROUGH

# MAGNETISM.

VOLUME II.

CONTAINING PERCEPTIONS OF FIFTY MORE PERSONS WHO DIED AT DIFFERENT PERIODS — A PERSONAL DESCRIPTION OF THEM, CONVERSATIONS HELD WITH THEM, AND CERTIFICATES AS TO THEIR IDENTITY. — ALSO, A NUMEROUS COLLECTION OF SUPERNATURAL FACTS COMMUNICATED BY MAGNETIZERS, AND QUOTATIONS FROM SPIRITUALIST PHILOSOPHERS ON THE IMMORTALITY OF THE SOUL, ETC., ETC.

"What magnetism rigorously demonstrates is the spirituality of the soul and its immortality; also, that souls separated from the body can in certain cases put themselves in communication with living beings, and convey to them their sentiments. The study of the phenomena of somnambulism is, in this respect, more important than in that of curing diseases."—DELEUZE.

WHEN, in January, 1848, I presented the public with the first volume of the "Secrets," I was unable to support the facts therein contained by any testimony but my own. My position as a simple workman — my very confined social relations, absolutely null in the scientific world — could give no weight to the persuasions I had just propounded: I felt that, despite their truth, and the facility of being assured of it, I should, perhaps, throw out only a few doubts, which would pass to the state of definitive beliefs, if I supported these revelations by honorable testimonials; consequently, to attain this end, I hastened to give apparition-sittings to persons who solicited them, and now I can surround my own name with names that the public venerate as authorities. In this second volume I present to the world a sufficient number of testimonials to apparitions obtained, recognised, and signed as true, by princes, counts, viscounts, generals, colonels, pastors of different creeds, landholders, merchants, men of letters, magnetizers, and artisans, personages of different nations, &c., &c., all ready to confirm by their verbal testimony what they signed at my abode.

I do not think that with such supporters, and such frankness on my part, any charlatanism, bad faith, and, above all, hallucination, can be suspected; my judgment may be confined to the little instruction I have received, and to a few persuasions more or less true and admissible; but the persons whose testimonials will be read are competent witnesses—*savans* interested in this question; magnetizers, who had not, till then, pushed their experiments in this direction, and who much doubted the possibility of causing to appear thus deceased persons, in conditions necessary to admit of their being recognised and holding converse with them: a great question assuredly was that, which I sought to resolve with all the force of my intelligence, and which I have succeeded in causing to be resolved by others with more facility than one could have ventured to hope.

I come, therefore, to present to the public this second volume, in which I have thought proper to answer, by way of refutation, certain objections made to different propositions set forth in the first volume.

I have thought fit to reconcile this faculty of clairvoyantes with that which our fathers must have possessed, as well in ancient times as in the middle ages, thus permitting them to open different schools, where similar beliefs were taught, which demonstrated, *à priori,* the existence of the soul after its separation from matter, living individualized in a better world under the human form, having recollection of its *self* and its terrestrial existence, reuniting itself according to its affections to its relatives or friends, dead like itself, and having sensations, usages, affections, as here below: this is what, in a few words, I have desired to demonstrate as mathematically as possible by the aid of somnambulism and apparitions. I may applaud myself for this undertaking, because, up to the present moment, it has completely succeeded with all those who have engaged in it. Some magnetizers have been so obliging as to respond to the general appeal I made, and have furnished me with several experiments, which will be read after mine and with no less interest.

May I not encounter on my road those bourns, obstacles past, present, and future, placed on all roads, to operate as a bar to the truths that enlighten the human species. I engage those who accompany me in these experiments not to halt from the desire of throwing light on any obscurity. It would be pure loss of time, and injurious to the proposed end.

### REPLY TO THE MAGNETIZERS WHO BELIEVE THAT THE APPARITIONS MENTIONED IN THE FIRST VOLUME OF THE "SECRETS" ARE BUT AN EFFECT OF TRANSMISSION OF THOUGHTS.

On the first appearance of the "Secrets of the Future Life Revealed," the spiritualist magnetizers, who had made similar experiments, gave a kind, I may say a grateful, reception to this work, because it strengthened in them beliefs which were yet in a mere nascent state. This work had necessarily to encounter adversaries in shallow magnetizers, who refer all the phenomena of magnetism and somnambulism to matter. I know not whether such kind of men believe in the existence of God and the soul. They say yes, for decency's sake, and deny through passion.

In such frame of mind, contrary to the spirit of this work, they exclaimed, with a certain assurance, "These pretended revelations are but a transmission of thoughts." I then wrote to M. Hébert de Garnay, editor of the "Journal du Magnétisme," to have the kindness to address to me one of those formidable *savans* who alone produce, see, and judge, in order to put to him questions worthy of his lofty intelligence; silence was the only adversary I found on the place of combat. As bourns are ever accidents, hidden and acting in the dark, I looked upon myself as warned.

I had dedicated the first volume of the "Secrets" to M. Dupotet, as being the most distinguished character in magnetic science, and consequently the fittest person to appreciate its value; he would naturally give an analysis of it in his estimable journal, in which he was so obliging as to announce the subscription. Several months elapsed before the subscribers to this journal knew what they were to think of this work. One evening, M. Dupotet came, in company with several persons, to ask me for an apparition-sitting: he was satisfied, as we shall see further on. But still this analysis did not appear. At length, on the 12th December, in the seventy-fifth number of the "Journal du Magnétisme," we read a critique, from which we extract the following passages:—

"1. M. Cahagnet dedicating to us his book, we are in a measure bound to say what we think of it.

"Wishing to assure myself of this incredible fact, I asked for a deceased friend of mine, wholly unknown to the clairvoyante and her magnetizer: this ecstatic described to me my friend, and enumerated all the singularities characteristic of him; nothing was forgotten, insomuch that I verily thought that I beheld him myself. This spectre disappeared abruptly, frightening the somnambulist; a single word had caused its sudden disappearance, and my astonishment was at its height, for this very word invariably tended to infuriate it.* This fact, which I guaranty, gives a sort of semblance of truth to M. Cahagnet's doctrine concerning the apparition of the dead. His book is full of similar phenomena; still, I am not fully convinced. In the first place, it is an intermediate who sees, and to any one familiarized with somnambulism it might be attributed to communication of thoughts."

2. Then comes a somewhat illiberal critique on the work as a whole, its poverty in poetical images, in scientific and logical solutions, accompanied with these words: "I renounce making

* *Vide* 117th Sitting.

quotations from the 'Secrets,' as some would prove too much for many persons, and others not enough."

3. Farther on we find the following: "Be that as it may, the 'Secrets' have created some sensation in the magnetic world. The book is a step farther toward the unknown."

4. And this observation, "How is it that in all the answers of the spirits, M. Cahagnet has not yet met with aught that distinguishes genii from simple mortals, nor collected any of those important truths with which heaven is full?"

I will answer, in a few words, these four principal observations of the Honorable M. Dupotet. With respect to the first, if you believed in the communication of thoughts, you should not have asked for a person of your acquaintance. If you are not fully convinced of the truth of these apparitions, how would you have the persons whom you invite to verify those that you publicly provoke every Sunday in your saloons, in a circle traced with charcoal, be convinced any more than you. As to the second, that the work is devoid of poetical images, scientific and logical solutions, ending with these words, "The 'Secrets' would prove far too much for certain folks, and not enough for others;" first, I am, as I have already said, the man of nature without any instruction, consequently as devoid of the genius of Virgil as of the captious definitions of Kant. The "Secrets," however, contain more than twelve hundred solutions, as well metaphysical as psychological, the analysis of which you neglect. If they are not scientific or logical, it was intended, at any rate, that they should be so; again, if they prove too much for certain folks, and not enough for others, there must be something in them useful or ridiculous. This seems to me logical. As to the third observation, you say that "the 'Secrets' have created some sensation in the magnetic world, that this book is a step taken toward the unknown." If they have created a sensation it is from pleasure or pity; let those who have read them judge. If it is a step taken toward the unknown, it proves, then, something more logical than you say. At the fourth observation M. Dupotet is astonished that certain genii did not come to reveal to me certain truths of which heaven is full. I will answer, that it is for the reason that like seek like; as I am not, and never shall be, a genius, I sought beings of my own nature. Still, the "Secrets" *have created a sensation, have proved, have caused a step to be taken toward the unknown!* The fact is, that those who came to inspire me knew more than I. M. Swedenborg, who, no doubt, according to M. Dupotet, never was a genius, has told me, however, that the sun which we behold was not a material globe, that thoughts were living beings; that a man had a universe enclosed in his sphere, and a hundred revelations of the kind. In one of the three that I have just mentioned, there is a total overthrow of all received philosophy and wherewith to acquire genius.

M. Dupotet is suprised, as well as many other philosophers, at learning nothing in what they read as to a future life, from the little harmony, as they say, which exists between the system of each clairvoyante. I am not surprised at it, not I. These philosophers did not write my book, and they wish to submit the whole creation to their own arguments, and, through affection, they argue incessantly. What would you say to us if we gave the key of these contradictions in three words; *ay, three words only.* We will do so; free to you to see opened to us the doors of Charenton (Bedlam); here they are: *All* is in all, *and everywhere.* The heavens of the clairvoyantes, the earth of mortals, are not places for them, but states. Each takes a delight in his own when it corresponds with his affection; he makes of it either a heaven or a hell. Swedenborg has told us this, and the state of our clairvoyantes proves it; they are wherever they will, in what they will, do what they will; without ceasing to be there, they are here below, they are *in all, everywhere, and all.* Judge, now, from such a property, whether there can be any agreement in what they reveal to us; it is the infinite of the infinite. I fear not telling you that the spirit can quite as well be in the *speech,* in *a single word,* as this *speech* and this *word* are in it. See whither I am leading you, since you drive me to it. Come, have a little indulgence, gentlemen of science, I am but a poor workman who earns his bread by the sweat of his brow, who meditates and writes at night. Aid me, and do not shackle me. I promise you that I will develop these propositions in another work which I am now about, merely wishing to prove to you in this the *individualized existence of the soul*, after its separation from matter, and the possibility of communicating with it. I return to our reply to magnetizers, on their argument as to the communication of thoughts.

I take the liberty of putting to them the following questions :

1. Is it true that a clairvoyante can see, hear, feel, and converse with another being, at a distance ?

2. Is it true that it merely suffices to put him *en rapport* with the names of the places and persons desired to be perceived at these distances, in order that he may perceive them ?

If you answer these two questions in the affirmative (and you can not answer them otherwise), you admit an intelligent being or fluid, independent (in this state) of the material body, able to know such things; such being or fluid rightly deserves a name; we will term it a soul.

This soul, no matter its mode of perceiving places or objects at a distance, proves to us that the material body is deprived of this faculty, since it is necessary that some agent or other should annihilate it (shall I say ?) to facilitate the intelligence which animates it in thus performing functions without. This soul, fluid, spirit, whatever you please, which encounters no obstacle, and finds itself independent of material laws, can not be more subject to annihilation than this matter, whose immortality, in an infinity of states, you acknowledge.

We can not admit a special law of annihilation for the spirit, when we admit none for matter, the soul survives its envelope ; we can not doubt it, or we must prove the contrary. If it survives its envelope, it is somewhere. It is not more *unfindable* for the clairvoyante than the place, the person, or the earthly object, which he sees at a distance, without being in communication with them; but, will you answer, the person consulting is *en rapport* himself with the thing asked for ? I will answer, in my turn, yes, in certain cases; but, in many others, he is not so. It happens to all magnetizers to make perceptible to their clairvoyantes, places, persons, or objects, of which the consulting individual, the magnetizer, and the clairvoyante, have no notion; the information and descriptions are found to be correct. These experiments are ordinarily performed, in regard to persons that have disappeared, objects that have been mislaid or stolen. The clairvoyante finds both the one and the other; it must, therefore, be that these objects present themselves to his view at his desire, or that he has a means unknown to us, of putting himself *en rapport* with them.

If you admit that at the mere desire, or at the mere mention of the name of the being or object lost by the clairvoyante, the being or object is forthwith present to his eyes, you will surely grant a being so intelligent as the soul when disengaged from and lost to matter, the faculty of presenting itself to the clairvoyante, according to its desire, as this apparently inert object did.

I have already observed, that it is needless conducting the clairvoyante toward the objects, that in order to see them at hand it suffices to desire their presence. The perception of lost or stolen objects is a proof of this; not knowing where these objects are, you can not conduct your clairvoyante toward them; they must, therefore, present themselves to him, agreeably to his desire. It may be the same, with regard to all views at distance. I ask for the place, without being acquainted with it, and it is instantaneously present to me. (These facts, which are within the reach of all, can not be denied.) If we can not refuse the clairvoyante this property, we can not, for the same reason, refuse him that of finding out the soul separated from matter; by this deduction, we shall come to enchaining ourselves by undeniable facts, and to confessing the possibility of the other proposition. Were we to conclude otherwise, we should be but an extinguisher. We may object, with our *ifs* and our *whys*, but we shall end by acknowledging what we can not deny; some formidable advocates of this sacrilegious cause of obscureness will argue thus: The clairvoyante, in all these facts, sees but material objects, for the reason that these objects exist; it may be the same with the soul, whose individualized existence after separation from matter, is still a problem.

My answer to such objection is, that in the search of these hidden or stolen objects, the clairvoyante sees not only these objects, he sees the traces left by them, he brings back to you the scenes, the words pronounced by the thieves; these traces or words exist not materially, how can he see them? How hear them? Hear what has been said, and is no longer being said! Does he not go further? does he not see a certain theatre, a certain battle-field, with what was acted on this scene, and the blood that was shed on the earth a hundred years before we were born? If he sees these things, in what state does he see them? No doubt, in the spiritual state, since this theatre or battle-field is replaced by other ornaments or constructions. Do you admit these facts? these revelations that you produce and obtain every day — that you mention in all your books? You will answer, yes. Then I will ask you why you should admit that this theatre, and what passed on it, should have left an image in the place where it formerly existed, so powerful that your clairvoyante could receive from it an impression as active as a similar existing or present scene could produce, and yet not admit that the beings that cooperated in the representation of these scenes were alive like them. (This is already the second time that I have made this observation.) After such a comparison, if you deny the individualized existence of the soul apart from matter, I say it with regret, you are extinguishers or of bad faith; in presence of such revelations apparitions are needless. If I continue collecting them, I do so less to demonstrate their reality than to console my brethren for the miseries of this sorrowful earthly existence; this is what I had to say to the detractors of "The Secrets of the Life to Come Revealed," and I terminate by saying to them: No, the clairvoyante sees not in your thought what can not be in it. No, the clairvoyante clears no space, and knows no time, in order to communicate with places, objects, or deeds remote, past, present, or future.

Let me once more remind you, since it is the fruit of our own experiments, that in the first views at distance you obtained from your clairvoyantes, you exclaimed: It is because

I, myself, have seen these places that he sees the image of them in me; the contrary was proved by describing to you changes operated in your absence, recounting to you what the persons were doing at the very instant you caused them to be visited hundreds of leagues off. You acknowledged that these things could not be in your thought, and you confessed that the clairvoyante really saw at a distance; now, you again take up this wornout argument to combat the perception of souls: but we have come to presenting you with apparitions that will remove all your doubts in this respect, and that you will read in this volume. We have perceived deceased persons, unknown to the asker, to ourselves, and the clairvoyante; we have obtained information that could not be in any human memory; where did the clairvoyante find these persons and this information? In the world of causes, which we term the spiritual world, wherein is found whatsoever was, is, and shall be.

Know, then, once for all, how to make a distinction between the communication of thoughts and the perception of the images which man has in him, representing whatsoever of material he has seen in the course of his life. The communication of thoughts is mental speech, it is the mental answer that follows this speech. No one exists, having obtained such apparitions, who can say that the details given him were a communication of thoughts, a mental answer to a mental question, forming no communicetion with the clairvoyante. Without questioning, and obtaining such information as can not be in the domain of their memory, in case there were communication, it would be merely a communication of images, the whole confined to those we might have in ourselves; but, going no farther, should it be admitted that such must be the case, it would remain to be explained how these images are alive, speak, and act? Should we succeed in this? it could be done only by admitting that one is a universe in abridgment? we should be then far from denying the existence of the soul, since we should have made of it an incomprehensible and admirable masterpiece, which would be the infinite of the infinite, and thousands of times the infinite of the infinite! Only think, then, possessing in yourself the whole universe in miniature! — all that has been, is, and shall be — all that has been thought, thinks, and shall think. Oh! you will not have this vast definition; your science is not sufficiently powerful to admit and explain it, you prefer returning to the simple existence of the soul inhabiting places appropriated to its nature and state; but I, without possessing your science, I repeat to you that *all is in all and throughout all.* Were you a little less learned you would give yourselves up to the study that I propose to you; it is well worth the pains. If you admit human immortality only in history, your progeny or your statue on a public monument, may you be placed in your niche to the admiration of gaping crowds, and let us venture into a world that you reject because you know that equality and fraternity reign there. Remain, I say, clad in doctorial ornaments, seigneurial or royal ones, in your niches, which are the emblem of the *statu quo;* we will practise science without you, and more consoling science than yours.

Fourier said: "The civilized are so hateful that they would disdain heaven, if every one entered it, and they delight in the thought that a good round number will go to the devil." Fourier knew you!

### REFUTATION OF A WHOLE LIFE OF BEATITUDE IN THE WORLD OF SPIRITS.

Some persons, after reading the "Secrets," have objected that there could not be any usages in the world of spirits as on earth, still less objects adapted for such usages; one of them thought it extraordinary that there should be houses, furniture, &c., and exclaimed while ridiculing this assertion: "Masons and tapestry-makers can't want for work there, then!" I have but a few observations to make in this respect: What is understood by life? Is it not thinking? Thinking of what? Of something. What is this something? All that can be perceived by the eye, heard by the ear, and that can fall under the other senses. 1. Places, accidents of places, ornaments of places. 2. Living beings and of our own nature, with whom we shall be in communication. To be in communication it is necessary to speak. Speak of what? Of things past, present, or future.

These somethings ought to represent images to our eyes as they do on earth. Without this I should not comprehend a life in which we should not think. Thought is the sight of something, speech is the name of this thing, sensation is the touch of this thing. Take away these properties from spiritual life, what remains for it? Nothingness! Give it these properties, they can not exist without the things thought. From the moment you admit thought, you admit the view of it; thus the thought of a place must represent a place in its entire form and with its accidents; there, a garden with trees, fruits, and flowers; an atmosphere, light of some kind; farther on, beings of a nature similar to yours, grouped, standing, seated or lying on what bears them. These beings can not remain standing or lying an eternity; they must admire these fruits, intoxicate themselves with the perfume of these flowers, breathe this sweet atmosphere, contemplate the light by which they see these things; but if a whole eternity were spent in seeing only trees, fruits, flowers, and grass, we should be soon tired of such a state; there must, we are sensible of it, be a progression, a succession in the thoughts to feed the sensations, and this succession of thoughts gives rise to the supposition, as I have said of thinking, seeing, and feeling something else. It is the infinite of the creation that is before us; palaces, houses, furniture, usages, in short, must exist there. If all this exists there, it is for the purpose of gratifying our sensations, our affections, and our infinite desires. It will be objected that all these things may exist in heaven without our being bound to fabricate them as on earth. I answer that that is true.

Scarcely have you desired an object than it presents itself to your view, because it is the type of your thought, and bears the very form of the object thought; but this does not do away with there being affections that wish to fabricate, co-arrange, or embellish the object thought as they do on earth. If man progresses in each of his thoughts and desires to take notes on what he observes, makes a book of them in order to communicate his observations to his fellow-beings, he must find paper and things necessary to form this book, another will have the affection of printing it, a third of publishing it, and so on. If I wish to play music, although it be possible for me to have or to hear it at my pleasure, if I prefer playing myself, I must have instruments that I can make or find, ready made it is true, without any other pains than merely desiring them; but he who has a taste for making such instruments has a right to make them, since for him it is no longer a necessity in order to live, but an affection that constitutes his whole happiness. An architect has the same right; it is his supreme felicity to produce a masterpiece; the mason's, to show his superiority in the details of this palace, and so on. Take away one of the things I have just enumerated from the spiritual life, because this thing comes not within the range of your tastes; your neighbor will have the same right. I, too, and we shall end with annihilating all that constitutes the future life. Heaven will no longer be even a place, a state, it will be nothingness. I do not think it necessary to carry these conclusions any farther in order to prove the absurdity of such an argument. Those who believe that singing the praises of God for a whole eternity is the sole occupation of spirits must necessarily divest spirits of forms, because forms demand usages, walking, seeing, hearing, feeling, touching, &c. There is no need of forms for singing; but what sing? The marvels of creation. And what marvels since you refuse them admission into heaven? Can it be those you have seen on earth where all is but wretchedness and grief? May God inspire you, bigot souls! I remain mute, and can not praise God for a creation which I do not understand; if he gives me the means of understanding it, being stripped of my material garment, it could only be from observation. Observation supposes two contrary things; if I annihilate these things and their typical forms, how should I observe and judge? Come, then, you who will have neither objects nor usages in the spiritual world, you shall be placed like Napoleon on the column Vendôme, when you are fatigued with the posture you will ask God to change it.

If we admitted such a state of—imbecility, shall I call it?—on our exit from this world, we must likewise be deprived of our respective sexes, for love supposes an agglomeration of sensations. What! feel where there is no usage? Wherefore, then, the creation male and female?

If it must be that one day I can not admire and render justice to the works of my divine Father, can not comprehend their beauty, the utility, the harmony of their creation, I am not the creature of his choice. If it be otherwise, he will make me comprehend the *pro* and the *con*. I must observe, compare, progress. If you take away from me the materials for comparison, I shall not know whether the arts, usages, or objects, which I have been acquainted with on earth were more or less perfect, more or less useful; if, on the contrary, you admit the future life as a sequel to the terrestrial one, without sudden transition, I comprehend in that case ETERNITY. I have, therefore, discovered nothing ridiculous in what my clairvoyantes have told me on this head, though not one of them has told me that usages similar to those I have just described caused excitement there. But I, for my part, comprehend them; I feel the utility of them as an affection of happiness, and not as a necessary impost, comparable to earthly wants. I have found nothing ridiculous in what the learned Swedenborg advances, in his works, on this subject. I beg my readers to consult them for more detailed information, and worthy of being meditated upon.

### OBSERVATIONS ON THE CONTRADICTIONS CONTAINED IN THE FIRST VOLUME OF THE "SECRETS."

OTHER persons have objected to me that the first volume of the "Secrets" contained a few contradictions of this sort: "Bruno, inspired by his guide, says that man is not free; Adèle, inspired by M. Swedenborg says the contrary!" It was because I wished to retrench naught from these "Secrets" that I allowed these contradictions and a few more to remain.

I owed to the science that occupies us, before all things, the truth. My opinions in this respect are not in favor of free will, as may have been seen in the course of this book by reasonings which all the works I have consulted, and the discussions I have had on this subject, have been unable to destroy. Man referring all in his scientific discussions to his pride, his wants and his manner of seeing, can but err. He who, on the contrary, detaches himself from matter, rises from humility above this human comedy, best discovers all its springs. I am bound, therefore, to enlighten the reader on this question. Adèle erred voluntarily. One day the abbé A——, M. Lemoine and myself, decided on summoning St. John to decide a religious question; it was the abbé A—— who was in communication with Adèle and questioned her. At the commencement of the sitting we all three prayed God to deign to enlighten us with his divine light. M. A——, in his capacity as a priest, was to preserve the clairvoyante from all evil influence, the more so as I had left him at liberty to exorcise and purify her agreeably to his desire. All the answers that he obtained were, according to the expression of this venerable abbé, strictly logical; he had not addressed any question on the subject of free will, but touching on one connected with it, Adèle said to him: "John, here present, orders me to tell you that man material is not free; that every being on earth has a mission to fulfil, from which he can not depart. I objected to him that I could not communicate such an answer to men; but he ordered me, in the name of God, to transmit it to you, and I do so." "Why," said I to her, "should you refuse revealing to us the truth?" "I have ever revealed it hitherto," replied she; "but I could not make up my mind to say to men, 'You are not free to do evil.' This doctrine was repugnant to my heart; it seemed much more just to let man believe that he is free in his good and bad actions; but John said to me: 'It is better to be silent than to alter an answer to the profit of falsehood; I advise you never to do so.'" Adèle, out of a religious feeling, had hitherto concealed from me this truth, and consequently had perverted the answers of M. Swedenborg. Her self-love seemed hurt at confessing this little subterfuge, which, however, can not be regarded otherwise than as favorable to virtue.

I was unwilling to make known this particular, because, I repeat it, I infinitely respect all beliefs; I wish not to speak against any, only I adhere to telling the truth and nothing but the truth. Had I not been guided by this feeling, I should have allowed no contradiction to subsist.

Let every one experiment without seeking in any manner to influence the clairvoyante, and in most cases the truth will be obtained. Adèle is not easily influenced, for she has ever maintained against me a position contrary to that we have just read. We must, moreover, be convinced that the spirit disengaged from matter is not the more for that freed from its errors. There is progression for it in its ideas; but if the ideas delight in such or such a system, they will run astray there as on earth, the Roman catholic will not depart from his beliefs, the Jew from his, and so on with all others, especially those who passionately delight in their beliefs. Many persons think that to know all it suffices to be a spirit; let them undeceive themselves in this respect; they can do so, it is true, if such is their affection; but as there is no sudden transition between one and the other state, the earthly affections are not forthwith annihilated; consequently, a man who on earth took a delight in the mechanical arts, will not give you the solutions of a jurisconsult; a miller will not demonstrate to you the science of metallurgy.

Behold a clairvoyante given up to himself, it is the exact representation of the first state of the world of spirits; ask him what he did or thought after remaining for a moment in this state, the answer he makes will give you a notion of his then predominant affection: thus you will not make of a clairvoyante who delights in travelling a famous mathematician. True, this comparison is liable to dispute, because the clairvoyante is still under the empire of material laws and impressions, but it gives an idea of the future life: thus the progression is not such as is thought, and I venture to affirm that many men in their material state are much more advanced than certain spirits that quitted the earth ages ago. It is a study that I propose to the spiritualists of a contrary belief; they will see that they will be disabused. For this reason, therefore, we ought to make mention of all the answers made us by clairvoyantes, the interpreters of spirits, without retrenching from them a syllable, in order to study what connection there is between them, and draw conclusions on certain points, as I have on these. 1. Spirits issuing from this globe progress in the affection which they have for such or such positive or negative science. 2. Hence it is that certain spirits, as we have already seen, wander about earthly places in which they took delight. 3. These spirits are attached to our globe, and have not yet passed into one of the superior heavens; hence it is that living in darkness they can teach but error. 4. Error is as common to them as upon earth.

Spirits accord only in these few truths:—

1. They live in a happy state.

2. None of them has seen God in any other form than that of the sun.

3. They obtain forthwith what they desire.

4. They have usages and experience sensations as on earth.

5. They know that they lived prior to their terrestrial life.

6. They acknowledge the utility of the earthly life in all its joys and griefs.

7. They are grouped in societies of kindred affections.

8. They have no knowledge of time or space.

9. They know that that there are different heavens in which we are very happy.

10. They are well aware of their immortality.

11. They have a recollection of their earthly existence, speak of it with more or less pleasure; but on a mass of details, they contradict each other, each letting his responses flow from his present affections, and referring them to the sects of which he forms a part: we ought, therefore, to be very circumspect in accepting such or such an answer more than another. It is prudence that elevates man—passion causes him to err: let us be content with what God permits to be revealed to us on the

future life, and not argue — we are too weak to handle this arm with success; let us humble ourselves before what we can not comprehend — hope that one day God will suffer us to know more, and give him a thousand thanks for the generosity he displays toward us! He only knows the truth and the utility of all the things he has created; let us walk with confidence in the road traced out for us;—it is useful for us!

---

## APPARITIONS.

I HAVE deemed it fit to continue the same order in numbering the sittings as in our first volume.

SITTING 98.—M. Lucas, a carrier at Rambouillet, was very uneasy as to the fate of his brother-in-law, who disappeared from the country twelve years ago, after an altercation that took place one evening between him and his father. This man, on quitting his family, made the observation that they should never hear from him again. Since that period his father died, and his succession (to which this man was the principal heir) remained vacant through the inability of obtaining any information as to his son's being alive or dead. This very much crossed the other heirs, whose affairs remained in suspense, as they could not produce, as legally bound, a certificate of his death. M. Lucas, having heard M. Renard say that I possessed a clairvoyante who could remove all his inquietude on this score, came and asked me for a sitting. Scarcely was Adèle asleep than she asked for this man by his name, as she usually does toward deceased persons. She then said to us: "I see him; he is not dead; on the earth is he, and not in the spiritual world." She gave so exact a description of him to M. Lucas that the latter, who no doubt for the first time beheld a somnambulist, was quite astounded at all he heard, and declared even the very gestures true to life. "I see him," said she, "in a foreign country, where there are trees like those in America; we don't see such in France: he is busy gathering seeds from small shrubs, not much more than three feet high. He has no wish to speak to me, and consequently does not answer the questions I put to him about the country he lives in; I see no one from whom I can obtain any information. I am afraid of meeting with wild beasts! wake me! wake me!" I did so instantly.

Both M. Lucas and myself would have wished to be made acquainted with this country. I told him that it was impossible to make a spirit speak despite itself, especially if such spirit is interested in concealing the place of its retreat, as appeared to be the case with this man. M. Lucas fully appreciated this reasoning, and left me quite convinced that it was really his brother-in-law whom Adèle had perceived, and seemed disposed to believe him as really alive as she declared she beheld him. I promised him that I would do my best by-and-by to learn more about the matter.

99. M. Lucas, the person interested at the foregoing sitting, returned a few days after to ask me if I had heard anything new respecting his brother-in-law. I had not paid any attention to the matter. The mother of the lost man accompanied M. Lucas, and asked me if I could give her a sitting. I made a slight objection, because I was holding a conference with several persons; but, on the observation of M. Lucas, who told me that this lady had come several leagues expressly to obtain fresh information, and that the coach was waiting for her, I begged the persons present to excuse me, and judge of the experiment about to take place. Adèle, once asleep, said, "I see him."—"Where do you see him?" "Here, present."—"Give us once more a description of him, as also of the place where he is." "He is a fair man, browned by the heat of the sun; very corpulent, features pretty regular, hazel eyes, mouth large, air sombre and meditative. He is in the garb of a working man—a sort of small blouse; as at the last time, he is at work, gathering seeds like enough to peppercorns, but I don't think they are, as they seem bigger. This seed is found in small shrubs about three feet high. I see a negro near, who is

doing the same thing."—"Try and obtain an answer to-day; let him tell you the name of the country where you see him." "He won't answer me."—"Tell him that it is his good mother whom he was so fond of, who is with you, and bids you inquire after him." "Oh! at the name of his mother he turned round and said to me, 'My mother! I shall not die before seeing her again; comfort her, and tell her that I am always thinking of her; I am not dead!'"—"Why does he not write to her?" "He has written to her, but no doubt the vessel was wrecked; at least he presumes so, as he received no answer. He tells me that he is at Mexico: he followed the emperor, Don Pedro; was five years a prisoner, suffered much, and will make every effort to return to France; they will see him again."—"Can he name the place he lives in?" "No, it is far up in the country; such places have no names."—"Is he with a European?" "No, with a man of color."—"Why does he not write to his mother?" "Because where he is no vessels come; he knows not to whom to apply; then, again, he scarcely ever knew how to write, and now less than ever; no one near him can render him this service, no one speaks his language; he has much pains in making himself understood; withal, he never was of an open or communicative disposition; he has a somewhat unsociable look. It is a hard matter to get a word out of him; one would think he was dumb."—"In short, how manage to write to him or hear from him?" "He can't tell; all he can say is, 'I am in Mexico, I am not dead, they'll see me again.'" —"Why did he thus forsake his parents without saying a word to them, since he was happy with them?" "This man was far from being communicative; he scarcely ever spoke, was very fond of his mother, but had not the same affection for his father, who was a stern, sour kind of man, and often used him roughly. The cup had long been filled up to the brim; it was not the slight altercation he had with his father, the night before his departure, that induced him to leave: it was a plan decided on long before; he communicated it to no one, and started off stealthily. Having embraced them all over night, he sneaked off the next morning, without saying a word. Make yourself easy, madam, you will see him again." The good woman melted into tears as she recognised the truthfulness of each detail given her by Adèle; she had not a word to retrench from this description; the character, the instruction, and the departure of her son, were precisely such as Adèle described; but what gives an air of greater probability to the clairvoyante's recital as to the country he lives in, is, that some of his relatives entertained the idea that he had enlisted into Don Pedro's army, and took steps at that time to acquire a certainty of it. M. Lucas furnished me with this particular some time after when on a visit to Paris: no information, however, could be obtained in this respect. What no less contributed to astonish this good woman, as well as M. Lucas and the person present at this curious sitting, was to see Adèle, who, to screen herself from the burning rays of the sun of these countries, put her hand up to the left side of her face as if suffocating with heat; but the most marvellous part of the scene was that she received a violent *coup-de-soleil*, that rendered all this side of her face, from the forehead to the shoulder, of a reddish blue, while the other side remained perfectly white; and full twenty-four hours elapsed before this deep color commenced disappearing. The heat was so violent there for a moment, that it was impossible to keep one's hand on it. Present at this sitting was M. Haranger Pirlot, formerly a magnetizer, and honorably known for more than thirty years in the magnetic world. He told me that he never saw the like of this. The good woman took her leave quite consoled, unable to account to herself how that her son, who was in Mexico, could be between her and Adèle, and how the latter could have received a *coup-de-soleil* when nobody felt the heat, the weather that day being very gloomy. I am not more advanced than she, and believe that many others in our place will be like us. We submit this question to the learned; awaiting their answer, let us pass on to another sitting.

100. M. Renard, whom we have already mentioned, begged me to address the following questions to M. Swedenborg, through the medium of Adèle; although they have been solved

in the first volume of the "Secrets," to make myself agreeable to my worthy friend, I felt bound to submit them once more, while Adèle was in her sleep, to this great ecstatico-prophet, who presented himself with his wonted kindness. "Tell this good brother that M. Renard desires to know from his lips whether Christ really existed." "Yes."—"Does he think that we might ask for him in order to address to him a few questions as to his life and doctrine?" "M. Swedenborg inquires whether you have a mind to cause all the spirits in heaven to appear, and if he is wanting in complaisance to answer the questions you ordinarily put to him. There is no inconvenience in asking for Christ: but M. Renard and you are insatiable. Spirits are like folks of the earth: when they pay a visit to any one with a view to oblige, they like confidence to be placed in them, especially when they do not deceive you. All spirits are not at your orders, nor as complaisant as M. Swedenborg; the mode of answering of one is not that of another; if the least disagreement is perceived, we profit by it to oppugn and deny all. Believe me, preserve M. Swedenborg, and put not yourself in communication with all the spiritual societies. He shows more kindness toward you than toward any other; if he sacrificed the same time to all those who should desire to speak to him, he would have none left for himself."—"I see no doubt nor harm in our questions." "There is no harm, but doubt: in short, what would you know of Christ?" "We desire to know whether Christ was God, in the full acceptation of the word, or merely the Son of God." "Christ was not God—he was, like us all, the Son of God: he had a special mission to fulfil: he acquitted himself of it, and returned to heaven as the rest: that is all."—"Is he the chief of the doctrine he taught on earth?" "There are no chiefs in heaven but God: all the members of the societies are there equal—some speak, propose, discuss; others listen, and think like them. There, where there is no disagreement, there is no occasion for chiefs or masters; harmony reigns there by the power divine. I have already told you this—you are constantly asking me the same thing."—"Do the celestial societies influence those of the earth?" "The celestial societies are occupied with themselves, and no longer think of the earth. If any earthly societies believe themselves in communication with heavenly societies, they are mistaken; and are so only with scattered members that wander around them, and do not yet make common cause with the heavenly ones. It is only when God sees fit that it is otherwise; but, in general, celestial spirits have no inclination for recalling to mind the earth, or holding communication with it, for they find our atmosphere heavy and bad; those that visit us must be good indeed to do so."—"For that reason, I beg you each time to thank them for me. Inquire, also, why we have a knowledge of a mass of apparitions of souls in pain, who claim the assistance of our prayers to procure them peace, as they say." "Those are persons who are pursued by ideas of remorse; they wander around the earth, because they have not an ardent desire to purge themselves of those thoughts that beset them; they believe that our prayers are beneficial to them—deem themselves unworthy, from their faults, of entering societies that would not admit them into their bosom, because they would create trouble; they are such men as Father Lauriot, who make mountains of a mole-hill; others that are really criminals, but suffer at not being called to God; they frequent the company of persons like themselves, with whom they form a society. It may be said that their ideas are not harmonized; they create for themselves false positions; they have no lively affection; but God insinuates into them, when he deems fit, other thoughts, and they enter heaven with the rest."—"How is Christ looked upon in heaven?" "As a very good spirit; he is dearly loved, that is all."—"And those who worship him as God, what does he think of them?" "Those who worship him as God, believe him such; and it is God who receives the homage of those adorations. I have told you that all religions were equally agreeable to him. Christ, knowing that he is not God, glories not more in that which he taught men than the other founders in theirs."—"His disciples declare to us that there is no salvaion but in his name: they teach us errors, then?" "All religions teach them. What they possess of pure ascends to God, who is the sole and only object to whom they address themselves; and what they possess of impure remains on earth, in the hearts of men who knowingly do evil."

This sitting confirms what we have already said on this subject. Heaven is but a compound of societies, each representing the religious or philosophical doctrines that have existed on earth; every one after his departure from this globe joins that which represents his predominant affection, and, through a gross error, each believes that his neighbor is damned if he has not the same beliefs as himself, without considering that religious beliefs are at bottom the same, inasmuch as they all address themselves to God, to receive his blessings or thank him for his generosity. The details alone differ; each believes himself more acceptable to God by offering him what he himself admires most on earth, without considering that what God prefers above all things is the heart and love of his children. Thus we are assured that these religious beliefs, so full of contrasts, have left such an impression on the spirit of the man who quits the earth, that they continue for a certain time to constitute all his happiness. Hence he seeks societies in which these beliefs are admitted, and becomes a member of the said societies until, elevated toward truer thoughts, he enters a heaven or superior state, where the pure truth shines before him in all its splendor; then the fusion becomes general. These souls become acquainted with the true light, the Divine light they have so ardently desired, and which they enjoy in happiness. It is, therefore, those different beliefs continually misleading man on his exit from this globe that cause our clairvoyantes to present to us in their religious revelations contradictions so obvious. They make acquaintance with spirits that possess their affection, and answer in accordance with this affection. If, on the contrary, the clairvoyante is not positively a slave to any belief, his magnetizer the same, and both address themselves to a spirit that on earth thought as they, there is a much greater chance of approaching the truth. This is what we have hitherto done, and I believe that the major part of the revelations made us bear with them the seal, not of absolute truth, but of an *ensemble* leading to it. What we can affirm is, that in the superior heaven there exists a perfect equality in age, beauty, form, position, affection; one has not a jot more than another; it is the reign of happiness of which we all dream, and which we shall all one day possess.

101. After many indifferent questions which I had addressed to M. Swedenborg, I put to him the following ones (through the medium, be it understood, of Adèle): "I have not the means of printing the first volume of the 'Secrets,' a good part of which you dictated to me. I have spoken of it to several publishers, who politely refused me because I had not a literary name; could you point out to me the means of attaining my object without their assistance?" "No; it is a very difficult matter. I know the trouble mine cost me to publish." —"Did you publish them at your own expense, or did God supply you with the means by occult causes or transmissions of money?" "I printed my works at my own expense, but sold very few in my time. Nobody would read them. In fifty years it will be the same with yours as with mine at the present time; they will be read with pleasure. I received nothing from spirits."—"Still they have the power of making such transmissions?" "Yes; but it is never good to ask them for them."—"Why so?" "Because it is ordinarily evil spirits that have this affection."—"For what object?" "To draw you into their society."—"What is the consequence of such alliance with them?" "Living with them, and doing for others what they have done for you."—"I can see in that but good." "Yes, so far; but this good is always done in some interest or other that must sooner or later be paid for."—"Is any suffering the result for the person obliged?" "Yes, in this sense, that he finds himself allied with a society whose usages are not in harmony with his affections. We can not extricate ourselves from this constraint before a certain time. If you had the affections of these societies, you would not suffer with them; but, not having them, I advise you to maintain your inde-

pendence."—"None but evil spirits have the power of making such transmissions?" "The good have likewise this power." —"Why do they not oftener make use of it?" "Because to deserve these favors of God, we ourselves must be as pure as beneficent. Few men exist who merit them. The good spirits know that the more we suffer on earth, the more agreeable we find the joys of heaven; and then, again, they trouble themselves so little about the earth!"—"One of my friends, M. R***, assured me that he found, some time ago, fifty francs scattered about the place where he locks up his money. He was in great difficulties, having but ten francs to last him out the month. He prayed, and the following morning he found the sum." "M. R*** may have been mistaken; possibly he had laid by this money somewhere, but could not recollect where; for my part, I do not believe that there is any transmission in this circumstance, but still I may be mistaken."—"You grant that there exist good and evil spirits that have this property?" "Yes."—"Could you direct one to me?" "No, I have no wish to do so; I advise you not to try it, we should be well acquainted with a spirit before thus giving ourselves up to it." Adèle is unwilling to proceed, telling me that she will never be an interpreter to such arrangements; that I have no reason to be uneasy about my book, as it would be published by some one who would appear in time for that purpose. I went on submitting to her several questions, which she answered agreeably to my wishes, and continued thus: "For my part, I do n't think it possible for me to tell you any more. Your work recapitulates, in this sense, all that it is possible to teach men as to the future life. Did they know more of it, they would bitterly curse the earth, and find the joys of heaven much less sweet. Though we can not form a just idea of celestial happiness, we find a pleasure which we trace little by little beforehand, less captivating. Besides, there exist mysteries which can not be explained. All this is so foreign to our material laws, that the time would be spent to no purpose in wishing to make you comprehend what it is not given you to comprehend.

We are conscious of these mysteries, but can not explain them by speech."—"In short, are all the deceased initiated into these mysteries?" "Yes; more or less promptly."—"Can they give an account to themselves of their departure from the earth, their present state, the places they inhabit, their spiritual form and that which they assume to appear to us on earth?" "They account for all this to each other, for each other, in their state, but they could not explain to you, material man, how it is they perceive that they are called on earth—how they resume their material countenance, and dress so faithfully—how they can appear to us if we desire it, in all the costumes they have worn on earth as in all the physiognomies they have had at different ages during their earthly existence. For this reason it is that a person who demands the appearance of a deceased friend, if he ask the clairvoyante—'Do you see him with mustaches (for instance) or whiskers?' The clairvoyante will be able to see what is asked of him for two causes: 1. Speech is a creator; it is never good to question in experiments of this sort, but let the clairvoyante give the description without interrupting him, unless such description in no wise resemble that of the deceased. 2. The deceased may have worn in the course of his earthly existence those mustaches or whiskers which we desire the clairvoyante to see, and yet not have worn them at the time of his decease. It is the same with regard to the dress and the color of it; whatsoever man has worn on earth is imprinted on him, nothing is lost. According to the penetration of the clairvoyante's view through these impressions, which are repeated hundreds of times in one and the same year on our bodies, the description will more or less correspond with the one desired. It often happens that at a later period, aided by some information, we shall know that the deceased was really in the conditions in which he appeared to the clairvoyante. He will never happen, for instance, to perceive a fair man for a black, a bearded man for a beardless one, an old man for a young one; but all the visions I have just detailed may take place, and this very often will cause a doubt as to the apparition. A skeptic may also, by ironical or captious questions, be the cause of the greatest mistakes. We must be penetrated with a certain religious respect, for the spirits of darkness are ever ready to lay hold of the least opportunity to sow error. He who seeks to make the clairvoyante err is punished in his turn; he sought error, and he finds it. There are also, some that may be involuntary on both sides, some a rising from the want of habit in the deceased of setting in play all the springs of the seemingly material envelope in which he appears; speech is as strange to him as the earth on which he lived. He may render his thoughts badly, seeing that in heaven language is wholly made up of sensation; thus you perceive that matter can neither appreciate nor judge of spiritual laws as it would wish."

I leave to the reader the task of judging of the precious information of this sitting. Is this the language of a madman or mere visionary? I think not.

As we have seen, Adèle tells me not to be uneasy about the printing of my books; *that some one will come to my assistance.* I will not attempt to retrace here the history of the tribulations this publication gave me, but I will say with gratitude that one day M. Pirlot, a respectable old man, presented himself at my house to inquire whether the subscription I had opened was filled up. On my reply in the negative, and telling him how uneasy I was, seeing that I had not required beforehand from the subscribers the amount of their subscription, this leaving me in the same embarrassment as if I had none at all, inasmuch as the printer was unwilling to take this subscription as payment, this gentleman drew out of his pocket-book a bank-note of 500 francs ($100), and handing it to me, said: "This will do away with all your difficulties." I knew not whether I was dreaming or awake. I offered a receipt, which this gentleman would not accept, saying to me: "You will return it me when your money comes in. I would that it were in my power to make you a present of it, but I am not rich, and have sufficient confidence in you to trust to you." This was the second time of my seeing this gentleman. I cultivated the acquaintance of this honorable citizen, and received with pleasure wise counsels from him whenever I stood in need of them. Another beneficent friend of science, equally unknown to me as the former, made up the remainder of the sum necessary for the printing, which, as Adèle had predicted, was not to disturb me. Oh! Secret Power that directs us, who can divine thee?

102. Madame Lorme, a grocer at Rambouillet, having heard speak of Adèle's speciality of communicating with the deceased, having long been desirous of making sure by herself of the degree of belief due to such recitals, undertook this journey expressly to solicit the apparition of her grandmother. Adèle, after having visited (spiritually) this lady, says that she sees the person asked for giving the following description: "This woman is not so tall as the lady here present; she appears to be stronger, and about seventy or seventy-two years of age; she seems to me still very fresh; her hair is gray—it must have been of a chestnut color; her chin is rather long and face wrinkled, like that of all old people. I see her in a cap with flat bands that go round just so (Adèle designates the form of a cap worn by country people); she has over her shoulders a red square handkerchief; her dress is that of a countrywoman—a flat corsage and a striped woollen under-petticoat. I see her with something in her hand; if not a snuff-box, it is a spectacle-case. This woman has surely been very mirthful, good, and dearly loved. For my part, I should be very fond of her. She suffered much during her life, is now happy, and would not come back on earth for all the gold in the world."

Madame Lorme declares herself highly satisfied with the exactitude of these details.

103. Madame Lorme, of whom we have just spoken, on her return to Rambouillet, received a visit from M. Renard, who had addressed her to me, and on the inquiry of my friend, this lady told him that Adèle had rightly hit upon the sufferings she experienced; but that she had made a mistake as to the apparition, it not being her grandmother that she had perceived. My friend sent word to me what this lady had told him, regretting that the apparition experiment had failed. I was

naturally astonished at such a communication—I who had heard this lady say at each detail given her by Adèle on the person that appeared—"'*Tis just so, 'tis just so.*" I forthwith forwarded to my friend a copy of the testimonial, and begged him clear up this affair. A few days after I received the following letter:—

"I have good news to tell you. Proceeding forthwith to Madame Lorme's I showed her your letter, when she said to me: 'Good heavens! the clairvoyante hit rightly enough on my bodily ailments, but it was not my grandmother who came.' The following Saturday, I again spoke to her about it; same answer. 'Perhaps,' said I, 'there are two ladies of this name in your family?'—'No,' replied she. I returned the next day, Sunday evening; Monsieur Lorme was absent. She exclaimed: 'Oh! my poor M. Renard, yesterday, when you were gone, it all at once came into my head that I had an aunt, Dame Vallée, which is indeed the name of my grandmother, and who was her sister-in-law; she lived at Nogent, and died four or five years ago at the age of seventy or seventy-two. She was small, very mirthful, a *Roger bon temps.* She wore caps with flat bands, a square handkerchief, a striped woollen under-petticoat, and a bodice without skirts, such as is worn in Beauce; she had always her spectacle-case about her, as she often sewed up coarse linen bags. Ah! she is, indeed, the woman; 'tis I who was wrong; goodness me, how I repent,' &c., &c. She repeated this version to me a number of times. You may imagine, my friend, what pleasure this recital gave me; I am still quite joyous at the thoughts of it. You know me; having an idea that the good Dame Lorme might tell me this to console us, I repaired to her mother's at Grenonvillers; there the same account. M. Millard, her father, told me the same thing. It is, indeed, our aunt, a merry little creature; in short, such a one as your clairvoyante described. This fact confirms us in the belief that Adèle has not the *communication of thoughts.* I will write to M. Dupotet; I should think that he will insert this fact in his Journal while speaking of your work. If Adèle had the transmission of thoughts, she would have depicted the grandmother of Madame Lorme; seen her in her brain. This is a very precious incident."

As my friend, I look upon this incident as a very precious one. But, it will be asked me, why Madame Lorme replied, "*Just so, just so,*" when it was not what she desired ? To this observation I will reply, that this lady lost all consciousness when Adèle visited her (spiritually) ; it was not without some trouble that I restored her to the use of hèr senses. This lady found herself in this state for the first time in her life ; she knew not what to think of it, and I believe that she was in haste to quit us, fearing a relapse. This, no doubt, induced her to say, "*'Tis just so, 'tis just so.* Let me escape as soon as possible, for I no longer know where I am." Without the perseverance of my friend, this precious apparition would be looked upon as false. My friend, in his letter, that was delivered to me by Madame Lorme, gave me merely the surname of the deceased. I asked for her by this name only, and hence, no doubt, the mistake. We have already made mention of two similar ones in our first volume, others will be seen in this ; great precautions, therefore, should be taken in this respect. A false application of names would cause a failure in the desired apparition, and often lead to the rejection of a truth, which would be perverted only through the fault of the asker. Take note of all the incidents, however strange they appear ; by-and-by we shall find the solution of them.

In the apparition we have just cited, the communication of thoughts can not exist, as rightly observes my friend, who thus terminates his letter :—

"Madame Lucas afforded me much pleasure from the account she gave of your admirable sitting, when your good clairvoyante had a *coup-de-soleil,* in the perception of Mexico. These facts confound all the religious and philosophical *writers.*

"Receive, &c.,

"Ch. Renard.

Employé aux hypothèques de Rambouillet."

104. M. Renard, whom we have just mentioned, begged me to get a small bottle of water magnetized for him, by Adèle,

when she should be in her sleep, in order to cure or calm an irritation of the conjunctiva, which prevented him from reading and looking steadily on an object. I begged Adèle, while asleep, to render my friend this slight service. M. Swedenborg was present at the sitting; Adèle begged him to strengthen by his action the virtue of the water; this good spirit did so with pleasure. Adèle held the bottle up, presenting it thus to M. Swedenborg, who magnetized it, and breathed on it. She returned it to me, saying, "It is good." I was about to paste some labels on different bottles; I put one on this bottle, on which I afterward wrote *magnetized water*. Three hours had scarcely elapsed when I no longer saw on the label but the word *water*, the other word had disappeared. I again wrote on it the word *magnetized*, and, next day, at the moment of sending this bottle to my friend, the word *magnetized* had again disappeared, leaving no trace behind it. I wrote it a third time, then forwarded the bottle to its destination. I was naturally surprised at the disappearance of one word out of two. I had written with a goose-quill, touched no acid, made this label as large as a liard, out of the same paper as the rest. On none had the ink disappeared—the paste was the same; what, then, could have caused this disappearance? Why had the word *water* undergone no alteration?

Already had I forgotten this incident when my friend wrote to me that he had received the bottle, bearing a label with merely the word *water* on it; he gave me to understand that I ought at least to have indicated what water it was, since I had put on a label. I answered him that I had even written on it three times *magnetized water*, and could not understand how it was that one word only should remain. I could not inform myself better in this respect than by applying to M. Swedenborg. I begged Adèle to mention to him this phenomenon, in order to know what he thought of it. M. Swedenborg replied to her: "I told you to beg your magnetizer to put on the bottle *divine water spiritualized*." Adèle confessed that she had forgotten this injunction. I inquired why it should be more necessary to put on it *divine water spiritualized* than water magnetized.

She answered: "Because it was by the permission of God that M. Swedenborg spiritualized, and not magnetized it. It is only material men who magnetize, spirits spiritualize."—"For my part," replied I, "this action seems to me similar to the other, since this water has not passed to a spiritual state, as we see by our distillations," "Who tells you that it has not been in the spiritual state? Let M. Renard preserve it, it will do him a great deal of good."—"It was M. Swedenborg, then, who took care to efface the word magnetized?" "No, he no longer thought of the matter; it is the water itself that carried away this word while filtering through the pores of the glass." —"I can't understand that; it could not have filtered, or the label would have come off, and the word *water* would likewise have been effaced. Explain this phenomenon more clearly." "There is no phenomenon: the will and the fluid of M. Swedenborg were in this water, which was not to bear the word *magnetized;* consequently the water caused it to disappear." —"You affirm that it was not M. Swedenborg, nor any spirit, that effaced this word?" "It was the water itself."—"To perform such a work this water, then, has a will? It is alive, then?" "It had the will and the fluid of M. Swedenborg, that sufficed it."—"Then this is as much as saying that it was M. Swedenborg himself who effaced this word?" "He troubled himself no more about it; be content with this explanation. I find myself forced to be so, let every one do as I." My friend wrote word to me that he was cured in two hours; he applied it, also, to a contusion, the consequence of a fall he had had; at the lapse of a few instants he felt nothing more of it. I looked upon this fact as marvellous enough to take its place in the "Secrets."

105. M. Mirande, director of the printing-office, Belin-Mandar, at St. Cloud, to whom I intrusted the impression of the first volume of the "Secrets," experienced much pleasure in reading the proofs, and knew not what to think of such marvellous facts. One day he confided to me that he was acquainted with magnetism only by name, and begged me to tell him sincerely whether all I said in this work was strictly true.

I repeated to him what I said in my introduction, that "I should deem myself the most contemptible being on earth if I speculated on such falsehoods. All that I recounted was the sacred truth." He then said to me: "Would you be so kind as to give me a sitting?" I eagerly offered to gratify his wish. Adèle visited (spiritually) his daughter and wife, who could not for a single moment doubt her excellent clairvoyance. Madame Mirande can not make use of the thumb of her right hand. Adèle asked her if she had not magnetized some one? This lady replied that she was acquainted with magnetism only by name; but that from what she had seen Adèle do, when showing M. Mirande how he should magnetize his daughter, whose arm is paralyzed, she recollected that a doctor had once taught her how to perform frictions on the arm of one of her friends who had lost the use of it. She had rendered her this service for nearly a fortnight; but finding that it fatigued her and gave her pains in the thumb, she left off; and it is only since then that her thumb has been in this state. Adèle said to her: "It was magnetism that you performed then; the doctor ought to have warned you to shake your fingers to disengage yourself from the bad fluid you absorbed, and wash your hands in water acidulated with vinegar, as I recommend your husband to do after each magnetization." This lady acknowledged that Adèle's was a just observation, since her thumb was not in this state previous to the above time, and that she had received no blow or any injury that could have occasioned what she felt. (A warning to those who do not believe in the transmission of disease.) M. Mirande, from the first sitting of somnambulism he had ever seen, was convinced of the reality of what was said with respect to maladies. But he wished to know what opinion to come to as to the revelations of the "Secrets;" consequently he begged Adèle to ask for the apparition of his brother, whom he believed killed in the Russian campaign. Adèle, not seeing him in the spiritual world, said that he was not dead; that she saw him on earth. She gave the following description of him: "I see a tall stout man, with brown hair, fine black lively eyes, and of a tender expression; a mouth neither large nor small, beautiful teeth, nose well made, cheeks colored, air gracious, and very cheerful. He seems to me about thirty years of age, and is rather taller than M. Mirande. He wears the uniform of a sub-officer (I believe), because I see him with only one epaulette, blue coat, pantaloons of the same color, with scarlet edgings, shako with visor; altogether he is a fine man."—" Ask him in what country he is?" "He does not know, *or he has no mind to tell me.* He says that he has undergone much suffering. He was made a prisoner and sent to the very interior of Russia, in countries bordering on China, *I believe;* he tells me that his brother will see him again." "Why has he not written to him?" "He did write, but the letters have either been lost or miscarried."—" Why does he no longer write?" "He knows not whether his brother is still alive."—" Tell him that he is alive and takes upon himself to find out the place of his retreat." "He answers that he can not say when, but that he is in hopes, one day, of taking his brother by surprise."—" What does he do there?" "He is very comfortable, has lands of his own, turns them to account, and employs many persons. Could he have managed to dispose of his property, he would have been before this in France; but thereabouts purchasers are not to be found as with us; he can't tell when he shall succeed in selling off."—" Let him write to his brother." "He has no opportunity. You think it an easy matter; he is very far from the sea; then again he has a wish to take his brother by surprise, when he returns, rich and happy. He is not selfish, he has an excellent heart, but he is not free from ambition; he always was ambitious. He has dreamed of only one thing in his life,—being rich in his old days, and he is at the height of his wishes."—" Is he married?" "Yes; but he has no children. Next time I will beg him to show me the country he lives in, as well as his house and wife." Adèle is fatigued, and desires to be roused. M. Miranda asks for further particulars as to the costume of his brother. Adèle repeats what she has already said, and adds that "she believes she saw gold lace on his breast, what we call *brandebourgs;* she likewise thinks that he had white facings to his coat." M. Mirande acknowledged that all the details as to the personal appearance were exact, as well as those in respect to the character, and so forth, of his brother. The brother of this gentleman had served in the departmental guard, previous to the Russian campaign. M. Mirande believes that such was the costume, only he did not know that he was a sub-officer. He is much surprised that his brother, who must be fifty-six years old, should look no more than thirty. Adèle makes the observation to him that she sees him at the moment he left France. "At that time," replies M. Mirande, "he was not above one-and-twenty. He looks to you full thirty; no doubt the fatigue he underwent made him grow old soon." Adèle resumes: "As you knew him only a soldier of one-and-twenty, he appears to me an officer, and older. Several years may have elapsed since that time and the moment I see him. This is very admissible. If I beheld him at the age one-and-twenty, it would be said that I see in the thought. If, on the contrary, I saw him at the age he is now, fifty-six, his brother would not recognise him." M. Mirande can very well understand this. He has not the least doubt but that it was his brother who appeared. He can not recover his astonishment. I will add, as a reflection to this apparition: 1. If Adèle had seen this man in M. Mirande's thought, she would have seen him as a private soldier, about twenty-one years of age. 2. It would have been sufficient for her to have given this gentleman a few particulars, then to have broken off with the observation that his brother was dead. Such was M. Mirande's opinion. Adèle, on the contrary, gives details as to the existence and life of this man; she makes judicious observations. If she saw him at his present age, and in his present dress and occupations, his brother could never have recognised him. The only objection admissible is, that he ought to have given the name of the place he lives in. It remains to know whether he is able or willing to do so. To be able, this place must have a name; and all the countries of the globe are not like France, where each hamlet is dependent on a city, this city on a department, &c. Those uncultivated, remote countries, but little known to geography, possess not names so easy to class as with us. We experienced the same difficulty in our perception of Mexico. Then, again, if this man is unwilling to acquaint us with the place he lives in, for reasons of his own, we can not force him. He evades the question by saying: "I have been a prisoner; I have written; I have no opportunity; I know not whether my brother is still living," &c. The future will tell us more about it. This apparition proves to us that if men still on earth can appear in the dress, the features, and age, they no longer have, souls disengaged from matter may surely have the same power; and we acquire the certitude, by this fact, that all that I have said, in this respect, is correct. Each garment, each year, imprints an ineffaceable image on our bodies, which may be found again, at all times, agreeably to the desire of the spirit. I have made this experiment several times; I have asked for persons living on earth at different periods of their life; they have appeared at the age demanded, clad in the costume they then wore. I have made inquiries of them, and obtained the assurance that this was correct. I was far from having known these persons when of the age at which I asked for them. In somnambulism, there is a continual source of observation. To succeed we must not argue; we must study—not believe without proofs, and not deny without knowing. I will even go so far as to say that we have no right to deny what we can not comprehend.

106. I take advantage of a visit paid me by Emile Rey, of whose sittings we have read in the first volume of the "Secrets," to beg him to allow me to magnetize him, as I had a few questions to put to him. It was not without some trouble that I could prevail on him to consent to my wishes, his family having told him that such experiments would make him ill. This child is but twelve years of age, and would be an excellent clairvoyante if conducted with perseverance; but he prefers playing to sleeping, which is natural enough at his age. A few days before I had submitted to him a few questions which his guide was unable to answer; I had a mind to get a solution of them. Once asleep, I tell him to ask for his guide. "Here he is," said he.—"Ask him if there are any books in heaven." "He tells

me there are none."—"Ask him, once more, if we have already lived on a material globe before appearing on earth." "He answers, 'No.' "—"What is the festival called, at which, the last time you saw him, he told you he had been crowned?" "The feast of the angels."—"What kind of pleasure did they take that day?" "They danced a great deal in a circle."—"What is this day called?" "St. Nicholas' day, it was Monday."—"But you saw your guide before Monday, and the feast had already taken place; ask him again, very slowly." "He replies that it was St. Nicholas' feast."—"Your guide, then, is very fond of dancing in a circle, that he took so much delight in it." "Ah! yes."—"And while he was dancing, what had become of his horse; no doubt he had put it in a stable?" "There are neither stables nor houses in heaven; there is but a large garden, a beautiful one. He put his horse in this garden. Horses are not so vicious there as on earth, they destroy nothing."—"Are they all little boys together?" "Yes; but there are also little girls."—"Do the boys play with them?" "Yes; each plays with his own."—"How his own?" "Each little boy has a little girl, whom he terms his companion, and with whom he always plays."—"Has your guide also a companion?" "Yes."—"Does she ride on horseback with him?" "No, she is not adroit enough."—"Could he let you see her?" "He is going to fetch her." Emile waits a moment, then exclaims: "Here she is; she is a black."—"A black, what do you mean?" "Yes, she is a negress." Fearing that it might be an evil spirit that had a mind to play us some trick of his own, I attempted to drive her away in the name of God, but Emile said: "They are really sent by God, and you can't drive them away."—"Then, tell me how this negress is dressed?" "She is in a beautiful white robe; she is rather taller than Aïs."—"Where was she born?" "At Neva."—"That is a cold country, *I believe.* Was it not rather at Java, or Nouga-Hiva?" "No, she says Neva."—"Did Aïs know her on earth?" "Yes, at Paris, but he saw her only twice; she lived opposite his house."—"Has she any relations with her in heaven?" "No."—"And Aïs?" "He has an aunt."—"You once told me that he had his father there?" "He replies that he never told me so; 'tis I who made a mistake."—"The parents of this little negress, are they still in Paris?" "She says that she believes that they have returned to Neva."—"Is she black in heaven, as she appears to you on earth?" "No, she is as fair as Aïs."—"What is the color of her hair in heaven?" "'Flaxen."—"And Aïs?" "He has fine black hair."—"Of what color are their eyes?" "Both of them have blue eyes."—"Do they never quit each other?" "Aïs says no; but," observes Emile, "since he came to see me without her, he must surely quit her."—"Ask him again." "He replies that he leaves her only to come and see me, and to go and see his aunt in heaven."—"Has this little creature also seen God?" "Yes."—"In what form?" "I have already told you, in the human form."—"How is he named?" "Our Lord Jesus Christ."—"Is it Jesus Christ who is the God, Creator of heaven and earth?" "No."—"Who then?" "It is God."—"Who is Jesus Christ?" "The Son of God."—"But you say that in heaven he is called God." "He is called God, but he is not God; he is the Son of God."—"What you tell me, is that really the answer made you?" "Yes."—"Does your guide eat in heaven?" "Yes."—"What?" "Fine fruits."—"What fruits are they?" "Such as on earth."—"Does he undergo any sufferings; experience any fatigue?" "He does not suffer, and is never fatigued."—"Does he sleep sometimes?" "Yes."—"On what does he lie down?" "On a beautiful turf in the garden."—"Ask his companion if she dearly loves him, and whether she makes much of him?" "She says that she does, indeed." I awake Emile.

As I have already observed, it is very difficult to put questions comprehensible to children of this age, and from Emile's answers we perceive that he is in accord with many of the revelations we have read. This way in which children perceive God proves to us that each enters the society that corresponds with the belief in which he was brought up on earth, and continues there the same usages. Christ is the God of the Christians; the Mahometans, Jews, &c., have each their own. The true philosopher has but one who is neither the one nor the other of these teachers, but who is all, in all, and throughout all. It remains for us to know if in heaven a negro preserves his color, and can be united to a white; in Adèle's next sleep we will submit to her these questions, though she has already answered the first one. We see that Emile has sufficient judgment not to be the dupe of an illusion, by the judicious observation he makes when his guide tells him that he never quits his companion.

I will observe, for my part, that I should not comprehend the utility of a guide such as that of Emile, and all those who are, it is said, constantly beside us. If I admitted that they were charged with a continual surveillance of our actions, they would be slaves like ourselves, by sacrificing to us all their time. It must be otherwise, or our life would be theirs. I do not believe that they are bound to us in any other way than in proffering us counsel when we address ourselves to them; were it not so, it would be difficult to reconcile their happy occupations with our troubles. We see that we are not called on to explain all in our present state. Eternity is before us!

We will study in this the question of free will; for either we are or are not free. If we are free, why influence us; if we are not free, the influence becomes in like manner unlawful. We will refer, on this head, to what has been said in our first volume.

107. Adèle is not apprized of Emile's sitting. I have prepared the following questions, which I beg her to submit to M. Swedenborg; "The two beings created for each other, are they in every respect alike as to physiognomy?" "No, they are only exactly similar as to affections."—"May one be a white and the other a black?" "Yes."—"Can a white be united to a negress?" "Yes."—"Do negroes preserve their black complexion in heaven?" "In heaven all men are white; it is only on earth, from the effect of climate, that they are of different colors."—"When blacks reappear on earth, do they resume their black color?" "Yes, it must be so, otherwise they would not be recognised."—"Negroes among each other

do they see themselves black, if such is their affection?" "There are no negroes who like their color. When they compare it with that of the whites, they envy the white color. They prefer us in all. Black women seek after white men, and black men after white women. They have no affection for their color, had they any they would be deprived of it in heaven where all men are white."—"Can a black child be united with a white child, each having died in its own color?" "Yes."—"Have children, among each other, books to study?" "Those that desire it have them."—"Is each pair of children under the special care of a superior spirit charged with their instruction?" "The spirit charged with this instruction has not less than a number of children, and that number is twenty."—"What kind of instruction is given them?" "That which God deems suitable."—"Are children crowned at a feast which is general with them?" "There are religious festivals and usages in heaven as on earth; but all children are generally crowned at the age of seven years."—"There are years, then, in heaven?" "Time, as I have before said, is not reckoned there as on earth; it is no longer a necessity, one is not obliged to put off till the morrow the desire which is satisfied as soon as formed; the calculation of time becomes needless there. It is only for children still subject to the usages necessary to complete their instruction that time is counted."—"Children, from their earliest age, can they be united if they died at about the same time?" "Yes, but they are not ultimately united before the age of fifteen years; it is the age of eternal union."—"Can a child be ignorant of its having lived spiritually on another globe before appearing on earth?" "No one is ignorant of such existence; it is for want of thought if some do not speak of it."—"Children perfected, do they caress each other by kisses or other demonstrations?" "Yes: but their ordinary caress is shaking hands affectionately until they are ultimately united."—"There have appeared to us children who did not seem to have made any progress since their departure from the earth; do they remain long in such state?" "A time more or less long."—"Can they, like grown-up persons, remain an unlimited time in innocent pleasures?" "Yes."—"Do children believe that they speak through speech or thought?" "They believe that they speak through speech." I had put this question to Emile's guide, and he answered me in the same sense. Having exhausted the questions I had prepared for this sitting, I was about to rouse Adèle when she made a gesture of surprise, and tendered, with the greatest vivacity, her hand to some one who was near her, and caused her so powerful an emotion that she shed tears in abundance. "What creates in you this surprise?" said I to her. "It is Alphonse."—"What! Alphonse, who for so long a period has not paid you a visit?" (About eighteen months.) "He, himself," replied she.—"Has he anything to tell you?" "It seems to him, he says, but two days ago."—"He does not grow weary where he is." "I perceive as much." Adèle expressed a wish to chat with this cherished brother; I left her a moment, but soon perceived that she was entering the complement of ecstasy. I felt her pulse, to guide myself by its pulsations, when I thought it time to recall her to earth; I did so, and she obeyed me without a murmur, exclaiming: "Yes, our departure from this miserable globe, our descent into the grave, is the first step we take toward perfect equality; fortune, title, grandeur, ugliness, deformity, grief, misery—all this passes under the spiritual level, and emerges from it, equalized for ever; love, fraternity, replace egotism and ambition. Oh! my God, wherefore men do they not appreciate thy divine mercy? wherefore dost thou send me back among them? My time is not ended, let us re-enter this prison and hope!" I had sacrificed this sitting, as I have said, to verify whether all that Emile's guide told me was correct; we have seen that there is accord: 1. As to the color of the hair, which may be different between two beings, as we have the proof direct in Aïs and his companion, hers being flaxen and his black. 2. As to the possible union of a white with a negress. 3. As to the disappearance of the black color in heaven, where all beings are white. 4. On the necessity of appearing on earth in the color we bore there. 5, On the possibility of having books in heaven, if children are fond of them.

6. On a mentor, who superintends their education; Aïs had told me in a former sitting, that a saint instructed them. This child is so lively that he scarcely awaits the answers made him; to this may be attributed the mistake he made as to the decease of the father of Aïs. We see by M. Swedenborg, as by M. Mallet, that a number consists of 20. 7. There is also accord as to the coronation. 8. As to the festivals. 9. As to the possible union and caresses of two children. 10. As to their belief, in communicating with each other, through speech; this, also, Emile had told me, when, on the contrary, it is through thought, through sensation. Here, then, are ten secrets in which they perfectly agree. It is necessary to observe that I did not magnetize this child once in two months, his mother having an objection to it. We may judge what facility is prepared for somnambulists in communicating with the deceased, especially when rightly brought up for this purpose, and prudently guided in this speciality. I return to an observation to which I did not give sufficient importance: that is, to prepare the questions we desire to address, not to suffer ourselves to be led away by those raised by the answers we obtain; keep them for the next sitting, you will have had time to reflect on them, and prepare them better. They may, sometimes, accord with others that have preceded them, which would be a needless repetition, for we have been enabled to appreciate that an answer very often contains several solutions; hence it is, that at the first sitting, Binet used to say to me: "You have already been answered that question."—I did not believe it; I had not comprehended him, and I found at a later period that he was right. Such conversations, likewise, present in the reading a void which is, at times, painful. It will be understood that this is not a history whose every detail should be consigned with harmony and a certain elegance of style, in order to amuse. Here we instruct ourselves, pick up information in the road of the infinite, the unknown, to construct the universal history of creation and the human destination. We are but a very poor workman for a monument so colossal. A skilful architect will one day come to unite these materials, and adorn with them the

edifice at which we have been courageously working for so many years. Many questions, also, are found unanswered; the spirit, no doubt, perceiving that our intelligence is not open to such revelations. It is silent—and we insist not. We ask for the spiritual obole with humility, and stop in time when we find that we are importunate.

Many magnetizers are easily enough disgusted with somnambulism; good somnambulists are always useful to consult; it is very frequently the magnetizers who disorganize them by the strangeness of their questions. We should be convinced, once for all, that it is necessary to train every somnambulist to one speciality, suited to his tastes and the kind of instruction we desire. How conceive that a somnambulist should answer at the same sitting questions hurried, and so little in accord as these: "Can you tell me what I have in my pocket?" "Can you read this letter?" "Can you see where I suffer?" "Can you tell me what my brother is doing in Africa?" "Can you see whether I shall gain such a law-suit?" "Can you tell what such a person thinks of me?" "Will the lottery-ticket I have purchased turn up a prize?" "Can you tell me what has become of my husband, whom I have not seen these twenty years?" and a thousand other like questions. The world thinks that a somnambulist who sees and knows a certain thing can see and know all. The magnetizer himself is no less insatiable. Consider that mistakes must be the consequence of such a mode of operating; too many are often made even in following a route with great circumspection. What can we expect from such a chaos of questions? Deception for all, shame and vexation for the magnetizer, and insanity or stupidity for the somnambulist thus tortured; fortunate for him if physical tortures be not added to moral ones. I am not at all surprised that somnambulism should lose in the public mind its sacred and divine character. You wish to learn so much from it that you know nothing. If, in spiritual researches, we were to proceed in this way, we should obtain but very little. It is necessary, as I have said, to write down beforehand the questions we intend putting—acquaint the clairvoyante with them, that he may prepare for them. These questions should be clear and few in number, touching only on one subject, with no objections, and thus terminating the sitting. The answers obtained will supply new questions for the following sitting. *Never make two similar experiments at the same sitting*, if you would succeed; no pride, no interested calculation. Be patient, kind. The stone that caused your fall to-day should warn you to pick out a better road. It is for you to guide your clairvoyante in it carefully and firmly.

108. When I intrusted to the printer my manuscript of the "Secrets," I had not a duplicate of it, my employment permitting me not to copy such a work: I recommended it, therefore, to M. Mirande, director of the printing-office, harassed as I was by a secret inquietude, still further augmented by the somewhat unfavorable disposition of mind into which my prospectus had thrown certain members of different sects. Several of them having come to me for more ample information as to the religious tendency of this work, I had frankly answered them that my object was to tell all that had been revealed to me, without, in aught, perverting the meaning to the advantage of any particular belief. I agreed not with these gentlemen for two reason: 1. I believe God to be infinitely good—not subject to fits of vengeance and cruelty. 2. I believe that in all religions we might be saved. No more was necessary for these stupid and egotistical men to make them augur ill of the soundness of my work. One day a disciple of Swedenborg quitted me, saying: "Monsieur, with such disposition of mind, you can but have written your work under a very bad influence. It could not have been M. Swedenborg who came to you; but I predict to you that in a few days he will appear in person to you yourself, to undeceive you and forbid you printing it." I answered this gentleman, that "the day I should have the honor of such a visit would be one of the happiest of my life." He quitted me in a very bad humor, being unable to contain his displeasure before a lady present, who was a follower of Swedenborg, and worthy of respect from her great age and enlightened understanding, the fruit of long and

painful meditations. Matters stood thus. A vexatious idea came into my head, that if it were possible, certain persons inimical to this work might make away with it. One day I received a proof to correct, with a part of the manuscript, of which it was the reproduction. What was my surprise on seeing that twenty-six pages of the manuscript had been so burned that it was very difficult to read their contents: these pages were actually those containing all the revelations of M. Swedenborg. I was confounded. Next day M. Mirande came to my house: I begged him frankly to tell me, since this accident had been attended by no untoward results, whether it had occurred before, during, or after the composition. This gentleman replied that it happened before the composition, in the room of the reader. The latter was about looking over the manuscript; some one came to speak to him; he laid down this part on the top of his stove, which was very hot at that moment, and perceived his distraction only from a strong smell of burning; he instantly withdrew my manuscript, which, had it remained there a second longer, would have been annihilated. I knew not what to think of such an accident, when yesterday I asked M. Swedenborg the cause of it. He replied: "This accident was prepared by evil spirits, who wanted to annihilate the truths I have revealed to you."—"Is it to you that I am indebted for its non-execution?" "Let it suffice you to know that good spirits watched over its preservation, as they watch over yours and your clairvoyante's. Had these evil spirits the power, they would lay a spell on you. But fear not; those who conceived such vengeance will be the first to read you, and will learn to repent of their error. You ought to remember that I came the morning after this accident, to assure you that your work would appear unshackled, for such is the will of God. Be calm: among my disciples, as in all religions, there are false men who pervert to their profit my writings; but they will not succeed in establishing their doctrines." I did not exactly recollect, not having taken down the date, whether M. Swedenborg came to see Adèle the morning after this accident; but I still await the fulfilment of the prediction of his disciple, and I think that, after reading this work, he will be enabled to judge whether it has been dictated by the evil one, or by a beneficent spirit. I availed myself of the presence of M. Swedenborg to put to him the following question: "At the last sitting you explained to me how years were estimated in heaven; but I did not perfectly comprehend your explanation: could you furnish me with a little additional information on this point?" "In heaven there are no years as on earth; I have told you that children dying before the age of seven years, were all crowned at that age, and those fifteen years old in like manner. I merely borrowed the word 'years' as a figurative expression, to make myself understood by your clairvoyante, for in heaven they are degrees. The age of seven years represents the degree of knowledge; that of fifteen the degree of love, and so on." Adèle said to me: "It is true that M. Swedenborg always spoke to me of degrees; but, not comprehending these degrees, I begged him to explain this to me otherwise, in order that I might the better reproduce to you what he said to me; for if I do not myself comprehend, how should I make you do so? Then again, he told me that time was not reckoned in heaven, where all was by degrees of affection. On earth, children seven years of age, are, it is said, at the age of knowledge; it is this want of knowledge that is crowned in heaven: the child, were it not to enter this degree till after twenty of our years, represents the child of seven years with us. It is the same with respect to the age of fifteen, when we feel on earth the first approaches of love. In heaven it is a degree—an affection similar to that of the child entering the state of knowledge. There is no limited time: when this affection enters the person, we say he is in the degree of love, which corresponds to the age of fifteen on our earth." I am aware that some of M. Swedenhorg's works treat of degrees, but I am not acquainted with them. (I leave the reader to judge of the revelations of this sitting, in respect to the accident that befell my manuscript.)

109. The count D'——, honorably known to all the magnetizers in the capital, one of the most devoted and generous

disciples of magnetism, a subscriber to the "Secrets," consequently aware of Adèle's speciality, solicited from this clairvoyante a sitting for the apparition of a deceased person, possessed, at the time of his death, of a brilliant fortune, and having made a will in favor of devoted servants and other persons. At his decease all papers of this kind disappeared, and it was to obtain information in this respect, without informing us of the object of his solicitation, that this gentleman requested me to magnetize Adèle. I asked for the deceased, this gentleman being in no wise *en rapport* with Adèle, and the latter, not knowing the object of the apparition, she said: "I see near me, and seated, an old man, who says he is M. D——; he is wrapped up in a sort of dressing-gown, of a brown color; he must surely support himself difficultly on his legs, which I see trembling under him, inasmuch as he has just risen. He seems to me not quite so tall as M. D'——, here present; he is thin, but his frame is sufficiently developed, betokening that he must have been pretty strong; his hair is gray, no doubt it was once brown. He has a very open and remarkably fine forehead, hazel eyes, his face, though thin, is pretty wide, his nose rather pointed, the complexion fresh and healthy enough. He must have been a fine-looking man, what we term *a nice old man*." The whole of this description is exact, with the exception of the dressing-gown; this gentleman having worn only a riding-coat when at home. Adèle observes that in that case it must have been wide enough to cross over the chest like a dressing-gown, and over his knees where he crosses it as if afraid of the cold." This observation is acknowledged as true; M. D'—— can not call to mind whether his nose was pointed; Adèle takes her own in her hand and gives it the form of the one she wishes to describe, what we term an aquiline nose, but somewhat sharp at the end. We verify a portrait which M. D'—— has in his hand; the nose in this is of the same shape as Adèle has shown, the nostrils having this remarkable peculiarity that they are much shorter and more arched than the part separating them, thus giving it the form described by Adèle. The latter could not have seen this portrait, which she did not know was in the pocket-book of M. D'——, particularly as she had not the faculty of seeing objects at hand; had she seen it she could not have described the old gentleman as seated. The portrait representing only the bust, she had seen him in a riding-coat and not in a dressing-gown. Let us continue. "This man has a very meditative air, he was not very communicative with persons of a different persuasion to himself; he was well informed, and possessed a fine library. He has an excellent heart, upright, just, and open; he is much hurt at the turn his affairs, relative to the property, have taken. He had with him two women, one taller than the other, one older than the other. The tallest often entered his room; through her ministration is it that important papers have disappeared to the profit of a third woman who stood in no need of this increase of fortune, but she has a hard, selfish, covetous heart. She possesses those papers which have made her richer and at the same time more detestable, by the spoliation she operated to the prejudice of unfortunate creatures who had more need of the property than she. This woman is not alone, she has accomplices: in the first place those who gave up to her these papers, inasmuch as she did not take them herself; she could not do so, but there were others deposited with certain persons, which she knew of and bought up. This is the cause of her present uneasiness; she is far from being happy; she fears their indiscretion, she will give up the papers, and the unfortunate persons they concern will enter upon their rights." At my observation that it depends only on her will to destroy these papers, Adèle resumes: "That does not depend on her, the finger of God is there; she can not do it, she has taken them up several times to throw them into the fire, but an invisible hand held her back, and she was let off to hide them anew; they were first in a clothes-press, then secreted in the wainscotting, then under the floor; she knows not where to put them. She is already eaten up with remorse, and the beneficent spirits will so prevail over her that she will find an opportunity, a pretence, to deliver up these papers. This gentleman assures me that the heirs whom they concern have no reason to be discouraged—that right will be done them without any legal proceedings; for nothing could be proved. It must come of itself through obsession, and this will take place sooner than it is thought. This woman is so monstrous that she herself accuses the unfortunate creatures she has robbed. Oh! miserable wretch, you already suffer much; your torments are not at an end!" exclaims Adèle.—"By what means can they recover this succession?" "Through the means of M. D'——, here present, who was left executor to the will; who is the only one who can do it, and is interested in it by his duties as testamentary executor."—M. D'—— is so moved, and convinced of the reality of what he hears, that he is unable to hide a few tears offered by his sensibility to misfortune. A servant of the deceased, who faithfully discharged his duties to his master for twelve years, and who is better enabled than any other to recognise the truth of these details, asks if he was not put down in the will? "Yes," replies his master; "I am grieved at the injustice of this woman, whom, when on earth, I knew well enough to mistrust her, but not well enough to baffle her intrigues. You will lose nothing, justice will be done."—"Did you not put out at interest some money for me?" "No, I did intend doing so, but I put you down in my will. I spoke of this, my intention, to some one."—M. D'—— says that it was to himself that this gentleman made this confidential communication, and that he is the only person who can settle the business, provided he had the papers. The poor servant cries out to Adèle: "Could we not seize these papers?" The latter replies: "You want to know if I could deliver them up to you? I see them very well; but to take them, where they are, we must be authorized. How effect a legal seizure without more proofs? She is rich and you are poor; do not grieve, He who rules all is more powerful than this wretch. Let those act who concern themselves themselves spiritually with this affair; it can not long resist their obsession."—Further questions being needless, I rouse Adèle. M. D'—— congratulates her on her excellent clairvoyance, and declares himself convinced of what

I have advanced in the "Secrets." Persons who can see only matter will never believe but that this woman would make away with these papers; but materially speaking and thinking, she would make away with them, as she would fear the indiscretion of those who gave them up to her and those who aided her in this spoliation. The papers by this fact being a primary cause, would become a secondary one. This woman must have made this reflection, which diverted her from all thought of destruction: she still finds it in her power, by preserving them, to repair at a later period the wrong she has done; no longer having them, and being denounced by her accomplices, she would fall into greater difficulties than ever, having thus no proof of the quantity and value of the gifts, which might then be estimated at more considerable sums. Without admitting the intervention of spirits, if we stop at this thought it is sufficient; but, for my part, I believe what I heard. Adèle was so lucid in all she said, that she surely spoke the truth as to the spiritual obsession this woman would undergo, and which, sooner or later, will force her to repair her wrongs.

110. The abbé A——, a doctor of divinity, a man of profound learning, travelling to acquire fresh knowledge, of an open and sincere heart, a Spaniard by birth, on his arrival in Paris, heard in all quarters much talk of the phenomena of magnetism; which so piqued his curiosity that he addressed himself to the baron Dupotet, as the man of the highest standing in this science, and best enabled to demonstrate its reality, possessing saloons, and a journal, in which the most curious and novel facts are brought to light after verification and an impartial judgment. M. A—— became acquainted, through this channel, with the publication of the "Secrets of the Life to Come Revealed," to which he subscribed, as it might possibly be in consonance with his beliefs, and throw light on a few psychological questions which had hitherto remained unsolved. Scarcely had he read the work, than, as a studious man, he hastened to pay me a visit, and submit to me some reflections suggested to him by different passages in my work. I took upon myself to give him a proper solution of them; he then

said to me: "Monsieur, it is a matter of discussion between us, if you wish to accept it; but there is a more positive fact on which I desire to be enlightened, that is, to see, by myself, whether it be possible to evoke the souls of the deceased. I believe, above all men (by my ministry) in their existence; but I very much doubt the possibility of our entering into communication with them in the manner you announce." "Try," replied I; "you will better believe by your own experience than my word." "To try," resumed he, "there must be suitable subjects, and I have none. If a clairvoyante could only describe to me a brother I lost now about two years ago, I would then believe in what you announce, and, what is more, I would say that your book is an immense event for psychology." Adèle, present at these observations, seeing how desirous this gentleman was of being convinced, and assured, above all, of his good faith, said to me: "If you wish to send me to sleep, we will beg of God to grant us this favor." As we perceive, all was improvised, and the gentleman stranger, delighted at Adèle's offer, eagerly accepted it. Scarcely was she in the state to answer, than I asked for the name of the deceased, not wishing any communication to exist between him and Adele; he answered me "Joseph A——." We asked for the latter. After a moment's waiting, Adèle said: "I see before me a man rather taller than the gentleman here present, with brown hair, a mild and expressive look, of a pretty good mien, slightly colored. He seems to me an affable man, but severe in his ministry, for I see him in a very droll dress; he has a sort of wide pantaloons made in a queer fashion, and of the color of pansy; I can't see the colors very well, he is rather too far off. He has small open shoes, and I see a sort of mantle over his shoulders. Oh! but it is a fine costume, I never saw anything like it; this mantle seems to be a silk one and of a deep scarlet color, it comes down to a point as far as his knees; he wears also a small white collar that comes down over this mantle or cloak; I don't know what it is called, but it has no cowl, such as our priests have to their cloaks. Ah! good heavens, 'tis pretty, this costume, I should never grow tired of looking at it; he has a small hand. What could this man be? Not a priest, he has not the dress of one."—"Ask him where he died?" "He is a foreigner, he answers me a droll name, I can't repeat it. He could not speak French, he makes signs to me."—"Did he not say Alicant?" "Yes, with two other outlandish words. I'faith, I don't know, not I."—"Of what disease did he die?" "A disease of the chest. Oh! he was long ill, he supported his illness with great resignation and fortitude. I am certain that he was a good and open-hearted man; he was very fond of his brother. I told him that he was here, and he made signs to me that he was always thinking of him."—"What age does he appear to be?" "I should say about five-and-forty."

Observations.—M. A—— acknowledged the exactitude of all these details. What Adèle takes for a sort of pantaloons is an ornament similar enough to a priest's stole, appearing to the eye like the two legs of a pantaloon. This gentleman was fifty-one years of age; he did not look so old. He was a Spanish canon, and unacquainted with the French language. M. A—— finds not a syllable to retrench from these details; he puts his hands up to his face, and exclaims: "'Tis enough to upset all reason—all received ideas; I am convinced—thanks, thrice thanks. The details of the dress were sufficient for me; there is nothing like it in France; you can have no notion of it." Astonishment, admiration, were the accompaniments of this sitting. It remains for me, however, to explain why this man could not answer. When I said that the language of spirits was *unique*, universal, the language of sensations, still there are exceptions; the fact being that the clairvoyante must be in a very elevated state to communicate by sensation, and interpret the meaning of it in material language. Adèle gave us a proof of her good-will, by answering us questions which she herself must have interpreted to the deceased by the aforesaid language; but as this requires much study on the part of clairvoyantes, in order to steer clear of errors, they generally dislike this kind of communication. If clairvoyantes answer not suitably the questions put—the effect of a bad interpretation—it appears ridiculous, as we have seen in the case of Father Lauriot; they feel that they can not thus compromise the truth of these perceptions by needless questions in the very presence of the apparition. This proves that there is no communication of thoughts, as they would answer all. I am not always able to know what I desire; and what I do not desire is often explained to me with details that leave less room for doubt than the solutions I demand. Therein, then, is a mission which God alone knows.

111. M. B——, a magnetizer and subscriber to the "Secrets," desires an apparition-sitting. No sooner is Adèle in the required state than we ask for M. B——, Earnest Paul, a deceased brother of M. B——; the mother of this gentleman is present at the sitting. Adèle says, "Here he is."—"Give us a description of him." "I see him with bright chesnut-colored hair, and fine open forehead; eyes approaching a hazel color, brows sufficiently well arched; nose somewhat coming down to a point; mouth middling size: he wears mustaches, which are lighter than his hair; he has a clear, pale, delicate complexion; round chin; delicate frame, though he must have been pretty strong; illness has weakened him considerably; he wears a dark-colored coat—an olive color, I believe; he has a doleful, calm, suffering look; he has surely labored under some affection of the heart and chest, and experienced great weakness in the legs. He was not without his sorrows—he inwardly tormented himself without showing it; he was at times meditative and absorbed in gloomy ideas; he loved some one, and this was the principal cause of his sorrow; he was very sensitive."—"How old does he look?" "About one-and-twenty; his stomach has been greatly weakened by youthful excesses."—"To whom is he united in heaven?" "I know not whether it be his sister that he points out to me. I see a dark young girl, with fine black eyes and rosy cheeks."—"Ask him who this young girl is; he has no sister dead; is it a relative?" "No, this young man did not always live in Paris; he knew this young girl in the country."—"Is it his companion?" "No, his companion is still on earth; this young

girl is a friend."—"By whom was he received in heaven?" "By his grandfather."—"His father had a dream, in which he beheld his son in heaven with his grandmother." "The dream is true, but the first person who received him was his grandfather, his father's father—he whom he knew on earth; he opened to him his arms, the young man rushed into them: his grandmother was among the rest of the persons who awaited him. It is impossible to seize at once the picture of such a reception. He still found himself under the influence of a sort of bad dream; it was his grandfather whom he first recognised. He had scarcely any agony. He did not believe in magnetism; he desires me to tell his brother that he believes in it now."—"Who watched over his dead body?" "His family."—"Where was it deposited?" "In Père-La-Chaise."—"Did it remain in the same grave?" "No, it was removed to that of his grandfather, the person who first received him in heaven."—"Who were the persons who followed him to the grave?" "He noticed his brother more than any of the rest." Adèle is fatigued, and we leave off. M. B——, the brother, is quite delighted at this experiment, but his mother is plunged into the most profound grief: her son tells her, through Adèle, not to mourn for him, as he is much happier than she is; he would that her time of trial were over; he came to visit her several times in her sleep, in order to comfort her; he did not come to remind her of him in order to add to her grief, as he well knew the bitterness of her regret. He appeared likewise to his brother; he will appear to him again: he thanks his brother for having buried him. M. B—— finds not a syllable to retrench from this mass of details; his mother preserves but a single doubt as to the shade of the eyes—they can not exactly recollect what color they were. God has permitted that our faith should be strengthened more and more. M. B——, desirous of concealing his name, out of family considerations, signed the duplicate of this sitting, to guaranty me in future against the reservations that some forgetful and wrangling men might raise as to the reality of what they have heard and acknowledged as true. Henceforth, I shall act in the same way. The morning after this sitting, M. B—— came to my house to tell us that he had called together his family, to make sure of the precise color of his brother's eyes, and that the generality of reminiscences was in favor of the color described by Adèle. This particularity gave me great pleasure, inasmuch as this gentleman having said to Adèle, "You are wrong; my mother thinks his eyes were blue; do you persist in seeing them of a hazel color?" Adèle replied, "It would be very easy for me to say as your mother, since she believes them such, and that would add to the truth of all I told you; but I should be telling a falsehood and not saying what I saw: to me they are as I have described them." It was in consequence of this declaration that the gentleman convoked a family meeting, and thought himself bound to inform me of the result. M. B—— confided to me that he had often had a visit from his brother in his dreams; that some time ago he dreamed, that after his brother was dead and laid out, he beheld the lid of the coffin raised, his brother rise up on his feet, extend his arms, tearing the shroud, and say to him in a calm, steady voice: "Why do you weep for me? Don't you see that I am not dead; on the contrary, I am born to life—this is the entrance to it [pointing to his coffin]—we shall meet again; be calm and hope."

When M. B—— found a somewhat similar phrase in my *Secrets*, he was struck at the coincidence of such revelation with the assertion of his brother. This coincidence alone—God be praised—made a spiritualist of a materialist.

112. The abbé A——, already mentioned—appearing to be no longer convinced by the details given him by Adèle, on his brother's apparition, which he solicited at the 110th sitting—came to acquaint me with his doubts on this head. At this moment Adèle was asleep. He proposed calling for the sister of his maid-servant, whose name was Antoinette Carré, and who had been dead many years.* I asked for this person,

* This gentleman afterward told me that all the details of the apparition of his brother were strictly true; but some doubts had been raised in his mind by the observation that "these apparitions were but a transmission of thought." It was to convince himself of the contrary that he asked for a person unknown to him.

and Adèle said: "I see a person of middling stature, with light-brown hair, about five-and-forty years of age, not pretty, small gray eyes, large nose, rather thick at the bottom; sallow complexion, wide mouth; she has what we call a thick neck; she has lost some of her front teeth, and the remainder are little better than stumps; she wears what is termed in the country an undress—corsage of a brown color, striped under-petticoat, somewhat short; a full apron, such as countrywomen wear; she has a square handkerchief on her neck; her hands betoken hard work. She used to work in the fields; she had a brother, who died after her, but he is not in the same radius as she, for, without being altogether a worthless fellow, he was not very steady. This woman seems to me to have been a very good kind of creature."

M. A—— took away in writing these details, and answered me through the same medium. I extract the following passages: "After four times reading over to Marie-François Rosalie Carré the above description, she declared it so exact that she could not do less than recognise her own sister, Antoinette Carré, in the woman who appeared to the somnambulist; as to her brother, she declares that he died after her sister, as Adèle has said. She couples with all this a circumstance not unworthy of attention. She says that she dreamed, on the night of the 30th January (the eve of the sitting), that she was by the graves of her brother and sister, but that her attention was directed most to her sister's grave. (She had never before dreamed of her since her death.)" Signed A.

I will observe, in my turn, that M. A——, as well as his maid-servant, were not aware, not even the very day of the sitting, that we should ask for this woman. It was quite on a sudden that I put the following question to this gentleman: "Do you know any deceased person whose apparition could convince you?" To which he answered: "Ask for the sister of my maid-servant; so there will be no influence or communication of thought, as she is not here, and is wholly unaware of what is about to take place." As we have just seen, we met with perfect success; this woman, the better to prove to her master that what he had heard was true, declared that she herself had given her sister the square-necked handkerchief described by Adèle. The apparition of Antoinette Carré must destroy the malevolent objection of the transmission of thought; or, indeed, we are all insane in attempting to prove the *existence* of a soul to fools.

Fresh Particulars.—M. A—— came a few days after this sitting to my house, and informed me that his maid-servant had seen, the night before, a man from her own part of the country, to whom she read over the description given of her sister, which she had in her hands, asking him if he knew such a person. The man replied: " Why, it is your deceased sister whose portrait you have drawn; there's no mistake about that." —M. A——'s maid-servant observed to him that the description made mention of a small pimple on the cheek, and that she had never seen on her a mark of the kind." The man replied: "You are wrong, for she had one there," pointing out to her the place. This woman at last recollected it, and was but the more convinced, as well as M. A——, who desired this perfect exactitude, that left no room for doubt. The arrival of a third person was necessary to confirm the truth of this particularity, which, consequently, could not have been seen in the thought of any one. (I had forgotten to make mention of this little mark in the description that has been read.) M. B——, of the 111th sitting, came yesterday to tell me that he had a female somnambulist, who perceived his brother precisely as Adèle had seen him; she had told him the very same thing as to his reception in heaven by his grandfather. M. B—— asked her for a few particulars as to the young person who accompanied him at the time of his appearing to Adèle. His brother replied: "You knew her at Paris: you have been in her company. Don't you recollect an excursion that a party of us made on the water to a certain place, where we spent the whole day? there were two persons with us—it was this little brunette, to whom some one you know paid his court." M. B—— has a perfect recollection of this particularity. Here, then, is a fact extraordinary enough, to which I had attached no importance at first. This young girl, who appeared unasked for, and to whom we paid no attention, finds herself described and recognised by a second clairvoyante, whom M. B—— questions on this subject. In these experiments, there is a concatenation which it is not given to man to define.

113. M. Favre, of Lyons, a subscriber to the "Secrets," being at Paris on business, came to ask me for an apparition-sitting; he expressed a wish for Adèle to see his wife, Madame Favre (Marie Hélène, *née* Mathieu). Adèle said: "I see a woman still young, of middling stature, with auburn hair, hazel eyes, hollow and encircled with black and blue spots; nose pretty well formed, rather long than short; middling-sized mouth, thin lips, pale complexion, set off by a slight color, chin rather long, beautiful hands, although thin, well-formed nails, physiognomy mild and languid. Her ailing condition grieved her very much from the pain it occasioned her husband, and the persons who nursed her. She must have had an inflammation of the stomach; she was not treated rightly; she must have suffered, too, from the chest, and an affection of the heart. I perceive that she was greatly beloved, for she seems to me of a very sweet disposition; she had so little will of her own that she must have pleased everybody; she suffered with fortitude. Without her disease she would have been of a pretty strong constitution. She is an angel, this woman. She is very happy, but her happiness will not be perfect till she is reunited to her husband. They were born for each other, she dearly loved him: she is often with him; though, fearing to affect him, she keeps his material body in ignorance of this, but she promises me that he shall see her in a dream. I see beside her an aged woman, smaller than she is; she tells me that it is her mother who died before her, and received her in heaven; she had always dearly loved her, and prayed God for her. This woman has gray hair, but it must have been darker than her daughter's; she stoops a good deal, and this makes her look as if hump-backed, and gives her a very ungraceful air. She had an asthma, from which she must have suffered much."

"All these details acknowledged quite correct.

"Favre, of Lyons."

M. J. Vermale, of Paris, who had accompanied M. Favre, begs Adèle to ask for Madame Anne Louise Vermale (*née* Chardon). Adèle says: "I see a very little old woman with gray hair, she is very gay, lively, and cheerful; she has a very pleasant air, and is always smiling. She has very expressive eyes, a very open forehead, thick eyebrows; she is open-hearted and frank, not in the least afraid to offend persons by telling them her mind; her thoughts are as lively as her movements. This woman tells me that she is your mother; she was very fond of you, she had no other son but you, you were very good to her, so that she was able to appreciate you. She suffered in her legs which were very swollen and painful. Her death was easy enough; her stomach was swollen in her last moments, she was very much oppressed, could scarcely breathe; she must even have had the death-rattle, this was caused by the inflammation of the stomach. She was very courageous; she has small feet, and must have been very pretty in her day. She is very happy, always thinking of you as when she was upon earth; she tells me that she has already appeared to you in a dream, and will appear to you again."

"Acknowledged as perfectly exact all the above details.

"J. Vermale."

These two gentlemen, as magnetizers, appreciate with enthusiasm the precious lucidity of Adèle, take her by the hands and thank her with an overflowing heart. One would say that their soul was confined in the sphere of the departed spirits; no more constraint, a demonstrative happiness; a few tears are almost always the result of these sweet emotions. We see in this sitting three persons appear, one of whom was unasked for. The details, this time, speak not of their dress, but, by way of a change, give a description of their qualities, their ailments, their sufferings; all this proves to us that if the body or the image of the material body as well its accompaniments are not annihilated, the actions, the sensations, even, are from all eternity! In presence of such facts not a single doubt can be raised.

114. Adèle was suffering from a nervous pain throughout the entire left part of her head. At first we thought it a fluxion.

then an epidemic malady attacking all nervous constitutions. This pain varied in its crises; we thought it over at night, on the morrow it returned. Adèle could not visit herself (magnetically) in her accesses, which were not unlike fits of madness; her face became of a dark purple color, the lower jaw trembled convulsively, a tremor that gained the whole body; anger was the result, she struck her head with her fists violently. Scarcely could I prevent her from becoming a victim to her passion. In the intervals of these crises she no longer felt anything, and was unwilling to visit herself, for fear as she said that the pain would return. As I have before said, Adèle is very obstinate, and independent of my influence in her sleep as in her watchful state. I could not by any means induce her to procure for herself relief; we employed fumigations, cataplasms, cleared the lower passages, and I magnetized her perseveringly, but all was of no avail. Nearly three weeks had passed away, and we still had the misfortune to see her suffering without being able to afford her any relief, when I had recourse to another somnambulist, who prescribed a few remedies, which, however, were attended with no favorable result. I was ill myself, consequently not in a fit state to magnetize her. If I attacked the part affected by passes, I only made her suffer more. At first I took this additional suffering for favorable crises, and as the precursors of a cure; but it was no such thing. An idea came into my head to magnetize her at a great distance, by the look only, fixing the extremities of her feet for a longer or shorter period of time. This kind of magnetization procured but momentary relief. We were in hopes that, cleared of the redundancy of blood, she would be cured; such, however, was not the case. M. Blesson, a friend of mine, and a magnetizer, one of the best-hearted men on earth, perceiving my inability to perform a cure, proposed trying himself. I accepted his offer with joy and confidence, thinking that it was a beneficent spirit which, having pity on us, animated M. Blesson, and would remove all our inquietude. Under any other circumstance I should never have allowed any one, however well-intentioned, to operate on Adèle, but at this moment it would have been egotism; she suffered too much, and my impotence commanded me to attempt all. This gentleman did all that it is humanly possible to do under like circumstances, and obtained no better result than myself. On the 19th of February she took it into her head to snuff up powdered camphor in great quantities; this so irritated her that she found fault with my purchasing a pair of under-stockings, which I had procured her for that very morning, in the idea that they would keep up a gentle heat in her feet and disengage her head from the blood or fluid which might thus cause her suffering. At any other time Adèle would have thanked me for such attention, being as she was, of a just, upright, and grateful disposition. It was otherwise: she tried to pick a quarrel with me. I did my best to persuade her by calm and logical reasonings, but this brought on in her an alarming fit of madness. Her face became injected with a dark blood; she took up a table and dashed it aside, opened the window, and was about precipitating herself from a fifth story, when, as quick as she, and endued with a strength I never before knew, I seized her round the waist, pressed her against me with violence, and breathed coldly on her forehead, with such conviction, such power, that her teeth clacked, her whole body bent backward, and she uttered shrieks of pain, as if I were breaking her bones. (Adèle is a very stout, strong woman.) She begged me to cease this powerful breathing, which I can not too highly recommend to magnetizers, as having succeeded with me in many circumstances wherein all medical and human means appeared impotent. Could man produce, by other emanations of the body, what he is capable of producing, through breath, he would fancy himself a God. His error would be a very pardonable one; for it is necessary to have done what I have many a time done to appreciate so magical a power. When her head appeared to me cool, and her mind calm, we advised her to go to bed, which she did without any resistance. The blood flew up to her head, and an hour's delirium was the consequence. I magnetized her to bring back the blood to the extremities. Exhausted as I was, obtaining no result, I threw myself on a seat, my heart broken with grief and fear, the tears in my eyes.

I entered the state I have already once known, and the result of which I mentioned in my "Secrets," under the article, "Can Cures be performed through Prayer?" I prayed the Lord to extend his infinite goodness even to me, to restore to reason this unfortunate creature, who, I believed, had lost it for ever. I called to my aid the good Emmanuel Swedenborg, who, in so many circumstances, shielded us with his powerful protection, and enlightened us with his divine light. I remained at prayer for some time; half an hour had scarcely elapsed when we saw Adèle kneeling in her bed, turning toward the right, and apparently speaking to some one. I asked her who was there. "It is M. Swedenborg," replied she; "he is good, he is just, all-powerful, humane; he magnetizes me, and wishes me but good." I thought that she was still in her delirium. I attached no importance to this scene, which however greatly affected us; she lay down again, after an instant, and appeared pretty calm. I then proposed replacing her handkerchief on her head to keep away the cold, which was so inimical to her pain. She said to me: "My pain! M. Swedenborg has taken it away. I shall have it no more; he has thoroughly assured me of that." I perceived that she was asleep. I said to her: "Who put you in this state?" "M. Swedenborg. You may wake me; I am well." I opened her eyes. She was in her ordinary state, very much astonished at finding herself in bed, and having no recollection of what had passed. She was calm all night. The next morning she had no pain; the external sensibility, which had not left her for a minute since the invasion of the malady, as well as a few small ulcers and large swellings gorged with blood, which she had on her gums, all had disappeared. She could eat at her ease, which she had been unable to do since the commencement of the attack, especially of warm dishes, which redoubled her pain. I was disposed to believe in a miracle—if there be any miracles in nature—at any rate, in a superior action. On the 21st, I threw her into a sleep for the preceding apparitions, and asked her what we were to think of her pain. She answered: "We ought to thank God, who, alive to your prayer, favorably heard it. Our protector, M. Swedenborg, magnetized me, and removed my pain; he sent me to sleep, and assured me that I should feel it no more."

I leave every one to think of this cure as he deems fit. I prayed mentally; Adèle was in a delirium, and certainly did not hear me. Half-an-hour after, at the moment I least thought of it, so invaded was I by a thousand confused thoughts, M. Swedenborg took possession of her, agreeably to my wishes, and performed in a few minutes, what, in three weeks, the magnetism of two persons — somnambulism and medicaments — had been unable to effect. He restored reason, health, and peace, to a heart that was bereft of them!

NOTE.—Adèle has never since experienced a similar attack. Thrice thanks, Lord! thanks, good Swedenborg.

115. The 6th March, the abbé A—— asked of me a medical consultation for a person at a distance, in whom he interests himself. The consultation over, this gentleman desired to put the following questions to Adèle: "Which is the state of mind or thought most agreeable to God?" "That of having a holy confidence in him, and an ardent love for our neighbor." —"Are all religions agreeable to God?" "Yes, when they are founded on these two principles."—"But the practices of these religions, are they approved by him?" "Yes, when they aim at the object I have just defined."—"Still, human reason is less repugnant to accepting the offerings or sacrifices made to God in certain mild religions than in others which seem ridiculous or savage." "There are no ridiculous or savage practices in the eyes of God, the disciples of such religions believe they make themselves agreeable to him by offering him such a thing, or praying to him in such a manner. It is the love with which they are penetrated for God that animates them, and God accepts with the same impartiality whatsoever is offered him with a view of being agreeable to him!" —"There existed, and there still exist, nations that offer up human victims to God in their sacrifices; is that agreeable to God?" "Yes, for these men offer up to him their dearest possessions in the persons of their children, brethren, and friends; they give him a proof of a superior love which

God can not reject, especially when these men are convinced of the value of their offering, and make it not with indifference."—"In that case, in what does evil consist?" "In doing it wittingly."—"Deign to be more clear?" "The rational being who coolly resolves on an action which he knows to be bad in itself, and the results of which he has the conviction must create trouble, and are condemned by morality, such a one does evil, since he calculates it, appreciates it, and executes it for pleasure's sake."—"What punishment does God reserve for him?" "God consigns him after his material death to a place apart, where his thoughts are gradually purified, and make room for thoughts of love toward his neighbor; thoughts he has never known."—"Why has he not known them?" "Because he has had no confidence in God, who is the principal basis of all happiness."—"What is the effect of this confidence?" "That of receiving in one's heart a ray of the divine light, and driving from it darkness."—"What do you understand by light and darkness?" "Good and evil thoughts."—"How unravel these thoughts?" "This divine ray thoroughly unravels them; it gives birth to all the good thoughts that seek its influence, and drives away the evil ones that dread it."—"And in what way?" "In this way: the heart of man is more and more purified, stripped of the evil thoughts that oppressed it, and becomes acquainted with the greatest happipiness desirable—the love of God and the love of all!" M. A—— says that Adèle is in accord with the case of conscience we admit in theology; evil exists only in the knowledge we have of doing it. Reflect on this somnambulic morality, ye learned of the age! study it, and tell me if ever anything grander, more reasonable, and more admissible, ever emanated from your thoughts?

116. M. Duteil, a member of the Magnetological Society of Paris, and a subscriber to the "Secrets," desires like the foregoing persons to judge by himself of the precious clairvoyance of Adèle; he solicits the apparition of Madame Duteil, his wife, by her maiden name, without apprizing us that it was his wife. Adèle sees a young lady, who may be from

about eighteen to twenty years of age (she was twenty-eight), whose hair is of a deep flaxen, eyes of a dark blue, forehead pretty open, smooth and handsome, nose rather pointed, slight rosy colored cheeks, ordinary mouth, thin lips, round chin, hanging down a little, and forming the hollow under the lower lip; doleful air; she is not stout, her hand is long and thin. She must have been of a very mild disposition and possessed of a good heart. She suffered in the chest and from violent palpitations of the heart. Her speech is gentle. "M. Duteil asks whether she was married?" She replies to Adèle: "Yes," adding, "you know my husband well enough, and so does the person who tells you to ask the question." Adèle says: "He may, but I don't." M. Duteil asks whether she had any children? She answers that she left behind her a little girl. "Has she been long dead?" "Yes," replies she (she has been dead six years). Adèle again asks her the name of her husband. She repeats: "You know him well enough and so does the person present." M. Duteil then informs us that he knows this lady's husband well, inasmuch as it is he himself; this removes the inquietude in which Adèle appears to be in trying to find out who this man can be, and proves to M. Duteil as to all those who believe in the communication of thoughts, that if such were the case Adèle would have seen immediately who this lady's husband was.

"I acknowledge the above details as exact, excepting the age.

"DUTEIL,

*Magnetizer*, 246 *Rue de Saint Denis*."

Adèle adds that she perceives near Madame Duteil an aged woman, sixty years old at least, with gray hair, face wrinkled all over; she must have been very corpulent; she seems to her rather shorter than Madame Duteil, whom this woman says that she received in heaven in her capacity as grandmother by the mother's side. She has a very cheerful and pleasant look, and wears spectacles; this seems rather droll to Adèle, inasmuch as it is the first person she has seen wearing them. This apparition uncalled for, so much the more astonishes M. Duteil as he declares he never knew or saw this woman; it was not without some trouble that he was able to gather the following particulars:—

"I, the undersigned, certify that the grandmother whom I never saw, and of whom I could not have been thinking, as she died a very long time ago, at the age of seventy, constantly wore spectacles, and was, in fact, of a very cheerful disposition; this I have learned from her only grandson.

"PARIS, 10*th April*, 1848." "DUTEIL.

117. The prince of Kourakine, secretary to the Russian embassador at Paris, having read the "Secrets," presented himself at my house with the baron Dupotet, M. Hébert de Garnay, and a fourth person, to ask me for an apparition-sitting. I sent Adèle to sleep, and told her to ask for the princess K——, the sister-in-law of this gentleman. Adèle replied: "I see a tall dark young lady, about 28 years of age (she was 22), with dark hazel eyes, rather small than large, pale complexion, fine forehead, nose rather thick at the top, but pretty well formed, upper lip thick, eyebrows pretty thick and arched; a supine carriage, speech mild, air calm and resigned. This lady suffered much from the heart and the left side of her bosom. I perceive that that side is quite black; she suffered also in the lower part of the body, in the bladder, and very much in the head. She was not much of a talker. I see beside her a little boy of a fair complexion, about five years of age; she was surely fond of children."

This gentleman acknowledged the truth of these details, apart the color of the complexion, which in her latter days was of a violet color. He does not know this child, and prefers addressing metaphysical questions to his sister-in-law, through Adèle, to obtaining any fresh particulars as to her dress. She gives him very satisfactory answers, among others she tells him that she has already appeared to her sister (the wife of this gentleman) in dreams; that is quite true. She speaks with difficulty, with constraint, as she did on earth; this arose from her sickly condition which caused her much suffering. I did not get this sitting signed by the prince as he was to return; but the events that suddenly took place in France forced his departure; the testimony of the baron Dupotet and M. Hébert de Garnay would guaranty, if necessary, the truth of the above particulars.

M. Dupotet desires in his turn to summon one of his old friends, Dr. Dubois, who had been dead about fifteen months.

Adèle says: "I see a man, whose hair is quite gray, and very scanty in front; he has an open forehead, prominent near the temples, thus making his head as if square. He may be about sixty. He has a couple of wrinkles on each side of his cheeks, a fold under his chin, making it appear double; neck very short—he is a short thick-set man; eyes small, big nose, mouth rather large, chin flat, hands thin and small. He does not appear to be quite so tall as M. Dupotet: if he is not stouter, he is broader shouldered. He wears a brown riding-coat, with pockets at the side. I see him draw out of one a snuff-box, and take a pinch. He has quite a droll gait; he did not stand firm on his legs, he must have suffered from weakness in them. His trowsers are rather short. Ah! he did not clean his shoes, for they are covered with mud. Altogether, his dress is not a rich one. He had an asthma, for he breathes with difficulty. I see also that he has a swelling in the lower part of his body; he wears something that presses on it. I told him that it was M. Dupotet who asked for him. He talks to me of magnetism with incredible volubility; he speaks of everything at once, mingling all together; I don't understand a word of what he says; he speaks so fast that he even sputters."

M. Dupotet begs Adèle to ask him why he has not appeared to him as he had promised. He answers: "Give me time to consider where I am; I have but just arrived; I am studying whatsoever I see. I will give you an account of all when I appear to you."—"What day did you promise me you would do so?" "One Wednesday." Adèle adds: "This man must have been forgetful; I am certain that he was very absent in mind."—M. Dupotet again asks: "When will you appear to me?" "I can not fix the time, I will endeavor to do so within six weeks."—"Ask him if he liked the Jesuits." At this name he takes such a leap in the air, extending his arms, and exclaiming, "The Jesuits!" that Adèle quickly moves away, and remains so alarmed that she no longer dares speak to him. M. Dupotet declares that all these details are so very exact that he can not retrench from them a syllable. "This man," said he, "was of an inexhaustible conversation, mingling all the sciences, of which he was a great amateur, and so voluble of speech that he actually sputtered, as your clairvoyante says. He was very careless of his person, and was so absent in mind that he sometimes forgot to take his meals. Whenever any one spoke to him about the Jesuits he would jump in the manner Adèle has described. He was always very dirty; it is not surprising that the clairvoyante should see him in shoes covered with mud." He had, indeed, promised M. Dupotet that he would appear to him on a Wednesday or Saturday. M. Dupotet acknowledged the exactitude of this apparition in No. 75 of the "Journal du Magnétisme."

113. Madame D——, possessing, like every one else, her share of incredulity, wishing to trust to her own judgment, in preference to that of her husband (professionally versed in such matters), desires in her turn an apparition. She is accompanied by M. H——; and begs Adèle to ask for M. B——, Jacques. Adèle says: "I see a man, about thirty-six years of age, of middling stature; black hair, rather long, coming down to the bottom of the ear, but not as is worn in the present day; complexion pale, face thin; hazel eyes, large and hollow, but of a mild expression, nose rather long and sharp, air sad and downcast." Madame D—— interrupts Adèle, to inquire the malady of which this man died. The latter replies: "I don't perceive any grave malady in him—I see only indisposition; but, good gracious! this man has been killed! by a firearm—a pistol. He has blown out his brains! Oh, the wretch! I can understand his sorrowfulness. I told you so, those who commit suicide enter not forthwith—they wander around the earth!" —"What, then, is their suffering?" "That of being unable to enjoy light as the rest."—"When does he hope to enjoy it?" "When the time that he should have accomplished on earth is

terminated."—"That is to say that he will thus wander to the age of sixty, were he to have lived to that age materially?" "Yes."—Madame D—— inquires whether this gentleman knows her. "Yes; she is related to him by marriage."—"This gentleman only knew madame by her maiden name; he could, perhaps, tell you the degrees of this relationship?" "I asked him whether madame was his cousin. He replied: 'She is more than that to me! more than that!' From this exclamation, one would say that madame is his mother, or as much as a mother—at any rate, he seems to be as attached to her as if such were the case."—"Tell him she has married the baron D——: and ask him if she has acted agreeably to his wishes!" "Oh, my poor wife!" exclamed he; "may you be happy—it is the sole wish of my heart." Adèle turns toward Madame D——, and says to her, with an air of astonishment, "You were, then, the wife of this gentleman!" The lady replies in the affirmative—Adèle continues: "He says that he applauds this union; but, at the same time, he seems pained at it, for he was very fond of madame. This man, without being positively wretched, is not happy: his ideas have suffered—they are still agitated, and under the influence of those that drove him to suicide."

When Adèle asked for this gentleman, there first appeared a person about sixty years of age—a tall, strong, handsome man, decorated with orders, &c. Madame D——, not recognising in this personage her husband, pays no attention to him, and has no recollection of his being, or having been, as he terms himself, a friend of her husband's. Toward the close of the sitting I put a few questions to him, seeing that he did not for a moment, quit M. B——. He answers me that he appeared first, because M. B——, his intimate friend, who was asked for, had no mind to appear; that he dragged him along—must we say, by force; that we are indebted to his entreaties for M. B——'s appearance. This gentleman says that he never quits his friend, whose mental condition gives him much pain.

Madame D—— acknowledges all the details of the apparition of her husband as quite exact, and is confirmed in the belief that it was impossible to read in her thought, seeing that Adèle would have forthwith seen and told her that she was the wife of this gentleman — a revelation, for which we were indebted as we have seen, to a question foreign to this communication. Madame D—— is also further convinced by the double apparition, which she had not asked for, and the personage of which is unknown to her, and, consequently, not in her thoughts.

119. M. Hébert (de Garnay) editor of the "Journal du Magnétisme," more inclined to believe in the communication of thoughts than in the reality of the apparition, asks for that of M. J. Hébert, his uncle, whom he says he never saw. Adèle perceives a man about the same size as M. Hébert, but stronger, with auburn hair, beginning to turn gray; he is round shouldered. Here M. Hébert interrupts Adèle, saying that he can not appreciate such description, and desires, in order to be convinced, but one thing — let her tell him of what kind of malady he died. Adèle replies: "His complaint lay in the head; this man was insane. Ah! how disordered are his ideas. I see that he died mad, but I could not affirm that madness was the cause of his death; I rather believe it was the treatment he underwent." M. Hébert resumes, "My uncle became blind in his insanity; is this accident to be attributed to his sad condition?" "I do, in fact, perceive that his eyes are shut, and this proves to me that he could not see; but they were not completely closed. I see them half open. I can not tell whether this arose from his insane condition; I believe it is an effect of it, a congestion of blood. Ah! how droll is a madman's head.

M. Hébert asks what could have been the cause of his insanity. Adèle replies, "I perceive that an idea of interest is predominant."—"Is it a commercial interest?" "No, not a commercial interest, but a private one." M. Hébert says that this man became insane at the age of eighteen or twenty, and died at upward of fifty, having been neither rich nor in trade. We think that if Adèle's judgment is correct, he must have been in love with some young person richer than himself, and wished to be wealthy enough to wed her. With madmen the objects of their insanity do not always correspond with their position in the world.

To the name of Hébert there first appeared a young man from twenty to twenty-four years of age. I ask Adèle who this young man could be whom M. Hébert had forthwith dismissed as not being the person he asked for. Adèle replies, " It was no doubt the same gentleman who wished to appear to me as he was before being insane. M. Hèbert having desired to know of what he died, he, perhaps, reappeared in the wretched state in which he ended his days. This is merely a supposition of mine," repeats Adèle.

" M. Hébert (de Garnay) acknowledges as true only the revelation of insanity, merely knowing," said he, " this particularity respecting his uncle. HEBERT (DE GARNAY)."

Next day I requested M. Hébert to sign his name to this sitting, and this he did with a very good grace. But, would it be believed that this gentleman, who ought to have been convinced by the revelation of the insanity alone, which for any other would not have been sufficient, seeing that it could be read in the thought, took advantage of this circumstance to give utterance to these absurd remarks: " The somnambulist has failed; she reads in the thought. I was aware that my uncle died mad, it was not difficult for her to read this in my thought." I reply to M. Hébert: " If she saw this particularity in your thought, she has not, therefore, failed; if she has failed, she does not, therefore, see in the thought. To be consistent and impartial, you ought not to have stopped her in the midst of the particulars she gave you of the person, whom, as you say, you had never seen. A reason the more to be convinced that you had not this image in your own thought. But no, you wish this system to prevail, and you hasten to put a question that deviates from the true one; you are answered right, and then you exclaim that you were aware of this answer. Why put the question? If you were answered wrong, you would cry out still louder.

120. Hitherto I have omitted no error of my clairvoyante nor any of her truths. I have said in my preface of the " Se-

crets" that I should deem myself the most contemptible man on the face of the earth if I speculated in falsehoods. Because penetrated with this truth, I make mention of the slightest details concerning these apparitions, of which I could give a summary without entering into these minute particulars for which the reader may blame me, but which he will not despise at the bottom of his heart. Since I have just cited an inconsistent contradiction, I ought to follow it up with a ridiculous personage who acknowledges the thing he denies. This type of a man will form a diversion by its eccentricity, to the types hitherto known. The abbé A——, whose curious sittings and frank conversion we have here, desired to have his conviction shared in by a protestant minister, named Rostan. The latter had two sittings, and was convinced at the last one, of which I shall make mention after this, seeing that at the first one there was an involuntary error on his part in asking for the deceased. This gentleman signed the testimonial of this sitting with pleasure, because he declared himself satisfied; he made known his conviction to one of his colleagues who is the person we are about to converse with, and whose incredulity and ambiguous answers will be appreciated.

He asks for M. Francisco Solano Constantio. Adèle says that she perceives a person from fifty to fifty-six years of age (true), a fine corpulent man—that is to say—very broad across the shoulders and chest (not very so), smaller than Alphonse (true), dark brown hair (it was black), half gray (true), high, open forehead (true), sensitive sight, what is termed weak sight (true), middling size eyes of a dark blue (true, but they were large), eyebrows turning gray (possible), nose broad at the top (I know not), I see a scar on his right cheek (I know not), countenance meditative and agreeable (true), rather cheerful than austere (true), he has a sweet smile (true); he has still all his front teeth (true); he has suffered from oppressions (true); he had an affection of the heart causing violent palpitations. He was weak on his legs and forced to sit, as if subject to fits of fainting (I know not), I presume that he had the gout in his right leg (I know not), I see no mortal malady in this man, only his ideas seem to me disordered, wild (he died of apoplexy). He often felt a great heat in the lower part of his body, and this often disturbed the whole system (I know not). He had gray whiskers (true); wore a riding-coat, white cravat, his shirt-collar turned down (I know not).

"He was exceeding corpulent; a particularity which the somnambulist neither made mention of nor saw.

"C. D. BOSNEVILLE,
"*Minister at Lisieux.*"

"Do you recognise in the portrait just shown you that of the man you asked for?" "No."—"For what reason?" "Because he was exceedingly stout, and his particularity has not been spoken of as very remarkable."—"When the clairvoyante told you at the commencement that he was a fine corpulent man, you replied: 'Not very so;' this scarcely accords with what you now observe to me. Did you know this man well, and did you see him at the time of his death?" "I knew him very well; I even dined with him a few days before his death." —"How is it that knowing him so well, you can not say whether he was dressed in the manner described to you? In this apparition are found six-and-twenty particulars, fifteen of which you acknowledge as true; to six of them you answer, 'I know not;' to one—'It is possible.' That which you acknowledged as possible, and the ten that you are not aware of, may very well correspond with the fifteen you confess to, thus not one could be rejected. You are not convinced; we will ask for another apparition, but first swear to me that the person you are about to ask for is really dead, and that your intention is not to gainsay or influence the clairvoyante in order to make her err?" "I swear it."—"What is the name of the person you demand?" "Robert Pitter."

Adèle says: "I see a person older than the first one (true); he is tall and rather thin than stout (true); hair more of a flaxen than auburn (true); face very thin (true); forehead rather prominent than flat (true); nose long (true); nostrils open (tolerably so); eyes hollow (on account of his thinness): they do not seem large (they were large, not extraordinarily so); cheek bones prominent (on account of his thinness); mouth rather large than small (true); chin long (true); the neck appears long (true); a frill to his shirt (sometimes); dark colored pantaloons (true); he did not wear boots, he wore shoes (true); he had a dry cough (pretty often); he suffered in the chest and stomach (when dying, yes). The seat of his complaint was there."

Now, this is what the gentleman writes at the bottom of the testimonial:—

"She presumes that his lungs were affected. The doctor says that it was the gout in his stomach. He had an aquiline nose. Apart this the description is exact.

"C. de Bosneville,
"*Minister at Lisieux.*"

"Well, monsieur, are you convinced?" "No; she did not say that he had an aquiline nose."—"Recollect, monsieur, that she could not find the expression, and the better to make you comprehend how she saw it, she dwelt upon the end of his nose, thus making it bent in the middle, and consequently aquiline." "I did not perceive that."—"M. Rostan, your friend, M. Blouet, and myself, all three of us perceived it and rightly understood it." "Possibly; but I can not believe that the person who came was the one I asked for."—"Will you read over again the written description, and point out in your handwriting where you find there is any error." "Yes."—This gentleman returns to me the paper we have just read, signed with his own hand, with the words as I have given them between parentheses.

"If I let you speak with this person and he answers your questions, will you believe?" "Yes."—"Ask what you please?" "Was Jesus Christ God, as to his human part as in his spiritual part?" "He was God in his divine part, and not God in his human part."—"In heaven is he looked upon and recognised as God?" "Yes."—"Was he conceived by the Holy Ghost?" "Yes."—This gentleman declares himself satisfied with these three answers; but Adèle seems not to be in the least so, she says to me: "I can but reproduce the truth;

these things were answered me, I was bound to tell you them; as they accord not with what M. Mallet once told me, aid me in asking for him that I may see what he will oppose to the minister who has just made me these answers." This observation of Adèle sharpens our curiosity; we are eager to obtain an answer. M. Mallet comes and throws light on the question by these words: "Monsieur is a protestant minister and belongs to a society of similar persuasions. It is the same with all spiritual societies, they continue holding the same beliefs as they had on earth." "But you, a catholic minister, what do you think of these things, your religion admits them likewise?" "I am not of the same opinion in this respect." I observe to Adèle that in such case it is very difficult for us to obtain the truth, and advise her to search for it by herself. She was very much fatigued, and unable to give us the solution.

M. Rostan asks M. de Bosneville what he thinks of an image that makes such answers. The latter says: "They would induce me to believe in the real presence of our pastor; but I am not convinced of it." "Where do you think that she could get the exact description she has given you, and the words you have heard?" "She may suppose all this." I ask this gentleman in my turn whether he could by the same suppositions reproduce to me the same amount of particulars as he has just heard, with respect to my mother, who is dead. He replies: "I could not; but that does not prove to me that this gentleman was present here." I reply to him in my turn, "God bless you." This gentleman finds himself in the sorry position of denying what he affirms, as I have already said. It is a contradiction that I should never have thought it possible to meet with in an educated man. What must he think of a testimonial which he signs as exact, and denies as true?

121. On the evening of the foregoing sitting M. Lemoine, a magnetizer and an excellent somnambulist, came to beg of me to magnetize a lady, his somnambulist, in order to see if I could obtain more decided effects than himself. Scarcely had I begun, than Adèle, having absorbed, no doubt, all the fluid that I gave this lady, fell asleep and into a state of catalepsy. I

quitted the lady to attend to Adèle, whose arms only were paralyzed. I asked her the cause of this; she replied that, having been magnetized in the afternoon, she was not yet freed from the magnetic currents passing from her to me; that these same currents had invaded her, bringing in their train the nervous irritability of the lady I was magnetizing, and this had occasioned the catalepsy. I disengaged her, and left off magnetizing the lady, seeing that a third person wâs beginning to feel my influence, M. Lemoine himself, who could scarcely keep himself awake. We altered the arrangements of this *soirée*, foreseeing that, otherwise, I should have three clairvoyantes at once to guide and question. This *soirée* was solely at Adèle's expense, and we had no reason to repent of it; she gave a medical consultation to the lady, whom she saw for the first time; this proved (from the lady's own affirmations) to all the persons present that she was as powerful a clairvoyante for diseases as for spiritual perceptions. I addressed to her the following questions, which the abbé A——, present at this sitting, begged me to put to her: "Was Jesus Christ God, in his humanity as in his spirituality?" "He was God only in his spirituality?"—"Had he two bodies, one material and the other spiritual?" "Yes, and for this reason he died materially and lives spiritually."—"Is he looked upon in heaven as God?" "Yes, by those who believe in his divinity."—"He was not, therefore, positively God?" "He was the son of God, like us all."—"Was he begotten by the Holy Ghost?" "Yes, it is the Spirit that begets all."—"Was he begotten like all other men, through the medium of a man?" "No, herein it is that he is superior to them."—"You fall again into the same error as just now, when the protestant minister put to you the same questions." "Just then I could not explain what I know now, that I am in a superior state. What raised Christ above other men is this—that, by the way in which he was made flesh, spiritually and not materially, he had a recollection of his former spiritual existence, the one we have all had, and which we do not remember, from the force of our materialization. Not having undergone, like us, the laws of matter, he was not subjected to them, and remembered on earth what we shall remember in heaven. He had, therefore, this degree of spirituality more than we; hence his saying—'I am not the Son of man, my Father is in heaven; and not upon earth.' If all men were aware of their primitive existence they would not call themselves fathers, they would all know that they have but one Father, who is the only true God, and they would term themselves brethren as Christ termed them. If the power of Christ was great, consider how great was his suffering—he who came down from heaven upon earth, where he was to fulfil a mission so painful—he who had constantly before his mind the joys, the felicity of heaven, and the troubles and anguish of the earth. If you can understand his position, you will conceive his having the right to speak as he did; but you will also know that he never said that he was God, he was but his son, his envoy on earth, and he was continually saying to men: "Pray to my Father, who is in heaven." "What, then, is the mission he had to fulfil?" "To instruct men in the existence of God, in which at that period there was little belief."—"If he had not appeared on earth, could men have been saved in the sense understood by the church?" "Those who lived before his appearance on earth are equally saved with those who since then have not heard and never will hear of him."—"The men who preceded Christ, were, according to Scripture, in direct communication with God—as Abraham, Moses, &c." "Those who put Christ to death were not in communication with him, since they disowned the word of God, which Christ came to re-establish among them."—"All men who exist and have appeared on earth, do they descend from one man alone named Adam, and one woman only named Eve?" "This first man and this first woman are but a fiction, an allegory. The world has always existed, and will ever exist, just as it is, or nearly so."—"Did the Virgin Mary really remain a virgin after bringing forth Christ?" "Yes, since he was begotten without the aid of man. She is not in the same condition as other women."—"Had Christ any brothers through the medium of the same woman?" "He did not want for brothers, since we are all his brothers; but never man knew the virgin. She had too high an idea of her mission, after bringing into the world such a son of God, to give herself away to a man."—"Are the Jews guilty of the sin of Christ's death?" "Materially, in our eyes, yes; and, spiritually, he was doomed to be crucified. All passed in his mission just as had been decided upon. They did but execute what they were destined to execute."—"Is St. Peter the representative of Christ on earth? Has the power to bind and unbind men?" "One being only has the power to punish or absolve—that is, God."—"Does he who observes the ten commandments of God stand in need of submitting to others?" "He who observes to the letter the ten commandments of God can dispense with the rest."—"Jesus Christ, however, conferred on the church the right of making commandments?" "Jesus Christ taught the sublimest of morals; and gave counsels, which, if followed, would not have given birth to all the calamities of which we have been, and still are, victims; but men have perverted his morals, his precepts, his actions."—"He did not teach the communion as it is practised; baptism, as it is administered, and all the other ceremonies, which the church practises in his name?" "There is very little of him in what the church teaches at the present time."—"The gospel, however, ought to be sacred in this respect?" "The gospel is like the rest—whatsoever the hand of man touches it spoils."—"Was the birth of Christ predicted, or not, by prophets?" "No."—"The prayers which are addressed to Christ as God, or mediator between God and man, are they more agreeable to God than through any other medium?" "In the first place, it is better to address ourselves to God than to his saints; in the second place, whatsoever is addressed to Christ in the name of God, reaches God, since whatsoever is addressed to God, no matter where we be, is known to him, himself being everywhere, and in all."—"God, then, has no preference for any particular religion?" "All religions, without exception, are agreeable to him."—"Still this diversity of creeds, which bring in their train so many disorders and errors, ought not to exist under a God who should wish to make known the truth?" "Much rather should you say that something else ought not to exist. If man retrenched all that displeases him in the creation, and all that he can not account for, he would find very few useful things; but God thinks otherwise, and we can not be judges of his actions."

I beg to observe that I am not responsible for the repetition of the questions that will be found in my work on this head. It was M. A—— who put all those mentioned at this sitting; and it must be granted that Adèle answers them quite logically. The definition she gives us of the nature of Christ and his properties is unexceptionable. Though matter has some difficulty in admitting it, it would account for the state we name the ecstatico state in which he lived.

This sitting merits the attention of studious men. M. A—— appreciates the powerful lucidity of Adèle without accepting all her definitions, and finds her very consistent in her answers. I make the observation to this gentleman, that if it be impossible for history to prove, documents in hand, the period of the appearance of Christ upon earth, he might very well have preceded the pretended prophets who announced his appearance, and would give ground for Adèle's reply on this point. But it remains for us to find out how a material being should be engendered without the participation of another material being. To enter upon the subject, we will observe, that if there was a first material man he was born without the assistance of his species, and still more miraculously than Christ, who was fecundated in the bosom of a woman to imbibe there all the juices necessary to form the material tissues. So, then, what God may have once done, he could do again; what even he may not hitherto have done he can do whenever he pleases! We have seen in the first volume, from the explanation given us by Binet of the act of procreation, that when a Newton, a Voltaire, a Napoleon, or any other superior genius, is to appear in the world, God intrusts the care of his introduction into the organs of the woman to angelic spirits, who strip the material seed (which serves as an envelope to the spirit becoming incarnate) of all the material particles that could disturb the ascension of ideas, and the accomplishment of the great things which these spirits are destined to promote. Is there not a certain affinity between this definition and that of the incarnation of Christ, the latter having a far superior mission to fulfil to that of Newton, Voltaire, or Napoleon; being about to be the direct intermediate between the word of God and the heart of men, between heaven and earth, to live in a continual ecstasy, work miracles, which matter approaches through magnetism, but which it can not produce in all their force and splendor. It is, therefore, matter only that paralyzes us in this property which we find more perfect in magnetic ecstasy, wherein cures, and the most miraculous things, are produced, because the soul is less dependent on matter, a property which we find divine, through the aid of prayer, wherein all men then are direct ministers of God. We, therefore, naturally acknowledge: 1. That if we perform not miracles, it is because matter is opposed to this. 2. That all spirits being created from all eternity, with the same faculties, the same number of thoughts, if they be not all equal in genius on earth, the fault lies with matter. 3. That this inequality presents itself from the cradle. Therefore, the germ must have been impaired in its course, or by long abode in the being from which it shoots. It is more probable that its defect lies in the germ, since Binet tells us that angelic spirits are destined to purify it at the moment of its introduction. If it be thus, wherefore should not God, desiring to form a man more perfect than the rest, deposite direct in the bosom of a woman (of a very pure material nature), a spirit, without having recourse to the assistance of a second being, which, in such a circumstance, performs pretty closely the functions of a machine, by depositing there an object which it has received elsewhere. The woman performs a contrary office, she supplies this spirit with the material dress. Had God dispensed with her assistance, he would have transgressed the laws that rule nature. I see no transgression in freeing the spirit from this law of cohabitation, which serves, as we have seen, only to impair the germ in the impure deposite wherein it is obliged to sojourn, without any utility to itself. I see nothing more incredible in the birth of Christ than in the creation of the first man; and what I have just said, proves the almost possibility of cabalistical, and even catholic assertions! But it is far from my intention to conclude that such is the case.

122. The pastor Rostan, of whom mention is made in the preceding sitting, after the conversion of the abbé A——, desired to obtain in his turn an apparition. He asked for a person unknown to him, whose name had been given him: but a mistake had been made in handing over to him the name, hence a person presented himself, whose description we took, but whom we could not recognise; such, at least, is the version of this gentleman, and I do not imagine that he wished to impose on me. I proposed to him a second sitting, seeing, above all, that he clings to asking for a person wholly unknown to him, so influenced had he been by the arguments of M. Hébert. He then requested his maid-servant to give him the name of one of her acquaintances, who had been dead some time; he came with this name, and asked for Jeannette Jex. Adèle replied: "I see a woman who is not tall; she may be from thirty to forty years of age; if she is not hump-backed she must be bent a good deal, for she has a very awkward deportment. I can't make her turn round. Her hair is of a brown color, approaching a red; she has small gray eyes and a large nose. She is not good-looking; she has a long chin, a receding mouth, and thin lips. Her dress is that of a countrywoman. I see her in a cap, with two flat bands rounded over the ear. She must have suffered from a determination of blood to the head, and she was troubled with pains in the stomach. I see a swelling on the lower part of her body, on the left side, and a sort of tumor on her bosom. She was ill a long time."

M. Rostan presented the written description of his maid-servant, and returned it to me after adding thereto his signature and the following observations:—

"This is true as regards the stature, age, dress, deportment, malady, and the deformity. "J. J. Rostan."

This gentleman went and called upon M. H——, accompanied by M. A——, to tell him that he was convinced, and could not doubt the truth of this apparition. M. H—— replied: "It is not thus that I should pretend to make an experiment; your maid-servant gave you the name of this woman; it suffices her, being in your service, for the clairvoyante to see in her thought." M. A—— observed to him that the clairvoyante had never seen this gentleman or his servant; that she had had no correspondence with any one; that she had been unable to tell him the name of his father, which he caused to be asked of his deceased brother. This name, and many other things which she answers not, are, however, in the thought. If a name pronounced be sufficient to create a speaking, gesticulating image, answering questions that have no material solution, representing maladies very often unknown to all, deformities that have been seen by none of the persons present, to obtain counsels, find out hidden things, why then, in faith, you present to me a much greater difficulty than that of admitting that the soul can come to a clairvoyante, as we cause to appear to them, every day, material places which are at very great distances. Then, tell me how you would go to work to believe. I would give a name to a person, who should transmit it to half a score more, from mouth to mouth, and the last one only should ask for the apparition. What you therein propose is the same thing. It is not because this name shall have passed through half a score of mouths that the clairvoyante will lose the trace of it; and if the person who shall have given the name recognises the apparition as true, you will say what you say of all those who confess to you that they are convinced—you will say that they are simpletons.

I should advise this gentleman to say at once, I believe not in the existence of the soul; 'tis sooner done. As a chemist, I admit the life of aggregation, but I refuse its individuality, for the reason that I can spread out or divide the elements into myriads of parts, and collect them into one and the same essence. I will ask chemistry, in my turn, whether, because it is easy for me to collect in a bag millions of grains and separate them individually—to form figures and numbers, *ad infinitum*, with their assistance—I can snatch from them, or deny them, their life individualized in each of them? Whether, for instance, because I should have the pretension to take from them a multitude of different species and make them one compact mass, from which I would draw a juice or different juices, and having no affinity with the nature of the species which they were each called upon to propagate—whether I am right in thinking that the multitude of essences composing them, because I have united them, will not separate hereafter, to return to their primitive individuality, without mingling and losing in aught their property, and one day again compose the same grain that I have pounded? If you answer in the negative, Monsieur Chemist, you will condemn yourself; for, if you compromise the forms and essences in the vast laboratory of nature, I know not how you will maintain the procreation of each species by the laws of affinity and attraction—those two great, intelligent creators, that know so fondly how to find and join each other again, to separate and still rejoin for an eternity, without having the power to annihilate themselves. *You hear!* Ah! *savans*, you wish to explain the possible by the impossible; you wish not to refuse a sort of intelligence to the flower, the mineral, to gas, to ethers, and you would refuse it to man, or at least, if you admit it, you do so only momentarily; you annihilate the intelligence we term "soul," to the profit of the mass, though you know that the mass is but the assemblage of the infinity of individualities. What! I shall hear you maintain to me that such a color, or shade of color, can not blend with a different color, that it will come to decorate this petal of a flower without ever being deceived—regenerate such form without ever changing it. This flower and this form will restore to space the particles of which they have been but an aggregation. These particles can never be annihilated, according to your physical notions, and can never reaggregate to create other forms. Thus the violet will be ever such; the rose in like manner, in the same corner of the earth, in the same pot; the molecules and the aroma composing these flowers will be individualized to eternity: that is to say, that the violet will not be formed of the particles of the rose, because each grain has its essences of attraction; and nature, to millions and millions of combinations, in no wise mixing them, will ever restore to the attraction of the grain the particles belonging to it. What! I shall see this with my eyes every year — all my life; and you would deprive my species of this individualized immortality. What! it shall not be possible for my soul to communicate with its species, as this flower communicates with the invisible colors which are soon to decorate it! What! this law of attraction, of universal individuality of all the particles of the creation, exists for all, excepting for me! Come, come, gentlemen-chemists! you take phlegm for spirit, corruption for a mattress; leave, for a moment, your distillations and your cohobations; convey your eyes to heaven, with your hand on your heart; pray the great Distiller of life and light to enlighten you on this question; meditate on the phenomena of somnambulism — and you will no longer believe that you are only mere clods without life and hope!

I still thank you for your kindness in conceding us such an album of images ineffaceable and full of life. In our first volume, we ventured to propound that we must have within us a sort of living panorama of all that we could have seen or known in the course of our existence. We confined ourselves to this, and did not think that you would be so well prepared to admit a proposition which appears at first sight so incredible; you who refuse to admit the soul — a thing, however, very admissible. No doubt it is because I expatiated less on the first proposition than on the second one, that you return to it now. Well! I am more generous than you: I grant you that a clairvoyante may see this impression of living images, or at least appearing such; but I will ask you, in my turn, how it is possible to have in one's self the impression of images of things or objects, one has never seen and heard of? You will say that it is by a sympathetic thread that, from body to body, the clairvoyante communicates to the object. In the sitting about to follow, you will perceive that you are wrong; for the person appearing died in 1578. No being on earth could have known him, consequently the sympathetic thread is destroyed. Since you do not admit it, you concentrate it merely in this material existence. How will you account for such a person being seen? That is beyond your proposition. There are more than ten persons forming the chain of 1848 back to 1578; you may, if you please, assure yourselves of the description, whether as regards the person or dress. As for me, I have no need of these proofs. Had you read those which I present in this second volume, you would not thus venture to compromise your reputation as *savans*. You must be aware, however, that I could not have known M. Swedenborg, Father Lauriot, and many others mentioned in this work, who came unasked for, and declared themselves either friends or relatives of the persons appearing, and wholly unknown to those who asked for the apparition. You perceive it; 'tis an infinite maze, that requires to be studied, and I can assure you that I will tell you much more about it in the aforementioned work. In this I content myself with establishing facts which shall serve me as materials for the other. Oh! then you will see that we shall be able to understand one another, especially by leaving to Cesar the things that are Cesar's. Now, only, as a guide to you, remember that the clairvoyante can spiritually see men, places, and actions, passed ages ago, that are in no human living memory; that he can also see places and actions that will happen but in the course of ages, and this is still less in the memory of any one!

You have written, and all magnetizers have made these experiments, and still make them every day. If these *things* exist, be so kind to this soul, this image of the Divinity, as to admit of its being one of these *things*, and you will believe in its individuality as in that of all these *things*. It will not be more difficult for the clairvoyante to perceive than the action which it is to perform in a century or two. You understand, the action is the effect, the soul the cause, in simple physics. Good faith, chemists; I know your sensitive part: *you did not write this book*.

123. M. Lemoine, the magnetizer, desires to enter into com-

munication (through the medium of Adèle) with a spirit that used to be engaged in astronomical pursuits. He begs of me to ask for M. Antoine Mizaud, the author of several works treating on this science, and who died in 1578. Adèle says that she perceives a man about seventy-five years of age. His hair is gray. He wears a dark-brown great-coat coming down to his legs, with black velvet cuffs to his sleeves; large buttons; white breeches made of stuff striped as dimity used to be; white ribbed stockings, sharp-pointed shoes with buckles; good broad countenance; eyes hollow and small; large nose, low forehead, face wrinkled, though pretty full; air cheerful, &c., &c.—"Ask him if he still pursues the study of astronomy and meteorology." "It is his predominant passion."—"Can he give me any information on this head?" "That depends."—"Does he believe it possible to foresee and predict the changes of weather, their influence on the earth and the harvests?" "It may be: but on earth he had not arrived at the degree of knowledge necessary for such results."—"Could he answer a few questions M. Lemoine would wish to put to him on this subject?" "He will answer what God permits, because there are limits."—"Could he tell whether there are any elementary spirits?" "All the elements are penetrated with spirits—are but a compound of spirits."—"That is not what I desire to know; the cabalists pretend that these elements are inhabited by spirits bearing the human form, which they name elementary spirits, and which unite themselves to men according to the desire of the latter." "This gentleman tells me that whatsoever exists materially, exists spiritually. Thus in heaven are found air, fire, earth, and water, as here below; the spirits disengaged from matter that desire to inhabit the elements can do so according to their affection. He knows no other spirits but these in the human form. He does not busy himself with cabalism."—"You are one of the oldest spirits inhabiting the spiritual world we have hitherto asked for; have you noticed this length of time, and do you think there are any spirits that reappear on earth?" This gentleman bursts into a laugh, and replies that where one is comfortable, there is no wish to change quarters; that he has had no time to grow weary, and that we come but once upon earth. When in heaven we are there to eternity, &c., &c.

I beg those persons who may be enabled to assure themselves of the exactitude of the description given by Adèle, to do so for their own sake. This apparition, of itself, destroys the objection of communication of thoughts.

124. General De Wagner, a Prussian, and a learned magnetizer, desires the apparition of Marie-Hélène Wagner, his wife, and best somnambulist, who died some years ago. Adèle says that she perceives a woman, from forty-six to fifty years of age, not very tall, having auburn hair, dark-blue eyes (this gentleman says that they were light-blue); a very expressive and lively look; a fine, smooth forehead, like that of a woman of thirty; nose well formed, but rather large; slight flush on her cheeks, proceeding from her illness; pale complexion, dimpled chin, thin breast, but developed; broad shoulders, small, well-formed hands, beautiful nails. The state of her blood was the chief cause of her illness; she suffered from violent palpitations of the heart (she had an aneurism); her stomach was also weak. She must have experienced an uneasiness in the lower part of the body; a heaviness in the matrix, the ligaments of which were relaxed on one side, and contracted on the other; she must have suffered from the stitch in her left side; the blood flew up to her throat and head; she must have experienced fainting-fits, syncopes. She was weak on her legs, for I see her seated; she also experienced a lassitude in the arms. She was assuredly good, frank, and, above all, endued with great fortitude; more ready to pity others than herself."

The general inscribes these words at the foot of the testimonial:—

"Very exact. "General De Wagner,
"39, *Rue de Grenelle, Saint-Germain.*"

M. Gilot L'Etang, a wealthy planter of the isle of Bourbon, a magnetizer also, having accompanied his friend the general, asks, in his turn, for Françoise Grayelle. Adèle says: "I see a woman, older than the last one, with gray hair (it was white), middling size (she passed as tall); she is thin, and has black eyes, that look hollow, on account of the thinness of her face; nose pretty long, chin long, hands thin, back rather crooked. She assuredly was subject to fits of passion, that were soon over; her movements are still lively. She suffered in her chest, and had a dry cough; she must have been very much oppressed in her last moments; she had great difficulty in digesting what she took; she suffered in the back—this pain reached up to her neck; she also experienced a pain in the right leg. She was a very religious woman; her being so tended to make her calmly bear her sufferings. She was also a good woman, but not very communicative out of her own circle of friends. Her physiognomy wears an air of marked dejectedness."—"Whence proceeds the pain of which you speak?" "From a fall."—That is true; she put her hip out of joint, and suffered much from this accident. "Did she take snuff?" Adèle immediately takes a pinch of snuff offered her by this lady. The gentleman says that this lady, who was his grandmother, merely inhaled the smell of snuff.—"What fruits was she, above all, fond of?" "Peaches, strawberries, and the quince."—"That is very true. What odor did she prefer breathing?" "The jasmine."—"It is true that she had one at the foot of her window, which she tended carefully and with pleasure. But there was another odor that she was fond of?" "The lady makes no answer."—The gentleman says that it was that of the citron, which she was constantly scraping in her illness. Adèle exclaims, when I put to her the question, "I did, indeed, see her with an orange in her hand, and not a citron." The gentleman says, "Possibly she prefers now the smell of the orange. Will you be so kind as to ask her whether she has not any recommendation to make her grandson?" "Let him observe moderation in an enterprise he is about to engage in, and abstain from obliging a gentleman who solicits or will solicit him."

This gentleman thus signs the sitting:—

"The whole is conformable to the truth.

"GILOT L'ETANG,

"*Quai de la Tournelle*, 43."

I forgot to mention, at the sitting of General Wagner, that

he begged his wife (an ex-somnambulist, as we have seen) to visit him, and acquaint him with a few remedies for his health. What she prescribed for him was precisely what he was then taking, and what she had already pointed out to him when on earth. Adèle at this moment appeared much astonished, exclaiming, "Here is a droll fact. I see this woman, of ordinary size, gradually entering her husband's body! I lose sight of her, find her again, and then lose her again. How can it be—since she appears to me as big as he—that she can thus dissolve herself, shall I say, in his breast, and in still less too? O my God, how great art thou, and insignificant are we to comprehend such miracles!" We have no time to discuss here these phenomena which theology remarkably well treated of in former times, and the solutions which it has given us in this respect—solutions that have not been accepted, for want of proofs: magnetism is destined to supply them, and to revivify many beliefs which have passed for so many follies. We will treat of this article in a work that will form a sequel to and the complement of this. I will observe that, in the two foregoing sittings, there is wherewith to puzzle the detractors of these apparitions. Let them be read over again, meditated upon, and the conclusion come to will be that the communication of thoughts stands for naught in them, from the few errors which ought not to exist in them, and which I have taken care to mention with exactitude, in order to disburden my conscience from all accusation of partiality, and prove to men that I seek the truth with all the strength of my soul, and will combat error with the like devotedness.

125. Colonel Roger, having read the "Secrets," and noticed in them an article respecting the son of Louis XVI., begs me to ask for the monarch himself, who could give me better information on this head than M. Mallet had done. Adèle says that she perceives a corpulent young man of handsome physiognomy; but she makes the observation that, having seen his portrait, she can but give such a description as every one is acquainted with, only she says that she sees him in a coat without any decoration; he wears a white cravat, and his hand appears

to her small and well made. "Ask him if his son is still living on earth?" He replies, "Yes."—"Does he know where he is?" "He does, but has no wish to say. He makes the observation, 'With your republic, did you find him, you would guillotine him!'"—"Observe to him that under our republic no one is guillotined." "'Oh!' says he, 'I have no wish to tell you; he has suffered enough as it is, poor child!' He weeps," says Adèle; the latter shares in his sensibility.—"How did he escape from the Temple?" "By the assistance of a man wholly devoted to him, and who himself suffered a great deal."—"Who was this man?" "He won't name him; he is always in fear of compromising."—"Will his son be one day called upon to reign over France?" "He answers, 'No; there is a sufficient number of pretenders without him.'"—"Can he tell us any more about him?" "No."—"Is he himself happy?" "Yes."—"Is he with his wife?" "No; he knows her too well now."—"Did he suffer much in dying?" "He did not suffer a single instant; he was no more, before the instrument struck him!"—"Still, he displayed much courage; he even wished to speak?"—"Yes; but he fainted away on the block, and felt nothing."—"What did he wish to say when he was forbidden to speak?" "He wished to make his confession to the people, for he was a very good man; he was by no means culpable—he was the victim of intriguers; he still weeps. I won't question him any more. I perceive that I recall painful things to him. 'T would be wrong in me to continue."

Copy given of this sitting to Colonel Roger, the 7th May, 1848.

126. The viscount D'Orsay, president of the Magnetological Society, an enlightened magnetizer, in no wise doubting the future life of the soul, but desirous of knowing how far a clairvoyante could communicate with it, begged me to give him an apparition-sitting the 11th May, 1848.

He desires that Madame Marie Rose Blanche Boulenger should be asked for. Adèle says that she perceives a tall woman about forty years of age (she was but thirty-five), with auburn hair, fine forehead, fine black eyes with long lashes and of a sweet expression, nose aquiline and well formed, cheeks slightly colored with a rosy tint, mouth small, beautiful white skin, very distinguished air, queenly port; sweet look, affable and severe in certain circumstances; small, well-formed hand, and beautiful nails. She must have suffered from the heart, and also experienced a heaviness in the lower part of the body; she was very courageous, and not sufficiently careful of her health. I think she died of an ulcer in the womb.

M. D'Orsay puts the following questions: "Is she happy?" "She is happy like all virtuous women."—"Does she think of and take an interest in her children?" "She was very fond of her children whom she left behind her with regret, especially her last child who was of a very tender age."—"Is she satisfied with all of them?" "Yes; excepting one whom she is unwilling to name; she says that her son knows this gentleman very well."—"Is she reunited to her husband?" "That is to say, her husband is reunited to her, because he died after her; they are together, because they were very fond of each other. This lady's complaint must have been the cause of her sitting a good deal, for I see her seated in an arm-chair covered with scarlet velvet. I see beside her a little boy from four to five years of age, with curly flaxen hair; she was very fond of children, she tells me that this child died before her; his name was Edward; you have seen him at times at her house, with his mother. On the answer of M. D'Orsay that he can not recollect this child, it is told him that he will do so. M. D'Orsay thus signs the testimonial:—

"I certify that the above details are perfectly correct, and that I was greatly astonished, as well as delighted, to find once more in this description all the reminiscences left me of my mother who died thirty-three years ago.

"VISCOUNT D'ORSAY,
"*Cité Véron, Montmartre.*"

At this sitting we see appear, before this lady, a child that died more than thirty-three years ago, and this child even now does not look above four or five years old. We have before seen that children dying at this age continued growing—a law to which, as some persons will say, this one appears not to have been subjected, had we not a declaration of the same kind telling us that children dying as such appear to each other as full-grown men, and that the latter see them as children only with respect to their affection, which is, to be fond of children. The law that prevails over all the laws of the spiritual world seems to be this—whatsoever surrounds us is conformable to our affection. Thus, if this lady be pleased to see this child, a time that corresponds with a thousand years of our earth, she will ever see it at such age, inasmuch as a more advanced age, requiring a more fully-developed form, will suit her less. It will be asked if, in fact, the child is full grown or not? I will answer: It is of the form and size of all spirits; but the spirit that sees this lady enjoys only faculties and appearances of properties which the child had at this age—properties that may be detached from him, *ad infinitum*, and may satisfy a whole multitude, without aught being taken away from his personal individuality, as the flame of a taper is in naught diminished because it has communicated a hundred or a thousand particles of its flame to a hundred or a thousand other tapers.

We need but meditate to come to a conclusion; in combating we come to no conclusion!

127. M. Blesson, a zealous propagator of beliefs in spiritualism, as a pure and beneficent magnetizer, brought to my house one of his friends, to whom he had praised up Adèle's lucidity for perceiving and conversing with the folks of the other life (as is vulgarly said). This gentleman asked for his mother. Adèle sees a woman of ordinary size, about sixty years of age (this gentleman observes that his mother was but forty-four when she died). I made the observation to Adèle, who answers: "Possibly; but in the state she appears to me I should take her to be this age. I am certain that it is the gentleman's mother. Doubtless her malady pulled her down very much." This gentleman grants that such may be the case. Adèle continues: "I see that she has light, even gray hair; a forehead more prominent than flat: eyes large, and very dark, but not black; nose rather sharp; and a very thin face. This woman

was very mild and kind-hearted, of a lively disposition, but good and frank. She has a very thin hand, even a skinny one. She breathes with difficulty. She must have been frequently obliged to unfasten her dress, which I see open in front; she suffered principally from a disease of the heart. Her chest, also, was out of order. Ah! I see a lentil on her neck." Her son wishes to know whether she is happy. She replies: "Yes; but I shall be more so when my husband has rejoined me." She adds that she was very fond of him. Her son again wishes the following questions to be put to her: "Have you anything to announce to me to my advantage? Do any misfortunes threaten me?" "No," replied she, "my son is as happy as one can wish to be on earth; but I strongly enjoin on him to be very prudent, or some misfortune might happen to him."—"Does she see her daughter who is dead? Are they in the same radius?" "No; they did not sympathize too much with each other on earth; she merely sees her at times."—"Does she see her son Auguste oftener; he, too, is dead?" "Yes; he seldom quits her. She was fond of him."—"Has she anything to say to her son Adolphe, who is still on earth?" "He has no fixed position. He will not be exempt from trouble, but eventually he will be very happy."—"And her other son, Victor, what does she think of him?" "He would not have been in his present position had he gone on with what he had undertaken: but he will succeed, God protects him." This lady, before disappearing, recommends her son present to take good care of himself. The gentleman thus acknowledges the exactitude of the above details:—

"I certify that all the particulars given by the somnambulist are very exact, and conformable to the truth.

"C. Witt,

"*Paris, this 22d May*, 1848."

Allow me an observation as to the remarkable mistake Adèle made in the appreciation of this lady's age, according to her son. If Adèle had not been sincere, she would have gone from this estimation, but, on the contrary, she answers that she should be more inclined to think her above sixty than under that age. This gentleman's lady, who was present at this sitting, makes the observation, that the great sufferings this person has endured have possibly made her look much older; that her son is unable to judge of this, inasmuch as he had not seen her for a long time when she died. This simple observation destroys all idea of communication of thoughts! The rest is perfectly exact. The answers made by this lady as to the position of her children, still on earth, prove that she is not so separated from them as might be supposed.

At the same sitting, M. Blesson desires the apparition of his grandfather. Adèle says that she perceives a man about seventy years of age. A stout man, with gray hair, very open forehead, the top of the head bald, eyes neither large nor small. By-the-by, he has a large nose, well formed, but prominent enough; the lower lip hangs over a little: this gives his mouth the appearance of jutting out instead of receiving, as is usual at such an age; air very agreeable. He is very upright, and still appears very nimble; he died from a rush of blood to the throat. He was surely very fond of walking, as it now forms his delight. He was very partial to M. Blesson, and has dandled him many a time on his knees. He recommends him not to torment himself, as all will turn out better than he thinks for; he prays to God for him. He says he is very happy. Surely he must have had a bad habit of shaking hands, as he gives me his, saying that he has business to attend to. He still thinks of his daughter, whom he was very fond of, and who was very good to him. He again recommends his grandson to make himself easy, as all will turn out well.

"Acknowledged the above details as strictly true in every respect. "BLESSON,

"*Entrepreneur de Peintures*, 36, *Rue aux Ours, Paris.*"

NOTE.—M. Witt came to me the day after the foregoing sitting to tell me that he had questioned a person who had nursed his mother in her last illness, and she had acknowledged all the particulars as quite exact, particularly those concerning the unfastening of her dress in front, inasmuch as she was unable to bear any pressure on the chest. M. Witt had not seen his mother for eight years before her death; he could not be aware of this particularity, which is no proof of the communication of thoughts.

128. Madame C—— asks for Madame S. B——. Adèle says that she perceives an old lady, with gray hair, projecting forehead, eyebrows pretty thick, fine large eyes, nose ordinary, mouth well made, rather small than large; chin well formed, a pretty cut figure, slight rosy color on the cheek-bones, small, well-made hands, middling stature, and altogether a lady-like looking woman. She was lively and good; of an open disposition, speaking freely her mind, and sorry for it the moment after. She suffered in the stomach, and from palpitations of the heart; she had rheumatic pains, and suffered from lowness of spirits. She was long ill, and supported her illness with fortitude, told no one the full amount of her suffering, took consolation in religion, but in a religion of the heart. She must also have experienced a sort of weight in the lower part of her stomach. I believe she died of a suffocation, which, I think, was the consequence of a neglected cold. I see that her lungs are choked up—this was the cause of her difficulty of breathing, especially when dying; her agony was a very long one. Despite her great sufferings, she has an air of sweetness overspreading her countenance. She is an angel, who quitted the earth, regretting only those she left behind her. From her virtues she had no fear of death; she tells me that she is your mother. She must have had a son whom she dearly loved as she did you. She is happy, and desires you to be informed that you have passed through trials that will never be renewed. She recommends you to take good care of your husband, saying that he is a worthy man, deserving all your attention; she adds that her position, happy as it was on earth, was not sufficiently so to prevent her from tormenting herself very much, and that she was not truly happy till she entered the world of spirits.

"Acknowledged all the above details as very exact.

"C. C."

Madame C—— expresses a wish that M. F. C. should be

asked for. Adèle perceives a man less aged than the lady who just appeared, with black hair mixed with gray — a fine, tall man, forehead open, eyes middling size, eyebrows thick, and standing out a little, nose ordinary, but pretty large, mouth middling size, chin round, forming a hollow under the lower lip, agreeable countenance, short neck, broad-chested, shoulders rather thick, a good round belly, fine manly air. He must have had something the matter with his right leg; he apparently died of apoplexy. I discover no disease; I only see the blood rushing violently to the heart, which, perhaps was taken for an aneurism. He was badly doctored, it was but a thick blood that stood in need of being purified — that's all. He has a fine constitution. He was, doubtless, brave, delicate, loyal; there are few like him. He is happy and even blesses the doctor who so ill understood his complaint. He would not have committed a base action, even to save his life; however, he was not unhappy on earth. He sees his family, with whom he is not, at all times, inasmuch as he was and still is fond of walking. He is always thinking of those he left behind, and still preserves for them all his affection, excepting one friend, who caused him much sorrow in return for the good he did him.

"Acknowledged the above details as very exact, leaving to the clairvoyante the responsibility of her opinion as to the malady of this gentleman, who really died suddenly, and was treated by the physician for an aneurism.

"C. C.

"*This* 28*th May*, 1848."

This lady desires, out of family considerations, to conceal her name, making no objection, however, to signing for me the testimonial, and affixing thereto her address to be made use of if necessary.

129. M. Petiet asks for M. Jérôme Petiet. Adèle sees a young man, about twenty-four or twenty-six years of age (he was thirty), not so tall as his brother now present. Auburn hair, rather long; open forehead, arched eyebrows, black, and rather hollow eyes, nose rather long, pretty well formed, com-

plexion fresh, skin very white and delicate, mouth middling size, round, dimpled chin. He was weak in the chest; he would have been strong had it not been for this. He wears a large gray vest, old-fashioned buttons, such as are scarcely ever seen now. I don't think they are brass ones, nor of the same stuff as the vest. They don't look to me very bright; his pantaloons are of a dark color, and he wears low-quartered shoes, without any instep. This man was of a stubborn disposition, selfish, devoid of sensibility, had a sinister look, was not very communicative, devoid of candor, and having but little affection for any one. His death was natural, though sudden; he experienced suffocation.—Adèle stops her breath as he did, and coughs as he did; she says that "he must have had moxas, or a plaster applied to his back—and this accounts for the sore I see there. He had no disease, however, in that part; the spine was sound; those who applied such remedy to him did not know the seat of the disease; his carriage is bad, back round, without being humped."

M. Petiet finds nothing to retrench from these details, which are very exact, and confirm him in his belief that the application of this plaster, advised by a man, a stranger to medicine, brought on his brother's death, which was almost sudden.

"Signed the testimonial as very exact.

"PETIET,

"19, *Rue Neuve-Coquenard*."

NOTE.—The buttons that Adèle was unable to define were in metal, of a dirty-white ground, and surrounded by a blue circle. In this apparition is a phenomenon extraordinary enough: that is to say, Adèle experienced the same kind of illness as this man. I was obliged to disengage her by passes; she suffered horribly. What answer can we make to such facts? unless it be that the past, present, and future, are only conditions of being with matter—only a succession of different states, which in a particular state are ever represented in the present—and this would confirm (for this state only) the belief in a creation without beginning or end; that is to say, an actual, momentaneous one. Stay not to observe what precedes and what follows creation; the state which it represents to you is for you whatsoever is. I shall be asked whether this man himself suffered at this moment as Adèle appeared to suffer. I will answer, no. He is in the world of causes, wherein harmony reigns. Had Adèle been totally disengaged from her material body, the latter would not have suffered; it is only the sight of the state of the material body of this man at the time he suffered, that awakens in Adèle sympathetic effects in the material molecules, and produces this suffering, the impression of which remained on the spiritual body of this man. We have already said that it was possible for a clairvoyante to perceive a deceased being at any age of his life, as well as in any dress he may have worn at different periods of his life. It must be the same with all external wounds and internal diseases: nothing is effaced; they are so many impressions left, to recall, no doubt, to the individual possessing them, what he has suffered or done at such an age, and to facilitate in him the comparison of his actual state with his prior one, and this must ever be to him a source of happiness; his present position is ever preferable, and that to which he aspires, as an eternal progression, must surpass all the rest. Thus, how many persons on earth are there who feel sick at the sight of a sore or the letting of blood; how many sympathetic effects are there that are communicated in all nervous effects, such as gaping, laughter, crying, epilepsy, convulsions; how many persons that are unable to follow the respiration or diction of another person without stifling, &c., &c. I once noticed in Adèle a fact of this nature, which I find it impossible to account for. She was consulted by an asthmatical person; she was seized with sympathetic fits of asthma, and in a few seconds expectorated great quantities of thick mucus of a yellowish-green, with the same effort and as often as the patient. Her pocket-handkerchief was full of these thick humors in a few minutes! Adèle never spits; and, habitually, she perceives rather than feels the ailments of sick persons, although she has the two properties at once. I leave medicine to explain this phenomenon, as I shall leave many others to psychology and physics.

130. I ask for my father, who had been dead two months. Adèle sees him as she knew him on earth. I put to him the following questions: "Well! you who dreaded death so much, are you satisfied with being dead?" "What! dead? who told you that I was dead?" He feels of himself, and exclaims: "Zounds! I am as much alive as you."—"But you have left the earth." "Zounds! that's true: I didn't think of that."—"Are you reunited to my mother? have you seen her?" "Yes, I am with her. Magnetism did me good; 'twas that that drew me out of this."—"What! drew you out of this! you don't think, then, that you are no longer among us?" "No longer among you! where am I, then?" "In the spiritual world." "Zounds! that's true: but I don't always go——" He feels of his stomach, and says to Adèle: "Something must be done for this." The latter replies: "In the place where you are, there are no like wants." "How stupid I am! that's true. I have some trouble to habituate myself; I always fancy I am on earth."—"What do you think of the contents of the book your son has published on the spiritual world, and which he was so pleased at communicating to you, to console you and give you hope of a better world?" "What book, pray? All right; I remember; it is the truth. When is he coming to see me?"—"You know that he is still upon earth, and can not come to you before his time." "True; I didn't give that a thought. And you—pray, are you going away already?"—"I am not going away; on the contrary, it was I that called you here. Tell me how you pass your time." "I admire whatever I see; all this is so surprising, that it can hardly be believed. Sometimes I see myself still in my own room; then I feel and see that I am no longer upon earth; it's enough to make one lose his wits. However, I no longer suffer, and feel very happy." Adèle breaks off the discourse, observing to me that my father has been in this state too short a time to be able to give a good account of it.

My father was eighty years of age at the time of his death. Formerly a captain in the merchant-service, habituated to an active life, and having lived sixty years with seamen, by whom he was generally esteemed, he had preserved in his conversation a few terms not in use with educated persons. Adèle says that she heard them. What will no less astonish those who read these curious observations, is the seeming doubt, the uncertainty he preserves as to his present state; at times he confounds it with the terrestrial state; and this sitting, strange as it may appear, fully confirms the assertions of Swedenborg, in this respect, in his "Treatise on Heaven and Hell," where he says: "Many spirits, possessing very strong earthly affections, can not, on their arrival in the spiritual world, believe that they have quitted the earth; they often remain a long time in this uncertainty." And this is what happens to my father on this occasion. Oh, men! study this science, and reject not the works of a great ecstatico-prophet, a profound thinker, as a heap of reveries or hallucinations, valueless to science, and by no means conducive to the happiness of mankind. We will pass on to another apparition of a similar kind to the last one, presenting in another way the same solutions.

131. M. Blouet, knowing the speciality of Adèle from experiments he had solicited of her, and verified by other clairvoyantes (in his capacity as a magnetizer), came one day to impart to me an idea that had just come into his head, and of which the following is a summary: One of his friends possessed a house at Beauvais, in which lived a woman who had, it was said, fifty francs a-day to expend. This woman, as the tale goes, did not expend this money, but every day put by two louis, which she took care to procure at a money-changer's. She died forty years ago. This gentleman purchased the house she lived in, ransacked it, and found nothing. He sold the property to a third person, reserving to himself the right of making, at any period of time, researches in this house, guarantying, however, to defray all expenses, make good any damage done to the premises, and reward the proprietor with an equal share of the treasure. This gentleman had told his tale to M. Blouet, when the latter entertained the idea of asking for the said deceased woman, and endeavoring to obtain information on this head. He asked his friend for her name: I magnetized

Adèle, and we summoned this person. Adèle saw a tall, thin woman, about sixty years of age, with gray hair, large nose, watchful air, sharp in speech, miserly, common, and maniacal. She was in bed over the shop. Said Adèle: "I see a large, rusty key in her hand; I perceive that she is afraid lest her gold should be discovered. I ask her where she hid it. She replies that she put none away. She must have been troubled with an asthma. She tells me that she had three cellars." Adèle tries to make this woman speak in a more straightforward manner; she can not succeed, and begs us to inquire whether the description she has just given is exact; this would encourage her to ask the woman a second time. M. Blouet having no knowledge of this person, took away with him the written description to send to his friend.

Second Sitting.—We again ask for the woman with the treasure, though we did not as yet know whether it was really she who presented herself, having no certain information on this point. Adèle sees her, and says to us: "This woman has preserved her earthly affection, the enjoyment of gold; avarice has not quitted her, I shall have a hard job to get anything out of her."—"Try and make her understand," said I, "that her material gold is no longer of any use to her, she may have as much of it as she likes spiritually." "She makes answer," said Adèle, "that she is well aware of that. But when she returns upon earth, how is she to live?"—"She thinks, then, of returning upon earth?" "Yes, she is the first person I have heard make this observation; she has not left the earth, she is ordinarily in her cellar, which is the place where I see her, and where I suppose she has hidden her treasure; she, but a moment ago, said, how shall I live when I return upon earth, and now she says to me that she did not so much as put by a couple of sous a day." Then takes place between Adèle and this woman a contradictory dispute, in which the former strives to entangle her in order to snatch from her her secret, but all the clairvoyante's efforts are fruitless. Adèle says to me: "This money must surely be buried at the bottom of the lowest cellar, at the foot of the wall; there must be in that spot a wooden box, under a large stone. Let me be put in correspondence with some one who has lived in the house, I shall see best by myself; it is useless trying to get any information from this woman, and I won't speak to her any more; she listens to nothing, she wishes to conceal from me her thoughts, and treats me as a thief." I make the observation to Adèle that it has often happened that she has seen places at a distance without being acquainted with them; that she may, in like manner, try and find out this house and these cellars. She replies: "I do not say that it is impossible; but it has never happened to me to see places without being in communication with persons who are acquainted with some one dwelling in those places; then, when the person who is in communication with me desires to render perceptible to me another person, whose place of residence, I suppose, he is ignorant of, I find that I have a starting-point and an object. I desire the fluid of the person at a distance to come and join that of the person whose hand is in mine; an effect of attraction is operated, uniting the two fluids which touched each other formerly, and thereby I obtain a conductor that directs me; but there is nothing similar to this with this woman, who is no longer of the earth." Adèle appears very much fatigued, and I rouse her.

Third Sitting.—M. Blouet gave an account of this fresh sitting to his friend, who came himself to the house a few days after, and assured us that, from the information he had obtained as to this woman, Adèle had given a correct description of her as well as of the place where she used to go to bed, and the three cellars which still exist. I put this gentleman in correspondence with Adèle, who told him the spot where she thought the treasure would be found. The gentleman acknowledged that the particulars relative to the cellars were exact, and as to the treasure researches only could prove how far she was correct.

Note.—A fortnight after the above sitting, M. Blouet and his friend searched the cellar in the spot pointed out by Adèle, and discovered, three feet under ground, a large stone, which they had much difficulty in raising even a little. M. Blouet slipped his hand underneath, and felt a sort of puddle; this discouraged him. They gave up their search. Three days after he recounted these particulars to Adèle, who declared that that signified nothing, as she had seen a treasure there; that he ought to have raised the stone and continued his search. Had he found nothing, the treasure must have been removed; but she was certain that, were it no longer there, it must have been there. He went after his friend. They raised the stone; dug to the depth of two feet; discovered a bed of flint-stones, and a good deal of mud, a consequence of the infiltration of water that rose to this height; they acquired the certainty that this stone had been cemented, that something extraordinary had taken place here. The stone was of granite, two feet and a half long, nearly as wide, and four inches thick. They thought that the treasure had been previously removed. For my part, I think that my friend was very wrong not to raise the stone higher; and to leave it thus for some days at the mercy of strangers, who, assuredly, would not hesitate, considering why and how it came to be cemented in such a place. Had the treasure been previously removed, no one would have taken the trouble to replace the stone in the same state and cement it again. My friend was more confident, and less curious, than I.

At these three sittings we have arrived at proving two truths:—

1. That a deceased person may be seen by the mere aid of his name, without leaving room to suspect communication of thoughts, which can not exist in this experiment as in many others we have already read, for M. Blouet and his friend never knew this woman; they can not, therefore, represent the image of her.

2. That spirit disengaged from matter is not, for that reason, disengaged from material affections, and that the elevation of the state in which it finds itself in the spiritual world depends much on the affection it had on earth for such or such celestial or terrestrial belief. The affection only constitutes the state in which the spirit finds itself. If you are under the empire of a fixed idea (would it not correspond with all the heavenly joys

which we figure to ourselves in the world of spirits), you are not the less its slave for a longer or shorter period of time. We are called, we acknowledge it, to register truths which it would cost many others much to unveil; but as we have not hitherto feared ridicule, we will say all we know; it is the duty of every man who loves science and truth. There are few magnetizers, engaged in treasure-finding, who have not experienced very great deceptions, which can be occasioned only by three causes: 1. The clairvoyante may be too weak in his lucidity, and suffer himself to be influenced by spiritual images, which will lead him into error. 2. He may still see the treasure in the spot where it was deposited, though it may have been removed since that time. It must be the same with treasures as with objects set in any place, and whose image remains in the same place, as I have said in my first volume. This fact can not be called in question. I have obtained convincing proofs of this, and here is one of them. One day a somnambulist, named Victor Dumez, then in great repute in Paris, told the abbé M—— that he perceived in a certain house a hidden treasure, and recommended this gentleman to purchase the house, which was then to be sold. The abbé paid down forty thousand francs (about $7,500) made researches on the spot where the clairvoyante assured him he beheld the treasure, but found nothing. The somnambulist was so convinced of what he saw, that he proposed being at half the expense in the search. The gentleman, encouraged anew, made fresh researches, without any further result. One day he came to my house to consult Adèle on the subject. She summoned the person who had concealed the treasure, and learned, through this person, that he had withdrawn it before his death; that it was useless troubling ourselves about it. He furnished Adèle with particulars as to what the hidden box contained, which details fully corresponded with what Victor had seen. The abbé was now enabled to make sure of the truth of this assertion, as the treasure had been hidden under the floor. All was raised, but nothing found. The image of the treasure had, therefore, remained in the place where it had been deposited. Adèle beheld it like the other clairvoyante, and had it not been for the information given her by the spirit, she would possibly have made the same mistake.

Not, indeed, in the present times is it that men believe that spirits, who have, during their materialization on earth, hidden treasures, still enjoy them after their departure from the earth, and fascinate the sight of those who attempt to discover them. Although these material treasures, as I have observed in the preceding sitting, are no longer of any use to the spirit disengaged from matter, they, nevertheless, remain the property of such spirit. There is no doubting it; if it is possible for an earthly man to say this piece of land, this house, or this furniture, &c., belongs to me, that constitutes a deed of property, as very justly observed to me my friend Binet; a spirit that has earned this gold, which he can hide more easily than a house or any other object, may surely, at his pleasure, make of it a deed of property which he has a mind no one should enjoy; the act of removing such a treasure is a positive theft—a bad action. He has a right to hallucinate you, the only means left him to defend this property, which he has honestly acquired. If we admit in them a series of terrestrial affections we can not refuse them this one any more than the rest, and the observation of my friend is strictly logical.

As to fascinations, there is no doubt of their existence, though they be not followed by more marked and dangerous effects. We may read on this head the ' Demonomania" of Bodin, 1558, where we shall find certain facts fully corresponding with these. I know a person who has passed through such deceptions and been unable to discover the treasure revealed to him by half-a-score of clairvoyantes. Three of them underwent hallucinations, which could not be recounted in this age without exposing one's self to ridicule. Every one has heard speak of the diggings at Mount Jalut, conducted by so many clairvoyantes of the first order and at different times; one beheld in one place, another in another, and all the shareholders in these diggings perceived that they expended therein their fortune to no purpose. I know a gentleman at Niort who found himself in the same conditions, and under the same influences. What he then experienced is still so fresh in his memory that his hair stands on end whenever he speaks of it. He was very near losing an excellent clairvoyante on this occasion. He could not wholly recall her to life till several hours after. He himself was, as well as two other persons who accompanied him, subjected to moral tortures impossible to describe. I am unwilling to be thought to accept tales which appear at first sight ridiculous; but I beg of magnetizers each to say of them as much as I, and the ridicule will be less overwhelming than on one alone. I will conclude this article by observing that out of a hundred indicated treasures, not more than two or three are discovered. There is, therefore, some cause for this, residing in hallucination. If it be possible for magnetizers to subject clairvoyantes to hallucination, all may be explained by this property which spirits disengaged from matter must possess, as well as those that are still confined to it.

132. Madame G. C—— desires the apparition of M. E. C. C——. Adèle says she sees a tall slender man, with auburn hair, splendid forehead, fine, well-formed eyes, long lashes, well-formed nose but rather wide at the bottom, large mouth, chin rather long, air severe; he is not very old, he wears a black dress, a white cravat. I perceive that he has a frill or a little lace on his shirt crossing his waistcoat, which is rather open; he suffered much from oppression in the chest, from palpitation of the heart; his moral sufferings were also great and of long continuance. During the latter part of his illness he was very weak in his legs; he did not complain in proportion with his sufferings; he was very courageous and well-informed. Though severe, he was affectionate, frank, pure, strong-minded; he loved above all what is good; he died in the conviction that his soul would survive his body. He says that he is very happy now; he is occupied in spiritual sciences, the conformation of the place he dwells in, and above all in the study of men. He had travelled a great deal on earth, and still delights in doing so in heaven. He tells me that it was not at the moment of dying that he suffered most, for his soul was already detached

from his body. He will not be perfectly happy, however, till those whom he loved on earth are reunited to him. I am much pleased with him, for he is a good and highly-educated man.

This lady, of high condition and elevated mind, acknowledges the exactitude of all these details: she begs Adèle to ask for a second person, so happy does she seem to be in the sphere of those spirits invisible to the eyes of our material body, but very sensible to persons whose hearts are open to their influence. We ask for M. W—— B——, who forthwith appears. Adèle says: "This man is older than the last one; his hair is almost white, and he has a bald place on the crown of his head; his forehead is not very high; he has fine eyes, rather hollow, and a benevolent look; flat mouth, rather long face—altogether a good-looking old man. He seems to me very cheerful and amiable. He must have been strong; he is corpulent enough; he had an asthma, and suffered shooting pains (from the gout); he was not long ill. He wears a riding-coat, rather long, and I see a stick in his hand. He tells me that he is fond of walking; his intelligence was of a less elevated kind than that of the preceding gentleman; he loved life also more than the latter, consequently he has some difficulty in comprehending the spiritual world; he tells me, however, that our life is not to be compared with his, which alone is life in perfection. I am much pleased with this man, on account of his amiable manners."

"Certified the above two experiments as perfectly correct.

"G. C——."

I ought to observe that some persons, holding a distinguished position in the world, beg of me not to publish their names, for fear of the ridicule that certain individuals, *too well informed to descend to such beliefs*, would not fail throwing on experiments of this kind; but I take care to make all persons who solicit these perceptions sign testimonials, observing to them that I shall hold them at the disposition of all my readers demanding such communication. Thus the abridged names are given in full length, with their address, in the said testimonials. If I make this concession to such timorous persons, it is only on the above condition; for I desire the truth, and nothing but the truth. If I do not fear ridicule, I wish to be able to prove that I am not deserving of it. I might have dispensed, some readers will say, with all these descriptive details, which are not very agreeable to read. I will answer that there would be nothing left me to say, and that these details present each in their individuality certain shades more and more persuasive. As in these last two perceptions, if we are disposed to find anything insignificant, we are forced to acknowledge that the *bald head of the old man, his stick, his long riding-coat, his tastes,* are persuasive details; so persons to whom merely one of these particularities is revealed, experience at each of the others a very decided movement of astonishment, which instantaneously overcomes their doubts, and gives rise to the exclamation—"'T is incredible! 'tis miraculous!" I say, with them: "Yes, it is miraculous; draw from it consoling conclusions, and death will no longer be to you a cause of anguish; on the contrary, it is the jailer who comes to restore you to liberty."

133. The lady who solicited the foregoing sitting (an Englishwoman by birth), after recounting what she had heard to one of her compatriots, brought him to me the following day. I shall retrench naught from this sitting, which demonstrates how far the eccentricity of this good people can go. The lady asks for Mr. John Wilson. Adèle perceives two gentlemen together, one an old man, the other younger. The old man has gray hair, is tall and thin, and wears spectacles; he has hollow eyes, a long, pinched-up nose, wide mouth, large dry hands; the general appearance of the countenance is serious. The youngest may be about forty-five to fifty years of age: he is of the ordinary stature, corpulent, and broad-chested; he has black hair, a prominent forehead, what we call an intellectual forehead; thick eyebrows, and this gives him a stern look; nose well formed, complexion clear, middling-size mouth, chin rather prominent and round, neck short; he wears a coarse blue coat. He died of an apoplexy. He was a very good man, of an enlightened mind; he seems to me even an extraordinary man, having very elevated thoughts.. He suffered much from

not being able to do all the good he desired. He must have been beloved; he would wish to be reunited to a person who is very dear to him.

This lady observes that she believes she can call to mind the old man, from the details she has heard, but she is not sure of it; it was the second one she asked for, who must have been the old man's grandson. She also observes that this man was ten years older than Adèle supposes him to have been, and that his complexion was not what is termed in England a clear complexion. For what concerns the elevated thoughts, she thinks the phrase might be rendered better thus: "He had good common sense, and elevated sentiments." All the other details are very exact. She refused to sign, for fear of compromising her name in the learned world; but I have the names of two persons accompanying her, who if necessary would affirm the truth of this perception, and the exactitude of the details acknowledged by the lady, to whom I observed that, if I had forgotten to acquaint her with this condition, indispensable to my sittings, I trusted she would have the goodness to inform those persons of it she was to send to me; for I make it a great point, in the interest of truth and science, to support my citations with the testimony of those who acknowledge their exactitude. It remains for me to observe what distinction may be drawn between what we call a clear complexion, and what the English, who have a superior color to us, call a clear complexion. We appear to them very dark, and a dark Englishman with them would appear to us of a fine carnation: this makes me think that the difference in the eyes of Adèle and this lady was but a matter of taste. Her second observation, as to the meaning of elevated thoughts, is sufficient to prove to us that we can attach no importance to the first one, because this man was not of illustrious birth, nor had he received a liberal education. He could have had but good common sense and elevated sentiments, although this lady assured us that he was habitually consulted by all the inhabitants of the town in which he resided in innumerable matters connected with art, mechanics, taste, and justice. Adèle having made the observation to her that he was not in her sphere, she replied: "No; he had no wit—received no education." I know not whether wit be included in education, or whether the latter does but give it the form; and whether elevated thoughts are aught else than elevated sentiments. I leave this question to be decided by those who have wit and education.

134. Madame C. C——, already mentioned, at sitting 128, desires another apparition. She begs Adèle to ask for Madame A. D——. Adèle perceives a lady about thirty years of age, with dark hair, white, smooth forehead, fine dark eyes, long lashes, rather large nose, middling-size mouth, an agreeable smile, and white teeth. I see an empty space at top, on the left side, and this makes me presume that she has lost a tooth on that side. Neck short, chest broad, graceful air and manners, easy carriage. This lady must have suffered at the heart. She died of an ulcer in the womb, not rightly treated; she was strong in the chest, but must have suffered from cramp in the stomach. She has not long been dead. She speaks to me of a child she was very fond of, though not her own. She would wish to be reunited to several persons whom she was very partial to. Her husband must still be on earth. No doubt she was beloved, as she herself was loving, good, and virtuous. I don't know whether she used to like flowers, but at this moment she is passionately fond of them."

At the request of Madame C. C——, Adèle follows the apparition to heaven—a period when ecstasy is at its height—for ten minutes. I call her back to earth. She then gives us the following account: "I followed this lady up, very high up. She was dressed in white, her hair in ringlets, a wreath of orange-flowers round her head. Oh, good heavens, how beautiful she was! why are we so ugly on earth? How graceful and pretty she was! Shall I one day be as beautiful as she? No matter what idea we form of heaven, we shall always come far short of the reality. If you did but behold the beautiful group of dark, fair, fresh-looking women, with white and transparent skins, modest looks, all crowned with flowers; one with white or red roses, another with jasmine, another with orange-flowers, each according to her affection! Some play music, others draw, others study; those singing, these promenading. Why, goodness me! what is this earth in comparison with heaven? a sink beside a palace! Fancy to yourself the Palais-Royal with its countless streams of gas, and a dark cave—it is still less than that. What light dresses they had! with what simplicity, what grace they wear them! When we compare our tanned, dark, wrinkled skins, our irregular features, our sorry looks, all our deformities, with these celestial bodies—O filthiness, O disgust! and we pity those who are dead—those who died at the barricades: why, my God, let the rest be shot! Why should I go to ask pardon for them? That they may live! that they may suffer! Oh, no! death is preferable to what you term life." Adèle is in a state of inconceivable exaltation. I make the observation to her that all these unfortunate creatures have wives and children, who stand in need of them. She replies: "What worse (according to us) can happen to them, in their turn, than death? Well, they will be happy: the sooner they die, the better for them. Those poor, misled creatures who fought, killed each other—only consider what was their surprise at meeting each other in heaven, without hatred, without vengeance, really alive, and satisfied of their earthly error! There, and there only, is the true reign of fraternity. O human weakness, pride, error! why can I not preserve the courage I at this moment possess? I would mount with them the barricades, and hearten them on to death! *For death is happiness!*

I succeeded with difficulty in proving to Adèle that she was wandering, and that she ought to return to sentiments, if not more true, at least more in consonance with our existence.

"Certified the whole as very exact.

"C. C——."

"PARIS, *this* 11*th of July*, 1848."

At this sitting it will be found that Adèle fails in her usual morality, by preaching up, in a manner, suicide. The observation I made to her was to this effect. But let any human being put himself for a moment in her place, issuing from a state so superior, returning to this sink of pains, passions, and saying to himself: "There, *life, happiness.;* here, annihilation and tears: there, *liberty, immortality;* here, slavery and death; I must descend again into this pitcher called the body, there to undergo for years the pangs of *what is termed existence,* and quit places where I feel myself so happy; is it not excusable in the galley-slave to curse his chains before garlands of flowers—in the old man, his wrinkles in the presence of youth—in the blind, the darkness before the light? O my God! Adèle is more virtuous than I. Were I but once, like her, to leave my body, I should never return to it, for I know nothing worse than it and the earth it inhabits!"

135. Madame Osborn asks for Madame Elizabeth Osborn, her grandmother. Adèle says: "I see a woman of about fifty years of age (she was older), of the ordinary size, broad-chested, figure pretty slender, hair gray, forehead prominent and open, dark hollow eyes, nose rather long than short, mouth rather large than small, chin somewhat long, and her hand, which must have been very beautiful, is long. This lady surely found it a difficult matter to keep on her legs during the latter part of her illness. She suffered from stoppages, and a pain in one leg; this, however, did not prevent her from being very alert. Though of a good heart, she was severe, open-minded, and possessed of much wit; she appears to me smiling, and very elevated in the spiritual world. She is surrounded by a brilliant light, and this, no doubt, contributed toward my taking her for a younger woman than she was on earth. She tells me that she is with her son, to whom she was very indulgent on earth; she loved him, and still loves him dearly. She was more indifferent about a daughter she had, and whose heart she can now better appreciate, as she has inwardly studied it. Consequently, she will be perfectly happy when she has rejoined her. She says that she lost one son, who perished at sea; she lost another, not less painfully, in battle, where he was killed by a cannon-ball. Adèle inquired the kind of death this gentleman met with only at the request of Madame Osborn. Consequently, she experiences an inexplicable shock at hear-

ing the report of the cannon, and seeing the unfortunate man mortally wounded. She perceives the battle raging, and turns away her eyes, to look no longer, as she says, on so frightful a picture. She recommends Madame Osborn, on the part of her grandmother, to take care of her health, for she has often pains in the stomach, and a very great oppression all over her, occasioned by the disordered state of the blood. She predicts that, in a short time from this, one of her granddaughters present will give birth to a little boy.

"Acknowledged all as correct, apart the age and prediction, which time only can prove. "E. Osborn,

"6, *Rue des Vignes, Chaillot.*"

Observations.—At the apparition of Madame Osborn we have heard this lady give a few details, not devoid of interest, as to the children she had lost. Scarcely had Madame Osborn, her grandmother, said to Adèle, "See to what kind of death my uncle was a victim," than the latter, instead of asking this of the grandmother, desires to see this man at the moment of his death, and does see him struck by a cannon-ball in battle. This scene appears to her full of activity; she hears the cannon growling, as if let off that very instant. Still, as Madame Osborn says, many years have passed away since then. This fact confirms what we have already said in the first volume (at sitting 93). The questions of time, produced by the state in which we find ourselves, alone engender the intervals separating the events. . But in somnambulism all is in the present. We are conscious, however short a time we dwell on this proposition, and inconceivable as it may appear, that it can not be in the world of causes as in the world of effects. . In the first, forms are eternal, and unalterable to the clairvoyante who is in direct communication with this world. When he desires to see a certain thing, it forthwith presents itself to his view as a certain volume presents itself to ours on a shelf of our library. It is impossible for us, in taking this volume to say: *It has been,* since it *is* whenever we think of it and desire to handle it. It is the same in the world of causes. A certain cause always *is;* it is only the material effect which such cause engenders whose action or form disappears from our sight, and fetters our judgment, that is to say—that has been, is, and will be. But, in a state where these things can not change their forms, they are ever in the present. Thus, an action consists not in the assemblage of several forms and the movement impressed on them. This movement itself is an action, a cause that ever vibrates to the clairvoyante, easy for him to comprehend, but quite negative for our state, which can assign it no form. It is the same with all the sensations of sounds and attractions; because we can not represent them ourselves by forms that catch our material eye, they, nevertheless, exist, since they so far touch us as to produce sensation. In metaphysics, as in physics, we can feel and see only what touches; therefore, sensations of any kind, or attraction. must be from bodies, since they make themselves felt by bodies; if they can not be proved by a view of their forms, they are proved by a sensation of their touch. Without losing our way in metaphysical figures, which would not be out of place in this work, we will say that this battle is represented in the world of causes by a living picture of a life present, not passed, nor to come. The existence of this book is what I have taken as a point of comparison, which is, and has not been. We will treat more amply of these questions in the work already mentioned, wherein we will point out the means by which a person may enter of himself into a particular state, independent of magnetism, and wherein this truth will be comprehended by a view of the solutions desired.

136. M. Roustan, a magnetizer, and member of the Magnetological Society of Paris, asks for M. François Xavier Roustan. Adèle perceives "a man with gray hair, about your size," says she to M. Roustan, "open forehead, pretty large eyes, but hollow, nose thick at the bottom, broad shoulders, back rather crooked. He died of an apoplectic stroke. He was a good-looking man, lively, and very agreeable, and of a mild disposition.—He tells me that he thinks of you. You have already had him asked for by other clairvoyantes, and have seen him yourself. He inspires you, but for some time past you have not

received the signs that he was in the habit of making you, because you are too absorbed in worldly affairs. You are very light in your thoughts and actions; then, again, there are persons about you who contest your opinions; you find yourself influenced by them because you are naturally fickle; your ideas are not matured. He tells that you had a twin-brother. He had something to enjoin on you, when dying; but matters having changed, he is no longer permitted to apprize you of it." M. Roustan puts a question to his father relative to Louis XVI.; he receives for answer that he still retains the same opinions respecting him as he did when on earth. Adèle says that this man is in the second radius.

M. Roustan finds these details in conformity with the truth, and thus signs:—

"This is exact. "ROUSTAN."

137. Madame Vedeaux, for fifteen years a student of magnetism, finding herself momentarily at Paris, desires to avail herself of this opportunity of paying a visit to several clairvoyant subjects. She took a sitting at a young person's, whose clairvoyance she had been previously enabled to judge of. To a question put by this lady, the clairvoyante replied: "I know but one somnambulist in Paris who can give you a solution to the question you ask: go to No. 17 Rue Tiquetonne; you will find there a subject surrounded by angels and departed spirits that direct her, so that she is much more elevated than I am." Acting upon this advice, the lady came and asked me for a distant-view sitting. I did not promise her a clairvoyance of the first order, such views not being Adèle's speciality, and not having for the moment any subject at my disposition. Agreeably to the wishes of my fair visiter, I begged Adèle to look over this lady's property, and tell us whether there was any hidden treasure there. She replied thus: "I see some water, apparently, to me, in a cistern; it is dark; then a turret, not unlike a dove-cot. It is contiguous to a house that stands by itself, and surrounded with fields. There is a room on the ground-floor with two windows; on the first floor there is a room which also has two windows. This house is three

stories high; the main building has two wings, with which there is a communication by the staircases and corridors where the turret stands; it is quite a small room, in which I see a spirit wandering: it is a person who was murdered there a very long time ago." Adèle shrinks back in affright: I quiet her, and she says that she is dragged toward a small store-room on the ground-floor, in which she can scarcely stand upright; she sees there some wine, and declares that under this spot has been hidden a treasure contained in a small strong box, in which she perceives jewels, silver, and plate. She goes on giving descriptions, superfluous for the reader to know, but very agreeable for this lady to hear. The day after this sitting, the lady returned to acquaint me that she had been again to see her somnambulist, who held with her, as near as may be, this discourse: "You ought to be satisfied with the clairvoyante I made you acquainted with. I fear but one thing, which is, that her lucidity should deprive me of your kind visits, for I am very much attached to you; it was to give you a proof of this that I feared not making you acquainted with another clairvoyante more powerful than myself. I perceive that she spoke to you of a spirit that wandered about the property she visited, the result of a murder: that is very true; I see it also. It is a pity that this clairvoyante should be too reserved and too much afraid of telling us all she sees; there would be moments wherein she would confound the most incredulous. She is too fearful of committing mistakes; her magnetizer ought to know that." I replied to this lady, that it was true that if Adèle was a little less afraid of committing mistakes, she would be capable of greater things. It is her reserve that proves her lucidity; she is aware how pictures which present themselves to the eye may lead to error, seeing that they represent the past, present, and future, as present, although in the world of causes, wherein are perceived the various states of their manifestation, there can be no errors: however, they are possible in their material effects, which are or are not manifested. If man studied with great attention this somnambulic or spiritual state, which he yet knows but imperfectly, he would not be so ready to inveigh against errors, especially if unable to verify the revelations of the clairvoyantes. I have spoken of this curious sitting merely to have an opportunity of repeating what I have already said in the first volume, that it was not necessary to guide clairvoyantes, step by step, toward the object we desire to have visited by them; for Adèle, at this sitting, formed no communication with the lady: she asked for the château, and it forthwith appeared. What has made me thus act, is, that knowing a clairvoyante able to find out the traces of an object stolen or lost, of a person missing, &c., in these researches, he can be guided by no human thought; the desired object, therefore, must present itself at the call of the clairvoyante, or the latter must proceed toward it without any itinerary. It may then, I say to myself, be the same with all views at a distance; of this I have obtained proof a hundred times. Even yesterday, a doctor of high repute, who believes in magnetism because he is so under my influence that I force him to confess it (whenever he seems disposed to deviate from the truth) that he can offer no opposition to my closing his eyes, for instance, if I will it, until he begs of me to open them for him (and he does not sleep)—he was in the same disposition of mind with regard to somnambulism and views at a distance, when yesterday, as I was saying, I somnambulized my little Emile, and intrusted him to the doctor to question him at his ease. Out of more than forty answers, he raised doubts only on two or three made by a spirit whom he caused to be questioned at a distance. His surprise was not less great when I assured him that the really living person whose spirit responded to that of my little clairvoyante, of twelve years of age, knew nothing of this little secret intriguing and those confidences, in which, however, he would have taken good care not to compromise himself by answers injurious to him. The doctor, before taking the hand of the clairvoyante, had already a description of the house into which he had sent him. On this simple invitation from me to the child: "The doctor desires that you should see a house into which he wishes you to enter." "I see it," forthwith said the child, "it is a new house," &c. This method of proceeding would not be admissible unless it succeeded as well as the other; but is it not demonstrated by the aforementioned experiment for researches, thefts, &c., so common in our days? What makes me more attached to these experiments is, that I wish to prove, that if an object unknown to the clairvoyante presents itself to his view, agreeably to his wishes—if actions passed like those attending all the circumstances of a theft, or the journey of a person whose trace has been lost, present themselves to him—I say, the person who has done or produced these actions, must exist equally as well as those actions which appear to our material eyes completely dead; and the soul which has produced such things can no more refuse to come, at the call of the clairvoyante, than these scenes refuse appearing. I wish also to observe, that the clairvoyante who addressed Madame Devaux has not the least knowledge of Adèle in her watchful state, and the same may be said of Adèle with regard to her. I will say, moreover, that in the view at distance Adèle took, it must be observed that she declares it impossible for her to stand upright in the store-room, which really is, as this lady has said, too small to admit of her doing so materially. It is, therefore, not the view alone that goes toward that spot—it is the whole spiritual individual, as I have already remarked at the commencement of this volume, in my answer to magnetizers who believe that apparitions are a transmission of thoughts, and as I have proved in the view Adèle took of Mexico, in which she received a coup-de-soleil (though it was rainy weather). It can not be for a moment doubted but that the clairvoyante is wholly in the places he visits at a distance, although answering our questions by the organs of his material body, as if still within it. If, perchance, it should be argued that he sees these things in the thought of the questioner, although the contrary is mathematically proved by the details present, which he gives you of places you have not seen for many years, and the changes that have taken place since your departure; these details can not be in your thoughts, since you are not acquainted with them, and ulterior information only proves to you their reality. This is a logical proof, admitting of no reply; but, as there are persons who have a reply for all, and who, prejudiced in their belief of the transmission of thoughts, see but it, I beg them to tell me how a clairvoyante can walk about in the least of their thoughts, which represents a place capable of containing thousands of spirits similar to the one visiting them. If I ask a solution of this from these *savans*, it is less to combat the truth of it than to fix for an instant their vast conception on this explanation, by which they believe they have nothing more to reply. I will tell them that it deserves a little more attention, and can not, though really existing, answer the question I address to them. Does the clairvoyante see only what you have seen or thought? Certainly not; since every day you obtain proofs of the contrary. In that case, then, where does he see these things? Where they are, no doubt. And they are, where we suppose them materially to be, far from us. If they are far from us, and the spirit goes to visit them, in body and not in sight—as it is easy for you to make sure of—who can convey it to these places, the doors being shut, and the walls well cemented? Answer, I say to you. Is it the places that come to your clairvoyante? Who brings these places into your room? I puzzle you a little more than I shall be puzzled, in answering you that the soul, disengaged from matter, has no more difficulties to encounter in coming at your request than the clairvoyante experiences in going unseen by your material eyes to those remote places, or than those places have in coming to you.

Madame Devaux, as a studious woman, whose position is as honorable as honored, desired, in order to complete her magnetic studies, to witness an apparition, in the second visit she paid me; we asked for M. Antoine Simon (her father). Adèle says: "I see a man, with gray hair not quite so tall as madame, pretty corpulent, neck short, fine open forehead; lively eyes, expressive and mild; countenance fresh; nose rather large at the bottom, middling-size; smiling mouth; chin round: altogether a good-looking old man. His death must have been caused by the state of his blood, as I perceive it is black, thick, and circulating with difficulty. He was subject to stoppages;

he was treated for an aneurism, but it was not one; his medical adviser ought rather to have diverted the course of the blood. He must have experienced a sort of weight in the lower part of the body, and lassitude in the limbs; also a pain in his left leg. I see him in a dark-colored riding-coat, light-colored waistcoat, coarse blue pantaloons; he wore shoes, and not boots; for his size as a man, his hand was not large. He had a look commanding respect, was good and just. In his last moments, he was easily provoked. He was not fond of showing off his kind feelings, preferring to keep them pent up within himself; this caused him to be looked upon as very cold, though he was not so. His domestic happiness was often disturbed, his wife's character not being in sympathy with his own. He tells me that your son is intended for the bar, that he will be an advocate. He often comes to inspire you with good thoughts. He has appeared to you in dreams; your position will be changed in two years' time, and you will reside in Paris." This lady is greatly surprised at the minuteness and truth of these details, especially those concerning her son; from the earliest age of the latter, the grandfather used to say, "My little grandson shall be a little advocate."

"Recognised as very exact, all these details.

"PAULINE VEDEAUX.

"*Château de Malbouquet, Toulon,*

"*17th August*, 1848."

138. M. Dejean asks for M. Joseph Noel Dejean, of Caderousse. Adèle perceives a bald-pated old man, with a few gray hairs. "He appears to me," said she, "rather taller than the gentleman here present: broad across the shoulders, high forehead, more prominent than flat, light blue eyes, lively and expressive, nose rather crooked, and slightly turned up at the tip, ruddy complexion, chin round, neck thick. He must have suffered in his respiration, and in the right arm, up to his shoulder, and also from weakness in the legs. I see that his chest and heart are affected, though not with any mortal disease; he was afflicted with an inflammation of the bladder and the lower part of his body; he limps on his left leg and leans on a walk-

ing-stick; this proceeds from a fall he once had. In the other hand he has a spectacle-case, which I took at first for a pipe. I believe that he has been a sailor. He used to wear a riding-coat folded across the chest, and longer than they are now worn; it appears to me of a coarse blue cloth: I see him in shoes, not boots, and dark pantaloons. He was very fond of walking; a quiet life was most agreeable to him; he was good, severe, but upright and just. He is not communicative with me. I believe that he suffered great losses; this made him taciturn. He lost also many objects of his affection; he says that he was wronged, deceived, absolutely cheated; he underwent many catastrophes; he must have had a large fortune. He was separated from some one, and this gave him much pain. At last he took to writing; he had a good head and a sound judgment. His advice was often asked. He tells me that this gentleman is his son. You have a share in some enterprise; you do not reside in Paris; he advises you to be cautious, as some losses threaten you; he recommends you to leave Paris as soon as possible, as grave events are about to take place there. He says that he is very happy; he has progressed; he has been long dead."

At every sitting I recommend persons before signing the testimonial to make mention of whatever in the given details does not appear to them exact; for I seek the truth with my whole heart, and always experience fresh joy whenever I give others satisfaction. The following are the observations of this gentleman:—

"The nose was not turned up, but large and aquiline; the cheeks were not ruddy, but pale; the neck was not long but short, and rather small than large. I never knew him to suffer in his respiration, in his right arm, or bladder. He had never been a sailor. All the rest is very exact.

"Dejean de la Bastie,

"*Delegate of the Isle of Bourbon to the Government,*

"*Rue Neuve-du-Luxembourg*, 18 *bis.*

"18*th August*, 1848."

There are persons who, when called upon to sign a testimonial, make it a case of conscience, and are unwilling to pledge themselves to the truth of a thing respecting which they have any doubts. Under the influence of this thought was it that M. Dejean made the foregoing observations. Adèle told him that the nose was crooked, which meant aquiline, but she maintains that it turns up slightly at the tip; she likewise sees the cheeks ruddy, and the neck thick (a short neck always seems thicker than any other), and as this gentleman had left his father many years before his death, at which he was not present, he could not be acquainted with his sufferings, or know whether the blood had not flown up to his head in his last moments. Adèle does not affirm that this person was a sailor, she says: "I think that he has been a navigator," because she perceives that his thoughts take a nautical direction. At last, his son observes to us that it was he himself who had been to sea, and that his doing so had caused his father much uneasiness. This explains to us why Adèle perceives his thoughts turned toward navigation. These five little observations remain therefore worthless, and prove that if these apparitions were transmission of thoughts they would not exist. We find in this apparition fully forty details acknowledged as true. I think that it ought to be received as one of the best.

139. M. Fandar, usher to the tribunals at Troyes, wrote to me about the beginning of August, to beg me to send him two copies of the first volume of the "Secrets," expressing, at the same time, a wish that I would cause his father, M. Nicolas Fandar, to appear, telling me that if I could give a description of him he should experience from it the greatest pleasure. I summoned the deceased. Adèle said to me: "I have but little liking for such apparitions, because the spirits themselves, conscious that none of their own friends are with me, come with more difficulty and answer my questions with constraint." I did not wish to refuse such consolation to this gentleman, whom we had not the pleasure of knowing; I desired, at the same time, to convince all that we may, by the mere assistance of a name, obtain apparitions as exact as if the persons were present; this does away with all idea of communication of thought, as may be seen in the following perception: Adèle says, "I see a man

with gray hair, full ruddy countenance, large nose, stern look, smiling mouth, and this betokens a lively and good disposition; short neck, and breathing with difficulty. I perceive pimples caused by heat of the blood on his face. He is pretty corpulent, and of middling stature. I should say that he suffered in his legs. He wears a brown vest, and I think, coarse, gray pantaloons. He is happy, and reunited to his wife, whom he dearly loved on earth, and who was, as he says, very kind to him."

I forwarded this description to M. Fandar, who sent me the following letter:—

"MY DEAR MONSIEUR: The indications given by our somnambulist are very exact; two years before death snatched him from me, my father suffered at intervals from oppressions, which so increased that the fatal day rapidly approached; his legs became so swollen that he was unable to stir a single step. My father usually wore a brown-colored vest, and coarse, gray woollen pantaloons; as he was of a very sanguine temperament, it often happened that he had large pimples on his face. He was very hasty, so that I am not surprised at your clairvoyante's having looked upon his countenance as stern; but his passion over, he was one of the best of men. You perceive, monsieur, that the indications of your clairvoyante are conformable to the truth. I authorize you to make such use of this letter as you shall deem fit.

"FANDAR,
"*Usher to the tribunals at Troyes,*
"*Rue de la Levrette, No.* 3.

"*The* 13*th August*, 1848."

I shall make no reflection on this letter. I thank the gentleman for his frankness: may it contribute toward convincing the adversaries of these apparitions! I beg the reader will pardon me my repetitions on this head; but having only one objection to combat—that of the transmission of thoughts, I am bound to set forth whatsoever each apparition contains contrary to this foolish argument, in order to disarm for ever the person more foolish still, who would wish to make use of it against so positive a truth.

140. M. Blesson asks for M. Pierre Blesson, his father. Adèle sees in this gentleman "a person about the same size as his son;" he appears to her "scarcely fifty years old; his hair is darker than yours," said she to his son; "he has a splendid countenance, fine forehead, soft, lively, and affable eyes; he wears a dark brown riding-coat with pockets at the sides, dark blue or black pantaloons; he surely died of the cholera, as I think I recognise the symptoms of that disease. He was buried in the common grave. His son inquires whether it really was his body which he caused to be exhumed and buried in a grave apart? He replied yes, and assures him that he is highly pleased with his regret, and also with his kind attention toward his mother. He tells him that he will succeed in his affairs, but not without some trouble, and gives him advice on this head. He assures him that he will be satisfied with his children when they are grown up. He often wanders near his wife, whom he loved and still loves very much. He awaits the happy moment of their being reunited to have no longer aught more to desire.

"Acknowledged the above details as perfectly exact.

"BLESSON,

"*This* 20*th August*, 1848." "36, *Rue-aux-Ours*.

This gentleman, after the perusal of the first volume of the "Secrets," and an apparition I had already given him, experimented himself on his somnambulists and obtained the same results. He handed to me a note of certain facts which will be found at the close of these sittings.

141. M. Dejean de la Bastie, already mentioned at sitting 138, desires a fresh apparition; he asks for M. Marie Joseph Théodore de Guigné. Adèle perceives "a man about forty years of age, pretty tall, and with dark hair." M. Dejean here interrupted Adèle, telling her that this is not the portrait of the person he requires. We see that this gentleman wishes for particulars admitting of no doubt. At the words: "He is pretty tall and dark," he says to us: "He was tall but not dark." Adèle replies that the person she was describing to him must certainly have borne his name and belonged to his

family, that she is conscious of it. But he asks again for this gentleman and a second personage appears, the first, however, still remaining. "This one," said she, "is about thirty years of age, tall and thin, with dark flaxen hair, pale countenance, dark blue eyes of a tolerably mild expression, nose long, mouth rather large than small, chin long; I see him in a sort of great coat, such as persons no longer wear, it is devoid of grace, and not unlike a dressing-gown; it is of a dark blue or black color; this costume denotes to me a man in office, a priest, or other functionary; he has an austere look; he must have suffered in the chest, I see that his lungs are gorged with blood. He suffered a long time. He was very weak. I believe that privations were the cause of his illness and rendered his chest so weak. I do not, however, see in him the seeds of any mortal malady, and this induces me to believe that he died a violent death, accidentally and unexpectedly. His hand is large and thin. I see a medal on his breast, about as large as the hollow of one's hand; he wears open shoes, such as are no longer worn. He is unwilling to speak to me, and this makes me presume that he did not speak French."

The following are the observations that precede the signature of M. Dejean: "This person had a position more remarkable for mildness and goodness than severity; he died of a violent fever, accompanied with a delirium that lasted several days, and attributed by the physician to the want of a vigorous constitution, worn out by absolute abstinence.

"Acknowledged the details as exact.

"DEJEAN DE LA BASTIE."

I pledged myself to making mention of the sittings just as I should obtain them, in the interest of truth, which I love and seek with a laudable intention; but, if I do so, and engage persons to make such observations as they deem fit previous to signing, I ought also to give notice that I have to fear intelligences little prepared for such revelations, and, on the part of my clairvoyante, moments more or less lucid; then, again, errors which spirits wandering continually around us strive to make clairvoyantes commit, as their whole affection consists in misleading, and we are their victims. However, we have no reason to complain of the preceding apparition; on the contrary, we ought to think that, if this gentleman accepts it in all its details, the observations that he adds do not destroy what Adèle has said—far from this being the case, they strengthen it; she perceives no germ of any malady; a violent fever that takes off a man in a few days, is, indeed, as she says, an unexpected, accidental death.

This gentleman observes that the physician accuses the abstinence, which the deceased imposed on himself, as being the cause of the destruction of his constitution, and having brought on death.

Adèle says: "He must have suffered in the chest, been very weak for a long time; I believe that privations are the cause of this." For my part, I see no difference between the word privation and abstinence; what we abstain from, we deprive ourselves of.

Adèle does not say that this man is wanting in kindness; on the contrary, she says that he has a mild look, but that, taken altogether, he seems to have an austere air. I will observe, in respect to this, that the gentleman was a priest, and so devoted to religious ideas that he constantly wore a hair cloth. Judge whether such a man should have a smiling air; thus, in the observation of M. Dejean, I see nothing that can cause us to suspect any reservation.

This gentleman asks for a second apparition, in the person of Olympe Pascale. Adèle says: "I see a little old woman of sixty." The gentleman forthwith wishes to stop Adèle, saying to me: "The person I asked for was but twenty-seven." I encourage Adèle, however, to continue, seeing that she seems vexed that persons unasked for should present themselves. She observes to this gentleman, that their appearing is to be attributed to his wishing for a multitude of persons at once. The mere thinking of one of them is sufficient for its instantaneous appearance in our sphere; hence it is that she sees them present themselves to her almost before their name is pronounced. She is certain that the first one who presented himself was a relative, of the same name as the person asked for, of whom, no doubt, the gentleman had been thinking. M. Dejean acknowledges, with me, the justness of Adèle's observation by saying: "True; all this is so surprising that a person would wish to summon all his friends to acquire the certitude of their all being really alive; and I do, indeed, desire to ask for many of them. It does not appear to me astonishing, when I think of a relative, that he should be near me, as he is near your clairvoyante, who is less acquainted with him than I. If the mere wish suffices, I ought to have a pretty good number around me." Adèle's observation refers to that which we have read in the apparition of M. Fandar, namely, "that spirits come with less pleasure when there is no one with the clairvoyante." We beg of her to continue her description: "She has gray hair," resumed she; "she was very lively, quick in her movements, well proportioned. I see a cap on her head; she has three small ringlets hanging down the sides in front; gray, hollow eyes; I believe she was a fair woman, and that her eyes were of a light blue; nose rather sharp, mouth somewhat sunken, and back rather round. She wears a dark striped robe, in the form of a peignoir, fastening in front; I see, too, that she wears a high collar."

The following is the gentleman's observation:—

"With the exception of the ringlets, these details appear to me to correspond precisely with the mother of the person asked for. "DEJEAN DE LA BASTIE,

"18 *Rue Neuve du Luxembourg.*

"*This 25th August*, 1848."

We have already made an observation to the effect that some persons may possibly experience a sort of weariness at reading this mass of testimonials; but if they have the good inspiration to remark that each apparition has quite a peculiar type, they will the better know how to appreciate the chain and *ensemble* they are called upon to form, to establish in them a firm belief, which should bring them sweet consolation and hope.

142. This is the extract of a sitting, written down by a third

person, who was witness to it, which will give a more exact idea of my not having amplified or omitted aught in the preceding sittings as to the futility of the details comprised in them, and as to the facility which Adèle possesses in expounding them.

Madame de Longueville, who has great doubts as to the possibility of spirits appearing to somnambulists, begs Madame Adèle to ask for her son and daughter, who had been dead some time. Mademoiselle Noémie appeared, as having died first; the clairvoyante thus describes her: "She appears to me taller than her mother: she has auburn hair, a fine forehead, beautiful eyebrows, expressive eyes, lively, intelligent, and steady; mouth small, chin round, slight rosy-colored cheeks, beautiful hands, roseate nails; she appears to be about two-and-twenty years of age; she suffered from an affection of the heart; she had a slight dry cough, and was troubled with pain in the back; the blood rushed to her chest, and caused an inflammation; she was also frequently troubled with a sore throat, and pains in the head; she wears a dark-colored dress."

Madame de Longueville acknowledges the exactitude of the description, and the morbid symptoms; there is but one particular inexact, that is the color of the hair, which was, as this lady expressed herself, of a mahogany color. Adèle replies that no doubt this young lady used a good deal of pomatum, thus making her hair look rather darker.

Not waiting to be asked for appears M. Emile de Longueville, whom the clairvoyante thus describes: "He has flaxen hair, very fine eyes shaded with long lashes; forehead not so high as his sister's; he is thinner than she, and yet he has a plump white hand like a woman's; he has a small mouth in the form of a heart, nose well formed, but not of the same shape as his sister's; chin rather longer than hers; he was melancholy and suffered in the chest; the cerebrum was too small to lodge all the great ideas that he would have entertained. He was unfortunate from his childhood, very good, much given to reflection, and this no doubt considerably enervated him."

Madame de Longueville acknowledges not only the exactitude of the physical, moral, and intellectual portrait of her child, but also the disease of the lungs of which he died.

The clairvoyante then sees what she never before saw: a ray of thread of a thousand colors, proceeding from the hearts of the two children, drawing them together and meeting in the heart of the mother; the two children say that they are constantly around their mother; it was them who gave her the strength to undergo all the trials she had passed through. The mother desires them to be asked whether she has any precautions to take in the political events which may endanger her life; their answer is to the effect that they could never think of warning her of obstacles that would prevent her from rejoining them. They are very happy, but they desire her to be with them. A lady present, who was acquainted with the two spirits in the time of their terrestrial incarnation, knowing that both, being *phalansterians,* believed in the renewed incarnation of souls upon earth, desires that Emile should be asked whether the soul is incarnated anew on earth; he replies, "No, the soul does not return into a material body, it is sufficient to have entered it once."

The clairvoyante says that the brother and sister are together in a beautiful light, more brilliant than that of many persons who died before them. She desires to see Mademoiselle Noémie in her celestial costume. Her hair is in ringlets, ornamented with a wreath of white roses; she is dressed in white. The clairvoyante accompanies her when the latter returns to heaven. She enters into the ecstatic state; her magnetizer brings her back to the earth. "You are insupportable," said she, "I should not have stayed very long. All is so beautiful there and she played such delightful music." "On earth, too, much is beautiful," replies M. Cahagnet. "Anything beautiful on earth?—what horror!" exclaims the clairvoyante. The apparition sitting terminates. She then visits (spiritually) Madame de Longueville and another lady present, whom she tells with great accuracy what they suffer. Left alone with one lady, she repeats to her exactly what the clairvoyante of this lady had told her a few days previously, discloses things it was impossible for her to have known, and gives her advice on matters this lady little expected, but which are perfectly true.

"Signed the whole as quite exact.

Mesdames De Longueville,
I. D'Hericourt,
Ve. Bimont."

143. M. Delaage, a skilful and conscientious magnetizer, the author of the "Initiations into the Mysteries of Magnetism," the "Classes Disinherited," &c., a grandson of the great Chaptal, a young man passionately fond of the study of the occult sciences, and better enabled than any other, from his profound knowledge of the Hebrew, Greek, and Latin languages, to make researches in the sacred sanctuary of mysticism, came one day to ask of me an apparition-sitting, desiring to converse, as he said, through the medium of Adèle with the solitaire D'Orval, whose prophecies he had commented upon in the "Almanach de la Science du Diable," of which he is the editor, and in which he was so obliging as to insert my cabalistic calculation as to the probable duration of the republic in France. I hasten to gratify his wish. Scarcely was Adèle asleep than we summoned the recluse by the title of: *The author of the D'Orval Prophecy.* This man forthwith appeared. I resolved to drive him away in the name of God, if he were not the person we asked for; despite this command he remained assuring us that he was the very man. Adèle says to us: "I am certain that he is the man. He appears to me endowed with singular goodness. He bears the stamp of gentleness on each feature of his physiognomy. He is not stout, far from it, he is very thin; he has very hollow eyes, a prominent forehead, sallow complexion, as if he had been subject to privations, or fatigued by deep study. He is surrounded by a very beautiful light. He tells me that he made his exit from the earth more than two hundred years ago. But you are not aware," observes Adèle, "that time being with them no more, it is very difficult for them to mark it."—"Does he still believe

in the fulfilment of his prophecies, concerning France and the destruction of Paris?" "Yes, but he says with M. Mallet that there will be much less mischief done than he predicted." —"Was he mistaken as to the dates?" "He thinks not; but possibly he might; at any rate these dates will be odd numbers, 5, 7, or 9."—"Who according to him, will succeed the republic?" "The young prince in question."—"I believe that this solitaire is mistaken. In short what means this cock and this lion spoken of in his prophecy?" "It is an alliance that he will contract with a friendly power, representing force by the lion and purity by the lily."—"Does he think that war between those who have and those who have not will exist?" "It already exists: it is those who have who make war on those who have not."—"But those who have not will they make war on those who have?" "Certainly, and they will prevail."—"What then will happen? Will the republic reign?" ". . . . . . . not more than it reigns at present; it will be terror, such as now r . . . . . (reigns); you will have wished it to r . . . . . (reign), you will have given the example."—"Who then will be the chiefs?" "They will emerge from obscurity. They will awaken like spectres. Oh! blood! blood! there will be oceans of blood!" Adèle is very much agitated. I beg of M. Delaage not to question her any more on this subject. She exclaims: "I see a 3. I know not whether it means three months or three years!!! Poor people, thus to butcher each other for one man!! Oh! grief; oh! civilization."

M. Delaage desires that his grandfather M. J. B. Chaptal should appear. Adèle forthwith sees him. "He has," said she, "gray hair; lively, intelligent eyes, magnificent forehead, smooth and not wrinkled as old men's usually are: there is a small protuberance on each side, complexion clear and rosy, nose well formed, but rather long, middling-sized mouth, thick lips, chin rather long, fine corpulence. He wears a great coat, such as we no longer see now-a-days, with large pockets at the sides, and trimmings to his sleeves of a very dark color; 'tis like hair, or, at least, it seems to me so. He was a meditative man, having very elevated ideas. Oh! how learned he was.

He devoted himself much to science, and believed in the immortality of the soul. This man wrote a great deal." M. Delaage causes several questions to be put to him concerning his future prospects. The gentleman advises his grandson to continue his researches in the occult sciences, and terminate the great philosophical work he is about. He promises him complete success. After several questions, quite personal to himself, M. Delaage thanks Adèle, and assures her that all the details he has heard are very exact. I was about to awaken her, when she exclaims: "Ah! M. D'Orval is still there. I no longer noticed him. This honest man appears to me so good that I repent not having bid him good-by."—"Since he is still present, ask him where he might find a copy of his prophecies?" "He answers that there are several of them with different persons, who would be unwilling to part with them. There is one copy in the possession of an old woman at Verdun." M. Delaage says that scarcely a week ago he heard what the solitaire has just stated—that an old woman at Verdun actually does possess a copy of the prophecies. The solitaire retires, and Adèle continues answering psychological questions put to her by M. Delaage, and also M. Roustan, who was present at this sitting. The latter desires to know whether we are born more than once on earth? Adèle says, "No," and strives to persuade him of this truth by arguments as ingenious as they are sensible. She loses her time, becomes fatigued, and I rouse her. M. Delaage shares not in the opinion of narrow-minded magnetizers. He is far from believing in the transmission of thoughts, and congratulates Adèle on the happy doctrine she has been called upon to teach men, by affording them the means of so easily verifying, through somnambulism, the immortal and individualized existence of the soul.

## OBSERVATIONS.

As I have said in the first volume, this work is far from presenting the interest of romance by its necessarily broken and abrupt style. Hence it will be found better suited to the amateurs of science than to readers passionately fond of the poetical descriptions in our romances of the day. I have sought to render the style as clear as possible by stripping it of that *entourage* of questions and scenes foreign to revelations of this kind. I hold less to writing well than to persuading thoroughly. Had I made my clairvoyantes speak like the actors in the "Thousand-and-One Nights," it might have been thought, and with reason, that I presented a sequel to it. No, I have remained within the limits of austere truth, acting the part of an impartial historian, presenting to the philosophy of the day facts in all their nudity, but also in all their sincerity. I have followed up each apparition with observations independent of any systems; connecting, in order, each fact with the *ensemble* of the facts pre-cited, in order to assist the reader in drawing from the whole the consequences he deems fit. I have not thought it necessary to offer him a greater number of testimonials, thinking that, if he admits but one, the rest are superfluous, and would appear to him wearisome. I have not omitted the address of the persons who signed them, and I hold the originals at the disposition of those who may think proper to see them. I believe I now ought to present the facts which have been communicated to me by magnetizers, and other estimable persons who have, like me, made a sacrifice of their name to truth, for they are aware of the appellation reserved for them. I beg the reader to peruse them calmly, and not reject the marvellous which some of them contain. If I give publicity to them, it is because I believe that I shall have it in my power to demonstrate the possibility of them in the work on occult philosophy I am about. Since I announced myself as willing to replace faith by experiment, it would be ridiculous enough in me to announce facts which could be accepted only through faith. To be consistent with what I advance, and not to be deserving of the name of a madman, which might then be rightly decreed me if I no longer kept in the path I traced out for myself, I ought to give a receivable explanation of what I take leave to publish, and I will keep my word.

The aforementioned facts are about to be preceded by two scenes of departure from this globe, which are not devoid of a certain interest for the science in which we are engaged.

---

## LAST MOMENTS OF ELIZA.

We were devoting all our care to a young woman, named Eliza, of whom mention is made in the first volume of this work. She was about twenty-four years of age, and dying slowly of consumption. Adèle followed the progress of the disease, without being able to arrest it. She knew what dread this frail creature had of death, and perceived the unheard-of efforts she made to cling to life. Oh, what a life was hers! for a thousand others it would have been a dreadful torture. This unfortunate came every day to receive the consolations of our good clairvoyante, who tried to persuade her that in less than a month she would be radically cured; to me, however, she would say: "In a month she will be no longer among us." How painful was it to see this poor woman ascend one by one our stairs, take rest by sitting down on the last stair of each floor, in order to come and hear her friend say that she would not die; with what an outpouring of the heart did she press her hands when she gave her this consolation! She would go away with renewed strength, to purchase a few drugs to make an emollient *ptisan,* and go to bed; it was one day more passed in this so cherished an existence. At length, one evening, a message was brought, begging us to visit her at a distance, inasmuch as she could no longer leave her bed. Adèle said: "She has not twenty-four hours to be among us." We were soon with her to assure her that she was in a salutary crisis, the issue of which would be a most happy one. "May God hear you!" replied she. We watched over her all night, and gathered the following words, which she addressed to each of us:—

To her husband: "Why do you weep since Adèle says that I am not consumptive, and that there is no danger? Still, I spit a good deal; how thick and disgusting are my expectorations! Oh! she is deceived; she sees me dying and strives to console me—'tis quite natural—'tis humane. Thanks, my good Adèle, thanks! But I—I too am a seer: heaven and eternity are open to me. I know what my complaint is now."

To me: "Alphonse, why are you so sad? Do you fear seeing me happy?" "No," replied I, "but I suffer at seeing you suffer."—"You deceive me. I read in the thoughts, and you are not sufficiently strong in your beliefs to see your friends pass into the future existence. It is needless any longer concealing from me my position. I see beside me this poor corpse in which I suffer so much, and which still makes me suffer so much in quitting it. Ah! could you but see within it; 'tis like a butchery in ruins, every morsel in which is spoiled; the heart is dead like the rest; and to think that I was and am able to depart only when I shall have turned out all this! Ah! there is enough yet for some hours. Do not grow out of patience—it must be so; I cling to it by its very rottenness. Oh, my father! you are happy—you—what! you expect me? and you, little angel! you that hold out to me your arms—pretty creature that I bore in my bosom. I am about, then, to be reunited to you, never more to part. A whole eternity you shall be with me. How foolish I was to fear death! I long now to be dead. I feel, on the contrary, that I am being born. What beautiful things the heavens contain! Ah, God of goodness! forgive me. Friends, pray for me—but no! it is I that will pray for you. I have no longer but a small morsel, about as big as the thumb, to spit out, but it still clings fast. My God, rid me of it! Alphonse, believe in another life; the only regret I have, is not seeing you reduced to my state. Adèle said that we had the same disease: she was mistaken. You have yet a long time to suffer; you—I am happy—I go. Believe in the Divine goodness. Farewell!"

Thus ended this young woman, who so dearly cherished existence—who used to laugh whenever I spoke to her of the life to come, while admiring her beautiful black hair and saying: "It is better to stand still than run. I do n't say nay, but I have no wish to assure myself of it."

For twenty-four hours she was in a continual ecstasy, describing her disease, just as Adèle had seen it; knowing our thoughts like ourselves; speaking of death with the irony produced by a contrary conviction; praising the beauties of heaven with that admiration of which all beings detached from the earth, and returning to the places of their first childhood, are susceptible. I wept; I know not whether it was from regret at losing her, or vexation at not being able to accompany her. Laugh, men of the age! the scene invites laughter: you will pass, like us all, through this last trial, which you can not shun. To prepare yourselves for it, be present at the last moments of the dying: they are almost all seers at this solemn hour. They will make you comprehend that between you and the grave there is but one step; and that between your incredulity and the truth there is an abyss, that you will never be able to clear, if you remain under the empire of your satirical judgment. Close not, therefore, your hearts and ears against men more humble than yourself—men who desire to cure you of the fear of death; for at this supreme moment you will be in fear, when you behold that lugubrious piece of furniture, composed of five planks, awaiting this dearly-loved body, which forms the ornament of your civilization: what! it must be thrown into this hole, where a multitude of worms await it to make off of it a splendid feast. What is it then to be the object of such abandonment and such contempt? What it was—nothing! It is because I know that you already tremble at the thought of this sad ceremony, that I write these lines, to teach you how to die—to calm the fear that gains upon you. If I succeed in gaining this victory by the experiments I recommend you to make, you will not treat me as a madman; you will believe in God—in a better life; and you will know how to prepare for this departure with calm and courage—ay, more—with joy!

---

## THE LAST MOMENTS OF MY FATHER.

THE 2d of April, 1848, I was devoting all my care to my dearly-beloved father, formerly a long-course captain in the commercial navy; a man possessed of a disposition far from credulous, and a soul thoroughly steeped in the effluvia of a materialism, admitting only what matter sees and touches. He was eighty years old, and greatly dreaded death; constantly repeating: "I well know where I am, but I don't know whither I am going. I cast anchor on this globe, and may God hold it here as long as possible."

I had rejoiced at the time of the printing of the "Secrets," thinking that I should dispose his heart, by their perusal, to beliefs more cheering as to the future than those taught by the philosophy of the day; he contented himself with a toss of the head, and said to me: "I like better to believe it than going there to see it; I believe, however, in the immortality of the soul, but am not sure of its individuality, though I am disposed to admit it, from the magnetic, somnambulic, and ecstatic experiments of which you have rendered me witness. Were I twenty years younger, I would study, with all my heart, to modify my belief in this respect; but now it is somewhat late to do so with success. Besides, I shall soon know what to make of it!"

In such a frame of mind was it that he fell ill, and remained eight days a prey to the acute sufferings of a suffocating asthma; the doctor could afford him no relief; several persons magnetized him as well as myself, each in his turn. His delirious state admitted not of his thinking himself so near to attaining this solution of the individuality of the soul, but, at the moment supreme, reason appeared to make a last effort, and tame the disorder of his ideas. He said to us: "What the doctor has hitherto prescribed has produced naught and will produce naught, because I am going! My body has already been dead for some hours. I am still bound to it by a few fibres that you can aid me to burst by magnetizing me to the tips of my toes. Give me but magnetized water, that's all I want for the moment." "Why speak to me of death?—why think of it? You are much better than you were yesterday, and, in a few days, you will be re-established."—"You are right, I shall shortly be better; my agony will be long, because the soul can not quit the body before casting out all that is destined to come out, and facilitate its passage. Hence it is that there still remains for me a great deal to spit out. The magnetized water loosens all this, give me some pretty often." —"Do not be thus cast down," replied I; "your condition is not so hopeless as you imagine." "My condition is not unknown to me: I see my body stretched out on this bed, it is really dead, and you will have it buried to-morrow; I am no longer within it, I merely cling to it by a few threads, the hour is not yet come. You will calm this crisis—but I shall have another, which will be the last. They expect me up above—patience, patience—I shall soon be with you." A few hours had scarcely elapsed, and this departure had taken place!

During this long agony I searched with my look and my thought on the edge of those lips through which the last breath was to pass, that breath named the soul, because it is the life of it! I looked by the bedside, saying to myself: "He says that his soul is there—and still causes his body to act! Oh! problem insoluble! speech, doubtless dragged from the soul to the body by a current, a sympathizing thread, which this half-disorganized matter still breathes, forms an echo in its interior, as we obtain an echo in places adapted to produce such effect. So long as this inappreciable breath is in activity, the whole machine works, though it is proved to me that the soul has issued from it through every pore; the breath, then, is the drop of oil which the wheels await in order to move!

O God, infinitely great! O departure infinitely desired, hurry me on in thy eternal course, that I may measure with the eye and the spirit that immensity which separates me from the true light; come and tear off the material bandage that covers my eyes! come and purify this atmosphere, which poisons my soul with errors; oh! divine light descend on me!

O, my God! couldst thou have animated me to refuse me reason? for what we term reason is folly—what we name life and movement is death!—is nothingness! Scarcely a few seconds ago, I had near me a father, a friend—where is he? Has he lived eighty years to arrive at the state of a corpse? Oh! no, he told me he was then departing to another world; at that moment supreme the word of man is sacred; I am bound to believe him, and hope to rejoin him. This departure is but an infinite chain, dragging after it myriads of beings in the stalls joined to each of its rings. He is in one, I in another, we shall arrive at the same port, within a few days of each other, never more to part!

---

## CORRESPONDENCE.

"TO M. CAHAGNET, AUTHOR OF THE 'SECRETS OF THE LIFE TO COME REVEALED'

"MONSIEUR: I have read your work of the 'Secrets,' and, though believing you sincere, its perusal, nevertheless, left a doubt, which I wished wholly to remove. Having sometimes the facility of being in communication with a somnambulist, whose excellent clairvoyance I am well acquainted with, I proposed to myself requesting her to ask for a few apparitions. If I succeeded, the evidence was there for me. If I failed, I should not from this infer that you were an impostor, but I should not be satisfied, and should have endeavored to seize another opportunity. At my first trial, however, I was destined to be positively enlightened; for this is what happened to me:—

"I will say, in the first place, that this somnambulist is one of my sisters, who resides at a distance of fifteen leagues from Paris, and this accounts for my not being often with her. On the 5th of February, 1848, I magnetize my sister, and hold with her the following discourse: 'Have you not already told me that we could cause deceased persons to appear?' 'Yes.' —'Will you try now.' 'Yes. What person do you desire to see?' 'My father.'—'Well, let us both ask for him.' At the lapse of a few instants she says: 'Here he is.'—'How do you see him?' 'In striped gray pantaloons, white waistcoat, brown riding-coat; he has the same features as we knew him to have.' —'Ask him if he will answer a few questions.' 'He makes no reply.'—'Earnestly beg him to answer you.' 'He tells me that he is willing to do so.'—'Ask him if he is happy.' 'Yes.'—'Has he seen God?' 'Not yet; but he is in hopes of seeing him shortly.'—'Has he seen our grandmother?' 'No.'—'How is that?' 'Because she is not with him.'— 'Does he think that you can see her?' 'Yes.'—'What means employ?' 'The same as for him.'—My father disappeared. This apparition is indeed real, I am convinced of it now; but I feared lest it should be the image of my father present itself to my sister's memory. Two days after I asked for another; this time it was my wife's brother, whom I never saw, and my sister has not the least knowledge of; he died eight years ago. All I know of him is his name; I asked for him. She says to me: 'Here he is.'—'On what side does he appear to you?' 'On my right.'—'Give me a description of him.' 'He is rather light, has dark blue eyes, long face; wears blue trowsers, dark brown waistcoat, dress-coat.'—'Has he already appeared to his sister?' 'Yes, once only.'—'Is he happy?' 'Yes.'— 'Where is he?' 'In heaven.'—'Are there several heavens?' 'Yes.'—'How many?' 'Three.'—'Has he seen God?' 'Yes.' —'Has he always seen him?' 'No.'—'Since when has he seen him?' 'Since his appearing to his sister.'—'In what form does he see God?' 'God is a spirit.'—'Could he tell me whether God has any form?' 'He sees him only in the form of a sun.'—'Can it be the sun that enlightens us?' 'Yes. But stop, he tells me that I am mistaken, that he did not say that; this sun can not be visible to us.'—'Is it true that we have each beside us a good angel and an evil spirit? I can't believe it.' 'It is true, however.'—'Is there a hell wherein we are everlastingly burned?' 'No.'—'Then what is the punishment allotted to those who have done evil?' 'They are deprived of the sight of God for a time more or less long.'—'The Jews, Mahometans, &c., do they, equally with the catholics, enjoy the sight of God?' 'Oh! yes, certainly.'—'Ask him if you can see your good angel?' 'Yes.'—'What must be done to effect this?' 'We must pray to God to grant us this favor.'—My brother-in-law disappears. We both put up prayers to the Almighty to permit his angel to appear; at the lapse of an instant, she says: 'Here he is.'—'Where is he?' 'On my right.'—'How does he appear?' 'In white; he has flaxen hair and wings.'—'What is his name?' 'Gabriel.'—'Has he lived on earth?' 'Yes.'—'When deceased persons appear, is it the body in which we have known them on earth that appears?' 'No.'—'Then why are they so much alike, and dressed as they were among us?' 'Because, otherwise, it would be impossible to recognise them.'—'What form, then, has this soul when separated from its material body?' 'It resembles the body in form.'—'Do we live in heaven as on earth?' 'It is not the same existence.'—'What do we do there?—have we desires, and can we gratify them?' 'Yes.'—'Do we see again the persons we loved on earth?' 'Yes, there comes a time when we meet again.'—'Are there houses, gardens?' 'It is a garden.'—'Could he conduct you to heaven?' 'Yes, by-and-by.'—He disappears.

"On my return to Paris, I hastened to make my wife acquainted with the description of her brother. She was quite astonished, and acknowledged the whole as very exact. What seemed to her most extraordinary was the apparition she had once seen just as my sister had said, and her brother wore the dress described by my clairvoyante, a dress precisely the same as what he used to put on every Sunday. My wife added: 'What is most singular is, that I never dreamed of my brother but this once I now speak of, till last night, when he again appeared to me just as before.'

"Thus, monsieur, as to the questions I addressed to her, as well as to my sister's angel, it was simply to see how far their answers would correspond with those you recount in your work. I have seen with pleasure that they were almost in all points alike.

"Since then I have obtained three more apparitions, which have succeeded perfectly well. I had but one error, in a date of thirty years instead of thirty-four, and I am surprised that the persons who appear thus do not make mistakes oftener; for all that has taken place on earth becoming quite worthless to them in the state they are, and no longer setting any value on earthly things, I can not conceive how they can answer with so much precision.

"Thus, monsieur, I have obtained five apparitions quite real in my mind. Three of the personages who appeared were wholly unknown to me, as well as to my clairvoyante. I can, therefore, no longer entertain the least doubt; and whatever be the opinion of simple or titled persons, who should attempt, from the Christian pulpit or the academic chair, to deny the truth of these perceptions, it would be impossible for them to shake my faith in this respect; and I say more — I do myself an honor in sharing the name they will give you, even were it that of impostor. We are now a great body of sincere magnetizers, who would say to them, 'We are in the truth, and you in the darkness!'

"Receive my sincere salutations. L. J. Lecocq,

"*Marine clock-maker*, 9 *Rue de Calais, Argenteuil.*"

I will not take the liberty of making any observation on the sitting we have just read, wishing to leave the reader sole judge in this grave question, and subject him to no influence. However, I begged M. Lecocq, when he should have an opportunity of seeing his sister again, to submit to her the following questions. This he did with an obliging eagerness, and sent me the answer we are about to read :—

"I caused to appear a spirit that has enjoyed for some time the presence of God. I suppose him in a fit state to answer your questions, the result of which I communicate to you. I caused this spirit to be asked—

"'1. On leaving its material body, whither goes the soul?'

"'In the first place, the soul goes straight up to its Creator, to be judged according to its works; then finds itself placed in a state correspondent with its actions. In this state we find ourselves in heaven.'

"'2. What does it do in those places?'

"'It ends with enjoying celestial happiness, perfect joy. It can no longer desire anything better.'

"'3. What is there in those places?'

"'Whatsoever we desire to see there.'

"'4. How long a time does it remain in those places?'

"'It remains there for ever.'

"'5. But, however, if it again inhabits material bodies, how can that be?'

"'Since it remains in heaven for ever, it does not inhabit again other material bodies. God has said, "Whosoever dwells in the heavens with me, dwells in them for ever!"'

"'6. Does every one finally dwell in heaven, or only a few?'

"'Every one finally dwells there: only there are some who are a very long time before being in this state.'

"'7. How does the soul know that it is asked for on earth?'

"'That depends in the first place on God, who permits men to be convinced, by these apparitions, of the immortality of the soul.'

"'8. How does it manage to appear thus in all the details of its material body, and in the dress it wore on earth?'

"'It is an image imprinted on it.'

"'9. At times there is something wanted in its features, or the *ensemble* of its costume: what is the cause of this?'

"'That can not and ought not to exist, but there may be causes which I am unable to apprehend.'

"14*th of September*, 1848."

If I caused these questions to be put by M. Lecocq to his clairvoyante, it was in order to obtain a clear solution on them as a whole, foreseeing that his sister was of an order sufficiently elevated to answer them.

To the eight questions she replies that the features and dress in which spirits appear are imprinted on them. Such is Adèle's explanation, and this accounts for the mistakes (very rare, it is true) which clairvoyantes may make in the descriptions they give us of these spirits. Each dress worn during the life of the individual being imprinted on his spiritual body, as each point of view or exterior image is imprinted in the domain of his memory, *better named imagination*, it is not therefore astonishing that if the spirit asked for wore a blue dress-coat at the age of thirty (for instance), and a surtout at fifty, the clairvoyante's eye, according as it is more or less piercing, will be able to traverse three or four similar impresses, which can not, as we may suppose, be very deep, and then commit involuntary errors, the cause of which, being unknown, would give rise to the supposition of a real error or a false apparition. Let the reader consult on this head what Adèle has said at sitting 101. I have deemed these observations necessary for persons who study this kind of perceptions, and warn them not to reject every apparition the details of which they may not recognise as very exact. The clairvoyance of the subject may be of great weight in the goodness of the perception.

"Monsieur: Allow me to discourse with you a moment on the extraordinary things I have read in your 'Secrets.' I thought myself knowing in magnetism before reading your work, but now I find myself like a man who springs out of nothingness, and only commences his birth. What obligation am I not under to you, monsieur, for having enlightened me on matters which I suspected, and left me tugging in a torrent of doubts! I required a little aid, and I have found it in your book. I return you my most sincere thanks for it, and beg you to thank in my name Madame Adèle, the earthly angel who has been so kind as to initiate us into the holy mysteries of the Divine power. How happy I deem her whom God has made use of as an instrument to reveal to men truths which had been hitherto almost hidden from or doubtful to their intelligence! I beg the Almighty to be pleased to continue his work, trusting, by his divine support, that all men will become less proud on earth, and learn that they are but atoms compared with the great Ruler of the universe. I venture to hope that the harmony which ought to reign among those infinitely petty beings is not, doubtless, far from its dawn. . . . . . . . I do not pretend to have a wish to refute anything in your excellent work; on the contrary, my feeble mind is assuredly unable to comment on revelations so sublime!

"Still, reflections innumerable have come to puzzle my brains when I read in many passages that *we eat* in heaven. I knew not what to make of this word *eat*, which was no longer in harmony with all that is so beautiful in the descriptions of your terrestrial angel. Most fortunately, I am somewhat of a somnambulist. I begged of my brother to be so kind as to send me to sleep, that I might clear up this expression, which offered me some doubts. When I was in a crisis, and after a short time given to reflection, I began to laugh. My brother asked me the cause of my doing so, and I said to him: 'Hark ye, my friend, I am about to make clear to you what just now engaged my thoughts. The expression *eat* is a terrestrial word which the spirit could not render otherwise to be understood of men; in many circumstances it is obliged to proceed thus—otherwise it would be beset with questions which, by being recapitulated, tend to fatigue it; for oftentimes a questioner reverts, unwittingly, half a score times, to the same subject, and the celestial spirit must be endowed with singular goodness if it does not move off and leave such catechiser unanswered.' To return to the word *eat:* it is correct enough, but it is understood in two different ways. The first is terrestrial eating which relates to matter; the second spiritual eating which relates to the Divine essence. The last is a problem difficult enough to solve, especially by men, seeing that in heaven all is ideal, and performed only through emanation. No matter what you desire to see or have, it presents itself to your eyes.

Thus I desire to eat a peach; it presents itself forthwith to my view, and then I can satisfy myself. But take care, earthly men, and consider that this peach is but a celestial emanation, and that the spirit desiring it can taste only its emanations: this fully satisfies him, without being any the more for that subjected to earthly functions. For instance, a person asleep dreams that he is eating a peach: certainly he savors in his state all its deliciousness—still he has not one; this prevents him not from having had the same enjoyment as if it had been a real peach. This spirit, disengaged from matter, has placed him on a level with the celestial essence, where he will be after his departure from this globe.

"Excuse me, monsieur, and accept the assurance of my high consideration. "LEMOINE.

"15, *bis, Rue de la Madeleine, Paris.*"

The observations we have just read are not those of a feeble somnambulist, as this gentleman has the humility to say. I ought to add that (now at the age of sixty) for thirty years he has been a magnetizer and occasionally a clairvoyante, and that the definition he gives us is not in contradiction with good sense, but quite the contrary, as it maintains what Binet, Adèle, and all good clairvoyantes, affirm in this respect. The celestial state is a kind of eternal creation. *I say a kind,* because God alone has created all from all eternity; but the facility which spirits possess of obtaining desired objects would make believe that they themselves create these very objects, had we not proof to the contrary. Let the sittings of Binet on this subject in our first volume be read over again.

As I have already said, for fear of rendering this work wearisome to read, I have not thought fit to continue giving an account of all the apparition-sittings I obtain: hence it is that I have made no mention of one which M. Lemoine solicited from Adèle, to assure himself whether she perceived his father as he himself perceived him in his dreams. This gentleman had taken a note of this sitting, and forwarded an account of it to me a few days after, with a request that I would insert it just as he had written it. This I hasten to do, as much to comply with his just request, as to give the reader one proof more, if he still needs it :—

"SITTING OF THE 10TH OF AUGUST, 1848, GIVEN BY MADAME ADELE, THE ESCTATIC OF M. CAHAGNET.

"I had been to M. Cahagnet's, to beg of Madade Adèle to suffer herself to be sent to sleep, in order to visit anew my body, which had been ailing for a long time. I had benefited by her former prescriptions, and this sitting has only confirmed the advice which she recommended me to follow about a fortnight ago. Finding myself much stronger and in better health, I am heartily glad that I availed myself of her speciality.

"I had long desired that she should summon my father, who died in 1824, at the age of sixty-six, in order to be more convinced, if that could be possible, than by what I am able to see myself when asleep, inasmuch as I have no recollection of it on awaking. It was no longer a doubt on my part—it was a want. Madame Adèle had never known my father; she kindly consented to ask for him. At the lapse of an instant, I saw her make a pretty decided movement which announced to me his arrival. In fact, it was my father. The ecstatic said to me, 'I see a man whose hair is quite white, with a pigtail and sides.' (This is true; my father preserved to the day of his death his old-fashioned head-dress.) 'He is a man of lofty stature,' said she, 'having sèveral scars on his face.'—(My father was above six feet, and had been ill-used by the small-pox.) 'His nose is broken and broad at the tip; he is very corpulent and round-shouldered.'—(All this is true.) 'He was afflicted with rheumatism in the arms, and particularly in the lower part of the loins. He died of this rheumatism, which flew up into his chest. He must have suffered very much; he used also to suffer pretty often from a cough, which was occasioned by a prickling he felt in the throat.'—(All this is true.) She says that my father 'is very happy, in a state he would not change to come back upon earth. He was,' continues she, 'of a pretty cheerful disposition; possessed a good and feeling heart; and was, in short, a thoroughly honest man. I like him very much,' says she, 'and have great pleasure in seeing him; I hope this will not be the last time.'

"I requested her to ask my father whether I should do right to go and settle in Touraine, in the *commune* of F——. 'As you will not go,' said he to me, 'I have no details to give you on the matter.' 'I perceive,' says the ecstatic, 'that you would be exposed there to vengeance, and that some misfortune might befall you; the persons you would have to do with are treacherous and wicked, and withal, not over-scrupulous.' As I had read the first volume of the 'Secrets' of M. Cahagnet, where similar sittings are found in great numbers, I was less astonished than any other person would have been. However, the presence of my father who had been dead so long a time, the pleasure of knowing that he was by my side penetrated me with a holy respect difficult to describe; the idea of knowing that he was happy: the hope of a future which would reunite me to him, made such an impression on me that my soul could at this moment have embraced death as a sovereign good.

"Yours in heart and friendship.

"LEMOINE."

I ought to add that M. Lemoine afterward made inquiries respecting the place offered him as a steward of a castle. He knew that the persons who had hitherto filled this place had been very severe with the people round about; this had rendered the latter disaffected toward the castle, and the person who should succeed the late steward might indeed suffer for him, seeing that the inhabitants of this part of the country are, as he was told, vicious and vindictive. He refused the place for this reason and others that remain unknown to me; the prediction of his father thus became verified.

"MONSIEUR: From the appeal you make in your first volume of the 'Secrets of the Life to Come Revealed,' to persons who may have any facts to communicate to you for insertion in the second volume you intend publishing, I beg to respond to this invitation in the interest, be it understood, of the occult sciences; and, in order to prove to you that I have been in nowise astonished at the contents of your book, which I have read with great pleasure. Formerly a theatrical artiste, I devoted myself passionately to the study of cabalism, as offering, by its studious meditations, a counterpoise to the lighter studies of the theatre. I made acquaintance with a society (of madmen, the world says; of *savans*, I reply), into which I was admitted, not without some difficulty. To tell you all that took place in this society, all the time I was a member of it, would be to undertake a work in three volumes. I will cite one fact, out of a thousand similar ones, which corresponds with what your somnambulist Binet says relative to the strength and power of spirits. The chief of our circle possessed a small, strong box, about a foot long, ten inches wide, and six in depth, in which he secured very valuable articles. One day it was stolen from him; he was in great distress, when he sent to sleep a young man whom we ordinarily employed at our sittings. He questionod him as to the disappearance of the box, and begged him to find it. He went further, he ordered the spirit, who habitually came at our call, to bring back to him the box. The somnambulist was lying on the bed, which was at the farther end of the apartment, in a complete state of catalepsy; I was in the middle of the room with this gentleman, and two other gentlemen, of the name of Revole, father and son. The clairvoyante issued a command, told us to open the window, which I did instantly, and M. Picolet beheld arriving the precious box, which he received in his hands at the moment I was going to take it myself. We saw nothing else; and were no more surprised at this conveyance than we were at all that took place daily before our eyes. Yes, monsieur, a spirit can convey objects. Write this in my name —say, moreover, that I am seventy-eight years old, and that I should not wish, at such an age, to be a madman, or to impose on my fellow-men.

"I assure you of this, in the presence of the Divine Power, whom I should dread offending if I fabricated such a falsehood.

"I have the honor to be, monsieur, &c.,

"Borde,

"24, *Rue Saint-Laurent, Belleville.*"

Shall I annex any observations to such a relation? I should not want for them, if I had a mind to seek for them in the library of supernatural facts, which would prove the possibility of them. It would be to enter upon a series of arguments on both sides, not suited to the limits of this work. I ought to say that I have studied this venerable old man, for the sole purpose of assuring myself of his moral condition; and I confess that I should wish to possess his excellent lucidity and superior information. He must be a man of veracity, since he is of sound mind, and calls Heaven to testify to the truth of his assertions. For my part, I never obtained any spiritual conveyance. One of my clairvoyantes once showed me one that he had received over night. I studied the fact, deemed it possible; but not having seen it with *my own eyes*, I made no mention of it. I set forth only what I have seen; however, I believe in such conveyances, and will demonstrate the possibility of them by laws wholly physical. I will treat of this proposition in the philosophical work I have already spoken of. If we ought to admit nothing without mature examination, let us, in like manner, deny nothing without mature examination.

We borrow from the journal *La République*, of the 3d February, 1849, a recital of this nature, extracted from the *Gazette des Tribunaux*. This fact is not the only one of which we have a knowledge; studious men will judge it with the impartiality necessary to examinations of this kind, and will not conclude, I am certain, as would the *savans*, who deny when they can not explain:—

"One of the most singular facts, a fact reproducing itself every night for the last three weeks, and baffling all imaginable plans that have been adopted to discover the cause of it, sets in commotion the whole of the populous quarter of the Montagne-Sainte-Geneviève, the Sorbonne, and the Place Saint-Michel. The double inquiry, judicial and administrative, which has been going on for some days past, verifies, in accord with public clamor, the following statement:—

"In the work of demolition commenced for the opening of a new street which is to join the Sorbonne to the Panthéon, and the Ecole de Droit, traversing the Rue des Grès up to the old church which has successively been used as a school and barracks, at the extremity of a piece of ground where once stood a public ballroom, is a wood and charcoal yard, bounded by a dwelling-house one story high, with lofts. It is this house, standing at a certain distance from the street, and separated from the adjoining buildings now in course of demolition, by the large excavations of the old enclosure wall of Paris, constructed under Philippe Auguste, laid open by the works, which every evening and all night is assailed by a shower of projectiles, which, from their size, and the violence with which they are hurled, produce such havoc that the windows are smashed, the doors broken open, altogether presenting the appearance of a place that has been attacked by the catapulta or grape-shot.

"Whence come these projectiles, consisting of paving-stones, fragments of ruins, huge blocks, which, considering their weight and the distance they come from, evidently could not be hurled by the hand of man? This is what it has been hitherto impossible to find out. In vain has been exercised, under the personal direction of the commissary of police, and able agents, a surveillance by day and night; in vain have been let loose every night in the surrounding enclosures, watch-dogs; nothing has been able to explain the phenomenon which, in their credulity, the people attribute to mysterious causes; the projectiles have continued showering down with a crash on the house, hurled at a great height above the heads of those placed on the lookout, even on the roofs of the neighboring houses, apparently coming from a great distance, and reaching their object with a precision in some sort mathematical, not one appearing to deviate in its parabolic course from the object invariably aimed at.

"We will not go into more ample details respecting this fact, which, no doubt—thanks to the solicitude it has awakened—will soon be accounted for. Already the inquiry extends over whatsoever could attach, in this object, to the explanation of the adage, *Cui prodest is auctor*. Nevertheless, we will remark that in circumstances somewhat analogous, and which equally created a certain sensation in Paris, when, for instance, a shower of small pieces of money attracted, every evening, the simpletons of Paris to the Rue de Montesquieu; or, when all the bells of a house in the Rue de Malte were set going by an invisible hand, it was impossible to succeed in any discovery, find an explanation, a first cause, whatever it might be. Let us hope that this time we shall arrive at a more precise result."

The *République*, of the 4th February, continues:—

"The *Gazette des Tribunaux* still speaks of the famous war-machine, so formidable, and above all so *mysterious*, which sets in commotion the inhabitants of the quarter Saint Jacques. To-day this paper says:—

"'The singular fact of the throw of projectiles against the house of a dealer in wood and charcoal, Rue Neuve-de-Cluny, near the Place du Panthéon, has continued being reproduced up to this very day, despite the incessant surveillance exercised on the very spot.

"'At eleven o'clock, although agents were stationed at all the adjacent points, an enormous stone struck against the door (barricaded) of the house. At three o'clock, the chief, *ad interim*, of the safety-service, and five or six of his principal subordinates, being busily engaged in making inquiries, concerning different circumstances, of the occupiers of the house, an immense rough stone fell shivering at their feet, like the bursting of a bomb.

"'We are lost in conjectures. The doors, the windows, are replaced by planks nailed up inside, to prevent the inmates of the house from being struck, as their furniture, and even their beds, have been smashed by the projectiles.'"

We possess a great number of similar accounts, which we shall not attempt to relate. We assure the police, that but one thing is wanted to discover the authors of this devastation, that is the somnambulic view. We will revert to this affair in our journal, the "Magnétiseur Spiritualiste."

"PARIS, 3*d September*, 1848.

"MONSEIUR AND FRIEND: The impression made on me by a perusal of your book is: That you seem to me a man who seeks after the truth, and that your desire has led you to raise a corner of the veil which concealed from mankind the future life — a life to me as certain as the present one. In your first volume, you ask magnetizers for facts similar to those you therein treat of; to comply with this request, I supply you with one which affected me personally. For the sake of truth, I will do my best to recount it to you. This extraordinary fact happened to me one night in the month of April, 1839. I woke up, about two o'clock in the morning, in a frightful state of moral suffering. I felt myself overcome by a secret power, that held me down, as if crucified on my bed, by the side of my wife, who was asleep, and whom the power that thus overcame me had prevented me from waking. All my moral force seemed to me concentrated in my heart. I retained my presence of mind, and, although it was impossible for me to move my body, I possessed my whole power of observation. I felt my heart full of a fluid, which made me suffer as if silken threads had been drawn through it. But, despite the power that thus grasped me, my resistance was in a ratio with my great confidence in God, and I doubted not being extricated from this miserable state. When my eyes opened, I perceived the moon reflecting her light into my room; and when I closed them, I found myself in conversation with a being I had known when he was alive, on earth. In the first place, he drew near and asked me for something; he was dressed in a sorry black riding-coat, and his shirt was very dirty; in short, his appearance bespoke the most profound misery: he concluded by ordering me to pray for him; but, as I hate constraint, I refused doing so, braving the consequences. I then felt his breath enter into my nostrils, and poison me with an insupportable and infernal odor; but, thanks to God, I made an effort on myself, despite those he made to prevent me. I roused my wife, and begged her to push me out of bed, which she did. I walked barefooted in my room; but I was still battling with this man by my interior senses. I drank a glass of fresh water, handed me by my wife, and begged her to kneel down with me and pray to God for my deliverance. We prayed fervently. I found myself better; there no longer remained in me but those pangs of the heart, from the force of the bonds in which it seemed to me grasped.

"In the morning, by way of diverting my thoughts, I walked to the exhibition of the products of industry, and this greatly alleviated me.

"I durst not speak of my singular adventure to any one, knowing how ignorant and incredulous the world is in such matters.

"Oh, monsieur, if, at that period, I had had the happiness of knowing a man as I now know you, your heart, I love to think so, would have become the refuge of mine; but poor and without support, against this world of wicked spirits, I remained in my painful condition for several months. The pain at my heart never left me; my physical faculties were not, however, disordered: God, I was sure of it, would, sooner or later, raise up for me a means of relief, and throw a light on this mystery of the human soul. However, I had given a hint of my adventure to our worthy friend, M. Pirlot. I perceive that my letter might become wearisome; but from the love I know you have for the truth, joined to that I have of rendering homage to Divine Providence, I beg permission to relate how I recovered my tranquillity. Now, it happened, one day, that the wife of M. Pirlot was indisposed, and Madame Pirou was sent for — a somnambulist whom I did not know, notwithstanding her high reputation for clairvoyance. As M. Pirlot knew what a wretched state of obsession I was in, he told me to come to the consultation that was to be held. I repaired thither, with the desire of getting myself visited by this lady. Colonel R—— was the person who sent her to sleep. I asked, in my turn, the favor of presenting my hand to the clairvoyante, that she might have the kindness to examine me. Scarcely had she touched me than she uttered a cry of alarm as to my condition, saying that I was beset by a spirit she saw, in a hideous form, coiled under my nose, and enveloped in a most disgusting atmosphere. The most infectious odors surrounded it; and she was not at all surprised at my unfortunate situation. She invited all present to join with her in supplicating the angels to intercede with God for me. A few days after this ceremony, I was wholly relieved.

"Here, monsieur, is a fact, in all its truth. You are quite at liberty to publish it, if you deem fit.

"Receive, &c., "BINET,

"*Manufacturer of Chemical Utensils,*

"*5, Rue Neuve-Saint-Sabin, Paris.*"

The fact narrated here by M. Binet has naught of ridiculous in it for me who was, through the effect of my own will, beset for three years, and saw infinitely more than this estimable and intelligent citizen, who had acquired, in his quarter, wherein he has lived full forty years, a claim to the esteem of all his neighbors, who occasionally find, in his wise counsels, hints that are not within the jurisdiction of a man laboring under the influence of hallucination.

"PARIS, *20th August*, 1848.

"MY DEAR FRIEND: Your work, of the 'Secrets of the Life to Come Revealed,' is the most curious and instructive book that can possibly be read. I congratulate you on the courage you have displayed by publishing it; for, sooner or later, it will produce beneficial effects.

"I do not expect that men in general will adopt the consoling truths you publish, and the practice of which you recommend, by employing the same means as you have employed in order to discover the mysteries of celestial happiness. I so much the less expect it, as I feel, on the contrary, rising up against the principles so true of the immortality of the soul, and the joys eternally in store for it, the cortège of materialists and skeptics, whose mind is fed only with ideas stamped with errors, prejudices, and religious superstitions;—people who believe only what they touch and see by their material eyes, rejecting as dangerous all that they have learned at the schools; and yet, if one and the other would but read your book, they would see that all that takes place in heaven among souls, is the most complete condemnation of the state of society on our earth. On the latter, man struggles incessantly against the storm of free-will—words ill understood. What victims fall into the abyss of evil. In heaven, the definition of good and evil is unknown; the latter never existed there! I pass on to the object of my letter. Initiated into, and familiarized for long years with, the world of spirits, I will not say that your work has taught me nothing; I should deceive you. You mention therein:—

"1. That spirits can see, touch, and carry, in certain circumstances, material objects.

"2. That a spirit can visit us on earth in a material form.

"3. That man material may render himself invisible. Your book is deficient in facts, in support of these assertions. Allow me, therefore (as you suspect neither my good faith nor my conscientiousness, and as I detest falsehood), to offer you some real facts on what you announce.

"The following are the initials of the persons who were present at what I am about to recount to you: 1st, M. Pi—; 2d, M. Bar—; 3d, M. Bou—; 4th, M. Rev—; 5th, M. A. Rev—, junior; 6th, Ad—, the somnambulist, and 7th, myself.

"FIRST FACT.

"M. Rev—, senior, and myself, were taking a walk on the high road of a town in Brittany. On entering the hotel, M. Rev— perceived that he had lost his gold seal, which was of great value. After dinner, he sent Ad— to sleep, saying to her: "Call such a spirit, beg him, and order him, if need be, to go and look for my seal among a heap of stones by the sea-side, at a league's distance from here.' The command was scarcely given, when the spirit delivered the seal to Ad—, who said to M. Rev—, 'Thank the spirit and dismiss him.'

"SECOND FACT.

"On our return to Nantes, whence we had first set out, Ad—, being sent to sleep, said to M. Rev—, sen.: 'The colonel is not wholly recovered from his illness; to cure him we must ask for a few drops of medicine, prepare a glass of sugar and water, and cut a piece of white paper in the form of a triangle.

Describe a circle on the floor, place the triangle in the middle of the circle, set down the glass of sugar and water on the triangle, and let the vertical angle look toward the east.' All these dispositions made, Ad— said to M. Rev—: 'Call the angel of the Lord, and beg him to pour into the glass of sugar and water the number of drops sufficient to cure the colonel.' While M. Rev— was commencing the invocation, Ad— stopped him, telling him that the triangle was not due east. As at this moment my eyes were directed toward the glass, I beheld with the greatest astonishment the paper triangle and the glass turn of themselves toward the east. After the invocation, and when the sugar-and-water was drunk up, God and the angel were thanked by us. Needless to say that, in less than an hour, I was wholly relieved. This took place in the month of April, 1827.

"*Apropos* of the facts, I ought to observe that the seal was brought back by a spirit of an inferior order, whom Ad— qualified as an elementary spirit of the earth, and whose name was Milknas; this was invariably the spirit we employed for sending or receiving material objects. As to the drops put into the glass of sugar and water, they were introduced into it by an angel of high degree.

"These observations are indispensable, to enable you to distinguish, in the divers facts I purpose revealing to you, by what order of spirits these facts were accomplished. Nevertheless, I believe that, when it concerns them to lend their aid to the man who fears and loves God, the spirits that he invokes are always good; for the bad, far from serving him, seek only to injure him, and excite him to evil by the most seducing and even the most atrocious temptations, when they perceive that the man yields to their attacks without the intention of having recourse to God. Allow me this reflection, which is rather a sudden inspiration than the result of long experience.

"THIRD FACT.

"Before returning to Paris, and while I was still residing at Nantes, those who received me at a later period into the bosom of their society, which was presided over by M. Pi—, a gentleman of great merit and extraordinary scientific attainments (it was he who magnetized Ad—), assembled one evening at M. Pi—'s, to take part in a ceremony relative to occult pursuits. M. Pi— sent Ad— to sleep, and each member sat down in a chair, placed for him within a large circle drawn on the floor, each having at his feet, and right in front of him, a lamp, the wick of which was burning in alcohol. M. Pi— having first called down the blessing of God on those present, the ceremony commenced. Scarcely, however, had it begun, than shrill cries, immoderate laughter, and horrible hissing, resounded in the room; the lamps were quickly extinguished, and on all sides fell pieces of old iron, bars of iron, &c.; but all these projectiles lodged on the edge of the circle, without striking any one. Forthwith, M. Pi—, armed with his talisman, drove out, in the name of God, these evil spirits, who decamped, leaving us their projectiles.

"This third fact responds in the affirmative to the questions you addressed to Swedenborg, to inquire whether evil spirits could create disorder in a room by displacing and upsetting the furniture. Swedenborg affirmed that they could do so, and I have just given you a proof of the truth of his assertion.

"I pause; my bad sight and trembling hand prevent me from continuing. Soon you shall have the sequel; in the meanwhile, believe me, &c., &c.

"Colonel Roger,

"4 *Rue Neuve de l'Université, Paris.*"

Well, my lords of science, we grow amusing, we take our patent as madmen, which we present to you to sign! What think you of it? We could have ventured to hope for absolution at the commencement of this work; but toward its close, we fall into the absurd. The absurd! be it so; I accept your definition, on condition that you will read us to the end, were it only to your children, by way of recalling to their memory their old ghost-tales. Thus you perceive that we are not very exacting; we know you to be infinitely learned, and that we do but excite your pity; consequently are we sure of success.

But you, men of good faith, we do not address ourselves to you to laugh at your expense or to make you laugh at ours; we certify to you that we will mathematically prove to you the possibility of these marvels; what we now present to you is but a sketch; we leave aside facts which will serve us by-and-by to regain your confidence should we lose it now. We assure you that we have frequented the company of Colonel Roger for these two years past, *with the sole view of studying him.* For we too have our share of doubts; we have caused him to be magnetically visited, and in his presence, by our best clairvoyantes; we have gone so far as to make inquiries as to certain acts (without his knowledge), and have obtained the assurance that he was in the full enjoyment of a sound mind, and that the facts recounted by him were true; eye-witnesses have affirmed this to us. It is from notions so positive that we give publicity to the three facts that have been read, out of twenty others which remain in my portfolio. But let us continue, all madmen are not yet at Charenton (Bedlam):—

"MONSIEUR: Having read with pleasure your first volume of the 'Secrets of the Life to Come Revealed,' and desiring to acquire by myself proofs of the facility which, as you announce. all good clairvoyantes possess of communicating with the souls of deceased persons, I actively busied myself in provoking such apparitions, and had the happiness to succeed more easily than by the aid of the magic mirror; the visions are much better delineated, make a greater impression on the clairvoyante, and offer him the twofold advantage of conversing with those blessed souls! As in your first volume you beg all magnetizers who may possess facts similar to those you publish to communicate them to you, I send you the following, taken from among many others, and authorize you to make such use of them as you deem fit.

"For a long time I have been in the habit of magnetizing a person whom I have known from my childhood, and who for some months was very ill and given over by the physicians; I had the happiness to restore her to health. From the first days of her treatment, she gave me proofs of singular clairvoyance, of which I took advantage to put her in correspondence with several deceased relatives and friends. I addressed to her questions similar to yours; all her answers were similar, in a religious and psychological point of view. Yesterday, I asked for a little sister of mine, whom I never saw and who died at the age of eight months. She forthwith exclaimed: 'I see a pretty little girl! oh! good heavens! how beautiful she is! But she'll fall, don't you see her? Hold out your arms to her.' I reassured her by telling her that a spirit could not fall. She resumed: 'The fact is that the clouds she is upon are so light! so transparent! that I can't understand how they can support this beautiful child.' 'Make her draw near,' said I. She keeps at a distance and smiles on me, but how pretty she is! Never before did I see such an angelic countenance.' 'What age may she be?' 'From about two and a half to three years of age.' 'How is she dressed?' 'She is quite bare.' 'What is the color of her hair?' 'Her hair is of a flaxen color and curly. But how beautiful she is!' I could not rouse this lady out of the admiration in which she was absorbed. Then, suddenly, she appears very much surprised, and exclaims: 'She is going away!—she is going away! Oh! I am wrong, she is going to meet her good mother. In fact, my mother was coming up stairs at this instant, for she entered almost immediately after. I was so much the more surprised as my clairvoyante does not see material persons at hand. I could not, therefore, doubt but that it was as she said. She resumed: 'Ah! how pleased she is at seeing her mother, she smiles on her with such a beautiful expression! Why can not her mother herself see her?' At this instant, she stretched out her arms and caught her? I told her to embrace her, but she replied: 'No, I should not dare. I am not worthy of doing so.'—'Do you really feel the weight of this child's body you hold in your arms, as if it were material?' 'Certainly, how can you doubt it?'—'I am far from doubting it,' replied I; 'for at this moment I feel something extraordinary passing within me; the influence of this little angel must surely be the cause of it. This would suffice to remove all my doubts had I any remaining.' I then inquired of my mother whether this child had flaxen hair, and whether she was as beautiful as my clairvoyante described her. She replied: 'All this is very true; the neighbors used to say that they never beheld such a beautiful little creature.'

"Only think, monsieur, what was my joy and whether I could still doubt the truth of such apparitions. I recognised in this one what your clairvoyantes affirm relative to children that die before the age of three years, that they seem not to exceed that age. Were it otherwise, it would be next to impossible to recognise them.

"I never knew this little sister of mine, as she died before I was born; my clairvoyante could not, therefore, perceive the image of her in my thought. Such supposition is as absurd as if it were said that a clairvoyante perceives in the thought places and persons that one has never seen one's self, as does Alexis and a thousand others, every day.

"I here give the result of the questions you begged me to address to my clairvoyante:—

"1. Whither goes the soul after leaving our material body?

"It ascends and traverses several radii, hears the voice of God who judges it, and consigns it to a place suited to its affections.

"2. What does it see in those places?

"Spirits like itself, open countries, gardens: in short, whatever it desires to see.

"3. What does it do in those places?

"Whatsoever it finds agreeable to do.

"4. What length of time does it remain in those places?

"It remains in them for a longer or shorter period of time; then passes into other places and remains there eternally.

"5. Does it return to take again a material body on this earth?

"Never.

"6. How does it know that it is asked for on earth?

"It is an effect of sensation. Our thought joins its thought in an instant, and it is with us.

"7. The dress which it wears when it comes to see us, is it that which it wears in heaven?

"No, it wears there much lighter dresses, a sort of gauze of different colors.

"8. Where does it procure the dress in which it appears to us?

"It is an effect of its thought; it can present itself in any form, assume all the costumes it has worn; it desires to appear to us in this or that one, and it presents itself thus.

"9. At times something is wanted in this attire, or in its personal appearance; how is this?

"It is to be accounted for in this way—in its haste to appear to us, it forgets something; for no longer having the same countenance, or the same dress, it may make a mistake. But on its second appearance this can no longer exist, it suffices to have a single doubt.

"10. We can perceive even the maladies it has had in the course of its earthly life, how is that?

"It desires to appear to us in such conditions; it is its thought, or, more correctly speaking, its *desire*, which supplies all; for, in heaven, there are neither maladies nor infirmities."

As may be seen, if I had it in my power to address the same questions to all the clairvoyantes in the world, I should do so in the interest of truth, and in order to avoid hearing say that it is an effect of influence on my part; it might be objected that M. Blesson having read the first volume of these "Secrets," drew therefrom answers which his influence over his clairvoyante might possibly reproduce; I will observe, that there are in the latter questions which are not to be found in the first volume; that they are to be met with only at the commencement of this, which M. Lecocq and M. Blesson have not read; their answers are in conformity with those of Adèle; there is no influence in the case.

"I can not resist," continues M. Blesson, "the desire of relating to you a fact for which I can not account:—One day I had just sent my wife, who is a somnambulist, to sleep; I begged her to ask for my father, who has been dead these sixteen years. Forthwith presented himself an individual, of whom she gave such a description as corresponded exactly with that of my father, with this exception, he appeared to her very stern; my father, on the contrary, was very affable. I entertained the notion that this might be an evil spirit, and, as you recommend, I ordered him away in the name of God, if he were not my father. My wife beheld him move off and replaced by an old woman of a hideous countenance, who caused her so much fear that she begged me to wake her, which I forthwith did, as she seemed to me very much agitated. Having no recollection of what she had seen in her dream, she set to work picking legumes to cook them for dinner; she lighted a large charcoal fire (for she was behind hand), set over it a pot of water, and was not a little surprised, after having used a scuttle full of charcoal in keeping up a large fire, at being unable to make the water boil. We were astounded, as well as the persons present, at this phenomenon, to me till then unknown.

"A fortnight after this, the weather was very stormy, my wife was close to me, and, as before, preparing legumes for dinner. She fell asleep, oppressed with the heavy atmosphere which prevailed this day. I took advantage of her sleep to magnetize her, and plunge her into the somnambulic sleep; I succeeded in doing so in a very short time. I asked for the apparition of a friend; an owl presented itself to her eyes, and so frightened her that I was obliged to wake her as before. She then put her water on the fire, this time in a copper vessel (the other was an earthenware one); the same phenomenon was reproduced, the water did not boil till after a lapse of six hours, and then not before I had addressed a prayer to God to disenchant our pot, in case there was a spell upon it. We were then able to cook our legumes.

"I know not whether there be aught ridiculous in these facts, but I do know that, being unable to account for them by the ordinary laws of nature, I am obliged to class them among the extraordinary ones. 'It was an evil spirit that played us that trick,' since said to me my wife when again in a somnambulic sleep. Believe me, most respectfully, &c.,

" Blesson,

*Entrepreneur de peinture*, 36, *Rue aux Ours*,

" Paris, *the 2d September*, 1848."

"Monsieur: The following I can vouch for as a fact, as it took place in my presence, at Lyons, in 1815:—

" Three females of my acquaintance, wishing to take tickets in the lottery which then existed, fancied that a death's head might be of service to them by indicating to them the numbers which would insure success. I will make no reflections as to the value of such a belief; it suffices me to say that such was the case.

" It was, therefore, settled that one of them should go to the cemetery of —— in search of a death's-head, and bring it home. The head was brought into the presence of the three women and another female who was lying ill in the room where the four persons were thus assembled. A discussion took place as to the sex to which this head belonged; one saying it was that of a man, another thinking it the contrary. At this moment there was a knock at the door; embarrassment and fear were manifested; the ladies resolved not to open; but the knocks redoubled, it was necessary to yield. In haste they placed the head under the pillow of the sick woman and then opened the door. A few minutes elapsed, when suddenly the woman who was in bed uttered a piercing shriek, drawing her arm out of bed. The persons present asked her the cause of her crying out, and what was the general astonishment when she declared that she had been bitten with great violence. Of this they convinced themselves by looking at her arm, on which were the marks of five teeth with the blood ready to gush out; the pain must have been acute. I will not say what passed at this moment; it may naturally be supposed that they got out of the scrape as well as possible, and that when once free they quickly carried back the head to the place whence they had taken it.

'This fact, which had no echo beyond the spot where it took place, was never, be it understood, made public. I can vouch for the truth of it, as I was a witness to it; I heard the shriek at the moment the pain was felt, and saw the marks of the teeth. Moreover, I certify that the woman had her arm in the bed at the moment she uttered the cry. So much is certain, and I guaranty the truth of it with all the force of my conscience. I affirm and set my signature to this statement, regardless of the ridicule with which some persons may treat it.

"DAME BELHOT, *Argenteuil*."

This kind of facts is not more incredible than those marks which have been seen at all times on the bodies of the possessed, or the clairvoyantes and ecstatics of our times. To admit the possibility of them, is to confirm that of conveyances. What can thus break into matter, can very well raise it; one is a consequence of the other. We have still at this moment the *stigmatized* of the Tyrol, &c., who have wounds out of which the blood is seen to run. There is no dearth of similar facts which it would be curious to verify, and there is a means of eliciting them. We will revert to the subject in our work on philosophy, under the head of "Magnetism," as we hold it a matter of greater importance to be true and frank rather than enthusiastic.

"MONSIEUR: To comply with the request made in your 'Secrets,' I transmit you a fact which happened to me in the month of May, 1818:—

"I had gone with my wife and young child to Vetheuil, a village situated near Mantes, to the house of my late parents, and which then belonged to one of my sisters. The ground-floor of this house was composed of a room at the entrance, in which we slept, and of another next to it, in which my sister slept.

"One night we were all in bed—I, my wife, and the child between us (in the same bed, be it understood)—when, at about eleven o'clock, my child, then about two and a quarter years old, was taken up from between us and conveyed to the foot of the chimney, which was about ten paces distant from our bed.

My wife, alarmed, uttered a cry that woke up my sister, who inquired into the cause of this noise. After being told, she replied: 'Oh! don't be surprised at that, it is Louis Metro playing off some of his tricks.' This reply was not of a nature to make us easy; but, however, I got up and went for the child, which, at the moment I picked it up, was accompanied by a strong light. I will not deny it—although an old soldier, I was frightened. I once more laid down the child in the same position; that is to say, between us two. Ten minutes had not elapsed, when it was again raised up, but only to the height of a foot, and then let down again in the same place.

"Now, here you have not a tale that was told me, but a reality that happened to me—an old soldier, living in the country, and following my old trade of a cooper. Moreover, there were with me at the time two witnesses, who can vouch for the truth of my statement. I am not an educated man, and consequently I am unable to account for it. I merely relate what happened to me.

"I remain, most respectfully, &c., &c.,

"*15th October*, 1848." "JEAN LEMAITRE."

Who could have removed this child? Those that convey objects.—Who convey objects? Those that have the power of doing so.—"You decidedly wish, then, my poor, senseless fellow," will those say to me who are rich in sense, "to make us believe that the spirit can act on matter!" To regain the esteem of those sensible persons, I will answer: "No, it is matter that bears the spirit; a spirit is air, and air can not bear matter. We perceive this by our globe, which is supported on the shoulders of Hercules, and the moon which is in the lap of Venus. What an error to think that a light body can support a heavy one!" Reasoning thus, the dose of physic which was being prepared for me will be diminished, and I shall not be sorry for it: long live the reasoning of our days!

We are about to pass on to an author well known by his *feuilletons* in the *Populaire* and other highly-esteemed works, who has had the kindness to communicate to me the paper we are about to read. An *esteemed* author is, however, a being recognised as superior by our *savans* to this good and honest soldier whose narrative we have just perused—a narrative as simple as it is full of truthfulness. After reading this one, they will be tempted to cry out, "Hallucination!" But there is no lack of hallucinated individuals of this kind: the satirical Balzac, the astounding Alexandre Dumas, the austere patriot Alphonse Esquiros, the piquant Alphonse Karr, the philanthropic Eugène Sue, &c., &c., all believe in magnetism and its marvels. It was to those well-taught men that it appertained to handle the subject which I have ventured to treat upon very superficially. What success would it not have obtained, set forth by those pens, as elegant as they are witty! In short, since I have opened the march, let us proceed; and you, readers, be indulgent:—

"MONSIEUR: Having perused your 'Secrets,' I am induced to relate to you a few facts from which you may possibly derive some information. As it seems necessary to me to make a few prefatory remarks in order to fix the amount of confidence that may be accorded me, I will do so, but in a few words.

"My natural tendencies are spiritualist ones; my aspirations are directed toward the world of causes; but three motives paralyzed my tendencies and my aspirations: the philosophy of our days, with which I was classically impregnated; my pride, which made me consider as weakness of mind the least faith in whatsoever departs from physical and chemical possibilities; in short, the fear of being a dupe, even to my own illusions—therefore laughed I disdainfully at the recitals of supernatural things. 'Your father,' once said my mother to me, 'was not a weak-minded man, and yet he affirmed having seen on two occasions, in the course of his life, two human forms clad in white: in one he perfectly well recognised his betrothed, in the other his aunt. In fact, these two persons were dying, far away from him, when he saw them.' At this affirmation I gave an incredulous shake of the head. 'Your grandmother, at the moment her father took to his death-bed, beheld him distinctly, wrapped up in a sheet, and seated on their garden-wall.' 'A mere illusion,' replied I; 'childish fright.'—'For several years we had not seen my father's brother: one night we were all aroused by his voice, which, from the yard, was calling my father. We ran out to welcome our uncle; no one was there, and we were all thoroughly convinced of the fact, since your grandfather had been thrice named.' 'Hallucination of the hearing,' replied I; 'a spirit can not speak.'—'When he whom I loved died,' added my mother, 'several blows were struck on a small spinning-wheel hanging from the wall, and it commenced rapidly turning round. Weeping, I conveyed the spinning-wheel to the bedside of my father, who laughed at me; and the fact was renewed in the presence of a score of persons, who felt the agitation of the air under the invisible wand, and beheld, not only the wheel turn, but a cloud of dust gather around it.'—'It was probably some sorry trick of legerdemain that was played you,' replied I. 'When my sister died,' resumed my godmother, 'I did not even know that she had been ill. I woke up during the night; the moon threw its light into my room, and I distinctly beheld my sister walking. When my husband died, far away from me, I felt myself raised thrice in my bed.'—'These are illusions, my dear godmother,' replied I, 'for such things can't be; the spirit has no form; the spirit has no action over the matter it animates, and acts physically only through the medium of organs.' My incredulity on such matters was so great, that I would not believe that three violent rings given at our door, while we were on the landing-place, were a sign of farewell sent by a female friend of my mother, although the hour of her death coincided with that of the three pulls at the bell. I preferred believing that a mouse had run along the bell-wire; and when my sister, at that time in Scotland, inquired of us by letter whether Madame O——, of whose illness we had not sent her word, had not died on such a day, at such an hour, because she had heard herself thrice called by the voice of that lady, although the coincidence was exact, my incredulity remained unshaken. 'Some such thing will happen to yourself,' said my mother, 'and then you will believe.'—'I will search into it,' said I, 'and find out, be you assured, some physical cause for it.'

"I was in this disposition at the age of eighteen, when, working at my thesis on the Divine presence and human free will, I heard a knocking over my head. The noise became so fatiguing by its monotonous continuance, that I went up to the room whence it proceeded: no one was there. I thought that it was some effect of acoustics. I was about to descend, when the same noise was renewed over my head in a garret. I went up to it. No one again. I explored the garret, and the rooms under it, looked out of the window: no physical cause within, no noise without that could possibly be repercussed. I once more took up my pen; but scarcely was I seated, than the same uniform knocks were again heard, and forthwith a thought took possession of my mind. Fritz is ill, and will not recover! This young man was my betrothed, and loved me with infinite sincerity and tenderness. I hastened to recount to my mother what had passed, apprize her of my intention, and beg her to accompany me to the abode of the parents of Fritz, who, in fact, was ill in bed. He told me that for several hours his wishes had been calling for me. Ten days after, he was very bad. My mother, at that time ailing, and my sister falling almost every night into horrible convulsions, I had made up my mind, in order to watch over these two objects of my affections, to sleep with the former, and make the other sleep in our room. On the night of the tenth day of Fritz's illness, a violent shock was given the bed occupied by me and my mother. Thinking that this shock had been imprinted by a kick from my mother, I did not trouble myself about it, but placed my hand softly on her leg, and assured myself, when the second shock arrived, that it did not proceed from my mother. The third was so violent, that my mother woke up in a fright, asking me what I was doing. After hearing my reply, she said to me: 'Fritz is dying, my child! he is come to bid us farewell.' I get up gently, light the candle, explore the room and the adjoining ones; then resume my place. Almost immediately after, at the foot of the bed, we hear the sound of two fists falling alternately on the bedstead, uninterruptedly and regularly. My sister, in her turn, wakes up in her fright, exclaiming, 'Good God! what noise, pray, are you making?' I speak to her, strive to reassure her: useless pains; she dares not remain in her bed. My mother goes to take her place, and she comes to occupy her mother's. The regular strokes pass along the side I lay on; the shocks made the candle flare. I commenced reading aloud to divert the attention of my sister, and the noise does not cease for several hours. In fact, my betrothed was dead! From that day my incredulity fell.

"Among facts of the same order, here are two which I have from persons worthy of belief. One of these persons, a grave and profoundly studious man, related that while he was a professor at the college of Aix, something quite inexplicable took place there. One evening, when the professors were assembled in the common hall, the laundress entered looking quite scared, and pretending that she durst not return home, because, no sooner did she set foot on the threshold of her room, than she heard blows struck on her furniture, and a great noise of broken dishes and plates. The professors, pupils of Voltaire and the *Encyclopædia*, burst out in chorus into a wild laugh; but, as the laundress persisted in her tale, one of them accompanied her home, and was thus enabled to make sure of the truth of her statement. Then he returned for his colleagues, who made the same trial, which was attended by the same result. The room was visited, every hole and corner explored, but nothing discovered that could be assigned as a cause for this strange noise. The following day the laundress heard that her father, a wagoner, had been crushed to death at the very hour all seemed as if being smashed at her abode.

"A lady recounted to me the following fact: Her niece fell ill at Paris. The aunt, who lived at Granville, is aware of her niece's illness, but makes no mention of the circumstance to her sister, the mother of the young woman. A few days after, the two sisters met; it was at dusk. The mother of the patient goes out of the apartment on the ground-floor, then returns to it in great alarm. All hasten to her — ask her what is the matter with her. 'Thérèse is dead! my child is dead!' exclaims she as soon as she could speak. 'I just now saw her standing under the peristyle; I recognised her full well, although she was clad in white!' In fact, young Madame B—— died that very day, at that very hour.

"Other facts, no less extraordinary, have happened to persons of my acquaintance; they have a different bearing, arising from the same order of things.

"One of my intimate friends, a woman scarcely believing in God, and not at all in the devil, related to me that, having passed the evening with a widower, and induced him to marry again, even offering to find him a wife, a very astonishing vision happened to her. She was in the habit of reading in bed: she held in her hand one of Paul de Kock's novels, and was laughing to herself at the countless comicalities of the author, when she thought she perceived something white. She raises her head; the widower's wife was before her, clad in a white robe; her thick, black head of hair, spread over her shoulders, enveloped her like a veil. She gesticulated warmly—her lips quivered. The spectatress of this apparition comprehended that she was entreated not to advise her husband to marry again. This lady, getting the better of her fear, and wishing to bring such a visit to a speedy termination, said to her: 'Make yourself easy—I will never speak again of matrimony to your husband.' The phantom disappeared, and never returned!

"A lady of Coutances had, for forty years, a sort of imp attached to her house. Two persons assured me that they had been victims to its malicious tricks. It used to snatch from them their cards, dice, or dominoes, while they were playing; knock at the doors; seat itself on the heels of the servants when at prayers; operate noises of broken dishes and plates. The lady to whom it thus clung, being at first very much alarmed, performed numerous acts of devotion, &c., but all to no purpose. Her house was exorcised, but the imp would not budge. She saw nothing but twice in her life: the first time a frightful man, the second a hideous woman. All her friends were so habituated to the malicious tricks of the imp, that they took no further notice of it than by giving vent to their laughter, and the lady herself philosophically made up her mind to tolerate the nuisance.

"A captain of the navy, who, from his triple capacity as a sailor, an Englishman, and a *heretic* [!], could not be accused of superstitious credulity, related, one day, to a friend of mine the following fact: He arrived at Lisbon with his wife and servants, and was unable to procure a lodging, except in a palace, which was forsaken on account, as it was said, of being haunted by ghosts. Our captain at first laughed, but so many details were given him that he came to the conclusion that it might possibly be a haunt for brigands or false coiners. He orders his servants to make up a bed for themselves alongside the doors of his room, leaves his candle burning, and lays a brace of pistols on his night table; then awaits, fully resolved to supply the place of the Portuguese executioner. All was sleep and silence in the city, when at midnight, the doors of his room appeared to open violently, and an impetuous wind forces its passage in, a noise of chains dragging along makes the floor groan. The captain, however, sees nothing, his doors had not been opened; he fires off his pistols, the light is put out, and all noise ceases; he jumps out of bed, gropes along all over the room, but can find nothing. He wakes up the servants, who had seen nothing, heard nothing — not even the report of the pistols. He explores the walls, the partitions; all attests that there is no vacant space. The next day he so stations himself that he may perceive the secret door, of the existence of which he has not a doubt, but no issue is disclosed, and the noise is absolutely the same, and the sleep of the domestics as sound. The third day, same phenomenon, and the cool Englishman would, nevertheless, have obstinately continued in his abode amid spirits, had his wife consented to so doing; but, pretending that she should be frightened to death, they quitted the haunted palace.

"A lady of my society, residing in a small town, hears that her curé is ill; she goes to see him, inquires into the cause of his illness, and is very much surprised when he tells her a tale, the substance of which I am about to recount to you: Three

30*

days, or rather three nights before, the sacristan starts out of his sleep, and perceives a light in the church. Thinking that thieves are there, he jumps out of bed, and cautiously advances toward the point lighted up; what was his fright, his terror on beholding at the altar, ready to say mass, a priest who had died some weeks previously; his hair stands on end, a cold sweat inundates his body, he runs off, and goes to wake up a priest who had been a friend of the defunct. Both return to the church, but nothing now was to be seen. The following night the church is again lighted up; the priest, no sooner informed, proceeds to make sure of the fact, but he is overtaken with the same fear as the sacristan, and dares not proceed. He gives an account of the apparition to his curé, a resolute man, who having had some trifling differences with the deceased, made up his mind to render him the service he solicited, and charged the sacristan to let him know whether the church was illuminated again. That very night it was once more lighted up. The curé advanced with a firm step. 'Do you desire that I should serve you by saying mass?' said he to the defunct. 'Yes,' replied the latter, and mass commenced. When it was over, the dead man turned round, and said to the curé, in a voice of emotion: 'I thank you.' Then all disappeared, the lights were extinguished, and the curé groped his way back to the vestry. But this half hour's tête-à-tête with a dead man made such an impression on him that he took to his bed, and three months after this narrative, the lady, who recounted it to me, attended the funeral obsequies of the good curé!

"This fact, the truth of which I can nót doubt, would sufficiently prove to me what you say, that man loses neither his beliefs nor his habits, on quitting the terrestrial life, and, indeed, the grand law of analogy demands that there should be progression and shades in the various states of man, as there are shades in nature. After all these apparitions, shall I speak to you of dreams? Are they not of the domain of the most clairvoyante somnambulism? Was not Mahomet right in saying that 'when man sleeps, his soul is with God—is no longer in his body?' Be that as it may, I have never been incredulous on this point, because my mother was a true Pythoness. Never did a relative, a friend die, without her being warned of it in a dream. She foretold the death of my father a year before it happened; on that occasion, she said to a friend, 'I shall fall ill, very ill, but I shall not die; my husband will die first, and my sister-in-law will soon follow him;' and all took place as she had predicted. Oftentimes would she say to me, 'So-and-so is happening to so-and-so; I am going to receive a letter, &c.,' and never was she mistaken. The eve of her death, she said to us, 'Prepare yourselves, my children, my mother has come for me, I depart to-morrow with her.' She had several crises previous to final dissolution. After the last but one, she calmly said to us, 'One more, and all will be over with me in this world;' as she said to us, before the others, 'Not yet; it is not the last!'

"This somnambulic faculty is in me for certain grand things; thus, on the eve of the fatal *ordonnances* of July, being a very young girl, and never hearing talk of politics, I dreamed that I beheld Christ in the clouds; in his left hand he held a number of tri-colored favors, which he waved in the eyes of the people, on whom he smiled while saluting them; and, in his right hand, he had a thunderbolt. I beheld his eyebrows knit when he fixed his looks on the royal family; then he hurled his thunderbolt. A few days after, the dynasty took the road to Cherbourg.

"'A prince will soon die,' said I to my brother, on the 13th of July, 1841; 'for I saw, last night, a magnificent hearse, preceded and followed by troops of all arms.' And, in the afternoon, the duke of Orleans was killed.

"'Has nothing been heard say of the king?' asked I, another day, of my brother. 'No, why?'—'Because I have had a dream, which signifies that an attempt will be made on his life.' Next morning Lecomte was arrested. On the eve of new-year's day, I ask of God to reveal to me the most important events that would happen to me in the course of the year. I behold, in a dream, a hearse; and my mother died on the 20th March. At the moment she met with the fall that caused her death I dreamed that we were removing, and that my mother was carried away. I was started out of my sleep by the cries of my sister. We placed our mother on a bed. Three weeks after, she returned to the bosom of her God.

"I was dreaming, one night, that I was in another world, with my father and godfather; the latter wished to detain me, but my father objected to this, saying: 'No, no, let her go, it would cause her mother too much grief.' At this time I was in very good health; two days after, I had so violent an attack of brain fever that it was near taking me off.

"What conclusion draw from all these facts, and many others I could cite? Is it not this, that the intellectual world is represented by zero in our philosophy, which is no less than what say our sages of the day? May we not ask ourselves whether the soul remains not in communication of love, of sympathy, of recollection, with those it leaves on earth? whether the communion of souls is not universal, and independent of the accidents of matter? whether time and space exist for the pure spirit? whether the soul is really in need of the organs of the body to operate physical effects? and whether it can not act on all matter, even foreign to that which constitutes its envelope? We may ask ourselves whether the spirit is not, or has not, an immortal form, an interior mould, as it were, of the body? whether, in short, it would not be possible to find out a law which might direct and regulate the clairvoyant somnambulism of magnetic and of natural sleep? Here is a pretty number of questions: their solution, I am certain of it, will destroy our philosophy, our metaphysics, considerably modify physics and chemistry. But what matters destroying a scaffolding raised on false hypotheses? Far preferable doubt than error; far preferable a truth painfully acquired than a system perfectly logical, but remote from the truth. Humanity marches: let us hope that a ray of the eternal sun will enlighten its intelligence, and that finally it will enter the road of truth.

"F. LAMB,
"17 *Rue Tiquetonne.*"

I will not take the liberty of making any observation on the interesting facts that have been just read; the person who relates them is worthy of all my confidence, and I recommend the reader to accord her his. I will merely take leave to reply to the questions of this lady with these words: Yes, you may address these questions to science and the *savans*, but beware of believing in the solution which will be given you by their mighty conceit; beware, at the same time, of communicating to them that which your judgment shall intuitively dictate; theirs would be the work of pride in your eyes, and yours would be in theirs that of a lunatic; ay, a lunatic, you hear, because you would indubitably conclude that there is an active, intelligent being seated in our material body, causing its springs to work, communicating to it all forces, thoughts, movement. Oh! utter not that word movement, for what internally moves a body may externally move it; they will grant you the one, but refuse you the other. You will answer, perhaps, by asking them whether it is the earth, the other globes and their kingdoms, that move of themselves or are moved; if they move of themselves, they are *the* life; if moved, they are death. As life is in all and throughout all—for our *savans* neither will nor can admit death, or nothingness, which is the same thing—they will wish to extricate themselves from the difficulty in which you place them, by replying, by way of criterion: Globes and reigns have their point of attraction. You will answer, what they attract is no more dead than they themselves; otherwise, attraction becomes impossible; life can not attract death, therefore the particles attracted have a positive individuality, forming *one* with the mass, but forming, likewise, *one* in the mass. They will reply to you: "Yes;" then, since this particle, attracting and attracted, forms one with the mass, and one again in the mass, its individuality is thus found guarantied, and the immortality of the soul, as an individual or particle of the mass, is found proved; that which is not so is the action of the particle on the whole. Thus the soul, which is but a particle of the human material body, can not dominate, raise at its will that mass a thousand times heavier than it; this is contrary to simple physical notions. Yes, in appearance; but have you discovered where the active force is? Can you say whether it is in the whole or in the particle? If you answer that it is in the whole, the material body could move without the assistance of the particle soul; if, on the contrary, it is the particle that possesses the active force, the more it is disengaged from similar aggregations, the more powerful it must be. See you not a proof of this in homœopathy? is it the part or the whole that operates? It is the part, there is not a doubt of it. By this fine discovery you obtain the material proof of the sublime axiom, *all is in all and throughout all.* The part, therefore, contains the force of the whole; containing the force, it contains all. You represent to yourselves force by the volume of the thing; that is, retreating, recoiling before the contrary demonstration of gunpowder, steam, galvanism, magnetism:—only study the last-named science, and you will see whether force is represented in it by volume.

Excuse me; this *sorceress*, Metaphysics, hurries me away despite myself: I had promised, however, that I would not touch upon this point in the present work. But if I made mention of all these extraordinary facts without offering the least observation, it would be said: This poor spiritualist is barely *spirituel;* let him hold his peace, or support his fantastical tales with some admissible considerations. It is because I hear the stern voice of the *savans* thus accusing me, that I throw out at random a few observations, which will be found more demonstrative in the aforementioned work.

So, my dear lady, content yourself with listening to what will be said to you respecting the tricks which are of the domain of physics; above all, make up your mind to hear this fine objection, that by a thread-conductor, cleverly concealed in certain places, we may turn topsy-turvy plate, furniture, men, and animals: ask them, then, whether this spark so powerful, accorded to the metallic kingdom, ought and can be refused to the soul, the masterpiece (say they) of the Divinity. The masterpiece ought, at least, to possess the property of the inferior part, if not more.

They will speak to you, also, of the havoc occasioned by the effects of the thunder-bolt, the grandest juggler in the universe. This *fluid* recoils not before conveyances; it would not dare compromise its high reputation by conveying a box, a letter, a seal, to such or such a place, for shame. Tell it, on the contrary, to tear out all the nails in the wooden shoes of those good villagers, who pray to God to preserve them for them, and it will acquit itself admirably. It will convey this rock to a distance of more than thirty feet; reduce this tree into finer lathes than man could; unshoe this horse without killing him; disarm this cavalier before he is aware of it; break all these windows; demolish this chimney; clear this table—and what more? This is not, however, the masterpiece of the creation, since you spit it with your pikes touched with loadstone. Oh, poor mortals! you believe and see these things—you know that it is an electric spark attacking, indistinctly, each kingdom—and yet you would refuse the divine spark, named the soul, the power of operating such things. Yes, you are profound.

"Monsieur: The prospectus of your work—'Secrets of the Life to Come Revealed'—having excited my curiosity, I hastened to subscribe to it; and after a perusal, which has made a deep impression on me, I was bound, before pronouncing on the value of the revelations it contains, to follow the advice you give to all magnetizers, viz., *to experiment.* You trace a route; I ventured to proceed in it, though fearful of missing my aim. At length I obtained a conviction of the reality of those apparitions, and surprising answers have been made me. Having called on you for information on this subject, the apparition that you had the kindness to procure for me, had already convinced me. Still, in consequence of what may be termed a remnant of doubt, I assured myself of the truth of this phenomenon by experiments of my own. I will not, however, tell you that all the clairvoyantes to whom I applied possess this faculty in a like degree. I don't think it necessary to give you the particulars of my experiments: I merely consider it a duty to render homage to this singular and useful truth in the common interest of men; thanking you, at the same time, for having received from you this key, which served me in finding out another phenomenon, well worthy, also, of fixing the attention of psychologists, and especially of spiritualists.

"This is the fact: *The mere Christian name* of a person who is ill, no matter where, suffices a clairvoyante whom I magnetize, to inoculate herself sympathetically with the malady, to any degree, whatever be its nature; above all, know that the thought has nothing whatever to do with it, since neither I nor my clairvoyante knows aught else but the name which, despite its infinite repetition in the material world, represents to us instantaneously all the details of the malady of the person who is suffering it. This sort of appeal, which I make in the world of spirits still on earth, confirms that which you make in the spiritual world with so much facility.

"Accept, monsieur, &c., &c., "DUTEIL,

"*Member of the Magnetological Society*,

"246 *Rué Saint Denis*.

"*20th October*, 1848."

The success which M. Duteil obtains in experiments of this kind confirms what we have said in our first volume, that it was losing precious time to make clairvoyantes travel step by step toward the place we wish them to explore. I ask for the place which I know not any more than my clairvoyante, and the place forthwith appears. If it is possible for the place which is devoid (no doubt) of a soul, to present itself thus at the mere call of its name, it ought to be as easy for a spirit to do so. It remains only to comprehend how Jean, who is, perhaps, the ten thousandth of this name in France, should present himself rather than another Jean? It may be replied to this question that there is a communion between souls in general; that the isolated scene which we play during the day is the result of a fact secretly determined on by our soul, which leaves its material body in ignorance of the cause and object of its decisions, and its relations with other souls: this would not prove the free will of the material body, far from it.

Here are two facts, one of which took place at my house while I was penning this reflection. Three ladies came to ask me for a view at distance. Having no subjects present for this speciality, I asked Emile, who happened at that moment to pay me a visit, to suffer himself to be sent to sleep; after demurring a short time he consented. I asked these ladies what they desired; one of them, Madame Bimont, an Icarian, told me that she was very uneasy respecting her brother, who had been among the first to set out with his brethren for Icaria. I inquired of her his name and summoned the man. Emile gave an exact description of him. I told him to see where this man was. "Oh!" immediately replied the child, "the road is not a good one to get there. I see, also, a very fine field—a pretty farm—a small pond—a well that looks like a new one—horses that are very vicious; I have no mind to mount them. They are white. The trees have droll kind of leaves; they are large and notched," &c., &c.—"Ask the gentleman why he does not write to his sister." "He has written to her."—"When?" "About the end of August. He is displeased with her for not having answered him." After several more questions of a like nature, I woke the child, and this lady (who was not *en rapport* with him) said to me: "So far as regards the description of my brother and the places, it seems to me to have an air of truth; but with respect to the letter said to have been written, it must be an error, otherwise I should have received it." Two days after this lady received the very letter, dated from the 25th August; she had the goodness to come and inform me of it. The child had therefore really conversed with the spirit of this man, while the latter was not aware of it.

The second fact is quite personal to myself. A respectable female neighbor of mine whom I had taught to magnetize, possesses a clairvoyante that promises being very powerful. She said to me: "Last night my clairvoyante declared that she beheld you taking the place of her good guide; she was quite surprised at it, she exclaimed: 'Ah! there's M. Cahagnet with his arms crossed over his breast, looking kindly on me.'—'Ask him what he wants with you?'" Then ensued a conversation between my spirit and this clairvoyante, which it is needless to mention; but what I can affirm before God is that this lady told me my inmost thoughts, which I had communicated to no one, and much less still, I am persuaded, to a clairvoyante whose influence I in nowise felt. At this moment when I was reading aloud, I had entertained these thoughts for the first time that day. What an abyss for our reason!

"MY DEAR FRIEND: Since its first appearance you have been aware of the opinion I entertain of your book: scarcely had I read it than I tried experiments of the same kind myself, and succeeded beyond my expectations. I will not recount to you here any of the sittings I had, you have so many similar ones, and more curious still, that it seems to me needless.

"However, I declare to you here, and publicly, that I have been fully convicted of the existence of a future life, by the perusal of your work. I believe that all those who make themselves acquainted with its contents, will think as I do, and will have no reason to complain of having read it.

"In one word, the opinion I come to respecting your 'Secrets' is that they are called to bestow happiness on humanity.

"Make my letter, my dear friend, as public as possible, and receive the assurance of my fraternal friendship.

"Wholly yours, "A. BLOUET,

"*Man of Letters, Rue D'Enfer*, 85.

"28*th October*, 1848."

"FROM MADAME LEVI.

"You would already have received, monsieur, my letter of thanks, had I not first wished to read your excellent work. Any one may clearly perceive that you have been inspired by very lucid somnambulists; as almost all the definitions are in accord with the works of the ancient sages. For my part, monsieur, I come to testify to you my gratitude for the disinterested obligingness with which you entertained my request of putting me in communication with your good clairvoyante. I herein bear witness to the truth; she perfectly saw and described the deceased person I desired, and every circumstance of the said person's relations with me. It can not be said that she saw all this in my imagination; for God is my witness, that

I was in ignorance of many circumstances, which, however, turn out to be true. . .

"Accept, monsieur, for yourself, and your obliging clairvoyante, the assurance of my esteem. "LEVI,

"*Publisher of the Journal L'Hermès,*

"*Boutigny, par Meaux (Seine-et-Marne).*

"18*th November*, 1848."

"MONSIEUR: Whatsoever I had read up to this day only tended to plunge me into the most desponding atheism; and, in moments of trouble, I had ever, to put an end to all, but one thought—that of self-destruction.

"I have read your 'Secrets of the Life to Come Revealed.' This book has given me a belief in God, toleration toward my brethren, happiness in my family, and sufficient moral force to support with fortitude all the misfortunes which previously caused my torments.

"Such happiness I prefer to any that the most splendid fortune could have procured me.

"I have no doubt, monsieur, that were it not for the political events which absorb all minds, these revelations would already have conveyed hope to the very bottom of a great number of hearts so much in need of it.

"Be assured, monsieur, of my high consideration.

"CONSTANT FLICHY,

"19, *Rue Vincent, Belleville.*"

"MY DEAR MONSIEUR CAHAGNET: Pursuant to the good counsels you were so kind as to give me relative to the apparition of spirits, I have convinced myself, by experiments, of the reality of such apparitions, and the non-communication of thought with somnambulists.

"Penetrated with this firm conviction, I authorize you to give publicity to my testimony; and I assure men that the soul exists in the future life, in the form of its material body, and having recollection of its individuality.

"Your devoted friend, "ROUSSEAU,

"*Post Office Employé (Dead Letter Office).*"

"My dear Monsieur Cahagnet: In support of the spiritualist doctrines which you seek to propagate with a zeal that does you honor, and prepares for you, at a future period, triumph and gratitude, you may subjoin the two following facts:—

"One night, about fifteen years ago, I was quietly sleeping, when all at once I felt myself struck on the shoulder, and suddenly waking, I beheld before me one of my uncles who lived at Châtellerault. He said to me in a strong and perfectly accented voice, 'Ninive is destroyed.' The trouble and emotion caused me by this apparition and these words were so great that my wife was suddenly roused, and quickly inquired what was the matter with me. 'Ah!' said I to her, in a voice of emotion; 'my uncle is dead: he was here just now, I saw him perfectly well; for he woke me up, and said to me in his voice of Stentor, 'Ninive is destroyed;' now, Ninive was he himself, he who had spent his fortune in leading the life of a Persian satrap.

"My wife, despite the trouble which had just been communicated to her, tried to calm me, endeavoring to persuade me that it was but an effect of my imagination or a deceitful dream; but all her reasoning could not drive out of my head the idea that my uncle was really dead, and that he had come to announce his death to me. I went to sleep again, but in the morning, on awaking, my first thought came and retraced to me this singular apparition; all day long I heard these energetic words—'Ninive is destroyed!' A few days after a letter came and announced to us the death of my uncle Fortin, my mother's brother. He had died a day or two before the fact which I have related took place.

"Second Fact.—During the winter of 1843, I was having some work done on my lands, which are about half a league from Niort. I had, by the means of somnambulism, discovered a spring of water at the top of a very high hillock; as water is a very useful commodity in the country, and spreads a great charm on all around it, I was insatiable, and often questioned the oracle which had already so fortunately directed me. One day from Niort, where I reside, a stream of water was signalized to me which was supposed to run under a large rock, which was scarcely visible on the surface of the soil. 'Have it removed,' said the oracle, 'and under its base you will have another pretty little fountain.' After having searched for and discovered this mysterious rock, I gave orders to Master Griseau, my gardener, to have it removed, and to look for the spring that was said to be beneath it; but Griseau, who was not fully convinced of the phenomena of somnambulism, represented to me that it was folly to go to such an expense in order to arrive at a discovery wholly improbable; in fact, how expect to find water almost at the crest of a hillock which looks over the river almost perpendicularly to a height of forty or fifty feet. These reasons appeared to me peremptory; but I wanted water, as, also, a proof more of the magnetic clairvoyance; so I rejected the advice, however just it appeared to me, and reiterated my orders, which were crowned with complete success.

"This fact, so far as regards the clairvoyance of certain somnambulists, did but confirm proofs already long before acquired; but the one which is about to follow cast into my soul new thoughts, which by-and-by, with God's help, were to be for me incontestable truths. No; man is not isolated on this earth, he is surrounded by benign spirits who protect him against evil; every being has his good genius, but unfortunately few listen to him. What mysteries surround us, and how ignorant we are! Somnambulism is a property that will, I am certain of it, reveal them to us sooner or later; for I am of the number of those to whom it is permitted to raise a corner of the veil which conceals them from our eyes. What truths must there be to alarm vice and console virtue! Pardon me this digression; I return to the fact.

"The rock, stripped at its base, remained half suspended, awaiting the brick-work which was to secure it firmly; the operations, interrupted by the bad weather, were about to be resumed, and I repaired to the spot over night. It was a Sunday, the keeper was absent, and I found myself absolutely alone. It was three o'clock in the afternoon; I took a gardening tool, animated as I was with the desire of finding water in greater quantity. I set to work, and dug up the earth with a courageous hope. I was wholly absorbed in this thought, when, suddenly, a voice struck my ears with these words, said in an abrupt and a hasty tone: 'Go away!' I made a bound backward, and precipitately withdrew from the spot where I was, leaving there one of the wooden shoes I had had on my feet. I then looked upward, to find out who it was that could have thus spoken to me, but I perceived no one. I was quite certain of being alone, so I intuitively perceived that some danger threatened me, inasmuch as the rock had only clayey earth as a base. Wholly absorbed, then, in my own preservation, I cautiously drew back my wooden shoe, and made all haste to get away. At a few paces hence, I asked myself what voice this possibly could be which had just struck my ear in so forcible a manner; it was sonorous, and its sounds still vibrated in my mind. It was, therefore, a warning from heaven, sent to snatch me from some great danger. But a few minutes more at this work, and I should have been killed. Being killed was not the worst that might have happened to me; but, hurled down by the mass, I might have been caught by an arm or a leg under this enormous burden. 'Oh! my God, my God! I thank thee,' cried I, raising my hands to heaven and falling on my knees, 'thou hast saved me, and I return thee my thanks.' I know not what passed within me for the few seconds I remained on my knees, but on rising, I found myself bathed in tears. After recovering from the emotion I had just experienced, I went and cast a last glance on my rock; it was still silently suspended. I moved away, turning round more than once with terror. It was five o'clock when I lost sight of it; at half-past five, the hour of the keeper's return, this superb mass had fallen in; falling at first on itself, it made a turn half round to precipitate itself side-wise, when it was stopped in its course by an accident of the soil. At the present time (1849) it is majestically seated under an enormous grotto, which I raised on the very spot where it once was. There, still proud and haughty, it preserves its threatening air; but pass, fearlessly pass, only bow before the words of my good angel, inscribed on its front: '*Go away.*' "J. B. BORREAU,

"*20th January*, 1849." "*A Landholder, at Niort.*

Our worthy friend, M. Borreau, has kindly granted us permission to give publicity to this communication; requesting us, however, at the same time, to defer to a later period another statement concerning facts, still more mysterious, applying personally to himself. We feel indebted to our friend, honorably known to the magnetic notabilities, for his generous confidence. He has comprehended that a spiritualist is not an egotist, keeping to himself this divine revelation of a moral world, which may convey the sweetest consolations to those who believe that nothingness is the apogeum of the creation.

Were it possible for us to make mention of all the persons who have come to submit to us similar facts, or acquaint us with their success in the experiments we have taught them to make, we should be obliged to go on with a third volume. We will now proceed to the questions we submitted to the venerable Almignana, for the purpose of knowing whether these apparitions are approved or condemned by the church.

"MONSIEUR: I herein reply to your letter of the 10th inst., in which you express to me the wish of knowing whether the belief in the apparitions of spirits individually, and in human forms, is contrary to the catholic faith.

"After God, a pure spirit, and the father of spirits, as says the gospel, theology admits two sorts of spirits dependent on God: these are the angels,—for the demons are fallen angels, —and the souls of men.

"I have looked over the Holy Scriptures, and it supplies me with different instances of apparitions of these two sorts of spirits, individually, and in human forms.

"ANGELS.—Those are three angels who, in the form of men, appear to Abraham, and even converse with him. (Genesis, xviii.)

"It is an angel, also, who, in the human form, appears to

Jacob, and wrestles with the holy patriarch to give him to understand that the weakest men may do much, with the assistance of heaven. (Genesis, xxxii.)

"It is also an angel, who, in the form of a man, appears to the young Tobias, and accompanies him on his journey into the country of the Medes. (Tobit, v., vi. vii.)

"In short, after the resurrection of our Lord Jesus Christ, it was an angel who, in the form of a young man, appears to Mary Magdalene and the other Mary. (St. Matt., xxviii.)

"SOULS OF DECEASED MEN.—Samuel, after descending to the grave, appears to Saul in the same form as he had on earth, through the means of the witch of Endor, of whom God makes use to execute his holy designs with regard to the Hebrew king. (1 Samuel, xxviii.)

"Moses, many ages after having rendered up his spirit on Mount Nebo, and Elias, long years after having quitted the earth, appear in human forms, though surrounded with glory, on the Tabor, a high mountain, to John and James, the day of the transfiguration of our Lord Jesus Christ. (St.Matt. xvii.; St. Mark, ix.)

"The 'Lives of the Saints' furnishes us with instances of similar apparitions, and especially the 'Life of St. Theresa.'

"M. Chardel, formerly a counsellor of the court of Cassation, and deputy of the Seine, whose learning and good faith can not be questioned, does he not recount to us, in his 'Essay on Physiological Psychology,' various apparitions of deceased persons, who, in their earthly forms, appeared to members of their family, asking them to discharge certain works of piety, such as masses and pilgrimages, promised by the deceased, but remaining unperformed at the time of their death?

"But what comes to confirm what we have just said, is the honorable testimony of a man as learned as orthodox, such as the abbé Duclos, who, in his reply to the sarcasms of Voltaire against chapter xxxii. of Genesis, relative to the angel who, in the form of a man, appears to Jacob in order to wrestle with him, when he sets forth his opinion, with respect to the apparition of spirits, says to us:—

"1. That God is surely the Master of appearing whenever he pleases, and in whatever manner he pleases.

"2. That the good or wicked angels and the souls of men may appear, but only at the order and by the permission of God.

"3. That God sometimes gives such order and such permission.

"4. That this occurred more frequently in the early ages of the world, for reasons deserving of it.

"5. That this may again occur, even now, because God is still as powerful as he was at first.

"In short, that the apparitions of angels and the dead contain not more difficulties than the apparitions of God himself.

"From what I have just quoted, I believe it may be rightly concluded that the belief in the apparitions of spirits, in human forms and individuality, is very far from being contrary to the catholic faith, the more so as the church has not yet pronounced against the apparitions of which you speak to me.

"As to me, monsieur, with this conviction was it, and not otherwise, that I permitted myself to wait upon you to witness a few apparitions, which, while surprising me, have become for me a fresh proof of what we read in the holy books with respect to the apparitions of spirits in human forms; and I shall never cease, while I live, returning thanks to God for having deigned to grant me a favor so great as that of knowing physically by myself the immortality of the soul.

"As to you, monsieur, allow me to congratulate you in this, that, in the midst of your humble position in the eyes of the world, God has made use of you and your modest somnambulist to confound the presumptuous *savans* of the earth, and, above all, the proud materialists, the scourge of religion and real plague-sore of society.

"Yes, monsieur, it is thus that I view the grand magnetic phenomena which engage our attention; and I am persuaded that it was in allusion to certain apparitions of deceased persons, seen by some somnambulist as privileged as our good Adèle, that the Rev. Father Lacordaire, in spite of the academicians and skeptics, proclaimed from the sacred tribune, in the month of March, 1847, that *magnetism was a Divine preparation to humble the pride of materialists.* For it is certain that among the arguments made use of by theologians to prove the immortality of the soul, that taken from the apparition of Samuel, of which I have just spoken, is one of the strongest.

"But, monsieur, if you and your modest somnambulist have a privilege so great, do not, however, glorify in it, seeing that it is from God alone that you have received it; for, as very wisely says the abbé Duclos, the angels, good or wicked, can appear only at the order of God or by his permission; and you yourself acknowledge this truth, since I have perceived that all your operations are invariably preceded by prayer, imploring the favors of Heaven.

"Thus, my good monsieur, far from being puffed up with your works, say with St. Paul: '*Non ego, sed gratia Dei mecum.*' ('Yet not I, but the grace of God that was with me.') It is not we who work these wonders, but the *grace* of the Lord, the Divine goodness, the omnipotence of the Eternal, who has been pleased to make use of us, beings weak and imperceptible in the eyes of the world, in order to confound the mighty, and the pretended philosophers of the earth. '*Infirma mundi elegit Deus ut confundat fortia.*' ('And God hath chosen the weak things of the world to confound the things which are mighty.') It is St. Paul who speaks.

"Accept, monsieur, I beg you, the sincere expression of my respectful sentiments, with which I have the honor to be

"Your very humble and most obedient servant,

"L. A. Almignana,

"15 *Rue de l'Eglise.*

"Batignolles, 14*th February*, 1848."

We are most happy at being enabled to publish the testimony of a priest so honorable as M. Almignana. It will tend to reassure a few timorous consciences, who fancied they beheld in the first part of the "Secrets" the work of the evil one. If the church acknowledges that no apparition can take place without the order and permission of God, we are, in this case, his most humble and obedient servant.

Thus, for want of space, we terminate a part of our correspondence, which we had no desire to keep secret, thinking it would be acceptable to a few readers who might wish to see new personages brought on the stage. It was to gratify this just wish, that we have published this extract of the most curious facts and particulars which have been communicated to us. and that we are now about to rummage in the history of the beliefs of different nations in the immortality of the soul, in order to prove, moreover — if possible — that we have been actuated by a desire to accomplish something useful, and at the same time show that we have been preceded, in all places and times, by hallucinated individuals of our species.

---

## ON THE IMMORTALITY OF THE SOUL:

### OPINIONS OF PHILOSOPHERS FROM ANTIQUITY TO OUR DAYS.

INDIES. — The belief in the immortality of the soul is inherent in the existence of man, from his first to his last thought. In fact, if we reascend the scale of ages in India, what do we find among those nations that reckon not 5,848 years of existence, as we pretend, but 131,400,007,205,000 years from the birth of Brama down to our days. In these countries — little known, badly explored, still worse described — we shall possibly find psychological science more advanced than among us. No: if we consult their sacred books, the true source of all earthly sects and superstitions, we shall find therein the belief in the immortality of the soul established from the most remote times, in the form of a polytheism which we seem unable, from the revelations of our "Secrets," to admit, but which we might possibly deduce from them were we to devote ourselves more positively to the detailed study of a multitude of propositions into which they lead us.

Unwilling, at any price, to fall again into metaphysical quotations, as so doing would destroy all the charm of this part, we accept, on the whole, our revelations, reserving to ourselves, for another work, propositions wherein the beliefs in the metempsychosis will find a place in certain acceptations only. We will restrict ourselves, for the moment, to quoting a passage from a learned work, entitled: "A Picturesque Voyage Round the World," published under the direction of the unfortunate Dumont-Durville, presuming that we shall find in this work information stripped of the marvellous things related by the old voyagers. We find, in page 140, vol. i.: —

"* * * * Such is a sketch of the Indian polytheism. As to the dogmas connected with it, a notion of them may be summed up in a universal metempsychosis; a certain quantity of spirit and matter, each imperishable, is found, according to them, in a perpetual state of transmigration. The punishment of spirits consists of a falling off in their material envelope. Thus, from the body of man they descend into that of the beast, following the progression of animals more or less noble, so as to run the risk of dwelling even in stones. In this comminatory part of their dogmas, the Bramins have never entertained the thought of threatening men with a perpetual hell; when we speak to them of such a place, they say that it is an insult to the Almighty, setting bounds to his right of mercy, prejudging his justice, and giving him hateful passions which are incompatible with his essence. 'However great be a crime,' add they, 'the Divine goodness is still greater.'

"This belief in the metempsychosis also serves them to explain the contrast of human conditions and the inequality of our destinies. With them compensation exists not altogether in another world, it is in this transitory world. That if, destined to the most humble lot, a mortal ends a meritorious and pious life, his reward consists in being born again rich, honored, amid all the enjoyments of luxury and comfort. Thus the Indian metempsychosis is somewhat mixed up with predestination and fatalism; free-will can not go so far as to efface a word of what Brama has written in the head of a man, but certain practices, certain expiations, can be set down to his account in the balancing of his good or bad works."

What logic Brama writes in the head of such man: Thou shalt do such a thing, and thou shalt ask pardon of me for having done what I commanded thee to do! Do we not recognise in this moral our sublime maxim: "Nothing happens in the world without the permission and order of God?"—therefore, you ought to ask pardon of him for having obeyed him!

CHINA.—If we extend our researches as far as China, we are assured of finding there this belief established from time immemorial, but under philosophical forms, or allegories, adapted to the wants and usages of the country. It is still the same encouragement to good actions, under penalty of being punished by a transmigration in the scale of beings, kingdoms, and elements, corresponding, by their life or state, with the actions of which man has been guilty, all this invariably ending in an eternity of happiness. God is still sufficiently respected among these people to have a confidence in his divine goodness and the hope of a better life. Eternal punishment forms no part of their creed.

OCEANICA.—If we come back among younger and less civilized nations (Oceanica), we find ourselves face to face with this polytheism, this transmigration of souls into such or such body, corresponding with its past affections, good or bad, and arriving in globes where the felicity is as sweet as our earthly sufferings have been painful. What is remarkable in the beliefs of all these countries, is, that our earthly globe is found to be the intermediate between a number, more or less considerable, of globes. Able only to progress or fall back in quitting it, man, in this mixed state, fills pretty nearly the *rôle* described in our first volume—a *rôle* that subjects him to trials of sensations, impressions, comparisons, hitherto unknown to him. Apart, the more or less admissible fictions of these doctrines, there results from them one fact—a belief in the individualized immortality of the soul, on quitting this globe, and its eternal felicity: this is more encouraging than the nothingness of our materialists.

Since we are in these countries, let us see what is thought there of ecstasy. We find in the occult sciences of the *Port-*

*able Encyclopedia*—a small work, written with great impartiality, and displaying much scientific knowledge—the following passage (page 203):—

"Without wishing to anticipate the discussions that will arise on this important question [ecstasy], we will nevertheless observe, in order to add a few facts to facts already known, that one of our friends who resided for fourteen years in the East Indies, has frequently seen Hindus fall at will into ecstasy, and become, in this state, an object of fear or veneration to their fellow-countrymen. The North and South Americans who are wrongfully classed among nations called savage, and who present in their customs and language the remains of an ancient civilization, have traditional reminiscences which deliver them up to a state of ecstasy, during which they believe themselves to be in communication with spirits. The phenomena of ecstasy are found in the most remarkable manner among the Kamtschatdales, the Yakoutes, and many other tribes of the north, where the soothsayers sometimes inflict on themselves horrible wounds, without apparently, and in reality, not suffering from them. The ecstatic state is also to be met with at Otaheite, at the Sandwich isles, in Polynesia, where a new religion is imposed on the natives, and where religious persecutions exalt the imagination of those who adhere to the old form of worship. Mariner, that young traveller unjustly accused of falsehood, but whose truthfulness is now acknowledged, during his residence at Tonga-Tabou, the metropolis of the neighboring isles, was a witness to extraordinary facts, proving in a positive manner the good faith of those who, among savage as among barbarous nations, are given up to a religious state of ecstasy. It is generally acknowledged at Tonga, that some persons are favored by the gods with their inspirations; the god who inspires them is found then in the person of the inspired priest who becomes capable of prophesying the future.

"Mariner so describes the ecstatic situation of the priests of this country as to leave no doubt with respect to the symptoms they experience, and the young traveller adds, that he has no reason to believe that these demonstrations are the result of imposture; he even produces proofs of what he advances on this head. Among the details he gives, there are two in particular worthy of examination, inasmuch as they above all attest the spirit of conviction of those who undergo the phenomena of the ecstatic state. The son of King Finow was often wont to repeat to the incredulous European that he was inspired by the spirit of Toogo-Ahoo, the last king of the isles of Tonga, that he no longer felt conscious of his own personal existence, and that his body seemed to him animated by a soul not his own. Having been questioned as to the nature of the spirit that disturbed him, and how this spirit descended into him, the young prince contented himself with replying, 'What a silly question; can I tell you how I know it? I know it because I feel a conviction of it, and because a voice warns me of it.'

"We might accumulate facts of this nature, but space is refused us, and we will content ourselves with reminding our readers that they exist in great number in the ancient and modern works of voyagers of all nations."

I will add to this curious dissertation on ecstasy, that the spirit that seizes the priests of these countries, taking possession of their material body to prophesy through their mouth, is not unlike the spirit that seized on Binet, the first somnambulist mentioned in this work, and caused him to say: "It is not I who always answer your questions, it is the spirit that speaks through my mouth, and I am a quiet spectator and auditor of its discussions with you." We, however, are neither among savages nor barbarians; no, but we are among madmen and visionaries; that amounts to the same thing.

We will now pass into Greece, and ask Lamprias, the brother of Plutarch, what he thought of the immortality of the soul.

Greece.—*Plutarch.*—Treatise on the "Cessation of Oracles, Annals of Magnetism," page 70:—

"One of the interlocutors of the treatise in question, having set forth that prophesying was merely the work of genii that animated the oracles and revealed to our souls what was passing at a distance and at a future time, Lamprias, the brother of Plutarch, combats this system, and thus expresses himself—

'Why should we deprive souls united to bodies of this faculty natural to the genii, of knowing and predicting the future? It is not at all likely that souls after their separation from the body acquire any properties they did not previously possess; they have ever the same faculties, but merely less perfect when souls are united to the body. Of these faculties some are obscure and hidden, others weak and languid; these grown dull and tardy, as are our looks through clouds, they stand in need of efficacious remedies to re-establish them in the integrity of their nature, and deliver them from whatsoever retards their activity. As the sun becomes not luminous on emerging from a cloud, and as ever brilliant by his nature he appears obscured only by reason of the cloud hiding him; in like manner *the soul acquires not the faculty of predicting when it has emerged from the body as from a cloud; it possesses this faculty while united to the body, but its intimate union with a mortal nature deadens its activity.*'"

Who at the present day could combat the opinion pronounced by Lamprias, and the fictions he employs to demonstrate the faculties of the soul in the material and in the spiritual state. It is right to admit that spirits can enlighten our clairvoyantes, to save them the trouble of making researches which very often fatigue them; but it is not less just to admit, that these clairvoyantes can dispense with their assistance, inasmuch as they possess this same property. What progress has psychological science made since that period? None; as at this day, with the demonstrative assistance of magnetism, somnambulism, and ecstasy, men still doubt the existence of the soul. Oh! reign of civilization, thy locomotives cause thy material body to clear space ten times more swiftly than of yore, but thy reasoning stands in great need of a spiritual locomotive to return to Lamprias, and listen to his lessons.

Let us ask Aristotle, while we are in the classical land of philosophy, what he thought of the immortality of the soul. In the "Explanation of the Doctrines of Aristotle," by Cicero, the latter makes the philosopher thus speak:—

"Souls derive not their origin from the earth. They admit

of no admixture, no concretion, no extract, or substance of terrestrial bodies, or that of water, air, or fire; for, in the diverse natures of these elements, there is nothing which is susceptible of the faculties of the memory, the understanding, the thought; nothing which is capable of retaining the past, foreseeing the future, embracing the present. All these can be but Divine gifts, and never will it be said from whom man received them, if not from God himself. The soul is, therefore, of a singular nature, and distinct from all other natures. So, whatsoever that be within us which feels, thinks, desires, and animates us, it is something celestial, divine, and, consequently, imperishable."

Since we are with Cicero, let us take advantage of it to inquire into his opinions on this head.

ROME.—*Cicero.—Book on Old Age.*—The orator puts in the mouth of Cato these remarkable words :—

"I am persuaded that your fathers, those illustrious personages whom I so much loved, have not ceased living, although they have passed through death; and that they are still living that sort of life which alone deserves being called by that name; for so long as we are in the bonds of the body, we are like slaves at the chain, since our soul is divine, which, from heaven, as the place of its origin, is cast down, and, as it were, buried in this low region of the earth, which is a place of exile and punishment for a substance celestial and eternal by its nature. * * * * In short, when I perceive what activity there is in our minds, what memory of the past, what foresight of the future; when I take into consideration the number of arts, sciences, and discoveries, to which they have attained, I believe, and am fully persuaded, that a nature possessing in itself the groundwork of so many things can not be mortal." * * * *

*Discourse of Cyrus, when on the point of dying, to his Children :* "Beware of believing, my dear children," said he to them, "that I am no longer aught, or that I am no longer anywhere, when I have quitted you; for, at the time I was with you, you did not behold my spirit; but what you saw me do made you think that there was one within my body. Doubt not, therefore, that this spirit will subsist even after it has been separated from it, although no longer perceptible by any action: * * * * * * * * * For my part, I have never been able to persuade myself that our spirits live only so long as they are within our bodies; and that they die when they quit them, or that they remain, stripped of intelligence and wisdom, when disengaged from a body that has by itself neither sense nor reason; I believe, on the contrary, that when the spirit, disengaged from matter, finds itself, in all the purity and simplicity of its nature, it is then that it possesses most light and wisdom."

In the same book, Cato exclaims:—

"For my part, I heartily long to rejoin your fathers, whom I so dearly loved and venerated; and not only those great men whom I knew, but even those of whom I have heard speak, and of whom I have read, or whose actions I myself have written. I go, therefore, to meet them with so much joy that it would be difficult to detain me; and it would afford me no pleasure to be cast over again, like Pelias, to renew me, and enable me to recommence life. No, though some god should wish to lead me back to childhood, and place me once more in the cradle to recommence a new life, I should oppose it with all my might, and from the end of the career in which I now am, I should not wish to be replaced at its commencement. * * * * * * * Oh! a happy day will be that when I shall leave this impure and corrupt crowd to rejoin that divine and happy band of great souls that left the earth before me. I shall find there not only those great men of whom I have spoken, but also my dear Cato, whom I can say was one of the best of men, of the best of dispositions, and one of the most faithful to his duties that has ever been seen. I placed his body on the funeral pile, whereas he ought to have placed on it mine. But his soul has not left me; and without losing sight of me, he has merely preceded me into a country where he beheld that I should shortly rejoin him. If I have borne the loss of such a son with some degree of firmness, it is not that I was not touched at it even to the quick; but I consoled myself with the thought that we were not separated for long."

I shall dispense with adding any reflections to so eloquent a *morceau*, I am too penetrated with admiration for these great men and the insufficiency of any observations of mine, to make the attempt. We will not leave the queen of the world, now simple Italy, before addressing ourselves to Campanella, that model of the philosophers of Christendom. We shall find him worthy, I believe, of the forementioned great men.

ITALY.—*Campanella.*—Madame Louise Collet's Translation.—"Poésies," page 67.

"Souls in the mask of the body present, on the theatre of the world, to the dwellers in heaven, the spectacle of their agitation.

"They perform the actions and say the things for which they were born. They go from scene to scene, and from choir to choir, sometimes joyous, sometimes sad, according to what is found to be ordained in the dramatic book.

"They neither know nor can do aught else but what infinite wisdom has inscribed therein for the good of all." (Page 142-5.)

"Death is sweet to him to whom life is bitter. He who is born in tears should die smiling. Let us at last give up these miserable rags to destiny that lends them to us at such a usurious rate. Before taking back altogether this mortal body, it demands of us our hearing, our teeth, and our eyes so dear. Take all that belongs to thee, O avaricious earth! and wherefore bearest thou not me myself away to the Styx. Happy he who escapes from time!

(6.)

"O my body! a living death, nest of ignorance, sepulchre I bear with me, garment of sin and grief, weight of misery, and labyrinth of errors, thou detainest me here below by caresses and by fear, lest I should turn my eyes up to heaven, the good supreme, and my true abode; thou fearest that smitten with its beauty, I should disdain and abandon thee—a dead coal."

(1.)

Page 132.—"Wherefore this despondency, O my soul!

thou fearest, perhaps, that I should die amid these immense griefs; leave terror to the vulgar, thou well knowest that dying means leaving what one loves. If nothing is resolved into nothing, never he who is not dead in himself should fear aught. He who has peace within him can dread no tribulation. Let no other reasoning prevail on thee, or thou wouldst be misled."

(2.)

"If a material person did not hold thee enslaved, no tyrant could do so any more than he could enslave the unchained winds, the angels and the stars. Thy torments are less hurtful to thee than to those who inflict them on thee; thy torments deliver thee, O my soul; they resuscitate thee and snatch thee from thy prison and thy grave, since, for thee the body is both."

(7.)

Page 136.—"By our weak understandings and confined movements we perceive only the material things which strike the walls of our prison: but things powerful and divine escape us, for they would burst our frail envelope. We are unable to become acquainted with the secret virtues of things because our organization presents an obstacle to our so doing. The most learned here below possess but the semblance of truth."

(2.)

Page 138.—"O my soul! when thou shalt have once quitted this body, which thou now fearest to abandon, thou wilt entertain such an aversion to it, that, were God to propose restoring it to thee, formed of iron and glass, that it might fear neither shocks nor obscurity, thou wouldst refuse with tears, unless it were restored to thee wholly celestial, like that of the Savior when he rose from the dead."

(3.)

"On beholding the immortal world, with its heavenly delights and the honors which spirits render to God, thou wilt be astonished that he should deign to cast a look on our circumscribed earth, obscure and devoid of beauty—on this earth, where resound so many blasphemies that one would say that

God has forsaken it—on this earth, inhabited by hatred, death, war, and ignorance."

(4.)

"Thou wilt behold heaven and earth combating even as heat and cold; thou wilt see how, for the diversion of superior beings, nature, with all this, forms wind, water, plants, metals, and stones; thou wilt perceive how pain and pleasure transform beings."

(5.)

"Thou wilt see the whole and the parts participate in the power of intelligence and reason, and how God, making use of destiny and harmony, ordains the universal drama, and disposes of souls with a view to the active and uninterrupted enacting of this drama."

Poor actor in his human comedy, who had a part so painful to play, how many times, from the bosom of its double dungeon, would thy soul have quitted thy body, loaded with irons, to draw from the heavens the courage thou knowest how to oppose to the executioners who tore off thy flesh with red hot pincers for the blind pleasure of seeing thy blood run. If thy happiness is as great as thy sufferings were acute, thou art surely one of the happiest in the kingdom of heaven. We are about to quit thee and pass into Sweden, to our dearly beloved brother Swedenborg, to demand of him some new revelations for those who have not read his works.

SWEDEN.—*Swedenborg.*—Page 9.—In a preliminary discourse, to serve as a guide in the perusal of the works of Swedenborg, by Captain Fraiche (brochure in 8vo., 1848), we find the following particulars respecting this celebrated ecstatico-prophet:—

"Emmanuel Swedenborg was born at Upsal, in Sweden, the 29th January, 1688, in a distinguished class of society. He was placed from his earliest youth in an important tribunal, and distinguished himself there by his knowledge and integrity; solid and numerous writings on mineralogy, physics, and astronomy soon made him known to the learned world. Esteemed and beloved for his knowledge and virtue, ever useful and irreproachable. Swedenborg gave up, about the year 1740, temporal affairs to engage only in spiritual matters. In 1743, he received the first favors and first orders from heaven." * *

From this period up to the time of his death, which took place in London, on the 29th of March, 1772, he published several works, all written in Latin, on spiritual matters.

NOTE 5.—"Independently of the communication with heaven, and the inspiration with which Swedenborg was favored the rest of his life, he astonished his fellow-citizens by several marvellous things. We will cite a few of the most interesting and best attested ones:—

"1. A demand was made on a lady of the court of Stockholm for a debt, which she well knew her husband had discharged previous to his decease; but not finding the receipt, and apprehensive of having to pay twice over, she went to Swedenborg. He told her, the following day, that he had spoken with her husband, who had told him where the receipt was. The deceased appeared also in a dream to his widow, clad in the dressing-gown he wore before his death, and told her that the receipt was in such a place, where she found it. She used to relate this strange adventure, which the queen of Sweden has since confirmed at Berlin, when on a visit to the king, her brother.

"2. Being at Gottenburg, sixty miles from Stockholm, he announced, three days before the arrival of the courier, the fire which ravaged Stockholm, and the precise hour it broke out; and, without having received any news, he also said that his own house had been spared by the flames.

"3. Embarking at London in the vessel of Captain Dixon, some one asked the latter whether he had laid in plenty of provisions, whereupon Swedenborg observed: '*We don't want such a plenty, for in a week hence, at two o'clock, we shall be at Stockholm.*' The prediction, as Captain Dixon has attested, was literally fulfilled."

NOTE 7.—"In 1758, a short time after the death of the king of Prussia, Swedenborg went to court, whither he was in the habit of going. Scarcely had he been seen by her majesty than she said to him: '*Monsieur, the assessor, have you seen my brother?*' *Swedenborg made answer that he had not; and the queen replied, 'If you should meet him, remember me to him.*' In saying this, she meant merely to pass a joke, and had no thoughts of asking him for any information concerning her brother. A week after, Swedenborg went again to court, bnt at so early an hour that the queen had not yet left her apartment, called the *White Room*, where she was chatting with her ladies of honor and other ladies of the court. Swedenborg waits not for the queen's coming out; he straightway walks into the apartment and whispers in her ear. The queen, struck with astonishment, faints away, and was some time before she recovered. Brought to herself again, she said to those around her, '*Only God and my brother could have known what he has just told me.*' She confessed that he had mentioned to her her last correspondence with that prince, the subject of which was known only to themselves."

NOTE 8.—"As a religion, the doctrine of Swedenborg is already propagated in Sweden, Prussia, the Low Countries, Switzerland, Germany, and even in Russia; in England, forty-four towns already number as many temples; in the United States there were seventy-two of them in 1827. Numerous learned journals propagate this doctrine in Europe, as also in the New World," &c., &c.

This is a slight sketch of the reputation of the man with whom we have entertained our readers; a man worthy of the respect, admiration, and veneration of all spiritualists; the greatest and truest genius of the eighteenth century.

Some *would-be philosophers* wish to refute his admirable writings by arguments worthy of their knowledge.

He was a visionary, say they. This name is well worth that of blind men, which rightly belongs to them.

He was a madman—whom, even up to this very day, they have been unable to do without in their works at the mines.

Let us not discuss with these learned gentlemen; we could not raise ourselves up to them, infinitely insignificant as we are; let us rather pass on to a few extracts from the treatise on heaven and hell, by this maniac — with whom, however, we should be most happy to play a game of *écarté* in the spiritual world: —

Art. 439. — " To throw more light on this truth, that man is a spirit as to his interior, I should wish to recount, from experience, what happens when man is removed from his body, and how, through the spirit, he is conveyed to another place.

Art. 440. — " As to what regards the first point of being removed from his body, this is the way in which it is effected: Man is conducted into a certain state, holding a medium between sleep and wakefulness; when he is in this state he can not know aught else but that he watches; for all his senses are so awakened that he finds himself in the most perfect wakefulness of the body; the sight and hearing are perfect, and most admirable in this situation; the touch also, which finds itself more exquisite and distinct than it could ever be in the operations of the body, is most perfectly awakened. In this state it is that I have seen spirits and angels — seen them *ad vivum* — even heard them, and, what at first strangely surprised me, touched them, without finding scarcely any difference in them from the touch of a body. This state is the one wherein we are said to be removed from our body, and not knowing whether we are in or out of our body. I have been three or four times transported into this state, merely that I might become acquainted with the quality of this state, and at the same time know that spirits and angels have the enjoyment of all their senses, and that man, in like manner, enjoys them as to the spirit when removed from his body."

Is it possible to describe ecstasy better?

Art. 447.—" The spirit of man, after the separation, remains a short time in the body, but only until the total cessation of the heart; this happens differently, according to the nature of the disease of which the man dies, for the movement of the heart in some lasts a certain time, and in others ceases at once; no sooner does this movement cease than man is resuscitated, but this is brought about by the Lord alone. By resurrection, we mean the spirit of man leaving the body, and introduced into the spiritual world; correctly speaking, this resurrection should be termed the awakening."

Art. 452.—"I have conversed with spirits three days after their death, and all the operations I have detailed in Nos. 449, 450, were already consummated. I have conversed with three spirits who had been known to me in their worldly life, told them that their obsequies were being prepared, and their bodies being buried at the moment I spoke to them; at the word *buried*, they were struck with the greatest astonishment, saying that they were alive, and setting in order what was of use to them in the world. Then, being better informed, they were quite astounded that all the time they had lived on earth they had not believed in the possibility of such a life after death.

"Hence, all those who come from the world into the other life are extremely surprised at perceiving that they live, and are men, as they had previously been; at perceiving that they hear, see, and speak; at perceiving that even their body enjoys the sense of touch, as before; but the most surprising of all to them, when they have ceased wondering at this new situation (No. 74), is perceiving that the church knows nothing of such a state for man after death, and, consequently, knows nothing of heaven and hell, when, nevertheless, all those who have lived in the world are now in the other life, and live as men, as they were astonished, also, that this truth was not manifested to man by vision, since it is so essential to the faith of the church. It was told them, from heaven, that this might be done; for there is nothing more easy when it pleases the Lord, but that never would those, who have been confirmed in errors against truths, believe those truths, even were they to see them."

Peruse once more the 132d sitting of the "Secrets," wherein will be seen, in the apparition of my father, the truth of what Swedenborg here reveals as to the momentary ignorance in which certain spirits find themselves who do not believe that they are dead.

Art. 493.—"The first state of man after death is altogether similar to his state in this world, because that then it is the same with exteriors; thus, his physiognomy, language, character — in short, his moral and civil life — are similar to what he has been in the world; hence, he who is in the world of spirits knows not but that he is still on earth, unless he notices the objects which are before his eyes, and the things which have been told him by the angels at the moment of his resurrection, in order to assure him that he was now a spirit (No. 450). Thus, a life is continued in another life, and death is only a passage.

"As the new spirit of man after his life in the world is such, he is then recognised by his friends and those whose society he was wont to frequent in the world; for the spirits recognise him not only by his physiognomy and language, but also by his sphere of life when they approach the newly-arrived spirit. Each, in the other life, while he is thinking of another, has immediately the physiognomy of the person who occupies him in his thought, and at the same time several deeds and actions of his life are retraced before his eyes; and when he is in this state of reminiscence, the object remembered becomes to him present, as if called for and brought before him. The same effect exists in the world of spirits, because the thoughts are communicated there, and because there space is no longer known as in the natural world (Nos. 191, 199). Hence, as soon as they come into the other life, they are recognised by their friends, their relations, their parents, by those even who had but a slight connection with them. They speak with each other, and, in short, renew the familiarities and friendships which had united them in the natural world. Several times have I heard those who came from the world which we inhabit; they were transported with joy at beholding again their friends, and their friends participated in this joy at seeing them arrive and become reunited to them. It is a very common thing for husbands to meet again with their wives, wives with their husbands, and congratulate each other at their meeting; then they remain together for a longer or shorter period, according to the degree of attachment they felt for each other in this world; and, in short, if a love truly conjugal had not united them (a love which is the conjunction of two souls by heavenly love), a short time after their new reunion they separate. If the souls of married couples have lived in dissension—if they have inwardly hated each other—they now display openly their mutual aversion, and oftentimes even abuse each other and fight, without being able, however, to separate till the moment of their passage to the second state, of which I shall treat in the following article."

We are conscious that it can not be otherwise: there is no possible transition between the two kinds existing; it must be, as we have seen, a continuation of affections which can not disappear suddenly. In the harmony of nature, there can not be any such escapements; there is progression, but by the catch of that universal and eternal wheel, a single tooth of which can not be broken without putting out of order the machine. Magnetizers, who know with what facility clairvoyantes communicate with places and persons at a distance, will readily admit that it must be thus in heaven, where spaces exist much less than on earth. It is not, therefore, incredible that so soon as we think of a deceased friend he should be forthwith with us; if we do not see him and feel him, it is because our organs are too paralyzed; but the clairvoyante soon proves to us the truth of this revelation, by describing him to us and conversing with him.

Who would still dare treat Swedenborg as a madman after so beautiful a description of the somnambulic faculties, which certainly were not known in his time as in our days?

Art. 507.—"When spirits are in this second state, they appear just as they were when in the physical world; then, the things which they have done and pronounced in the utmost secrecy are manifested in open day; for then, as external appearances no longer enchain them, they speak openly, endeavor to do openly things similar to those which they did and said in secret in their earthly life, no longer fearing the loss of their reputation, and no longer terrified by the other motives which kept them in check in the world; consequently, are they shown in their respective sinful states that they may appear just as they really are to the angels and good spirits who examine them. Thus it is that the most secret things are discovered, the most clandestine works unveiled. According to the words of the Lord: 'For there is nothing covered that shall not be revealed; neither hid that shall not be known. Therefore, whatsoever ye have spoken in darkness shall be heard in the light, and that which ye have spoken in the ear in closets, shall be proclaimed upon the housetops.' (St. Luke, xii. 2, 3.) 'But I say unto you that every idle word that men shall speak, they shall give account thereof in the day of judgment.' (St. Matthew, xii. 36.)"

On earth is there aught that we can hide from the perception of a clairvoyante? It is not, therefore, ridiculous to admit that in the world of spirits none is any longer able to conceal aught; it is the book of life which will be open to all. The masks of calm concealing rage, smiles concealing bitterness, virtue concealing vice, will be left on earth. We can not deny these truths after having studied magnetic somnambulism. Need we invite our readers to a perusal of the works of the learned Swede? No, these few passages, we are certain of it, will be a better invitation than any we could give. We abstain, therefore, from all insinuation in this respect.

We are about to proceed into Germany, to consult a philosopher highly extolled, and deservedly so, by our *savans* of the day.

GERMANY.—"Fichte, on the Destiny of Man:" Translation of 1836: page 254:—

"Moreover, it is not from to-day that this conviction exists in me. Long before conscience had spoken with its irresistible authority, I could not contemplate the actual world for a single instant, without feeling rise within me, shall I say hope? shall I say desire? No: better than that, more than that—the irrefragable certitude of another world. At each glance I let fall on men or on nature, at every reflection engendered in my mind by the singular contrast of the immensity of man's desires and his actual misery, an interior voice would raise itself within me and say: 'Oh! nothing out of all this can be eternal; be persuaded of it, another world exists, another and a better world. * * * I eat, I drink, in order that I may eat and drink again. The grave, incessantly open, seizes its prey; I descend into it to become the food of worms: I leave behind me beings similar to myself, that they may eat and drink until they die, themselves replaced by others, similar to them, who in their turn will do the same things. Such is my life, such is the world; it is a circle revolving eternally on itself; it is a fantastic spectacle, wherein all is born to die, and dies to be born again; it is a hydra with innumerable heads, never weary of devouring itself in order to reproduce itself, and reproducing itself to devour itself again. Shall I believe, then, that it is in the circle of those monstrous and eternal vicissitudes all the efforts of humanity must waste themselves in useless efforts? Shall I not rather believe, that if humanity undergoes them, it is but momentarily, with the view of arriving at a state which shall remain final, in order to reach at last a place of rest, where, recovering from so many fatigues, it will remain immoveable for eternity, above the agitated waves of the ocean of ages."

Page 363.—"While here below, we weep for a man, as we should have but too just a cause for doing so were he deprived for ever of the light of the sun, were he to go wandering for eternity in those immense solitudes wherein exists not the consciousness of self, where he sunk never to emerge from them in the sombre kingdom of nothingness; above us, other creatures, no doubt, rejoice at the birth of this man in their world new to him, as in this we rejoice at the birth of one of our children.

"May the day, then, whereon I am to rejoin him, quickly arrive! I will leave mourning and sorrow to the earth which I shall quit, and that day shall be to me the most welcome of all."

Let us return to France, our dear country, said to be the least philosophical and most light-minded of all nations. We will prove to its enemies that they have uttered a falsehood, and that our libraries swarm with works bespeaking great meditation of mind, and a love of spiritualism more refined than among many other nations. The limits of this work not admitting of our citing all the authors we are acquainted with, who have treated on this grand question, we will select from among them a few who have done so in our point of view:—

FRANCE.— *Pierre le Loyer.*—This writer of the seventeenth century appears to the eyes of the present generation as a superstitious character, who lived only among demons. Let us do him a little more justice; he deserves being admitted as a conscientious and enlightened writer, who—having been enabled, by his social position, to see, compare, and judge the facts which he relates—had a right to pronounce as he did. Had he been a little less of a devotee, he would have been but a still greater philosopher. One destroys not the other; it merely injures him in the judgment of a few persons who concede nothing to their fellow-men. Le Loyer represents the philosophy and beliefs of his age. In his treatise on "Spectres and Apparitions, or Visions of Angels and Demons, showing themselves sensibly to Men" (1586, 4th book, page 85), he says: * * * * "And after him [Mahomet], I find that King Avezoar Albuma, a great philosopher and physician, also believed in the apparition of souls; for he has left on record, that having a disease in one of his eyes, and no hope of finding a remedy, he beheld, while asleep, a deceased friend of his, a physician, who told him what remedies to apply to recover his sight;—and Avicenna follows, for the most part, the opinion of Plato as to souls; and as Plato has termed the body the grave of the soul, so by Avicenna the body is termed the paralysis of the soul, through which it can not freely perform its functions and actions; and as to the felicity of the soul after the death of the body, he still agrees with Plato, except in the damnation of the damned, the punishment of whom consists, he says, in a continual sorrow at being deprived of what they have most desired, believing that there is no other torment for the soul (which is the everlasting fire) than that of being deprived of the sight of God—which doctrine Plato did not hold."

Page 88.—"Certainly the Bramins, the priestly disciples of

the Bragmans, who dwell in Calcutta, in the East Indies, besides believing in the immortality of souls, think that they may be evoked by necromancy, and they are the greatest magicians in this part of the Indies."

Page 150.—"Do we require a more beautiful solution than that of St. Augustine, who, after having duly and diligently discussed the question of the apparition of the dead, at length unravels and disposes of it in this way: 'If,' said he, 'we consider as false the apparitions that the faithful and catholics declare they have seen, and if we set so little value on the testimony of those who declare that they have seen and heard with their corporeal senses the souls of the dead, we should be rightly reputed as too bold and incredulous.' Thus, St. Augustine founds his opinion upon what the generality of men believe, and principally good, faithful Christians, who, in his time, declared and maintained that souls had been seen after separation from the body."

What was believed at that time may surely be believed now, when God permits us to enter into communication with souls, through the medium of somnambulism, at any time and at any hour.

*Delachambre.*—The system of the soul, by Delachambre, published in 1665, gives a pretty good summary of the beliefs and long theological disputes of the seventeenth century. This work, highly metaphysical, is worthy of being studied by magnetizers. We find, at page 53, these reflections:—

"The greatest difficulty is to know whether the communication which men have with angels and souls separated can be performed in the same manner (by meeting forthwith); for it can not be doubted that there is some society between us and them, since there is such between all intelligent natures, and since the communication we must have together is a point of true religion; angels and blessed souls can, in truth, come to us, penetrate us, and unite themselves to our thoughts, but we can not go to them if they are in heaven. What, then, can become of our wishes and prayers with respect to them? how should they, being so far off, know our wants and wishes?"

Page 404.—"It must not, however, be supposed that the form of the soul and of angels is fixed and determinate, like that of solid bodies; it is vague and changeable like that of the air and the liquids, which assume the form of all the solid bodies surrounding them, and the difference is this, that the vivacity of the forms that supervene to the latter is of necessity, and that which is found in spiritual substances depends on their will; for, as they move as they please all their parts, they also assume whatever form they desire."

This proposition comes in support of what has been revealed to us relative to the forms which souls disengaged from matter can assume. In the first proposition, M. Delachambre (who may rightly pass for a philosopher of great merit) considers it a very rational idea that the soul of deceased persons should communicate instantaneously with that of terrestrial men, agreeably to the wishes of the latter. He thus draws his conclusions therefrom, by reasonings not systematical, but truly thelogical.

*Lebrun.*—Let us see what the Rev. Father Lebrun thinks of it in his "Critical History of Superstitious Practices," 2d edition, vol. ii., 1732, page 227:—

"Doubtless it was an abominable superstition to pretend to make the dead speak in order to pry into the future. God had distinctly said that it was consulting the Evil One, and was a crime deserving of death: still Saul, setting at defiance the prohibition and the penalty, ventured to consult a witch, and ask her to resuscitate, and cause to appear, Samuel. Although the Evil One had no power over this prophet, and could only assume his countenance and voice, God, nevertheless, permits Samuel himself to come and speak to Saul, reproach him for his crimes, and announce to him his destruction. I am aware that it is disputed whether what then appeared was the shade of Samuel or the prophet himself. I am also aware that some persons inquire whether it was supernatural or a sheer imposture! But this is a point on which there can be neither question nor doubt. Those who dispute have not paid attention to what is said in Ecclesiasticus, for this sacred book distinctly informs us that Samuel, being dead, made known to the king what would happen to him: 'And after his death, he prophesied, and showed the king his end, and lifted up his voice from the earth in prophecy, to blot out the wickedness of the people.' Here, then, is Samuel prophesying after his death, and God doing, among the abominable superstitions of the witch, what diabolic art could not have operated."

Don't let that astonish you, Father Lebrun; there was in the science of the witch nothing more reprehensible than what you may be pleased to approve in favor of your doctrine. *An apparition is a fact*, that is what we wished to register, since we are in the nineteenth century. Let us continue.

*Voltaire.*—Let us open for an instant the "Philosophical Dictionary," the panacea of materialists, in which M. Arouet de Voltaire condescended to write a few pages. Article—"Man," vol. v.:—

"Where is the man who, as soon as he withdraws into himself, feels not that he is but a mere puppet of Providence? I think, but can I impart to myself a thought? Alas! if I thought of myself, I should know what idea I should have in a moment; no one knows it.

"I acquire a knowledge, but I could not have imparted it to myself; my intelligence could not have been the cause of it, as the cause must contain the effect; now, my first acquired knowledge not being in my intelligence, not being in me, since it has been the first, it has been imparted to me by him who formed me and is the giver of all, whatsoever he be.

"I am altogether lost and humbled when I am made to perceive that my first knowledge can not of itself impart to me a second, as it would be necessary that it should contain it within itself.

"The proof that we do not impart to ourselves any idea is, that we receive many in our dreams, and, certainly, it is neither our will nor our attention which causes us to think in a dream. There are poets who compose verses while asleep, geometers who measure triangles; all this proves to us that there is a power that acts within us without consulting us.

"All our sentiments, are they not involuntary?—hearing, sight, taste, are nothing of themselves; we are conscious, despite ourselves, we know nothing—we are nothing without a supreme power, that does all."

Who now would venture to say that this article is the work of a materialist? What spiritualist ever better meditated?

Article—"Magic," vol. vi., ed. 1785.—"Magic is a science much more plausible than astrology and the doctrine of genii. No sooner do we begin to think that there is in man a being quite distinct from the machine, and that the understanding subsists after death, than we give to this understanding a delicate, subtile, aërial body, resembling the body in which it was lodged; two reasons, perfectly natural, invite to this opinion:—the first is this, that in all languages the soul was termed breath, spirit, wind; this spirit, wind, breath, was in something very small, and very delicate. The second—that if the soul of a man had not retained a form similar to that it possessed during its life, we should have been unable, after death, to distinguish the soul of one man from that of another. This soul, this shadow which subsisted, separated from its body, could very well show itself in a case of emergency, see again the places it had dwelt in, visit its relatives, its friends, speak to them, instruct them. In all this there was no incompatibility; what is, is able to appear."

Who, pray, after such a confession, would fear ridicule, by making a similar one?—To find, in the "Philosophical Dictionary," these words: "The soul can *see again the places it had dwelt in.*" What novelty is there in what we have just said? What, then, do clairvoyantes tell us that should be looked upon as incredible? Nothing. The "Philosophical Dictionary" has been as far as possible.

*Saint-Martin.*—We will pass on to the perusal of a few passages contained in a highly-esteemed work, entitled "Errors and Truth," by an unknown philosopher (attributed to Saint-Martin), vol. i., page 31:—

"No one of good faith, and whose reason is neither clouded nor prejudiced, but what comprehends that the corporeal life of man is a state of almost continual suffering and privation; thus, from the ideas we have formed of justice, it is not without reason that we look upon the duration of this corporeal life as a time of chastisement and expiation, but we can not look upon it as such, without forthwith thinking that there must have been for man a state anterior and preferable to the one wherein he now finds himself; and we may say that in proportion as his actual state is confined, painful, and sown with disgust, so the other must have been illimitable, and filled with delight. Each of his sufferings is an index of the happiness wanting in him; each of his privations proves that he was made for enjoyment, and his present subjection announces an ancient authority; in one word, to feel now that he has nothing, is a secret proof that once he had all.

"From the painful perception of the dreadful state in which we now see him, we may, therefore, form to ourselves an idea of the happy state in which he was previously. He is not, at present, the master of his thoughts; and it is a torment for him to have to wait for those he desires, and repulse those he fears; hence we feel that he was made to dispose of these same thoughts, and that he could produce them at will; whence it is, also, easy to presume the inappreciable advantages attached to such a power; he obtains, actually, a certain amount of peace and tranquillity, only by unheard-of efforts and painful sacrifices; hence, we conclude that he was made to enjoy, perpetually, and without labor, a calm and happy state, and that the abode of peace was his true dwelling. Possessing the faculty of seeing all and knowing all, he, nevertheless, crawls in darkness, shuddering at his blindness and ignorance. Is not this a certain proof that the light is his element? At last, his body is subject to destruction; and this death, of which he is the only creature in nature who has an idea of it, is the most terrible step in his corporeal career, the act the most humiliating to him, and the one which he holds most in horror. Wherefore, should not this law, so severe and dreadful for man, induce us to think that his body had received one infinitely more glorious, and was destined to enjoy all the rights of immortality!"

Page 43.—" It is, therefore, evident that this material body which we bear is the organ of all our sufferings; it is, therefore, it which, forming dense bounds to our view and to all our faculties, keeps us in privation and suffering. Consequently, I ought not any longer to dissemble that the junction of man to this coarse envelope is the punishment even to which his sin has subjected him temporarily, since we see the horrible effects that he suffers from it from the moment he is invested with it to that wherein he is stripped of it, and that hence it is that begin and are perpetuated the trials without which he can not re-establish the relations he once had with the light!"

I will make no observation on this passage, which is the full and entire confirmation of what has been revealed to us relative to a life anterior, in which we were, as St. Martin says, possessors of all we now stand in need of.

Here are a few fragments of the same author, extracted from his last pages on death.

" The society of the world in general has appeared to me like a theatre whereon we must continually pass our time in playing our part, wherein there is never a single moment to learn it. The society of wisdom, on the contrary, is a school wherein we constantly pass our time in learning our part, and where we only wait for the drawing up of the curtain, that is to say, till the veil of the universe has disappeared, to begin playing.

" From the way in which worldly folks spend their time, one would say that they are afraid of not being silly enough.

" Death is but one of the hours of our dial, and our dial must turn for ever.

" The hope of death forms the consolation of my days; therefore would I that men would never say 'the other life,' for there is but one life.

" I have seen that men were astonished at dying, and were not astonished at being born; this, however, should more justly excite their surprise and admiration.

"Is it not grievous to the thought to see that man passes his life in learning how he should pass it?

"Nothing is easier than arriving at the door of truth, nothing more rare and difficult than entering it, and such is the case with most of the learned of this world.

"If after our death this world should appear to us but a trance, wherefore should we not regard it as such from this moment? The nature of things can not change.

"As our material existence is not life, our material destruction is not death.

"Man has warnings of all, but he pays no attention to them; in fact, all is in our atmosphere, the secret is to know how to read in it."

What think you of this last passage, my dearly-beloved *savans?* Your spectacles are of an exquisite polish, but they do not penetrate so far, and yet this is, this can be seen, comprehended, demonstrated with little trouble and in little time; but we can not raise ourselves up to you. Let each remain in his place; ours is, you have said, at Bicêtre [Bedlam]; peace be between us. Be assured, dear readers, that the authors we quote have never been the inmates of Charenton [also a madhouse]; they have been forgotten at the door, where we made acquaintance with them. We will now introduce to you the famous, or if you please, poor Marmontel.

*Marmontel.*—"Lessons of a Father to his Children on Metaphysics," page 99 :—

"You perceive," said he, "by the functions performed by the soul of animals that its destination ceases with the term of its life, whereas the destination of the soul of man has barely commenced. Contemplative intelligence! it has seen but through a cloud the marvels with which the Eternal has been pleased to render it a witness, and only by disengaging itself from these material veils will it fully enjoy the sight of the great work, and that of its author."

Page 118.—"No, my children, if God has left to man the power of rendering himself worthy of reward and punishment, and if both are not distributed in this life with a constant and strict equity, there is for man another life in which God reserves to himself to be just; it must be so, otherwise he would not be God."

"Possibly I here make use of a very bold expression; for what is the right of the creature with respect to his Creator? What is the engagement and obligation of the Creator toward the creature? He owes him nothing, strictly speaking, but he owes it to himself, or rather it appertains to his divine essence and the excellence of his nature, to desire naught which is not perfectly conformable to the eternal idea of justice and goodness. We have reason to reproach men for having made for themselves a God after their own image, attributing to him qualities unworthy of him, and these are errors of the imagination from which I hope to preserve you. * * * * * Annihilation was ever the horrible hope of crime; immortality was ever the consolation of oppressed innocence and the support of virtue."

130. "It is this presentiment of a life to come which, in all times has imparted so much strength and elevation to virtuous souls, to such men as Socrates, Theramenes, Leonidas, Cato, Thraseas, and in an especial degree to the martyrs of this holy religion whose fundamental doctrine is the immortality of the soul. Man, occupied with a boundless felicity which it is permitted him to hope for, no longer regards this life but as a fugitive flash which escapes and vanishes through light clouds. A serene day is beyond, and this day which never night will darken awaits him. It is in eternity that he beholds what sort of being is his God, and there it is that he recognises him as supremely good and just. Physical evil, with respect to man, is therefore a fresh proof of the immortality of the soul; moral evil still adds to this proof, since it supposes a free will, and liberty in man is an infallible proof of immortality."

Let us now consult a few writers who have devoted themselves to the study of magnetism, for all bucklers are good to parry the blows aimed at us; we are not sorry at sharing ridicule in company. We will, however, first introduce the celebrated Ch. Fourier.

*Fourier.*—We find in his "Life and Theory," by Ch. Pellarin, 2d edition, 1843, page 394:—

"Fourier expressed himself as follows in a letter to Muiron, dated 3d November, 1826: 'It appears that Messrs. G. and P. have given up their work on magnetism; I would wager that they don't succeed with the fundamental argument. I mean that if all is knit together in the system of the universe, there must exist a means of communication between the creatures of the other world and this one; that is to say, a communication of the faculties of the ultra-mundanes or deceased, and not a communication with the latter; this participation can not take place in the watchful state, but only in a mixed state, as sleep or something else. Have magnetizers discovered this state? I know not; but in principle I am aware that it must exist, and if it is the state of artificial somnambulism, no advantage will be derived from it so long as we are ignorant of the calculation of the sympathies of characters in identities and contrasts. For want of sorting, according to this theory, magnetizers and the magnetized, we shall undergo a score failures for one successful result, and this will give a superiority to the skeptics and detractors.'"

What you foresaw I have put in execution. I wanted but your erudition to draw from it the sage conclusions that you—worthy man for such a task!—would have drawn from it.

*Bertrand.*—Let us pass on to Doctor Bertrand. "Treatise on Somnambulism," 1823.

"It is evident that those who admit an immaterial principle within us, can not consider it as confined or limited in any part of space, and that it can be no more placed in our body than anywhere else,* and, consequently, that nothing can limit the extent of its perceptions."

* "If we are induced to place our soul in our body, and to believe that it is maintained there, it is merely because we feel only in the extent of the matter constituting it, and because we can not act on any particle of matter beyond the limits. We ought not, therefore, to consider our body as containing our soul, as a thing material contains another, but only limiting the extent of the matter in which it is given it to act and feel."—*(Note to the above work.)*

For so confirmed a skeptic as Doctor Bertrand, this proposition is not a very materialist one! far from it.

"The soul can as well take cognisance of objects the farthest off from its body as of those nearest to it; for the view at the greatest distances once operated, there will be nothing to create surprise, or what may not even seem necessary; for, if our soul is quite as well at the antipodes as in our body, wherefore, if it desires to direct its attention on an object fifteen hundred leagues off, should it not equally as well take cognizance of it as of that within a few feet of it?

Page 257.—"Sometimes the somnambulist was shown absent persons, or those who had been long dead. When she opened her eyes, seeing before her a spectre or phantom, she was sensibly moved, and, at times, scenes occurred that might have injured her health. It would be dangerous to repeat such experiments often; I warn magnetizers who should be tempted to make similar ones, that serious consequences might be the result, alike injurious to the health and mental faculties."

I reply to Doctor Bertrand that the magnetizers who have made experiments of this kind, doubtless, knew not how to conduct them; this, it is true, might seriously affect the clairvoyante's mind; but those which I propose, and which have been read, can present no inconvenience of the kind, and ought, on the contrary, to establish demonstratively the existence of the soul after its separation from the body. The spectres or phantoms which the said clairvoyantes saw were naught else but the last state of the deceased patients, whom, in their ecstatic ignorance, they went to seek in the graveyards, and which the ignorance, not less great of the magnetizers allowed to subsist on the clairvoyante's awaking. This, it is true, must have produced injurious effects; but which ought to prove to the magnetizers that these corpses, reduced years ago to dust, nevertheless existed for the clairvoyante, and demonstrated to them the immortality of material forms in the world of effects, as spiritualism demonstrates the immortality of the causes in the type-world. Doctor Bertrand is far from wishing to believe in such communications between the two worlds, as will be seen by the following article; but his citing it is sufficient for us to reproduce it, thinking that those who may have been convinced by the experiments we have cited will explain it otherwise :—

"The members of the Exegetical Society of Stockholm were zealously engaged in magnetizing. In 1787 and 1788, they had come, I know not how, to the persuasion that the marvellous facts of somnambulism could not appertain to the material man, and that it must be some pure intelligence speaking through the mouth of patients fallen into this state! Well! all the sick persons sent to sleep by men persuaded of this idea, not only were persuaded of it themselves, but also, like the possessed, they identified themselves with the spiritual substances supposed to speak through their mouth; and when the magnetizer, after sending them to sleep, put to them the usual questions: 'Who are you who speak?' they replied, conformably to the ideas of the person questioning them, I am the brother, the father, the friend, or child of the person you have sent to sleep. And then he would speak of the dead, discuss points of philosophy, preach the doctrine of Swedenborg, and give information of what was passing in the other world. * * * * * * I could add to these examples, so conclusive, a great number of others not less so."

Doctor Bertrand apparently throws out a hint to the effect that he looks upon the members of this society (one of the most learned that ever existed), as poor visionaries, who were the sport of their imagination and of the more or less nonsensical ramblings of their clairvoyantes. Had the doctor thought of experimenting himself, he would have instantly recognised the truth or falsehood of these communications. To reject an assertion supported by well-informed men, without mature examination, is not being logical, and above all to terminate with this phrase: 'I could add to these examples, so conclusive, a great number of others not less so.' If these examples are conclusive, and you do not admit them, doctor, you know only how to cite, and not conclude.

*Chardel.*—We will pass on to another magnetizer, whose knowledge and veracity can not be doubted. M. C. Chardel, counsellor at the court of cassation at Paris, in his "Essay on Psychology," third edition, 1844, page 111, thus expresses himself:—

"The human soul seems, therefore, a stranger on earth—a prisoner in a new world; the body lends its organs to perceive it, and life gives it the means of making use of them, but in opening it to the material world it closes against it the spiritual one."

This passage comes to the support of the anterior existence of which we have already spoken.

Page 357 (Appendix).—"Antiquity believed in communications with the other world, it recounts numerous instances of such which the present age classes among fables; still, in our days, the apparitions of spirits are not more rare than formerly, only we conceal them in the veil of ridicule with which we can not hide the truth as well as error. I grant that facts of this kind demand an explanation, and I will give one, but to make it understood it is necessary that it should be preceded by an inquiry as to the mode of existence of souls; moreover, I beg to remind the reader that I have studied nature in a path but little known, and I make an appeal not to his credulity but his examination."

M. Chardel taking, then, his stand on the writings of Swedenborg, on facts of *ecstatism*, and several apparitions personal to himself and full of interest, concludes with a firm belief in the world of spirits, and the possibility of communicating with them; he believes in the recollection of *self*, and all that can constitute individuality in the world of spirits. He continues thus (page 384):—

"In the spiritual world there are no longer either fathers or mothers, brothers or sisters; the ties of family are broken, all the sentiments are laid bare, and the nature of the sensibility of each once determined no longer has occasion to change."

*Savans*, M. Chardel was in your ranks, and believed in spirits!

*Du Potet.*—While we conceal ourselves behind these bucklers, for the sake of a short respite, we will open the essay on the "Philosophical Teaching of Magnetism," by M. Du Potet, page 12, wherein we find these severe words, which you merit *savans*, and which this writer ought to have remembered before analyzing the "Secrets."

"You, *savans* of our country, you have not shown yourselves better informed than the Siamese, as, for these sixty years, it has been bawled in your ears: *The magnetizers march to the discovery of a moral world;* all the phenomena they produce indubitably prove its existence. You have declared that they were impostors, idiots, and of you all those are the most illustrious who have signed the judgment which will attest to all future ages your ignorance and insincerity."

Page 68.—"The knowledge of man and his destinies is within the science of magnetism; delay not too long to assure yourself of this, thy days are limited, no eagle-eye is required to measure their extent.

"Let thy actions be virtuous, for, know that thy soul will remember them all after thy life on earth and the remembrance of them will be ineffaceable. *Not on sand are human actions graven, but in the conscience. The torments of thy crimes will have no end. Thy heart may perish without removing the least stain from thy soul; this rust would be constantly gnawing it, for thou couldst no longer conceal anything, even from thyself, and thou thyself wouldst be thine own inexorable judge. Whatsoever thou shalt have thought shall be known by all who wish to know it. For thee no more dissimulation is possible; no longer any mask. As thou wilt be able to read in others, so they in thee, and thy most trifling actions will appear like a cloud under a serene sky.*

"Pray that thy life may be short; if thou hast lived well thy soul will quit the prison that confines it, it will issue from it radiant and full of light. This world of mockers and fools suspect not the object of life; imitate it not, it believes in a prolonged ball; whatsoever flatters its pride and intoxicates its senses is found assembled; but one day the Amphytrion of this banquet will dismiss his guests—their life will then be extinguished like the tapers that lighted up the fête."

Page 231.—"*The soul—What is a soul? Who has ever seen a soul? Where does it reside? Let it be shown to us.* Words as stupid as would be those of a person who should say, 'Where is the wind? Who has ever seen the wind? Let it be shown to us.' And many seek for their soul, as did the man for his horse when on his back. Oh! great geniuses of our time, illustrious mortals, strike but a blow on your shell, pain will answer you; you will have the consciousness of your existence, you will be warned that there is within you something that watches and is uneasy, not your *high reason;* strike again, and let the blood run, the occupant will take leave of you, quitting its domicile, and none of you will be able to repair it, and set it in motion. In vain may you cry, the air will resound in vain with your cries; the closed mouth will remain dumb. Should it be that of one of your orators, one of those mouths that in this world have a reply for all? Doubtless he who explains, accounts for all, has no need of having recourse to the Divinity; and hence it is that *savans* deny what they can not conceive or explain. A trumpery penny mirror, could it but speak on the objects it reflects, would reason like our *savans*; it would have, however, behind its surface but a little mercury and tin: of what, then, are the brains of our great men composed?

"Before the soul is disengaged from matter, it can already converse with pure spirits. God has permitted it, but in an imperfect manner. It can plunge its look even to the abode of those who have for ever lost the human form [material, meant by M. Du Potet]; it gives up its secrets, however, only with very great reserve."

M. Du Potet then cites several ecstatic facts, by which he demonstrates this truth. He assures us that he himself has received counsels from a spiritual voice similar to those given Bruno, of which mention is made in the first volume. We can not doubt the highly studious and upright mind of this *savan*, who may be heard every Sunday, at his conferences, developing his beliefs, which are, as we have just seen, as spiritualist as we can desire them. M. Du Potet has not become the apostle of such beliefs without mature examination, and thorough conviction of their truth. We venture, therefore, to hope that with support we shall appear less ridiculous, as we proclaim nothing more than he does. Had the limits of this work permitted us, we would have opened the numerous and estimable works of the rich library of magnetism, in which we could have collected as many facts of this nature as we could have desired; but this would have been abusing the complaisance of our readers; we will content ourselves with recommending to them the perusal of Mesmer, Puységur, Deleuze, Petétin, Despine, Billot, Charpignon, Ricard, the abbé Loubert, Loisson de Guinaumont, Teste, Gautier (Aubin), Possin, Delaage, and those whom we have quoted, &c. They will find in these authors an entire confirmation of the spirituel communications treated of in this work. After such perusal, we believe we shall no longer be in their eyes but a man who may have erred in certain propositions; who, for want of sufficient education, is unequal to the task; but who has done his best to communicate to his brethren, whom he loves with all the strength of his soul, ideas that may tend to mitigate their painful position on earth. He has done so conscientiously, truthfully, fondly; may he succeed agreeably to his wishes. I terminate, by solemnly protesting, before God, that in all that I have said, I have in nowise perverted the truth in favor of any system whatever; that of all the sittings that have been read, I possess certificates, and keep them at the service of all my readers, whom, moreover, I would recommend to experiment for themselves, according to the instructions laid down in the first volume. It is a general property, and will convince them better than all that could be written on the subject.

I receive, every day, fresh confirmations of the success of this property of the soul, from honest magnetizers, who wish, before judging, to experiment without partiality. To make mention of all the facts of this nature would far exceed the limits prescribed me in this work. Having just founded a society of spiritualists in Paris, which will publish its works in a journal entitled "The Spiritualist Magnetizer," the first number of which has appeared, we will report in its columns the most curious facts with which we may become acquainted.

---

## DEVOTEDNESS.

In these days of trouble, alarm, and mourning, in which we live, I despaired of the prediction which our good brother Swedenborg had made in saying to me: "Your second part of the 'Secrets' will be printed; such is the will of God. Do not be disquieted; when the time comes, some one will aid you." Who could have believed in the realization of this prophecy at a time when naught but falsehoods and enmities are seen issuing from the press; when not a single publisher dares venture to publish the least work; when each locks up his money in the painful prevision of events in which it may be found of absolute necessity. Having only just reimbursed myself for the expenses of the first volume, I had not at my command the funds necessary for printing the second, when the venerable and beneficent old man to whom I was indebted for publishing the first, one day came and handed to me the same note for five hundred francs, on the same conditions as before. At my observation that it was rash to venture a second trial—that this time I might not be able to reimburse him—he replied to me: "May God be with us, and his will be done! Should you be unable to repay me, you will not have to reproach yourself with having asked me for it; and, as for me, I shall think no more of it." Know you, reader, the age and the means of this devoted friend of the sciences? Why, he is seventy-eight years of age, and has an income of six hundred francs (about one hundred and twelve dollars)!

A few days after this offer, I received by post a letter, from the same person who had subscribed a hundred francs for the first volume, containing a bank-note of the same amount. as his subscription to the second, with a request not to mention his name, and, above all, to spare myself the trouble of thanking him. Oh, thanks, thrice thanks! generous men: this fine action will not go without its reward. I had asked nothing of these two persons who conducted this affair. I was bound to question M. Swedenborg, to inquire whether I ought to send this second volume to the press; and he said to me: "This volume must be printed by the 20th February, for certain ev— are drawing near; it is in like disasters that consolations are needed."

Here it is, dear reader, without having met with any accident. May it answer your kind expectations, and fortify you in these times of trouble, when it is precious to know how to die, and still more precious to know whither we go!

# CONTENTS OF VOLUME II.

CORRESPONDENCE.

THE IMMORTALITY OF THE SOUL—OPINIONS OF PHILOSOPHERS FROM ANTIQUITY TO OUR DAYS.



THE END.

# A CATALOGUE

OF

# BOOKS,

PUBLISHED BY J. S. REDFIELD,

CLINTON HALL, N. Y.

AND FOR SALE BY MOST BOOKSELLERS IN THE UNITED STATES.

## THE PICTORIAL BIBLE,

Price Six Dollars.

THE Pictorial Bible, being the Old and New Testaments, according to the authorized version: illustrated with more than one thousand engravings, representing the Historical Events after celebrated pictures: the Landscape Scenes from original drawings or from authentic engravings: and the subjects of Natural History, Costume, and Antiquities, from the best sources. With an elegantly engraved Family Record, and a new and authentic Map of Palestine.

"We have seldom seen a more attractive work, and have no doubt that the cost of the enterprise will be sustained by a large circulation."
*N. Y. Evangelist.*

"The type is fair and handsome, and the engravings are select and executed remarkably well. They are so numerous and good, as to be in themselves a *commentary*."—*Christian Reflector.*

"Its abundant and beautiful illustrations adapt it for a Family Bible, and will make it highly interesting to the young."—*Christian Register.*

"It is a superb publication."—*Zion's Herald.*

"The engravings are executed in a fine style of the art, and the paper and the type are all that the most fastidious eye could require."—*Hierophant.*

## THE PICTORIAL NEW TESTAMENT,

Price One Dollar and Fifty Cents.

## THE PICTORIAL NEW TESTAMENT, AND THE BOOK OF PSALMS.

Price Two Dollars.

BOOKS PUBLISHED BY J. S. REDFIELD.

JUST PUBLISHED,

*In one Volume, 12mo., cloth,* PRICE **$1.25,**

THE

# NIGHT-SIDE OF NATURE;

OR,

## GHOSTS AND GHOST-SEERS.

BY CATHERINE CROWE,

AUTHOR OF "SUSAN HOPLEY," "LILLY DAWSON," ETC.

### OPINIONS OF THE PRESS.

This book treats of allegorical dreams, presentiments, trances, apparitions, troubled spirits, haunted houses, etc., and will be read with interest by many because it comes from a source laying claim to considerable talent, and is written by one who really believes all she says, and urges her reasonings with a good deal of earnestness.—*Albany Argus.*

It embraces a vast collection of marvellous and supernatural stories of supernatural occurrences out of the ordinary course of events.—*N. Y. Globe.*

Miss Crowe has proved herself a careful and most industrious compiler. She has gathered materials from antiquity and from modern times, and gives to English and American readers the ghost-stories that used to frighten the young ones of Greece and Rome, as well as those that accomplish a similar end in Germany and other countries of modern Europe.—*Phila. Bulletin.*

It is written in a philosophical spirit.—*Philadelphia Courier.*

This queer volume has excited considerable attention in England. It is not a catchpenny affair, but is an intelligent inquiry into the asserted facts respecting ghosts and apparitions, and a psychological discussion upon the reasonableness of a belief in their existence.—*Boston Post.*

In this remarkable work, Miss Crowe, who writes with the vigor and grace of a woman of strong sense and high cultivation, collects the most remarkable and best authenticated accounts, traditional and recorded, of preternatural visitations and appearances.—*Boston Transcript.*

This is a copious chronicle of what we are compelled to believe authentic instances of communication between the material and spiritual world. It is written in a clear, vigorous, and fresh style, and keeps the reader in a constant excitement, yet without resorting to claptrap.—*Day-Book.*

The book is filled with facts, which are not to be disputed except by actual proof. They have long been undisputed before the world. The class of facts are mainly of a kind thought by most persons to be "mysterious;" but there will be found much in the book calculated to throw light upon the heretofore mysterious phenomena.—*Providence Mirror.*

This book is one which appears in a very opportune time to command attention, and should be read by all who are desirous of information in regard to things generally called mysterious, relating to the manifestations of the spirit out of man and *in* him.—*Traveller.*

This is not only a curious but also a very able work. It is one of the most interesting books of the season—albeit the reader's hair will occasionally rise on end as he turns over the pages, especially if he reads alone far into the night.—*Zion's Herald.*

A very appropriate work for these days of mysterious rappings, but one which shows that the author has given the subjects upon which she treats considerable study, and imparts the knowledge derived in a concise manner. —*Boston Evening Gazette.*

This is undoubtedly the most remarkable book of the month, and can not fail to interest all classes of people.—*Water-Cure Journal.*

To the lovers of the strange and mysterious in nature, this volume will possess an attractive interest.—*N. Y. Truth-Teller.*

The lovers of the marvellous will delight in its perusal..—*Com. Advertiser.*

# THEORY

OF

# PNEUMATOLOGY;

IN REPLY TO THE QUESTION,

WHAT OUGHT TO BE BELIEVED OR DISBELIEVED

CONCERNING

PRESENTIMENTS, VISIONS, AND APPARITIONS,

ACCORDING TO

Nature, Reason, and Scripture.

BY

DOCTR. JOHANN HEINRICH JUNG-STILLING.

TRANSLATED FROM THE GERMAN, WITH COPIOUS NOTES,

BY SAMUEL JACKSON.

FIRST AMERICAN EDITION,

EDITED BY REV. GEORGE BUSH.

NEW YORK:
J. S. REDFIELD, CLINTON HALL,
CORNER OF NASSAU AND BEEKMAN STREETS.

1851.

# PHYSICO-PHYSIOLOGICAL RESEARCHES

ON

# THE DYNAMICS

OF

## MAGNETISM, ELECTRICITY, HEAT, LIGHT, CRYSTALLIZATION, AND CHEMISM,

IN THEIR RELATIONS TO

# Vital Force.

BY

BARON CHARLES VON REICHENBACH.

**THE COMPLETE WORK,**

FROM THE GERMAN SECOND EDITION.

With the Addition of a Preface and Critical Notes,

BY

JOHN ASHBURNER, M. D.

FIRST AMERICAN EDITION.

NEW-YORK:
J. S. REDFIELD, CLINTON-HALL.
BOSTON: B. B. MUSSEY & CO.
1851.

BOOKS PUBLISHED BY J. S. REDFIELD.

# THE WORKS
OF
# EDGAR ALLAN POE:
## WITH NOTICES OF HIS LIFE AND GENIUS,
BY J. R. LOWELL, N. P. WILLIS, AND R. W. GRISWOLD.

*In two Volumes, 12mo., with a* Portrait of the Author.

Price, Two Dollars and Fifty Cents.

NOTICES OF THE PRESS.

"The edition is published for the benefit of his mother-in-law, Mrs. Maria Clemm, for whose sake we may wish it the fullest success. It however, deserves, and will undoubtedly obtain, a large circulation from the desire so many will feel to lay by a memorial of this singularly-gifted writer and unfortunate man."—*Philadelphia North American.*

"Poe's writings are distinguished for vigorous and minute analysis, and the skill with which he has employed the strange fascination of mystery and terror. There is an air of reality in all his narrations—a dwelling upon particulars, and a faculty of interesting you in them such as is possessed by few writers except those who are giving their own individual experiences. The reader can scarcely divest his mind, even in reading the most fanciful of his stories, that the events of it have not actually occurred, and the characters had a real existence."—*Philadelphia Ledger.*

"We need not say that these volumes will be found rich in intellectual excitements, and abounding in remarkable specimens of vigorous, beautiful, and highly suggestive composition; they are all that remains to us of a man whose uncommon genius it would be folly to deny."—*N. Y. Tribune.*

"Mr. Poe's intellectual character—his genius—is stamped upon all his productions, and we shall place these his works in the library among those books not to be parted with."—*N. Y. Commercial Advertiser.*

"These works have a funereal cast as well in the melancholy portrait prefixed and the title, as in the three pallbearing editors who accompany them in public. They are the memorial of a singular man, possessed perhaps of as great mere literary ingenuity and mechanical dexterity of style and management as any the country has produced. Some of the tales in the collection are as complete and admirable as anything of their kind in the language."—*Military Review.*

"A complete collection of the works of one of the most talented and singular men of the day. Mr. Poe was a genius, but an erratic one—he was a comet or a meteor, not a star or sun. His genius was that almost contradiction of terms, an analytic genius. Genius is nearly universally synthetic—but Poe was an exception to all rules. He would build up a poem as a bricklayer builds a wall; or rather, he would begin at the top and build downward to the base; and yet, into the poem so *manufactured,* he would manage to breathe the breath of life. And this fact proved that it was not *all* a manufacture—that the poem was also, to a certain degree, a growth, a real plant, taking root in the mind, and watered by the springs of the soul."—*Saturday Post.*

"We have just spent some delightful hours in looking over these two volumes, which contain one of the most pleasing additions to our literature with which we have met for a long time. They comprise the works of the late Edgar A. Poe—pieces which for years have been going 'the rounds of the press,' and are now first collected when their author is beyond the reach of human praise. We feel, however, that these productions will live. They bear the stamp of true genius; and if their reputation begins with a 'fit audience though few,' the circle will be constantly widening, and they will retain a prominent place in our literature."—*Rev. Dr. Kip.*

**BOOKS PUBLISHED BY J. S. REDFIELD.**

JUST PUBLISHED,

*In one Volume, 12mo., cloth,* PRICE $1.50,

# THE LITERATI:

SOME HONEST OPINIONS ABOUT

## AUTORIAL MERITS AND DEMERITS,

WITH OCCASIONAL WORDS OF PERSONALITY

INCLUDING

## MARGINALIA, SUGGESTIONS, AND ESSAYS.

BY EDGAR A. POE.

If I have in any point receded from what is commonly received, it hath been for the purpose of proceeding *melius* and not *in aliud.*—LORD BACON.

Truth, peradventure, by force, may for a time be trodden *down*, but never, by any means, whatsoever can it be trodden *out.*—LORD COKE.

---

Among the subjects treated of in the volume, are criticisms on the works of the following authors:—

J. G. C. BRAINARD,
FITZ GREENE HALLECK,
WILLIAM CULLEN BRYANT,
HENRY W. LONGFELLOW,
CHARLES F. HOFFMAN,
WILLIAM GILMORE SIMMS,
JAMES FENIMORE COOPER,
CHARLES ANTHON, LL.D.,
GULIAN C. VERPLANCK,
ROBERT WALSH,
PIERO MARONCELLI,
JOHN W. FRANCIS, M.D., LL.D
WILLIAM W. LORD,
SEBA SMITH,
THOMAS WARD, M.D.,
RICHARD ADAMS LOCKE,
RUFUS DAWES,
JAMES LAWSON,
PROSPER M. WETMORE,
GEORGE B. CHEEVER, D.D.,
FREEMAN HUNT,
NATHANIEL HAWTHORNE,
RUFUS W. GRISWOLD,
BAYARD TAYLOR,
CHRISTOPHER PEASE CRANCH,
JAMES RUSSELL LOWELL,
CORNELIUS MATHEWS,
HENRY B. HIRST,
LEWIS GAYLORD CLARK,
RALPH HOYT,
JAMES ALDRICH,
THOMAS DUNN BROWN,
CHARLES F. BRIGGS,
WILLIAM M. GILLESPIE,
EVERT A. DUYCKINCK,
JOEL T. HEADLEY,
GEORGE P. MORRIS,
NATHANIEL PARKER WILLIS,
HENRY CAREY,
LAUGHTON OSBORN,
EPES SARGENT,
E. P. WHIPPLE,
ROBERT M. BIRD,
WILLIAM ELLERY CHANNING,
WILLIAM A. JAMES,
CATHARINE M. SEDGWICK,
FRANCES S. OSGOOD,
ANNE C. LYNCH,
ELIZABETH OAKES-SMITH,
CAROLINE M. KIRKLAND,
ANNA CORA MOWATT,
ANN S. STEPHENS,
ESTELLE ANNA LEWIS,
ELIZABETH BOGART,
MARY GOVE NICHOLS,
AMELIA B. WELBY,
MARGARET MILLER DAVIDSON,
LUCRETIA MARIA DAVIDSON,
SARAH MARGARET FULLER,
EMMA C. EMBURY,
LYDIA M. CHILD,
ELIZABETH BARRETT BROWNING,
T. B. MACAULAY,
CHARLES LEVER,
HENRY COCKTON,
CHARLES DICKENS,
R. H. HORNE,
FRANCIS MARRYAT,
SIR EDWARD BULWER LYTTON,
THOMAS HOOD.

BOOKS PUBLISHED BY J. S. REDFIELD.

**For Schools, Academies, and Self-Instruction.**

THE

# AMERICAN DRAWING-BOOK.

**BY JOHN G. CHAPMAN, N. A.**

THIS WORK wlll be published in PARTS; in the course of which—

PRIMARY INSTRUCTIONS AND RUDIMENTS OF DRAWING·
DRAWING FROM NATURE—MATERIALS AND METHODS:
PERSPECTIVE—COMPOSITION—LANDSCAPE—FIGURES, ETC:
DRAWING, AS APPLICABLE TO THE MECHANIC ARTS:
PAINTING IN OIL AND WATER COLORS:
THE PRINCIPLES OF LIGHT AND SHADE:
EXTERNAL ANATOMY OF THE HUMAN FORM, AND COMPARATIVE ANATOMY:
THE VARIOUS METHODS OF ETCHING, ENGRAVING, MODELLING, Etc.

Will be severally treated, separately; so that, as far as practicable, each Part will be complete in itself, and form, in the whole, "*a Manual of Information sufficient for all the purposes of the Amateur, and Basis of Study for the Professional Artist, as well as a valuable Assistant to Teachers in Public and Private Schools*;" to whom it is especially recommended, as a work destined to produce a revolution in the system of popular education, by making the Arts of Design accessible and familiar to all, from the concise and intelligible manner in which the subject is treated throughout.

The want of such a work, has been the great cause of neglect in this important branch of education; and this want is at once and fully supplied by the—

AMERICAN DRAWING-BOOK:

upon which Mr. CHAPMAN has been for years engaged; and it is now produced, without regard to expense, in all its details, and published at a price to place it within the means of every one.

The Work will be published in large quarto form, put up in substantial covers, and issued as rapidly as the careful execution of the numerous engravings, and the mechanical perfection of the whole, will allow

☞ Any one PART may be had separately

**Price 50 Cents each Part.**

☞ The **DRAWING COPY-BOOKS,** intended as auxiliary to the Work, in assisting Teachers to carry out the system of instruction, especially in the Primary and Elementary parts, form a new and valuable addition to the means of instruction. They will be sold at a cost little beyond that of ordinary blank-books.

BOOKS PUBLISHED BY J. S. REDFIELD.

# CHAPMAN

ON

# PERSPECTIVE

**BEING PART III. OF THE AMERICAN DRAWING-BOOK.**

---

## NOTICES OF THE PRESS.

"The nation may well be proud of this admirable work. In design and execution, the artist has been singularly felicitous; and nothing can surpass the beauty, correctness, and finish of style, in which the publisher has presented it to his countrymen. The book is strictly what it claims to be—a teacher of the art of Drawing. The method is so thorough, comprehensive, and progressive; its rules so wise, exact, and clearly laid down; and its classic illustrations are so skilfully adapted to train the eye and hand, that no pupil who faithfully follows its guidance, can fail to become, at least, a correct draughtsman. We have been especially pleased with the treatise on Perspective, which entirely surpasses anything that we have ever met with upon that difficult branch of art."—*Spirit of the Age.*

"Perspective, is one of the most difficult branches of drawing, and one the least susceptible of verbal explanation. But so clearly are its principles developed in the beautiful letter-press, and so exquisitely are they illustrated by the engravings, that the pupil's way is opened most invitingly to a thorough knowledge of both the elements and application of Perspective."—*Home Journal.*

"It treats of Perspective with a masterly hand. The engravings are superb, and the typography unsurpassed by any book with which we are acquainted. It is an honor to the author and publisher, and a credit to our common country."—*Scientific American.*

"This number is devoted to the explanation of Perspective, and treats that difficult subject with admirable clearness, precision, and completeness. The plates and letter-press of this work are executed with uncommon beauty. It has received the sanction of many of our most eminent artists, and can scarcely be commended too highly."—*N. Y. Tribune.*

"This present number is dedicated to the subject of Perspective—commencing with the elements of Geometry—and is especially valuable to builders, carpenters, and other artisans, being accompanied with beautiful illustrative designs drawn by Chapman, and further simplified by plain and perspicuous directions for the guidance of the student. Indeed, the whole work, from its undeviating simplicity, exhibits the hand of a master. We trust this highly useful and elevated branch of art will hereafter become an integral portion of public education, and as it is more easily attainable, so will it ultimately be considered an indispensable part of elementary instruction. Its cheapness is only rivalled by its excellence, and the artistic beauty of its illustrations is only equalled by the dignified ease and common sense exemplified in the written directions that accompany each lesson.—*Poughkeepsie Telegraph.*"

"The subject of Perspective we should think would interest every mechanic in the country; indeed, after all, this is the class to be the most benefited by sound and thorough instruction in drawing."—*Dispatch.*

"Permit me here to say I regard your Drawing-Book as a treasure. I was a farmer-boy, and it was while daily following the plough, that I became acquainted with the first number of Chapman's Drawing-Book. I found in it just what I desired—a plain, sure road to that excellence in the Art of Arts, that my boyish mind had pictured as being so desirable, the first step toward which I had taken by making rude sketches upon my painted ploughbeam, or using the barn-door as my easel, while with colored rotten-stone I first took lessons from Nature. I am now at college. I have a class at drawing, and find in the several numbers I have obtained, the true road for the teacher also."—*Extract from a letter recently received.*

SAMUEL DICKSON, M.D.,
LATE A MEDICAL OFFICER ON THE BRITISH STAFF.

## THE PRINCIPLES OF THE CHRONO-THERMAL SYSTEM OF MEDICINE: WITH FALLACIES OF THE FACULTY:

In a Series of Lectures, originally delivered in 1840, at the Egyptian Hall Piccadilly, London. Now enlarged and improved; by Samuel Dickson, M.D. Late a Medical Officer on the British Staff. First American, from the third London (people's) edition:

WITH AN INTRODUCTION AND NOTES,

BY WM. TURNER, M.D.,

LATE HEALTH COMMISSIONER OF THE CITY AND COUNTY OF NEW YORK—MEMBER OF THE NEW YORK MEDICAL SOCIETY, &C.

1 Vol. 8vo. Price 75 cents.

"Dear Sir: I thank you most sincerely for your valuable work. I have not the least objection to being unchemical, if I can be useful; and I agree with you, that the living stomach is not a wedgewood mortar. Yours, truly,
"Dr. Dickson." "ASTLEY COOPER.

"LONDON.—My Dear Sir:—I have read with the greatest delight your Fallacies of the Faculty. Every word ought to be written in LETTERS OF GOLD. Yours, faithfully,
"DR. DICKSON." "M. FOGARTY.

"THIS work establishes the identity of Poison and Medicine, and proves to demonstration that attention to time (Chronos) and Temperature (Therma) comprehends the whole art of Physic. Favorable to Hydropathy, it deals tenderly with Homœopathy: while the Apothecary will find it a rich treat, being a complete death-blow to the drugging and drenching system."—*London Medical Times.*

"THE Chrono-thermal system of medicine, issued by Dr. Dickson, under the auspices of Dr. Wm. Turner of New York, is a curious eccentric and able production, full of new views and curious facts upon the interesting subject of medical science. Although enthusiastic, as are all the discoveries of new systems, yet he sustains all his assertions by facts. Time and observation will doubtless add to its claims upon the careful consideration of medical men."—*Sun.*

"DR. DICKSON'S Lectures will make a sensation. They will startle the medical community by their irreverence, amuse the people by their ruthless stripping of its hieroglyphics, and be read everywhere and by every man diseased, from him who is subject to the tooth-ache to the victim of the most complicated ailments—for all are claimed to be resolvable to one type. The book will make smatterers out of the ignorant, and set the educated to wondering what they have been about all their lives. We recommend every body to read it."—*U. S. Saturday Post.*

"THIS is a curious book. In the course of it a vast number of medical anecdotes and facts, are introduced. We are half inclined in many places to imagine that he [the author] studied English under Wm. Cobbett. By no other writer, since the decease of that original, have we been so forcibly reminded of him. With more polish of style, he has all his bluntness, much of his humor, equal directness, and more than a mere infusion of impudence."—*Courrier.*

# THE POETICAL WORKS
OF
# PERCY BYSSHE SHELLEY.

**EDITED BY G. G. FOSTER.**

**THE FIRST COMPLETE AMERICAN EDITION.**

In one volume, 16mo.

"Shelley has a private nook in my affections. He is so unlike all other poets that I can not mate him. He is like his own 'skylark' among birds. He does not keep ever up in the thin air with Byron, like the eagle, nor sing with Keats low and sweetly like the thrush, nor, like the dove sitting always upon her nest, brood with Wordsworth over the affections. He begins to sing when the morning wakes him, and as he grows wild with his own song, he mounts upward,

'And singing ever soars, and soaring ever singeth;'

and it is wonderful how he loses himself, like the delirious bird in the sky, and with a verse which may be well compared for its fine delicacy with her little wings, penetrates its far depths fearlessly and full of joy. There is something very new in this mingled trait of fineness and sublimity. Milton and Byron seem made for the sky. Their broad wings always strike the air with the same solemn majesty. But Shelley, near the ground, is a very 'bird in a bower,' running through his merry compass as if he never dreamed of the upward and invisible heavens. Withal, Shelley's genius is too fiery to be moody. He was a melancholy man, but it was because he was crossed in the daily walk of life, and such anxieties did not touch his imagination. It was above—far, far above them. His poetry was not, like that of other poets, linked with his common interests; and if it 'unbound the serpent of care from his heart,' as doubtless it did, it was by making him forget that it was there. He conceived and wrote in a wizard circle. The illiberal world was the last thing remembered, and its annoying prejudices gall him as they might in the exercise of his social duties, never followed over the fiery limit of his fancy. Never have we seen such pure abstraction from earthliness as in the temper of his poetry. It is the clear, intellectual lymph, unalloyed and unpolluted."—*N. P. Willis.*

# NAPOLEON'S MAXIMS OF WAR,

Translated by Col. D'Aguilar.

**WITH NOTES.**

In one vol., 32mo. Price 50 cents.

"The science of war, in its legitimate sense, is entitled to encouragement, and study, and we recommend that every man of military mind, should possess himself of a copy of 'Napoleon's Maxims.' The work is also one of interest to the general reader, containing, as it does, numerous brief historical facts connected with the most celebrated battles, and men of military renown of almost every age."—*Recruit.*

"It is a work of no little interest to those who wish to understand the principles upon which the greatest captain of the age carried on his operations, and who also desire to understand the errors committed by the inferior intellects brought into the field against him."—*Penn. Inquirer.*

"This work appears in its first American edition, with a recommendation from Gen. Scott, speaking of its utility to military men. That, indeed, is apparent enough; but it has occurred to us that the perusal of the little work, with its full illustrative notes, must be of great advantage also to the general reader, who desires to understand the tactics of the great Emperor. It will be a good companion to Thiers' History, now publishing."—*U. S. Sat. Post.*